Translators
Mystie Cho
Jean Yen

Editors
Duncan Cameron
Gina Kim

Marketing Editor
Nicole Curry

Production Artists
Walter Tsai
Kelly Lin
Atsuko Hattori

US Cover Design
Eric Lin
Hiep Ho

Lettering Fonts
Comicraft
www.comicbookfonts.com

President
Robin Kuo

Redmoon 5 © Mina Hwang
Originally published in Korea in 1988 by Seung-chul Pack
English translation rights arranged through
World Netgames, Inc.

Publisher
ComicsOne Corporation
48531 Warm Springs Blvd, Suite 408.
Fremont, CA 94539
www.ComicsOne.com

First Edition: January 2002
ISBN 1-58899-097-4

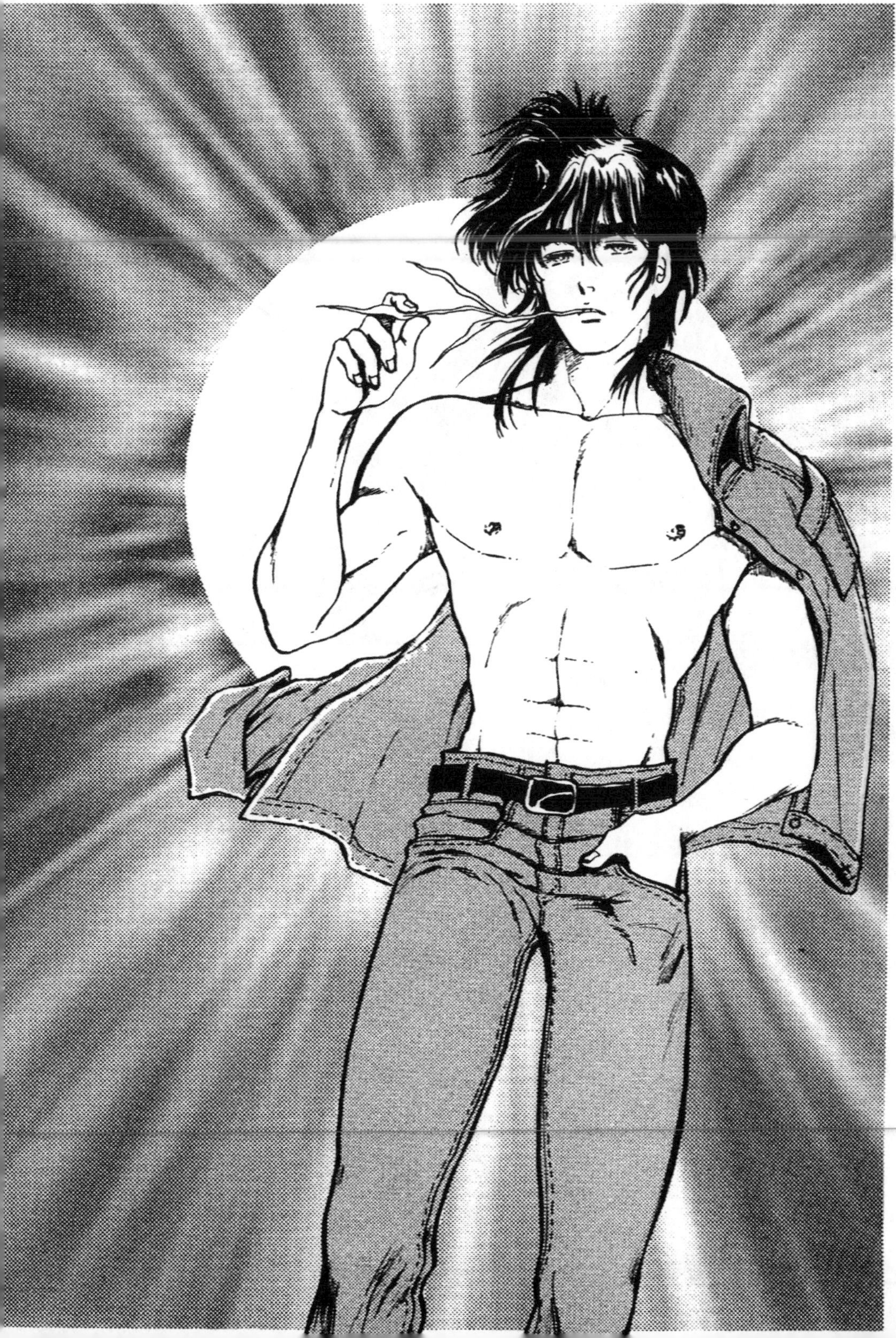

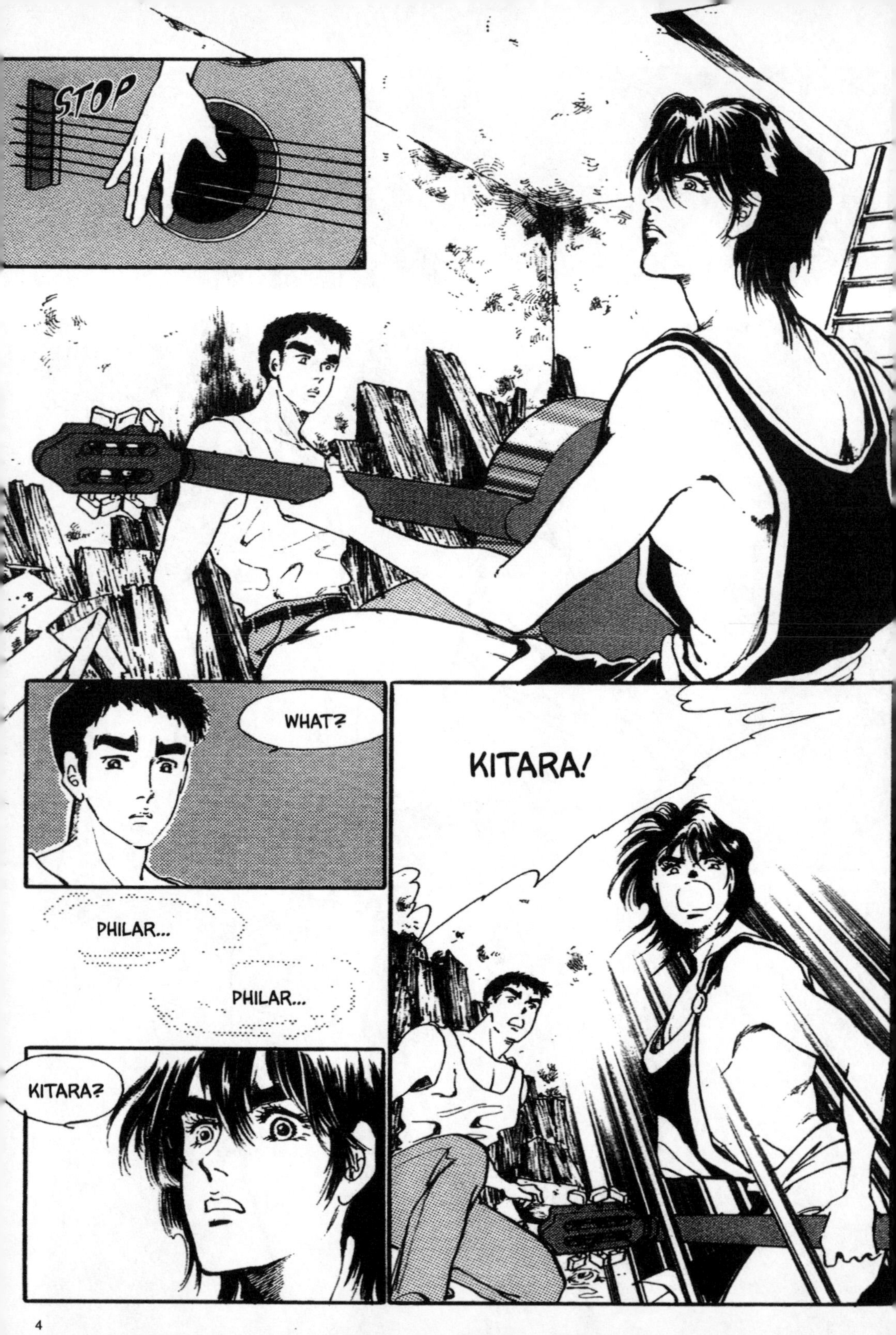
STOP
WHAT?
PHILAR...
PHILAR...
KITARA?
KITARA!

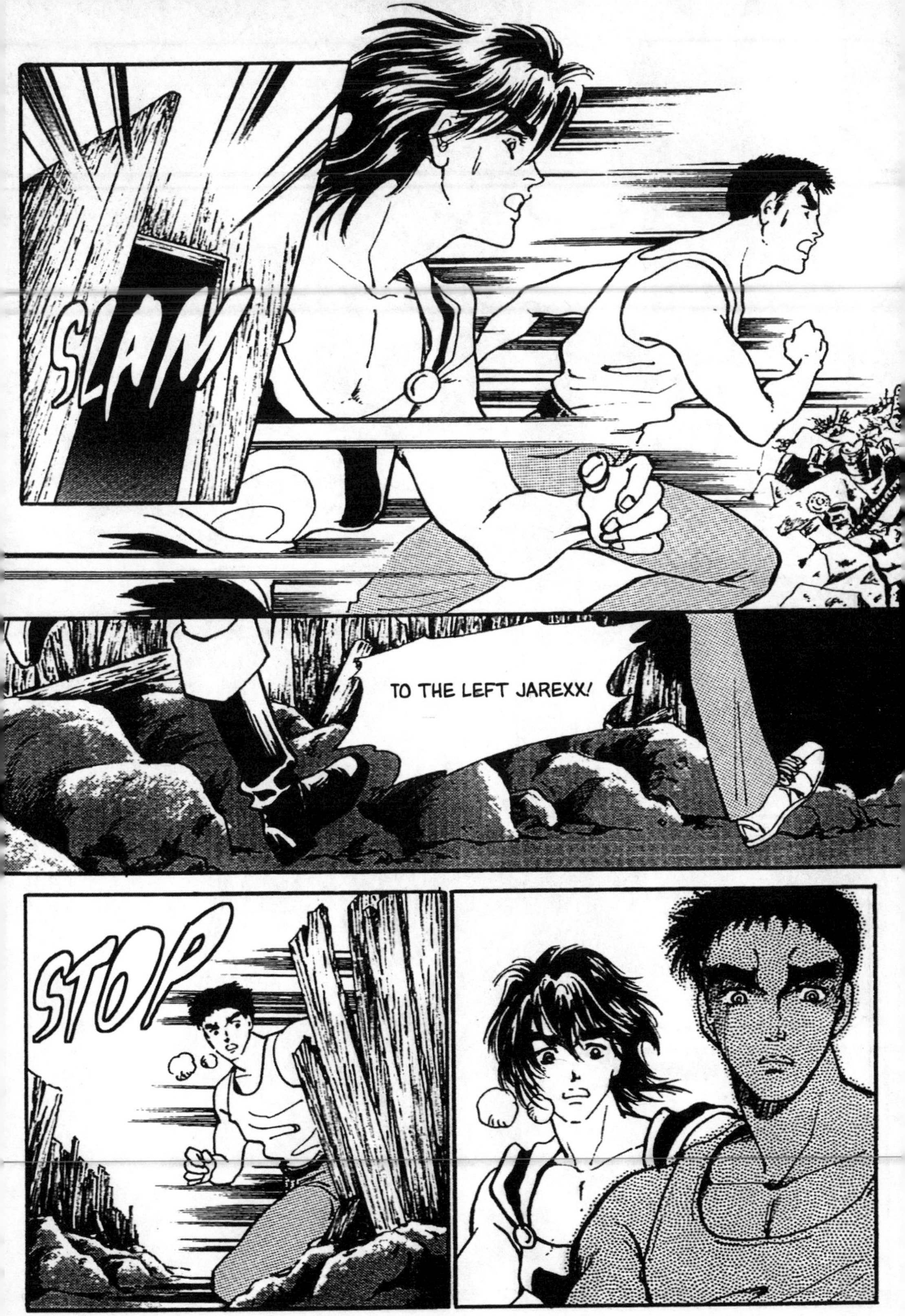
SLAM
TO THE LEFT JAREXX!
STOP

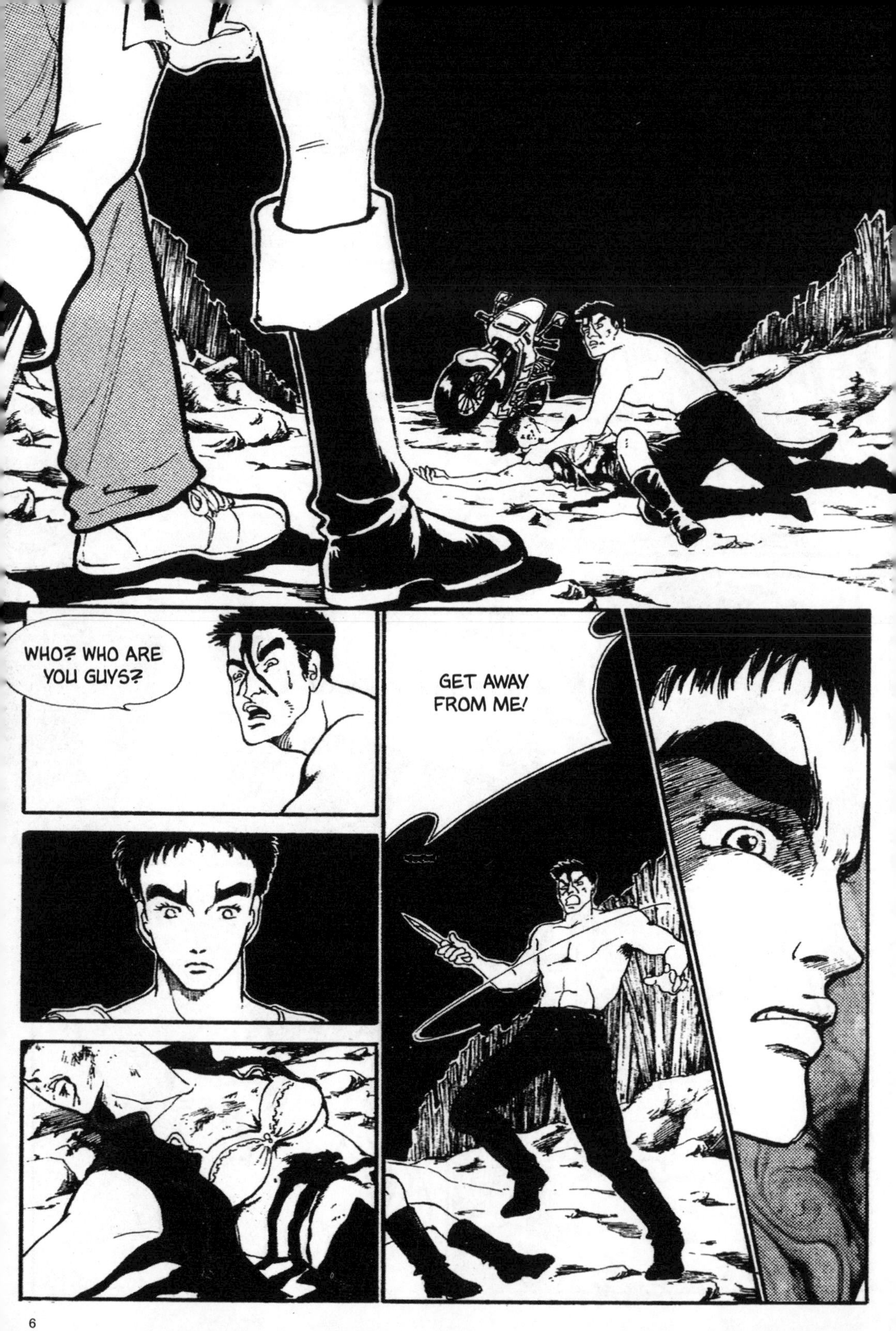
WHO? WHO ARE YOU GUYS?
GET AWAY FROM ME!

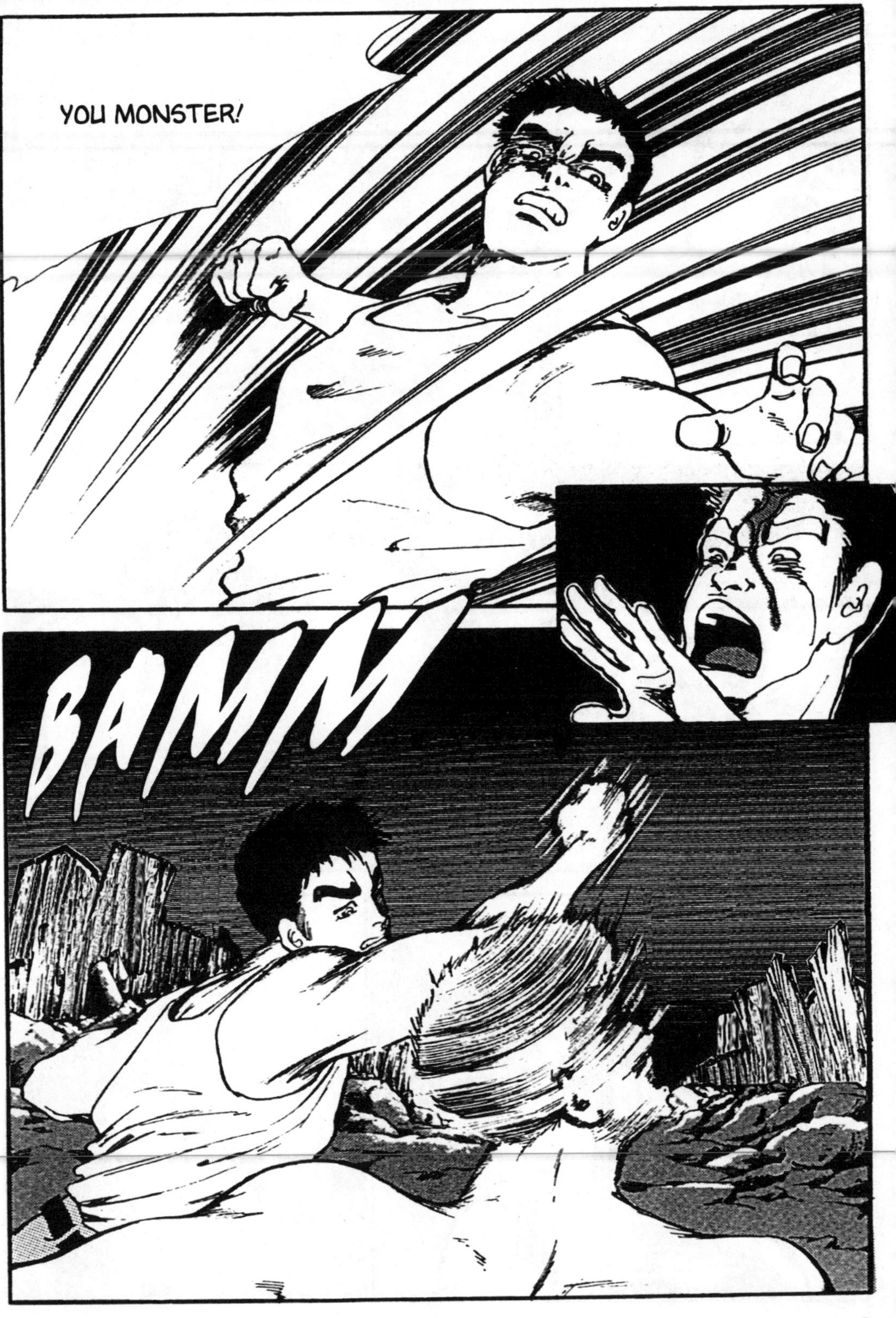
YOU MONSTER!
BAMM

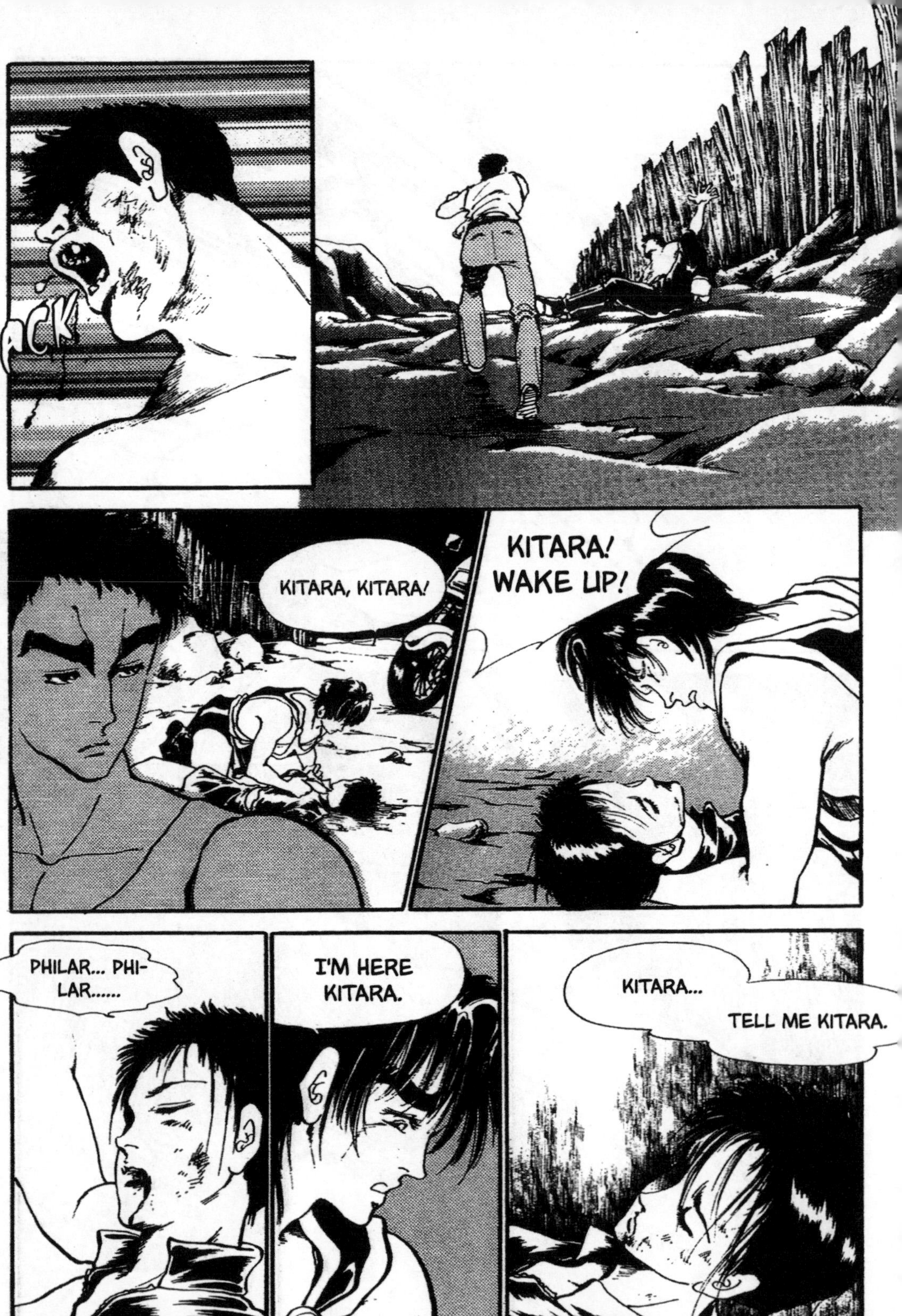
ACK
KITARA, KITARA!
KITARA! WAKE UP!
PHILAR... PHI-LAR......
I'M HERE KITARA.
KITARA...
TELL ME KITARA.

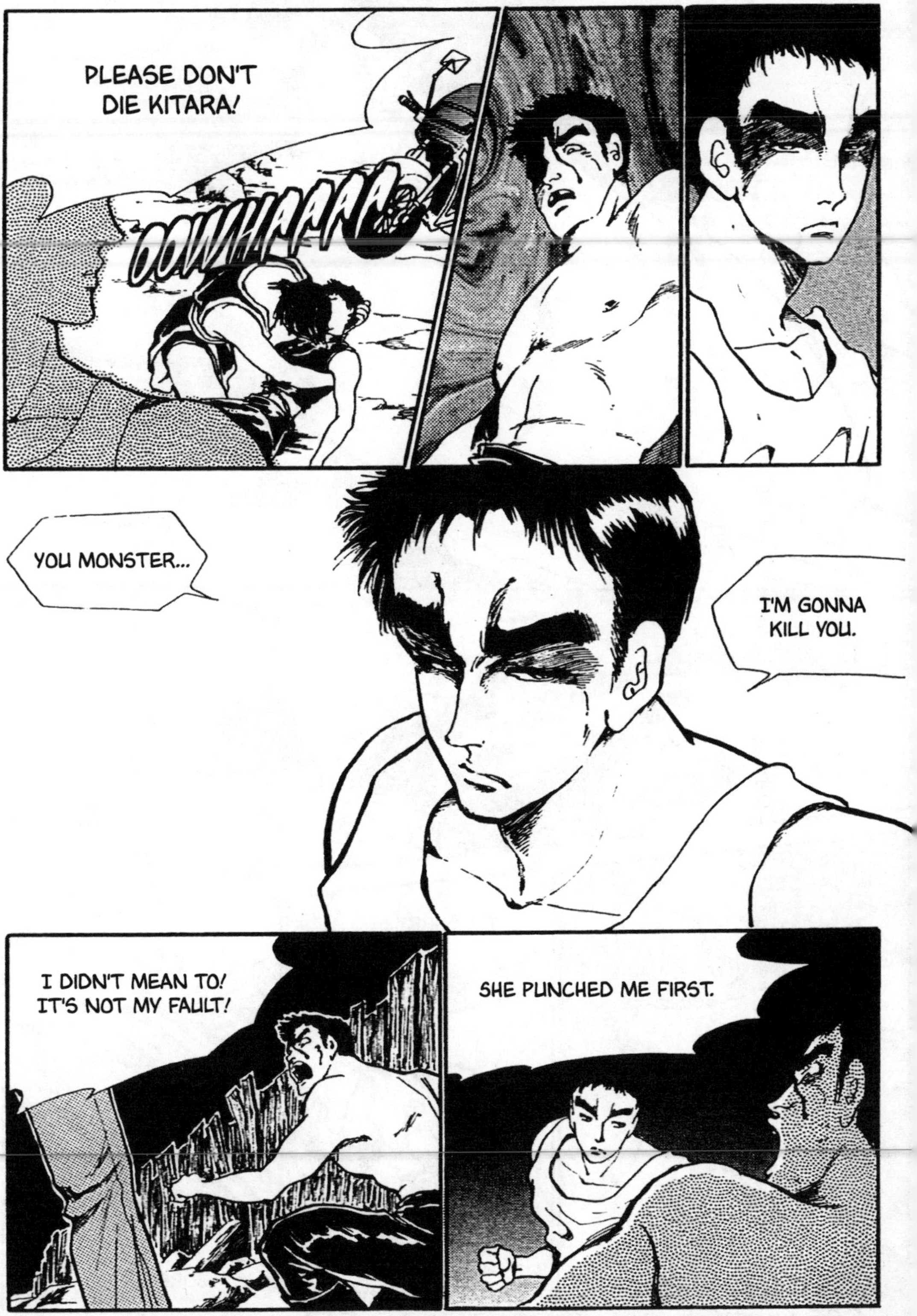
PLEASE DON'T DIE KITARA!
OOWHAAAAA
YOU MONSTER...
I'M GONNA KILL YOU.
I DIDN'T MEAN TO! IT'S NOT MY FAULT!
SHE PUNCHED ME FIRST.

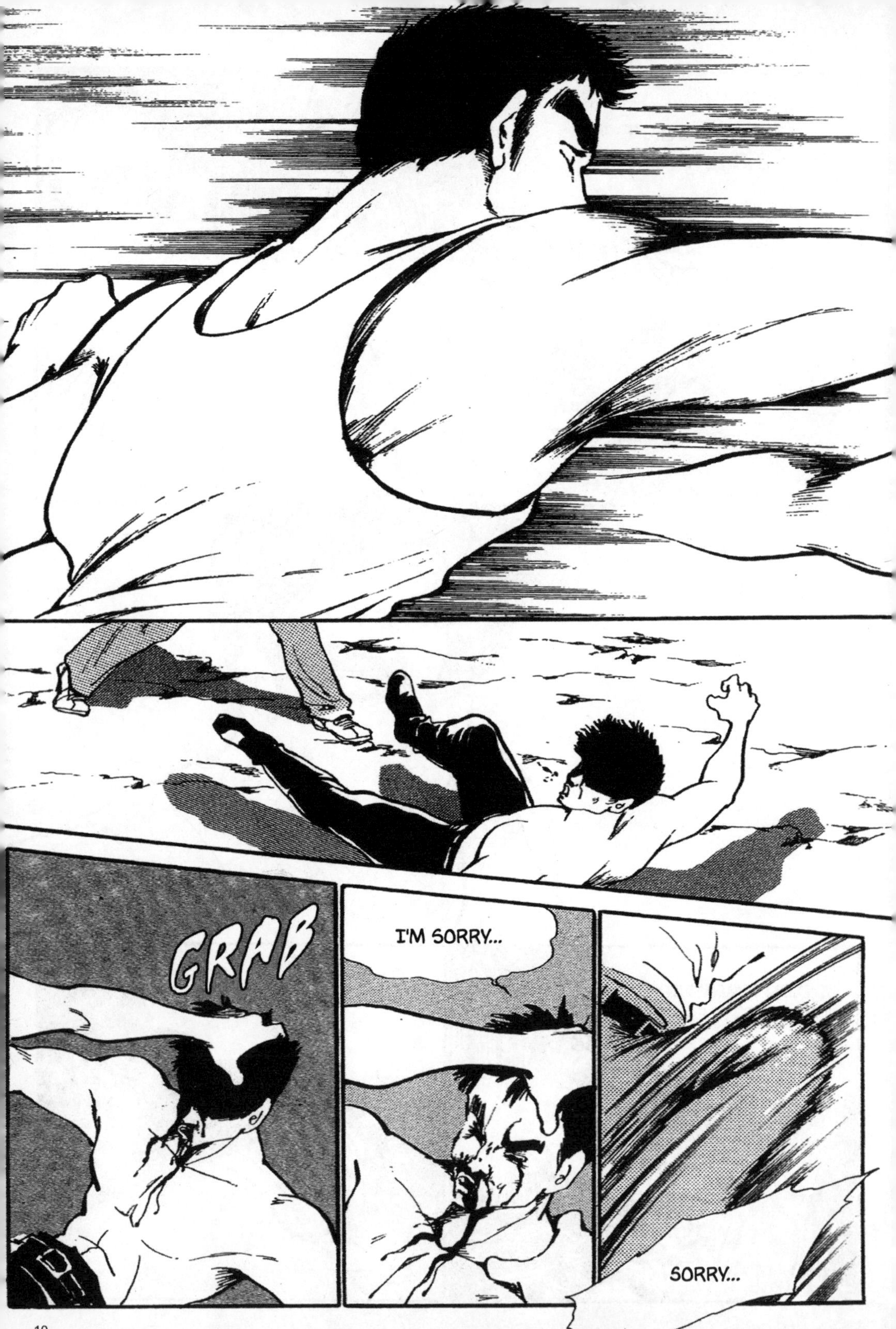
GRAB
I'M SORRY...
SORRY...

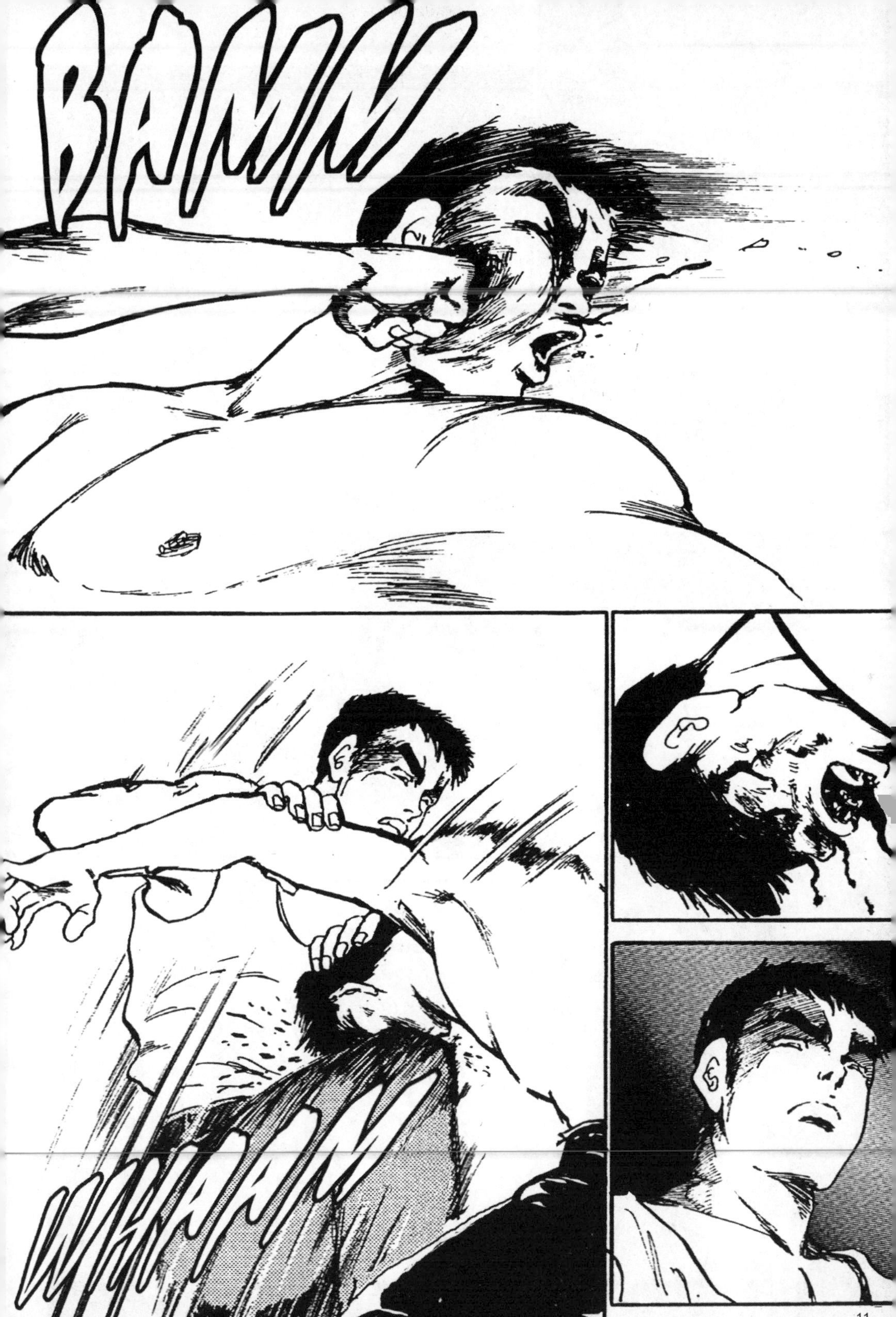
BAMM
WHAAAM

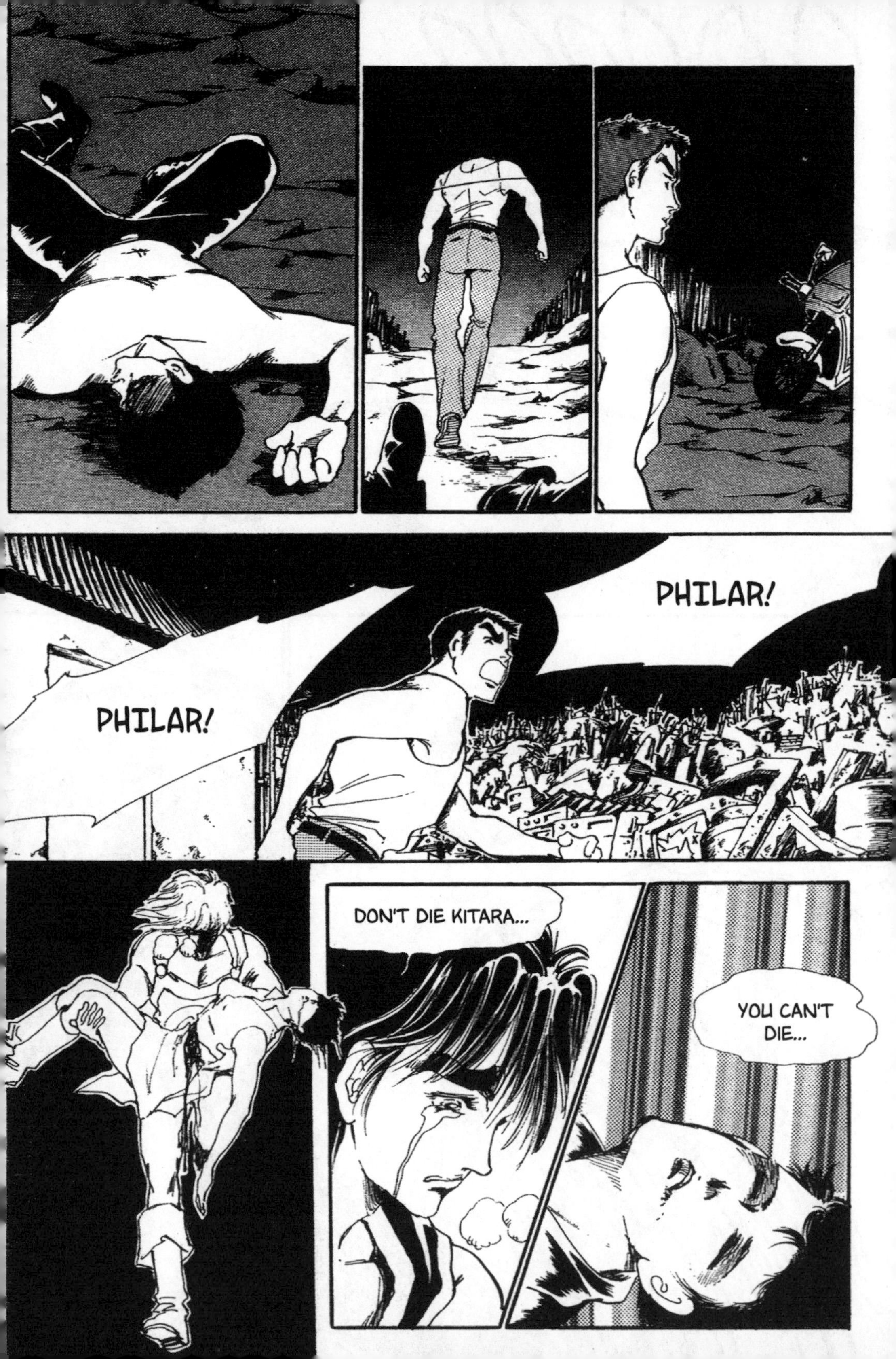
PHILAR!
PHILAR!
DON'T DIE KITARA...
YOU CAN'T DIE...

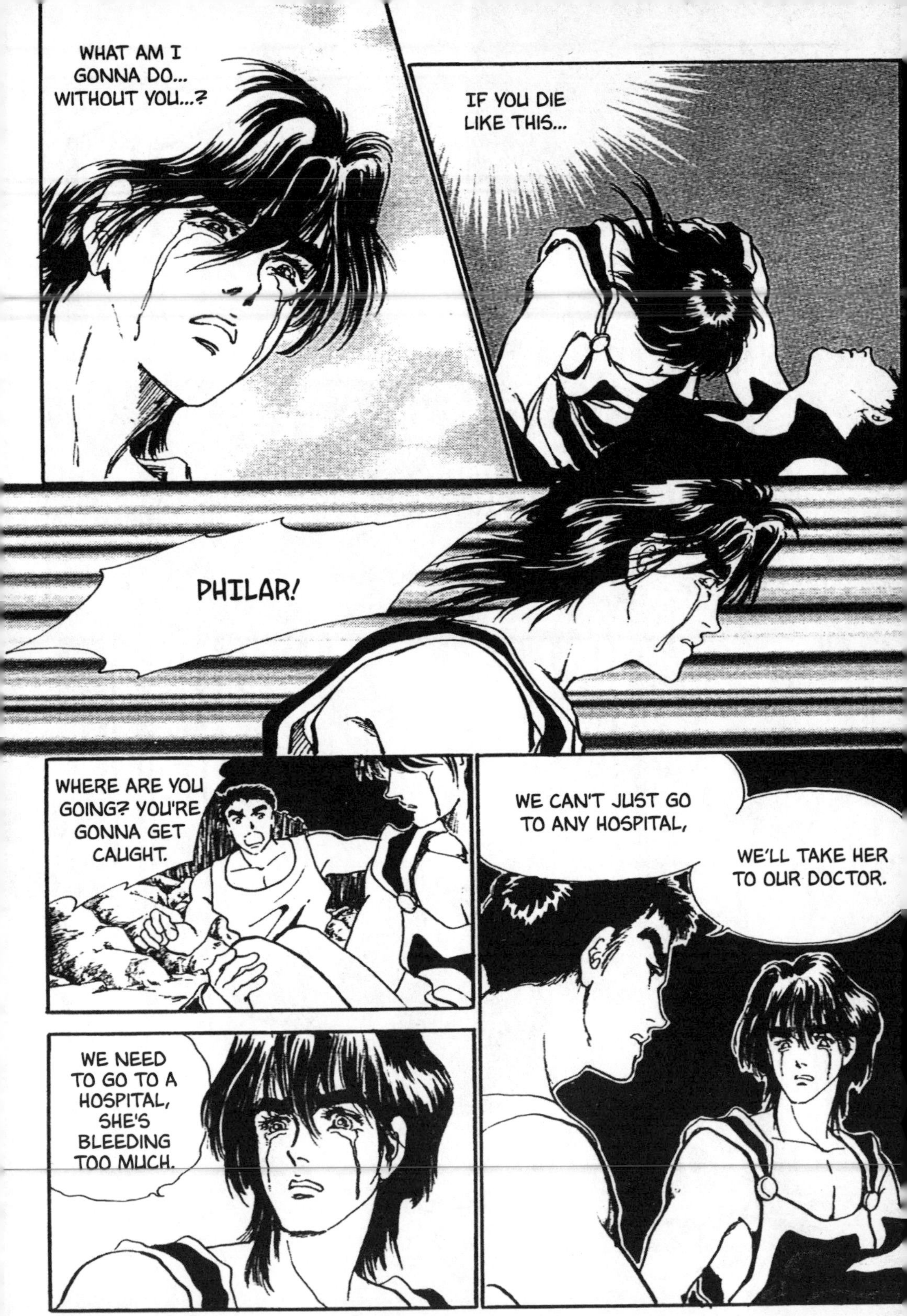

WHAT AM I GONNA DO... WITHOUT YOU...?
IF YOU DIE LIKE THIS...
PHILAR!
WHERE ARE YOU GOING? YOU'RE GONNA GET CAUGHT.
WE CAN'T JUST GO TO ANY HOSPITAL,
WE'LL TAKE HER TO OUR DOCTOR.
WE NEED TO GO TO A HOSPITAL, SHE'S BLEEDING TOO MUCH.

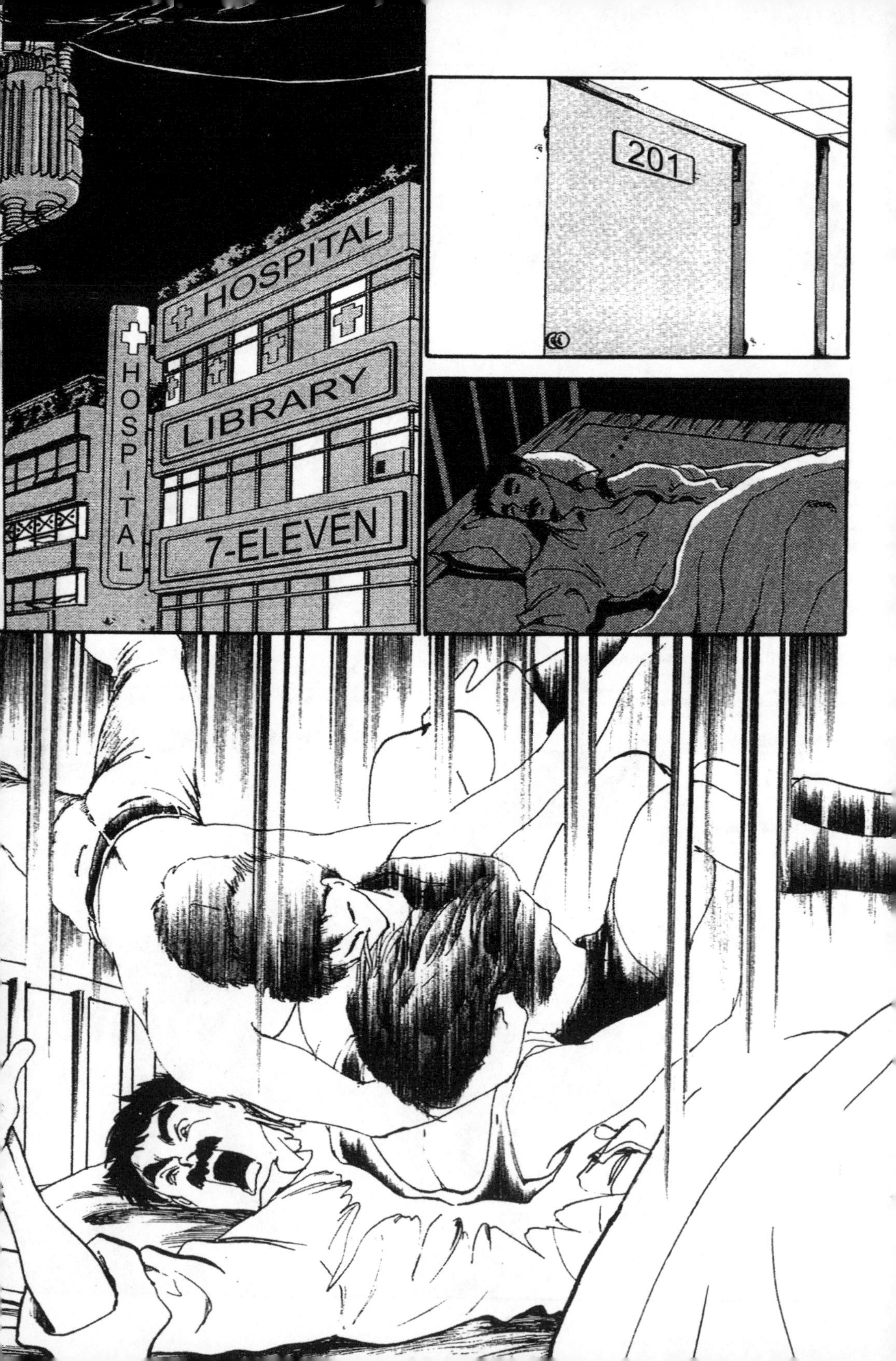
HOSPITAL
HOSPITAL
LIBRARY
7-ELEVEN
201

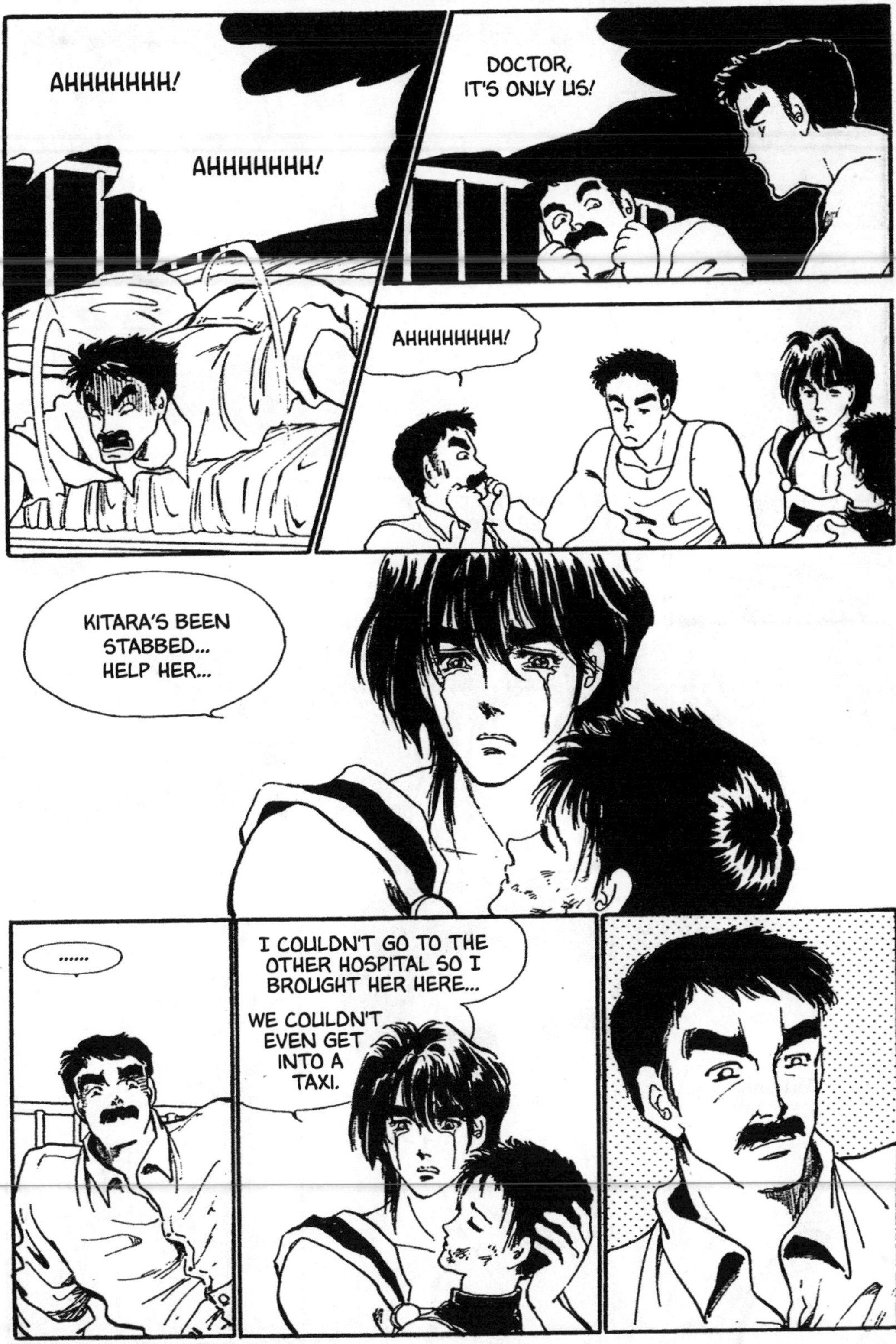
AHHHHHHH!
AHHHHHHH!
DOCTOR, IT'S ONLY US!
AHHHHHHHH!
KITARA'S BEEN STABBED... HELP HER...
......
I COULDN'T GO TO THE OTHER HOSPITAL SO I BROUGHT HER HERE...
WE COULDN'T EVEN GET INTO A TAXI.

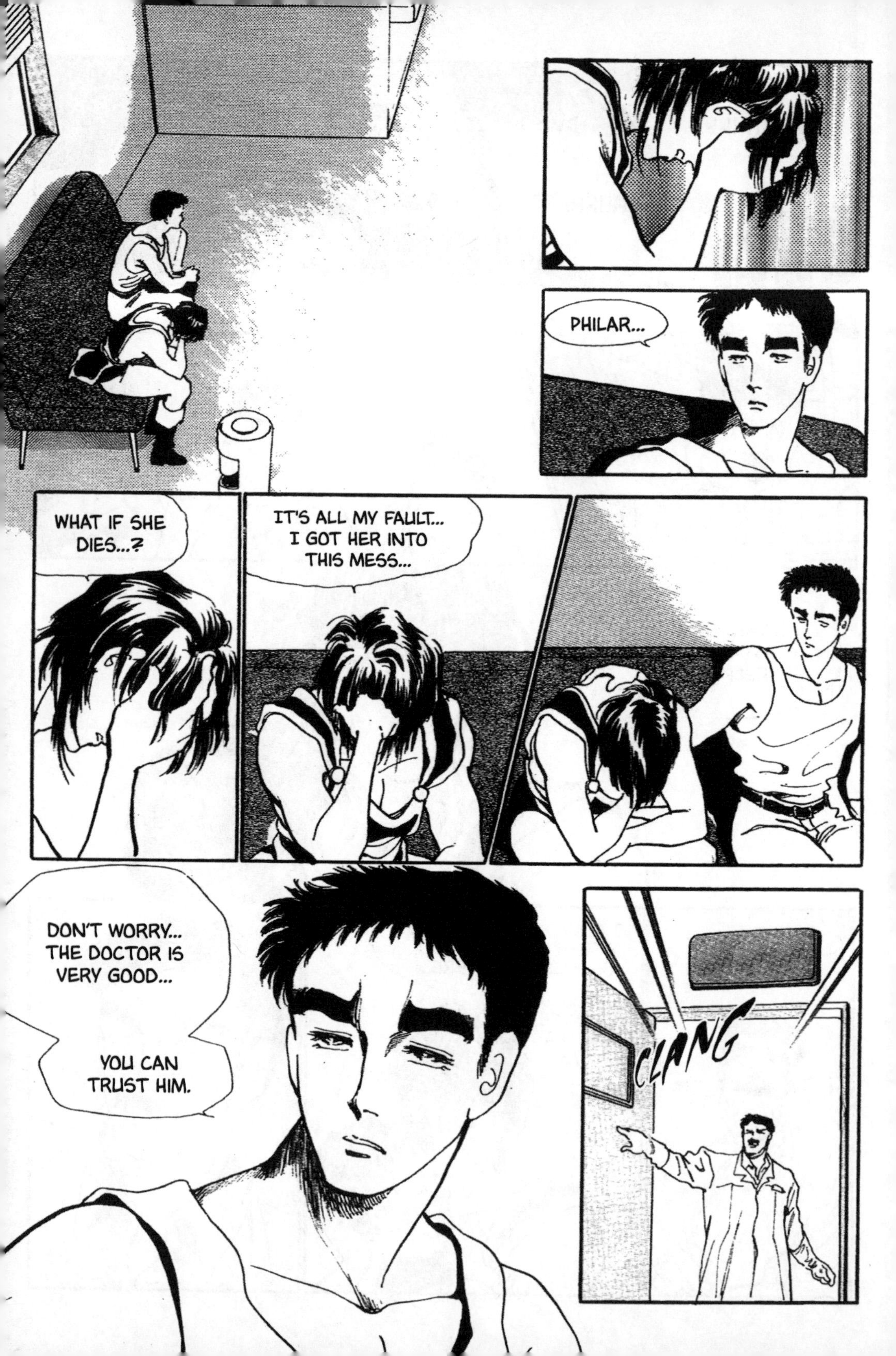
PHILAR...
WHAT IF SHE DIES...?
IT'S ALL MY FAULT... I GOT HER INTO THIS MESS...
DON'T WORRY... THE DOCTOR IS VERY GOOD...
YOU CAN TRUST HIM.
CLANG

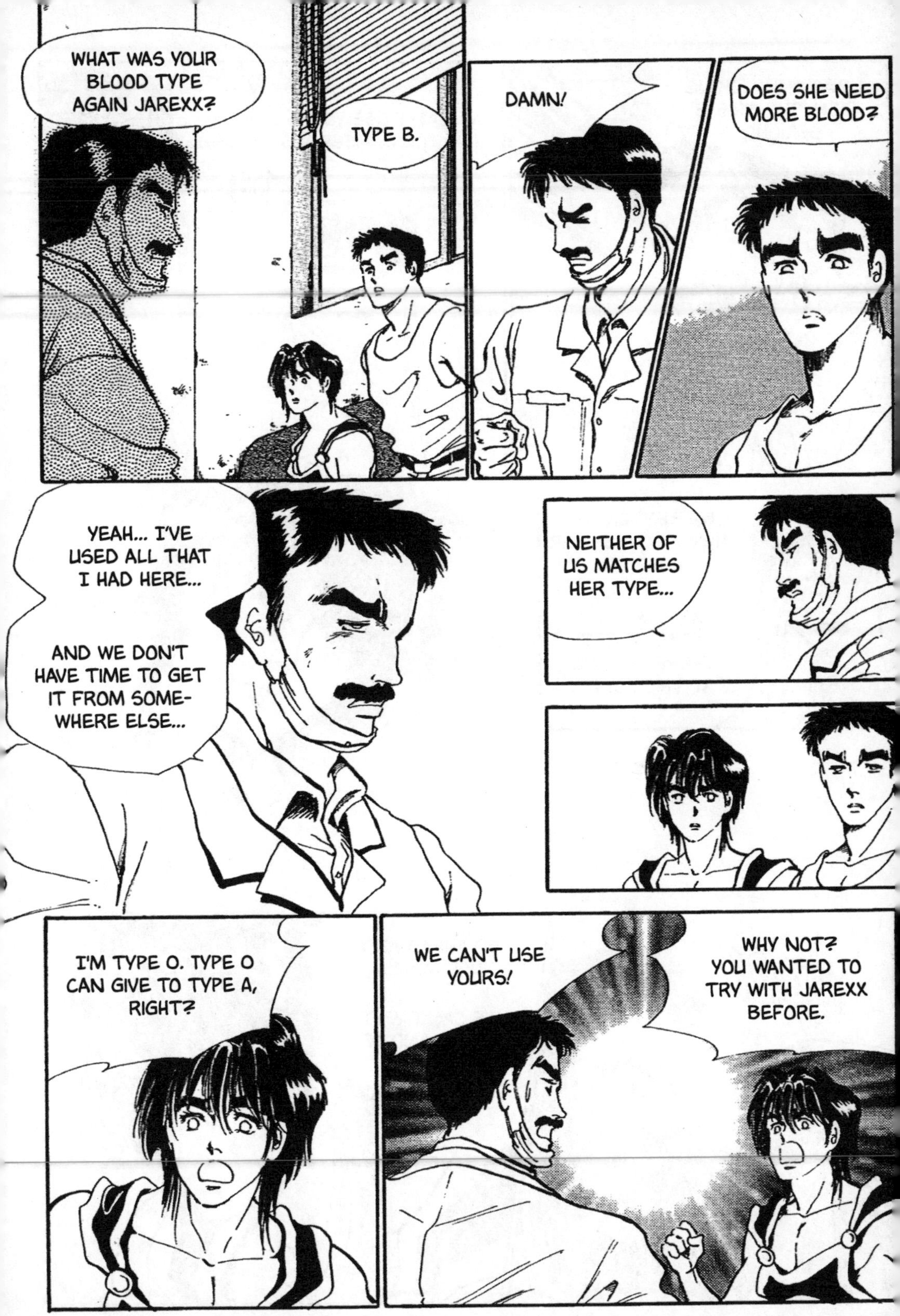

WHAT WAS YOUR BLOOD TYPE AGAIN JAREXX?
TYPE B.
DAMN!
DOES SHE NEED MORE BLOOD?
YEAH... I'VE USED ALL THAT I HAD HERE...
AND WE DON'T HAVE TIME TO GET IT FROM SOME-WHERE ELSE...
NEITHER OF US MATCHES HER TYPE...
I'M TYPE O. TYPE O CAN GIVE TO TYPE A, RIGHT?
WE CAN'T USE YOURS!
WHY NOT? YOU WANTED TO TRY WITH JAREXX BEFORE.

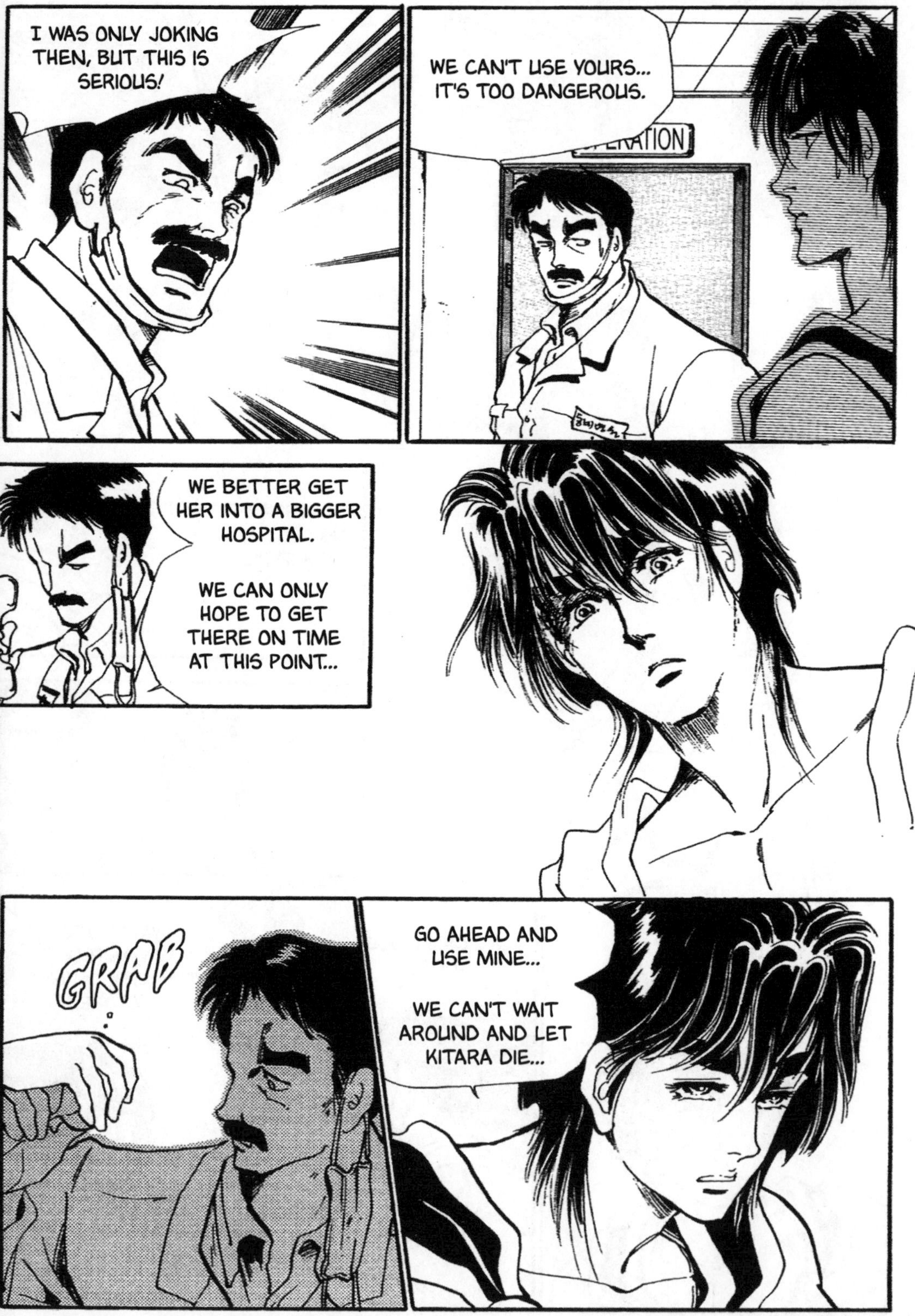
I WAS ONLY JOKING THEN, BUT THIS IS SERIOUS!
WE CAN'T USE YOURS... IT'S TOO DANGEROUS.
OPERATION
WE BETTER GET HER INTO A BIGGER HOSPITAL.
WE CAN ONLY HOPE TO GET THERE ON TIME AT THIS POINT...
GRAB
GO AHEAD AND USE MINE...
WE CAN'T WAIT AROUND AND LET KITARA DIE...

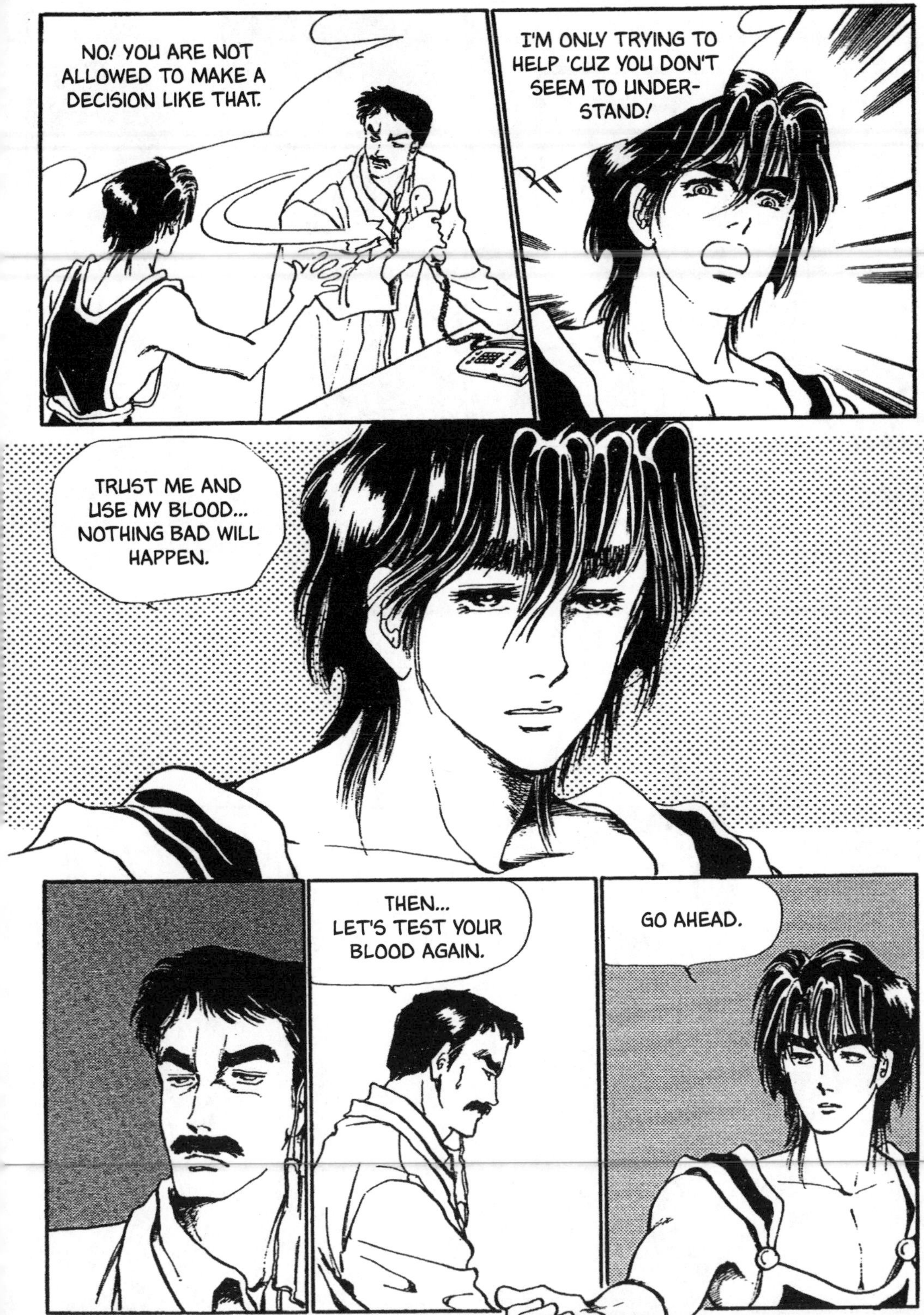
NO! YOU ARE NOT ALLOWED TO MAKE A DECISION LIKE THAT.
I'M ONLY TRYING TO HELP 'CUZ YOU DON'T SEEM TO UNDER-STAND!
TRUST ME AND USE MY BLOOD... NOTHING BAD WILL HAPPEN.
THEN... LET'S TEST YOUR BLOOD AGAIN.
GO AHEAD.

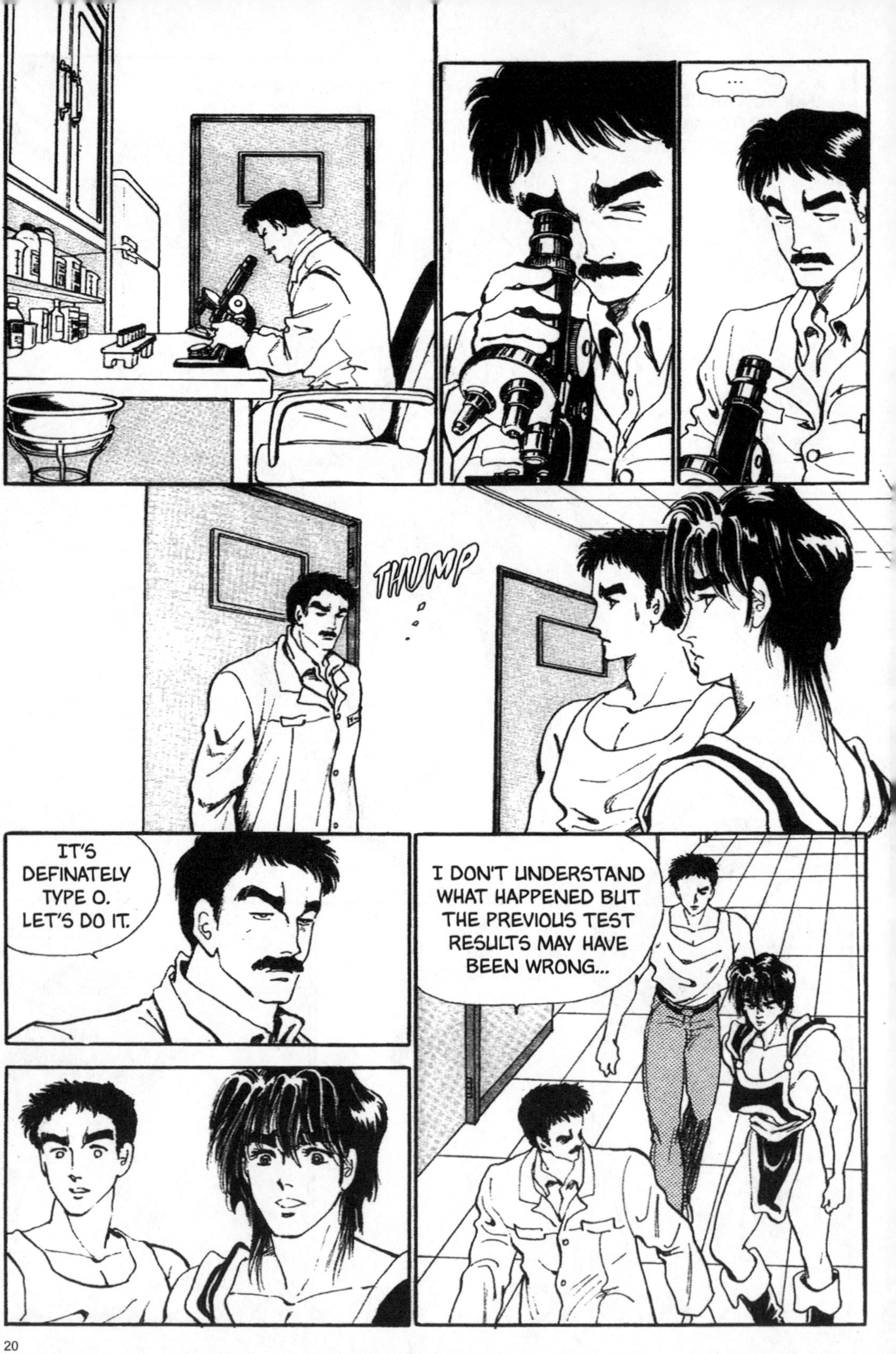
...
THUMP
IT'S DEFINATELY TYPE O. LET'S DO IT.
I DON'T UNDERSTAND WHAT HAPPENED BUT THE PREVIOUS TEST RESULTS MAY HAVE BEEN WRONG...

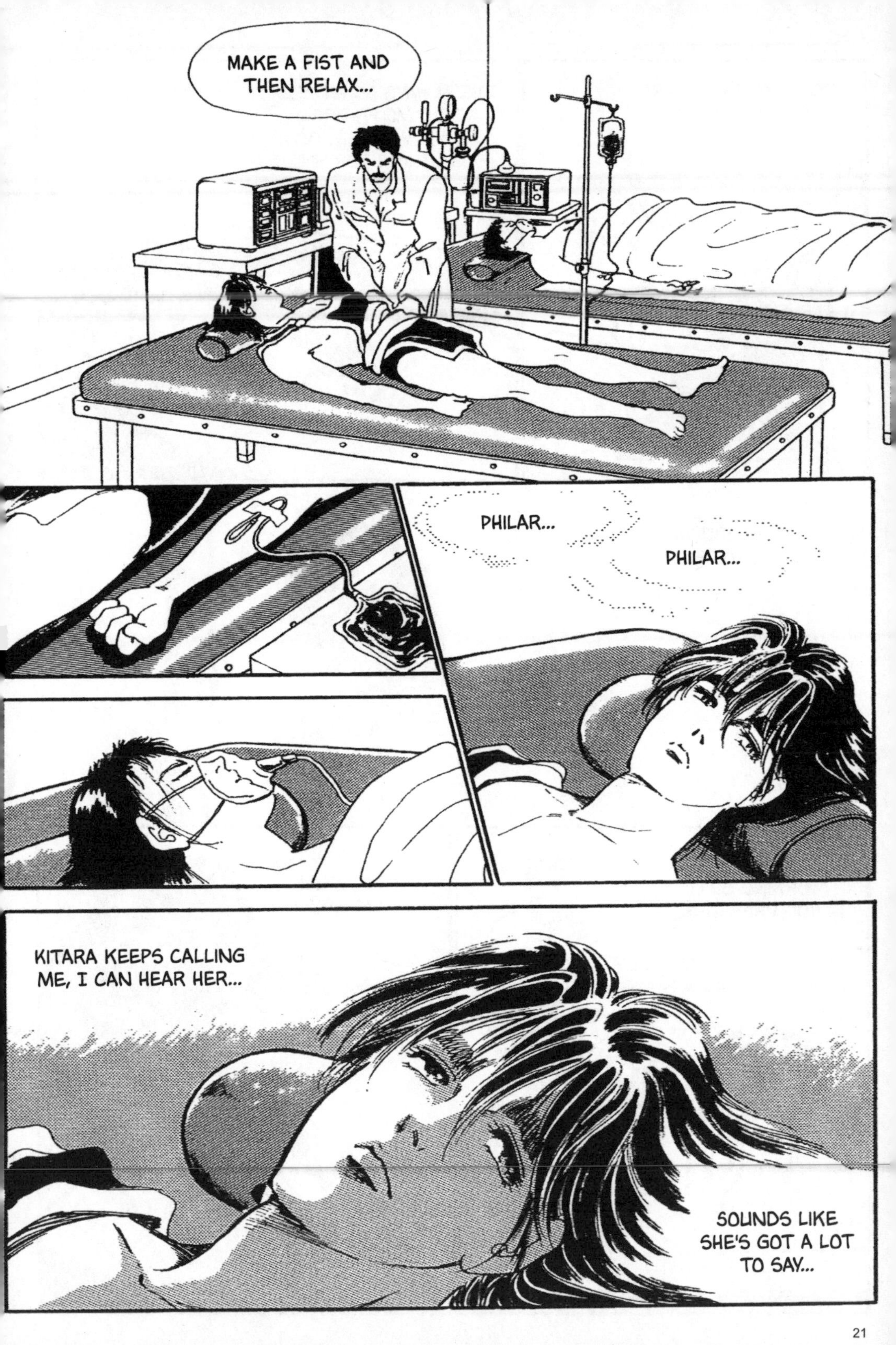
MAKE A FIST AND THEN RELAX...
PHILAR...
PHILAR...
KITARA KEEPS CALLING ME, I CAN HEAR HER...
SOUNDS LIKE SHE'S GOT A LOT TO SAY...

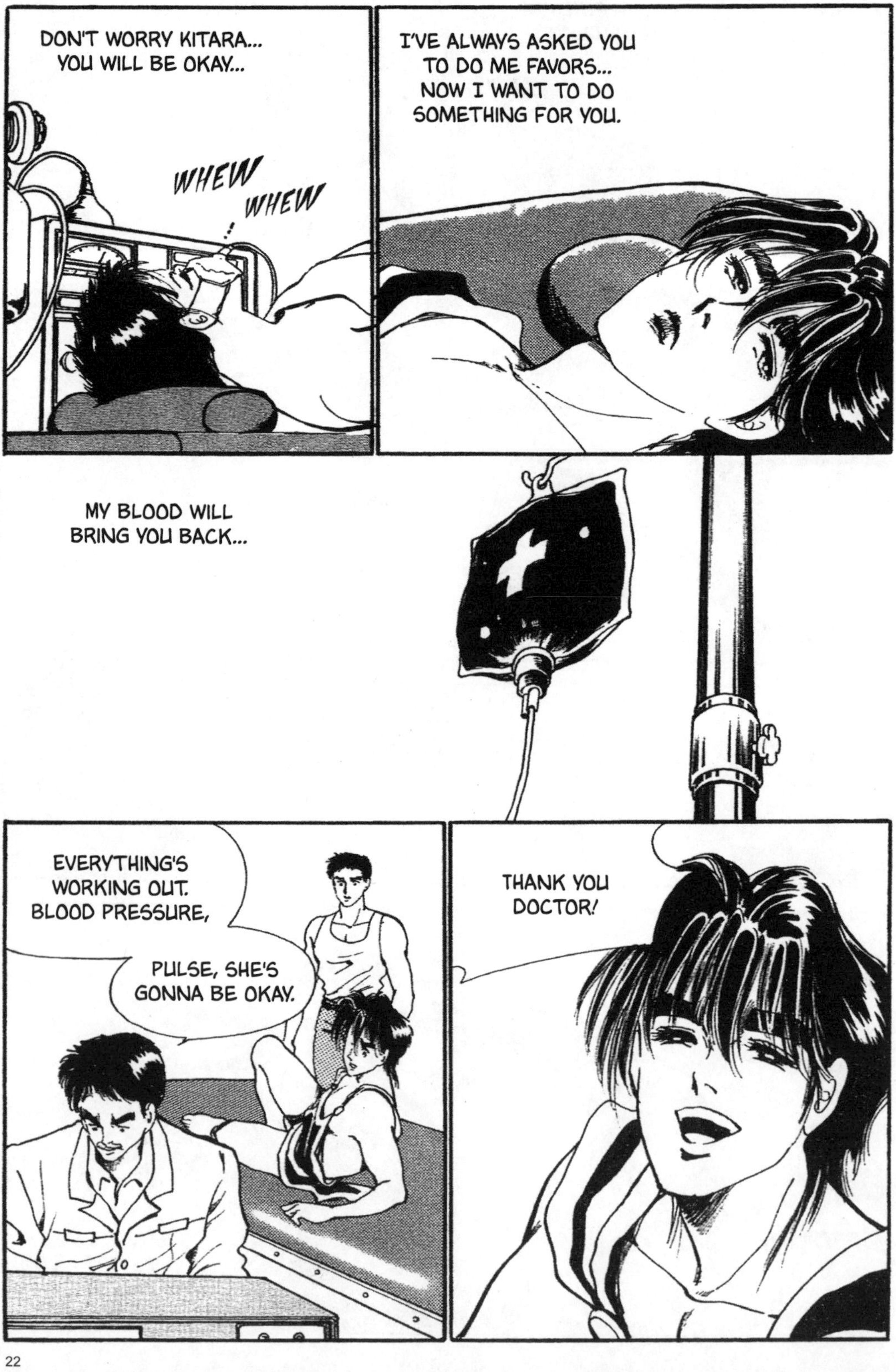
DON'T WORRY KITARA... YOU WILL BE OKAY...
WHEW
WHEW
I'VE ALWAYS ASKED YOU TO DO ME FAVORS... NOW I WANT TO DO SOMETHING FOR YOU.
MY BLOOD WILL BRING YOU BACK...
EVERYTHING'S WORKING OUT. BLOOD PRESSURE,
PULSE, SHE'S GONNA BE OKAY.
THANK YOU DOCTOR!

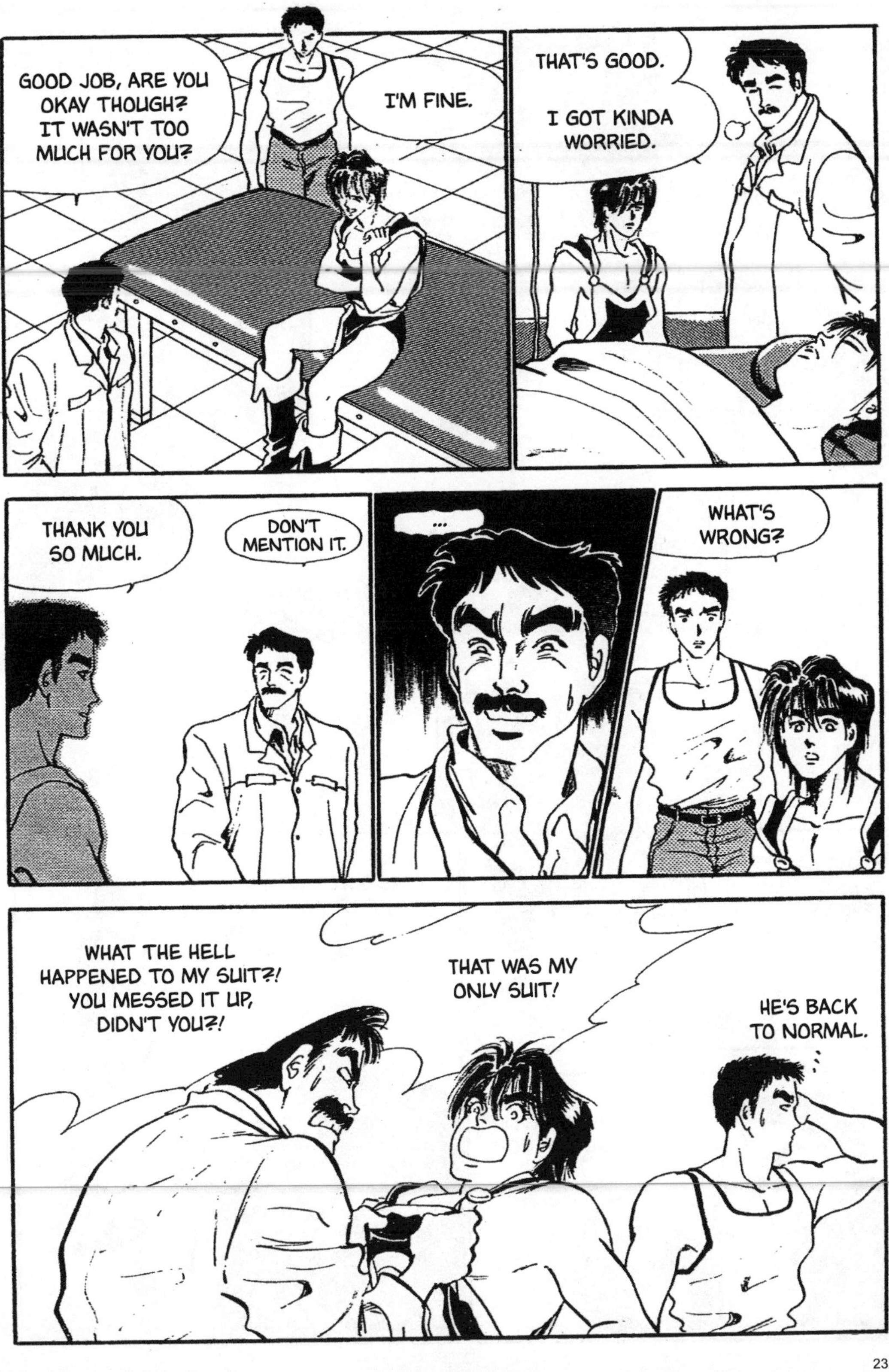
GOOD JOB, ARE YOU OKAY THOUGH? IT WASN'T TOO MUCH FOR YOU?
I'M FINE.
THAT'S GOOD.
I GOT KINDA WORRIED.
THANK YOU SO MUCH.
DON'T MENTION IT.
...
WHAT'S WRONG?
WHAT THE HELL HAPPENED TO MY SUIT?! YOU MESSED IT UP, DIDN'T YOU?!
THAT WAS MY ONLY SUIT!
HE'S BACK TO NORMAL.

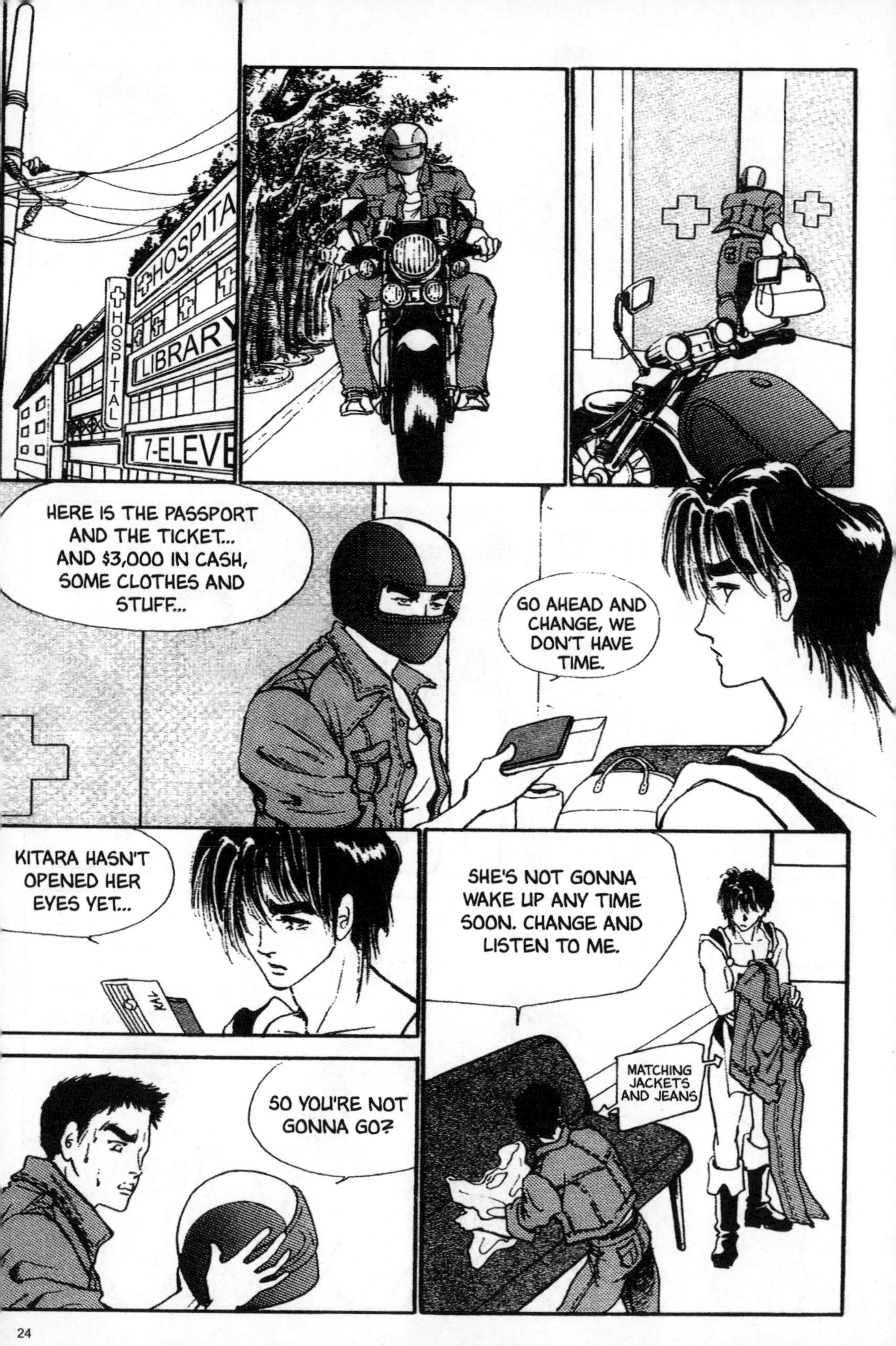
HOSPITAL
HOSPITAL
LIBRARY
7-ELEV
HERE IS THE PASSPORT AND THE TICKET... AND $3,000 IN CASH, SOME CLOTHES AND STUFF...
GO AHEAD AND CHANGE, WE DON'T HAVE TIME.
KITARA HASN'T OPENED HER EYES YET...
KAL
SHE'S NOT GONNA WAKE UP ANY TIME SOON. CHANGE AND LISTEN TO ME.
MATCHING JACKETS AND JEANS
SO YOU'RE NOT GONNA GO?

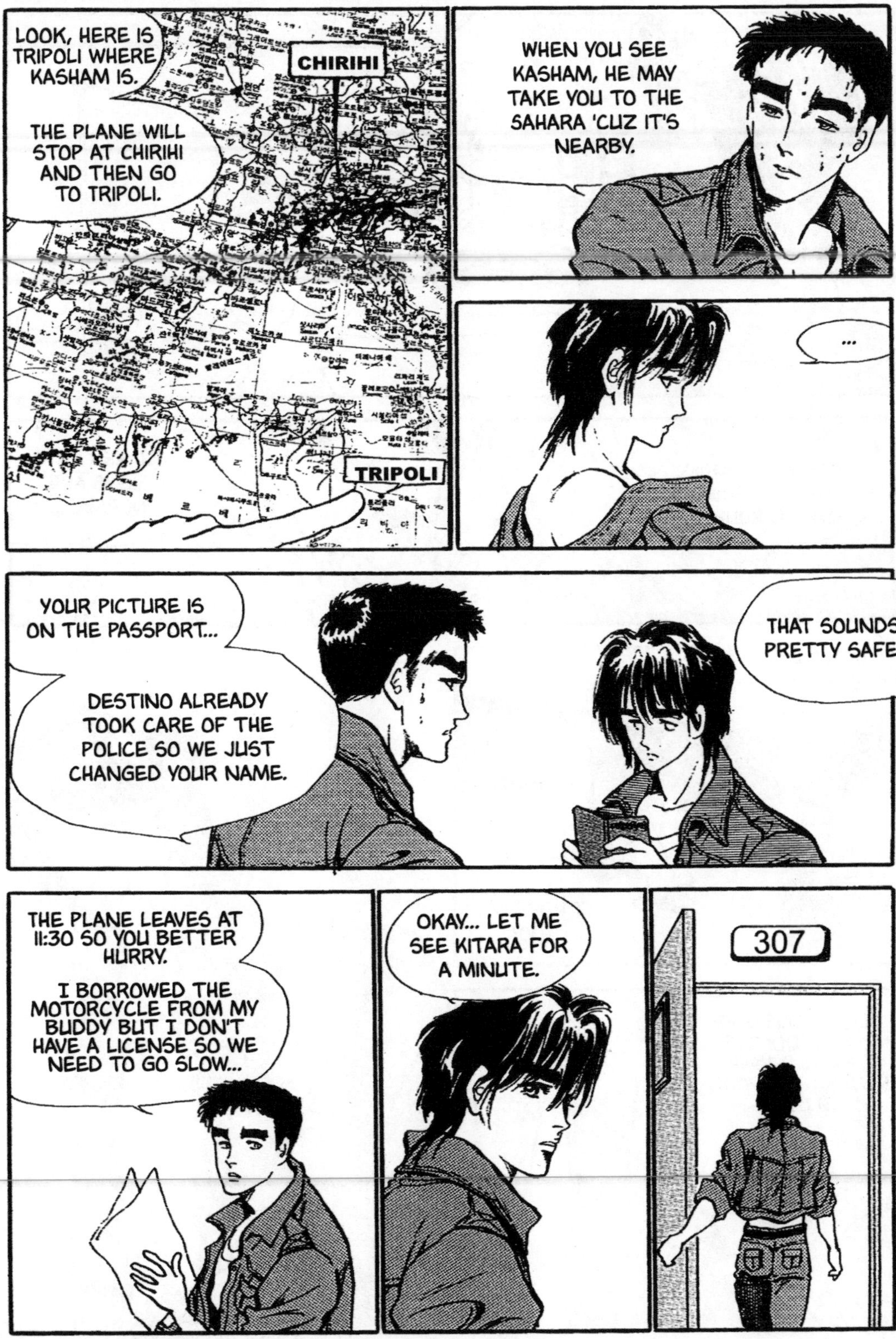

LOOK, HERE IS TRIPOLI WHERE KASHAM IS.
THE PLANE WILL STOP AT CHIRIHI AND THEN GO TO TRIPOLI.
CHIRIHI
TRIPOLI
WHEN YOU SEE KASHAM, HE MAY TAKE YOU TO THE SAHARA 'CUZ IT'S NEARBY.
...
YOUR PICTURE IS ON THE PASSPORT...
DESTINO ALREADY TOOK CARE OF THE POLICE SO WE JUST CHANGED YOUR NAME.
THAT SOUNDS PRETTY SAFE.
THE PLANE LEAVES AT 11:30 SO YOU BETTER HURRY.
I BORROWED THE MOTORCYCLE FROM MY BUDDY BUT I DON'T HAVE A LICENSE SO WE NEED TO GO SLOW...
OKAY... LET ME SEE KITARA FOR A MINUTE.
307

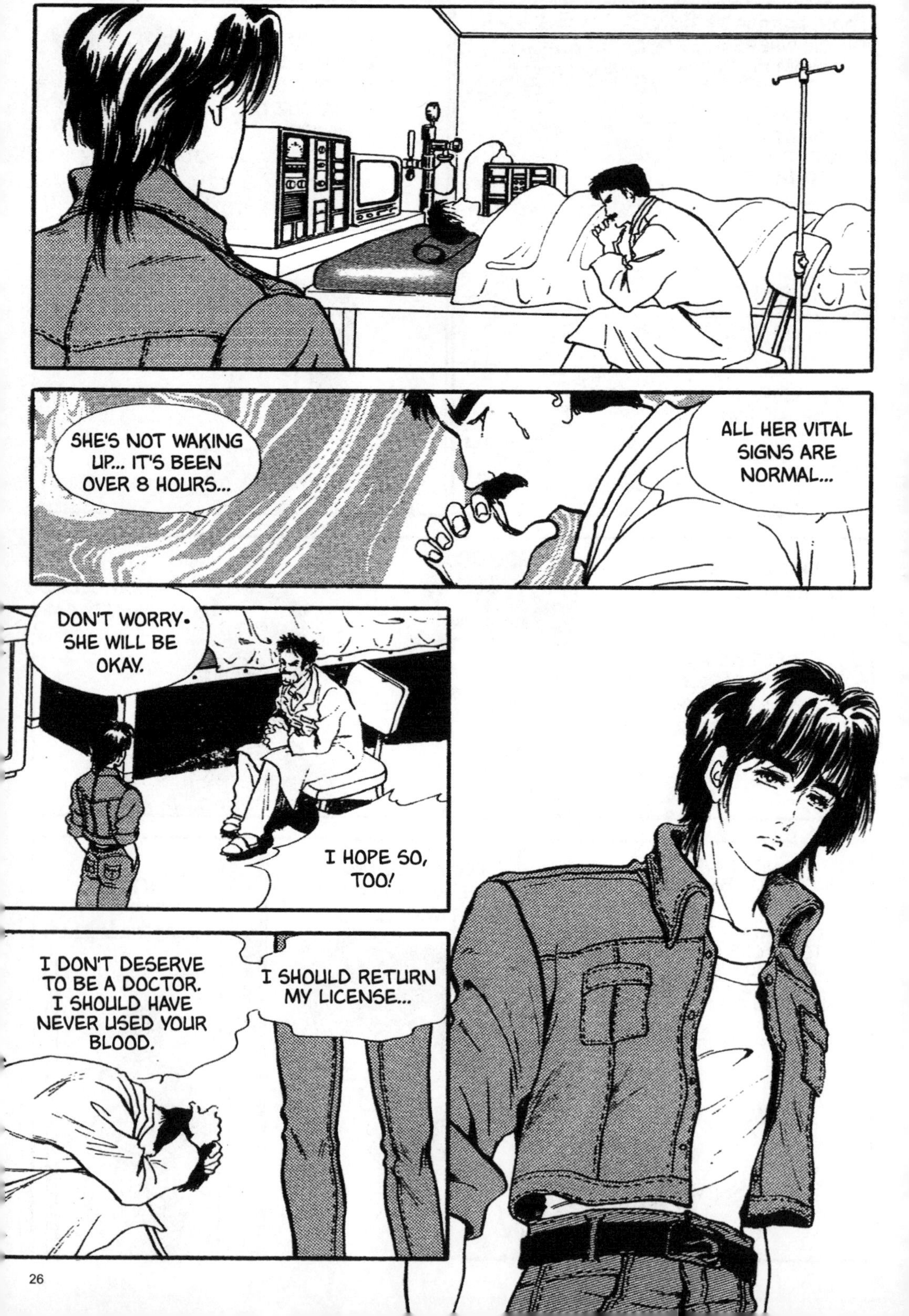
SHE'S NOT WAKING UP... IT'S BEEN OVER 8 HOURS...
ALL HER VITAL SIGNS ARE NORMAL...
DON'T WORRY. SHE WILL BE OKAY.
I HOPE SO, TOO!
I DON'T DESERVE TO BE A DOCTOR. I SHOULD HAVE NEVER USED YOUR BLOOD.
I SHOULD RETURN MY LICENSE...

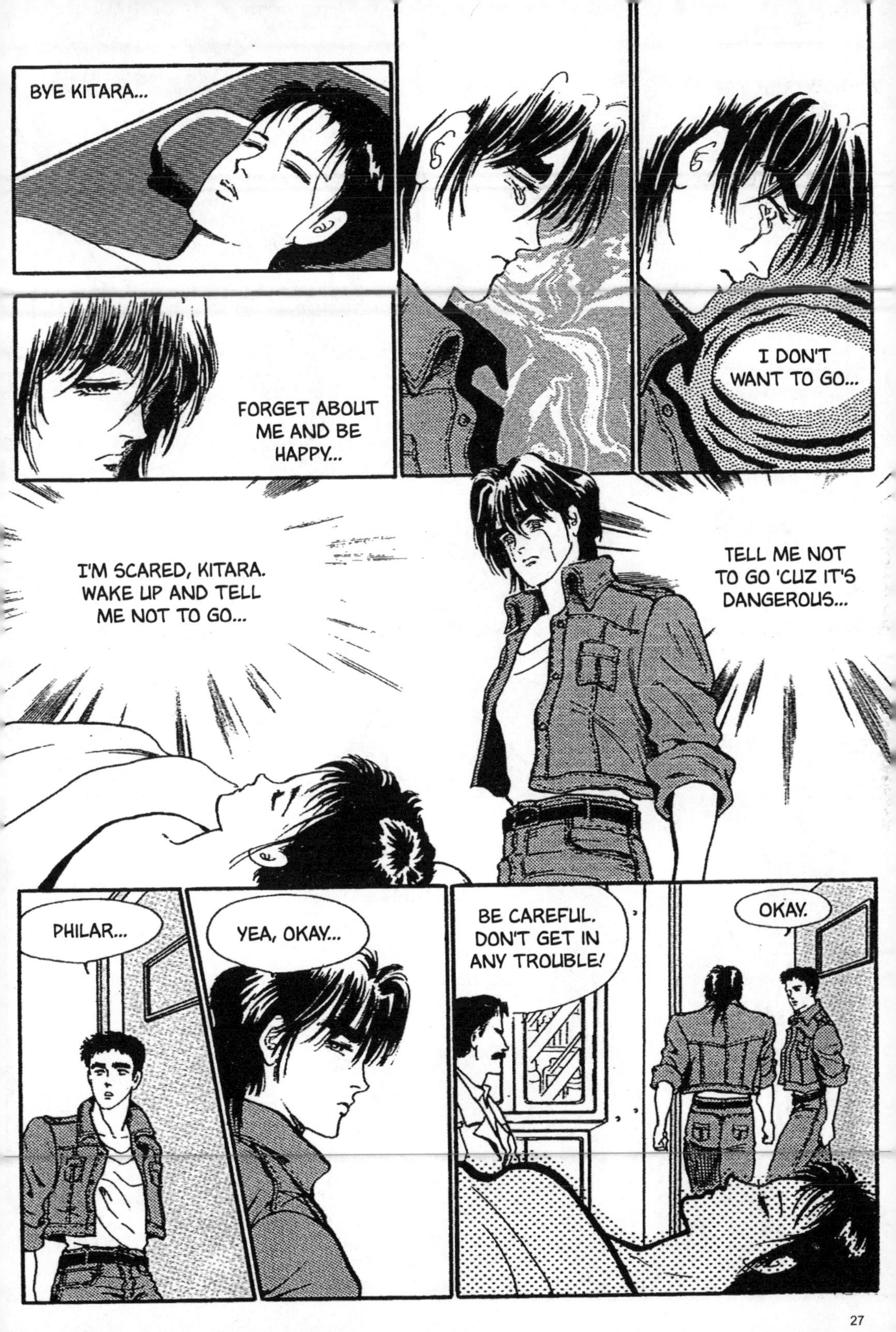
BYE KITARA...
FORGET ABOUT ME AND BE HAPPY...
I DON'T WANT TO GO...
I'M SCARED, KITARA. WAKE UP AND TELL ME NOT TO GO...
TELL ME NOT TO GO 'CUZ IT'S DANGEROUS...
PHILAR...
YEA, OKAY...
BE CAREFUL. DON'T GET IN ANY TROUBLE!
OKAY.

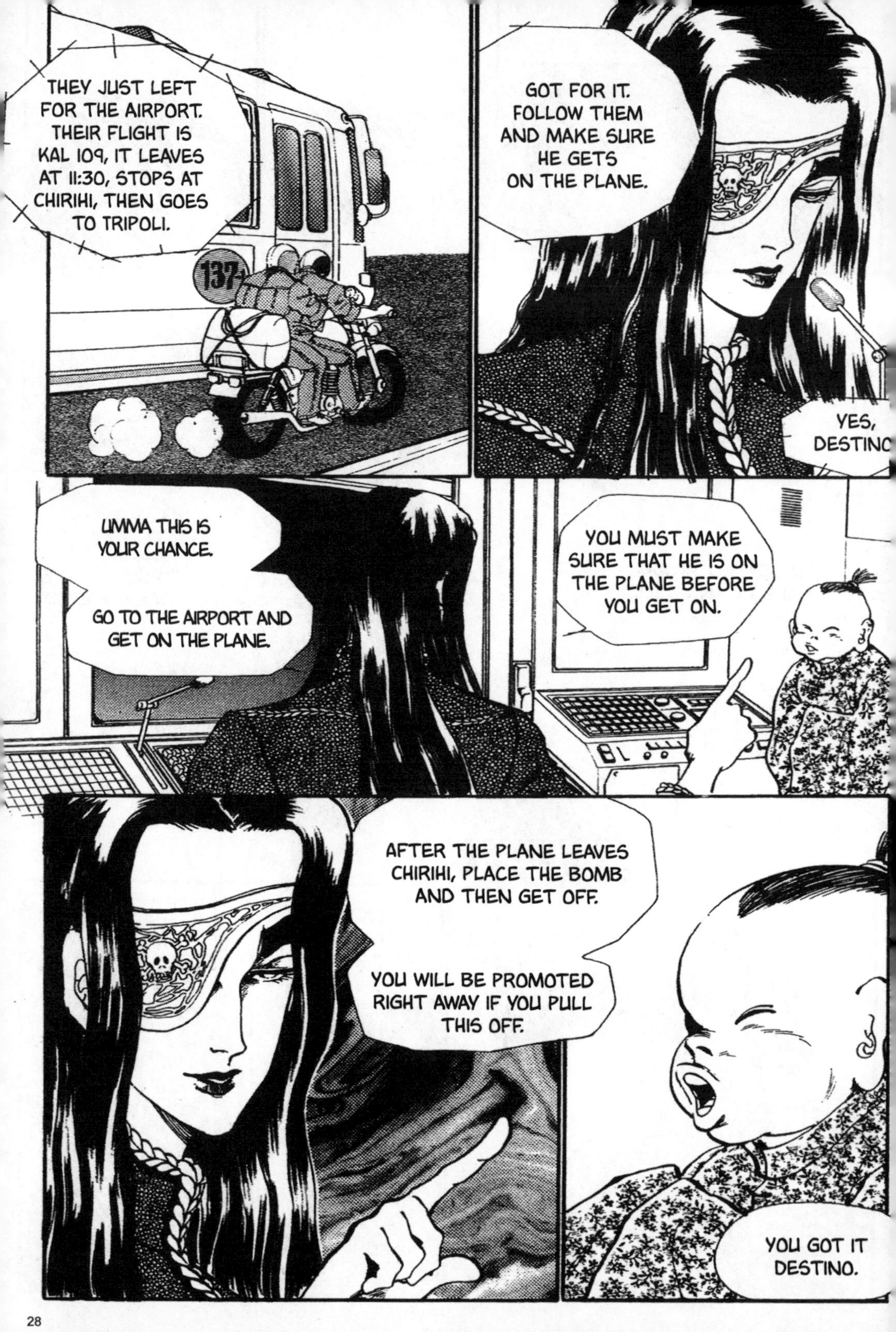
THEY JUST LEFT FOR THE AIRPORT. THEIR FLIGHT IS KAL 109, IT LEAVES AT 11:30, STOPS AT CHIRIHI, THEN GOES TO TRIPOLI.
GOT FOR IT. FOLLOW THEM AND MAKE SURE HE GETS ON THE PLANE.
YES, DESTINO
UMMA THIS IS YOUR CHANCE.
GO TO THE AIRPORT AND GET ON THE PLANE.
YOU MUST MAKE SURE THAT HE IS ON THE PLANE BEFORE YOU GET ON.
AFTER THE PLANE LEAVES CHIRIHI, PLACE THE BOMB AND THEN GET OFF.
YOU WILL BE PROMOTED RIGHT AWAY IF YOU PULL THIS OFF.
YOU GOT IT DESTINO.

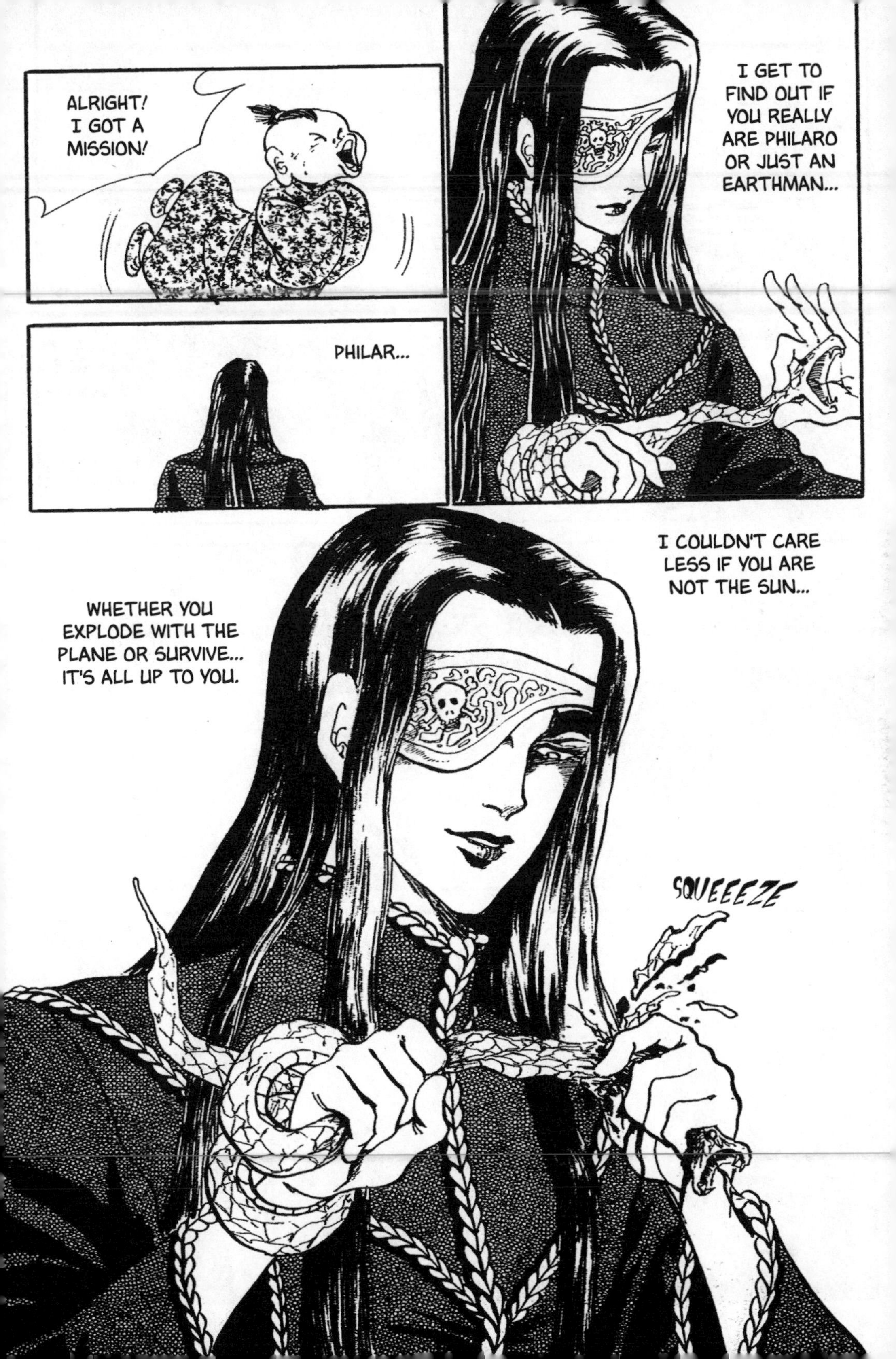
ALRIGHT! I GOT A MISSION!
I GET TO FIND OUT IF YOU REALLY ARE PHILARO OR JUST AN EARTHMAN...
PHILAR...
I COULDN'T CARE LESS IF YOU ARE NOT THE SUN...
WHETHER YOU EXPLODE WITH THE PLANE OR SURVIVE... IT'S ALL UP TO YOU.
SQUEEEZE

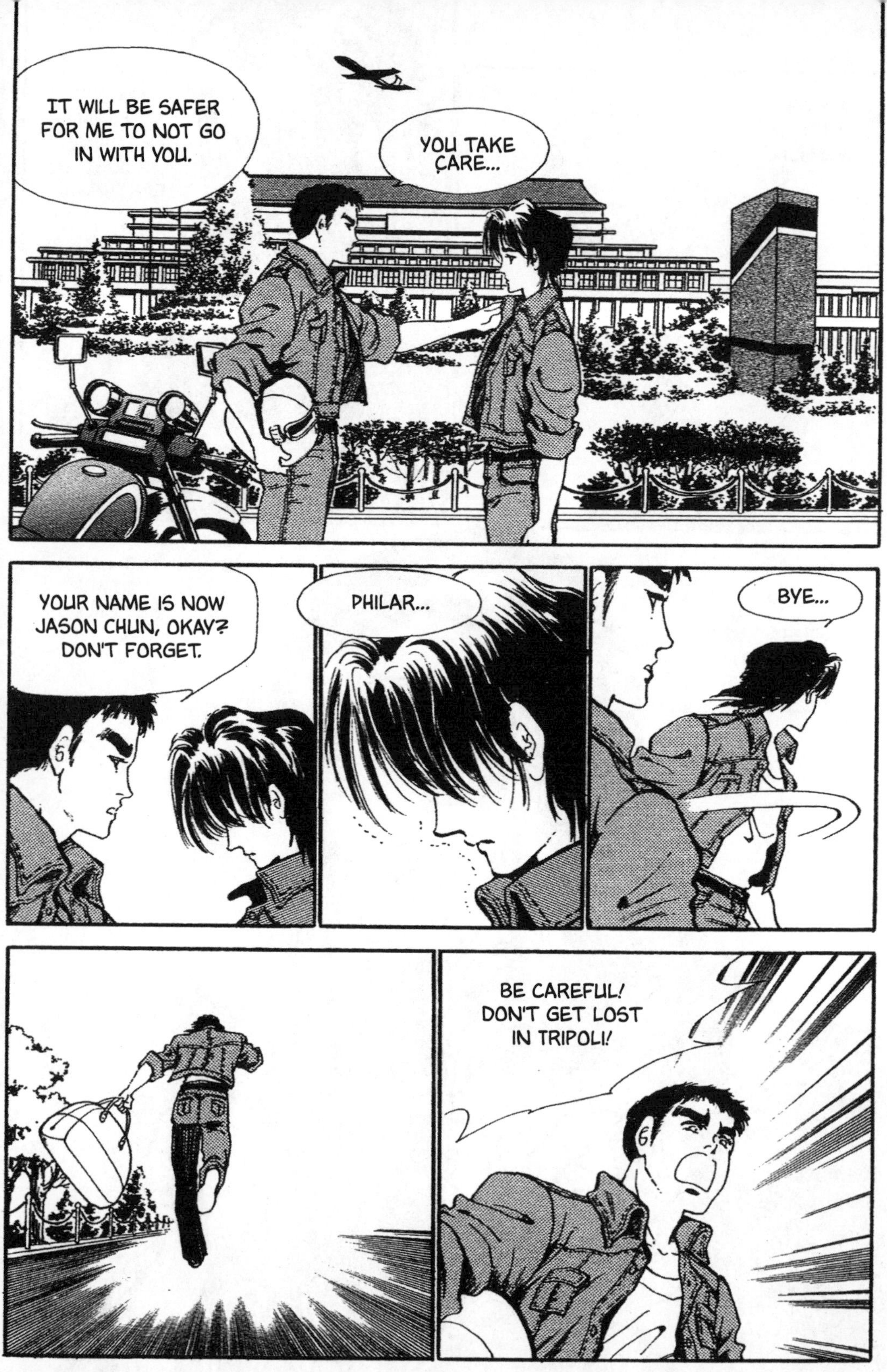
IT WILL BE SAFER FOR ME TO NOT GO IN WITH YOU.
YOU TAKE CARE...
YOUR NAME IS NOW JASON CHUN, OKAY? DON'T FORGET.
PHILAR...
BYE...
BE CAREFUL! DON'T GET LOST IN TRIPOLI!

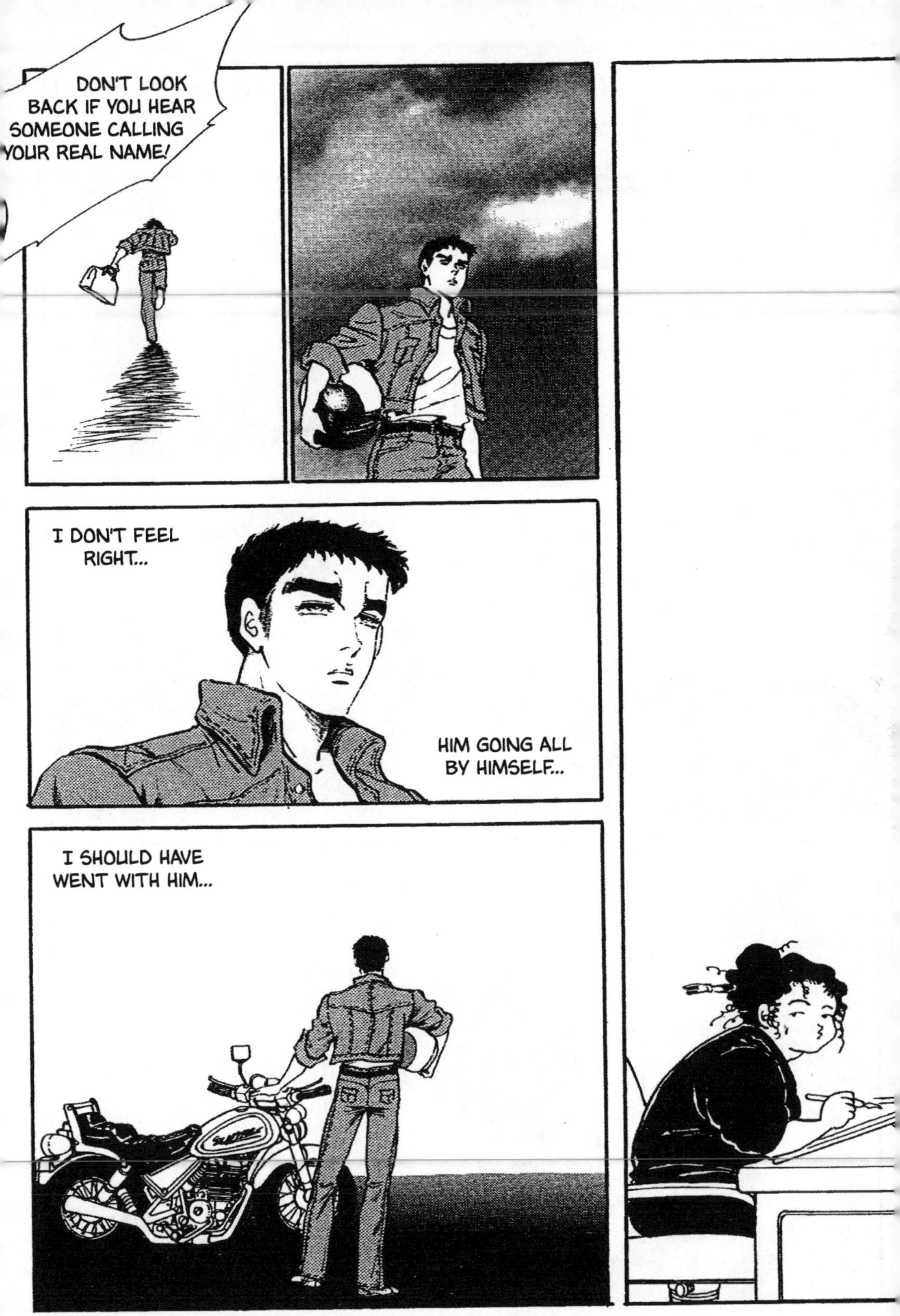
DON'T LOOK BACK IF YOU HEAR SOMEONE CALLING YOUR REAL NAME!
I DON'T FEEL RIGHT...
HIM GOING ALL BY HIMSELF...
I SHOULD HAVE WENT WITH HIM...

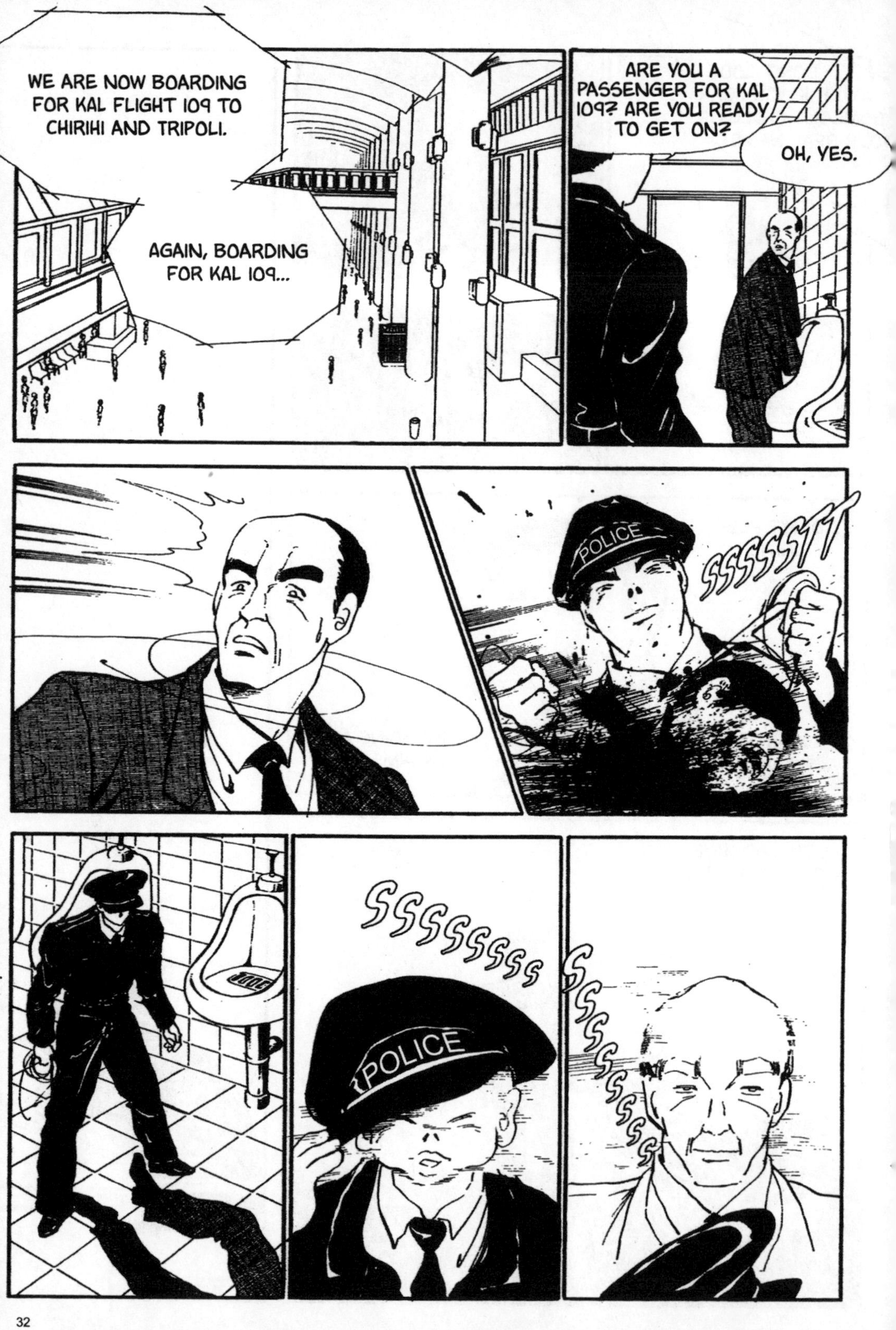
WE ARE NOW BOARDING FOR KAL FLIGHT 109 TO CHIRIHI AND TRIPOLI.
AGAIN, BOARDING FOR KAL 109...
ARE YOU A PASSENGER FOR KAL 109? ARE YOU READY TO GET ON?
OH, YES.
POLICE
SSSSSSTTT
SSSSSSSSS
POLICE
SSSSSSSS

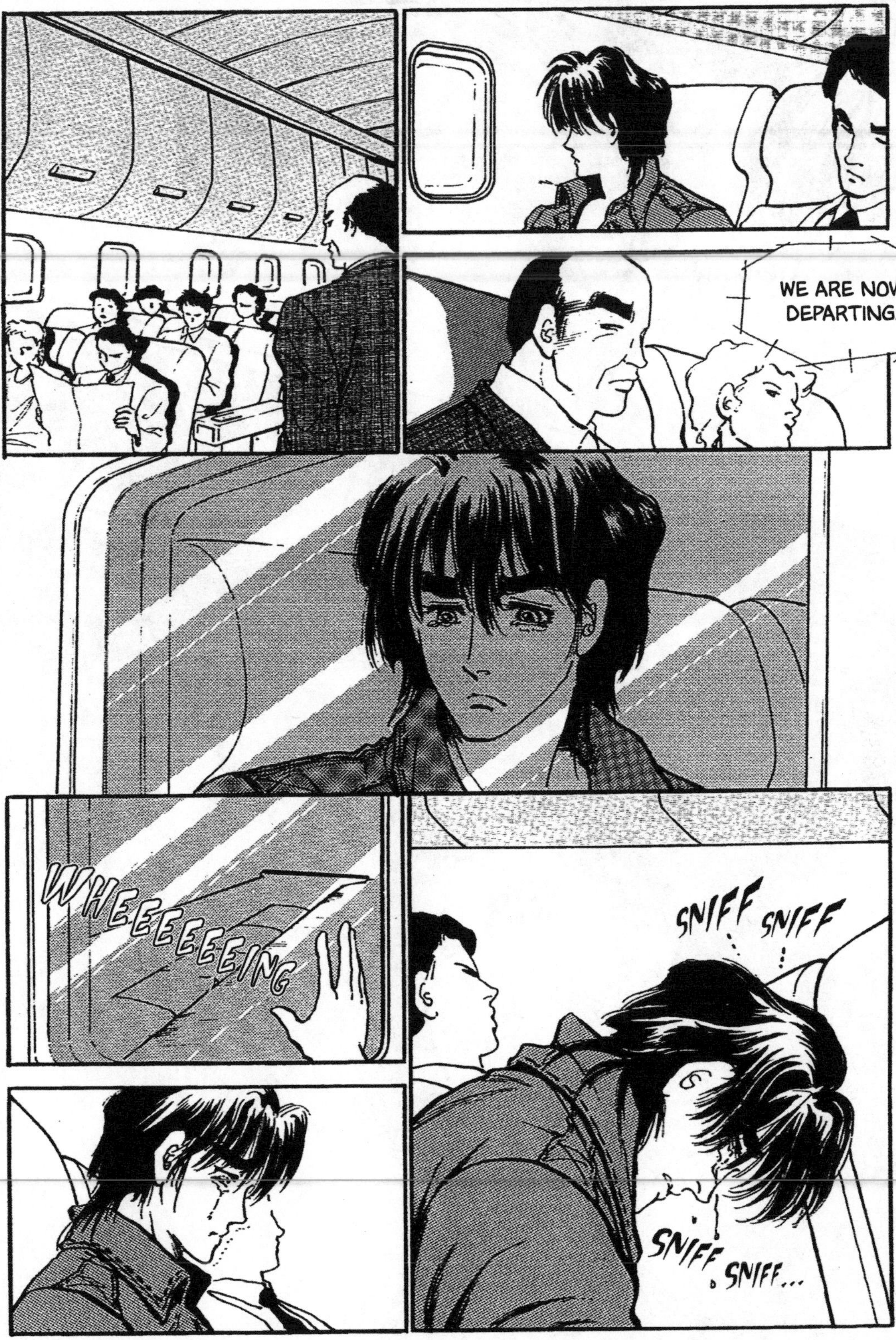
WE ARE NOW DEPARTING.
WHEEEEEEEING
SNIFF SNIFF
SNIFF SNIFF...

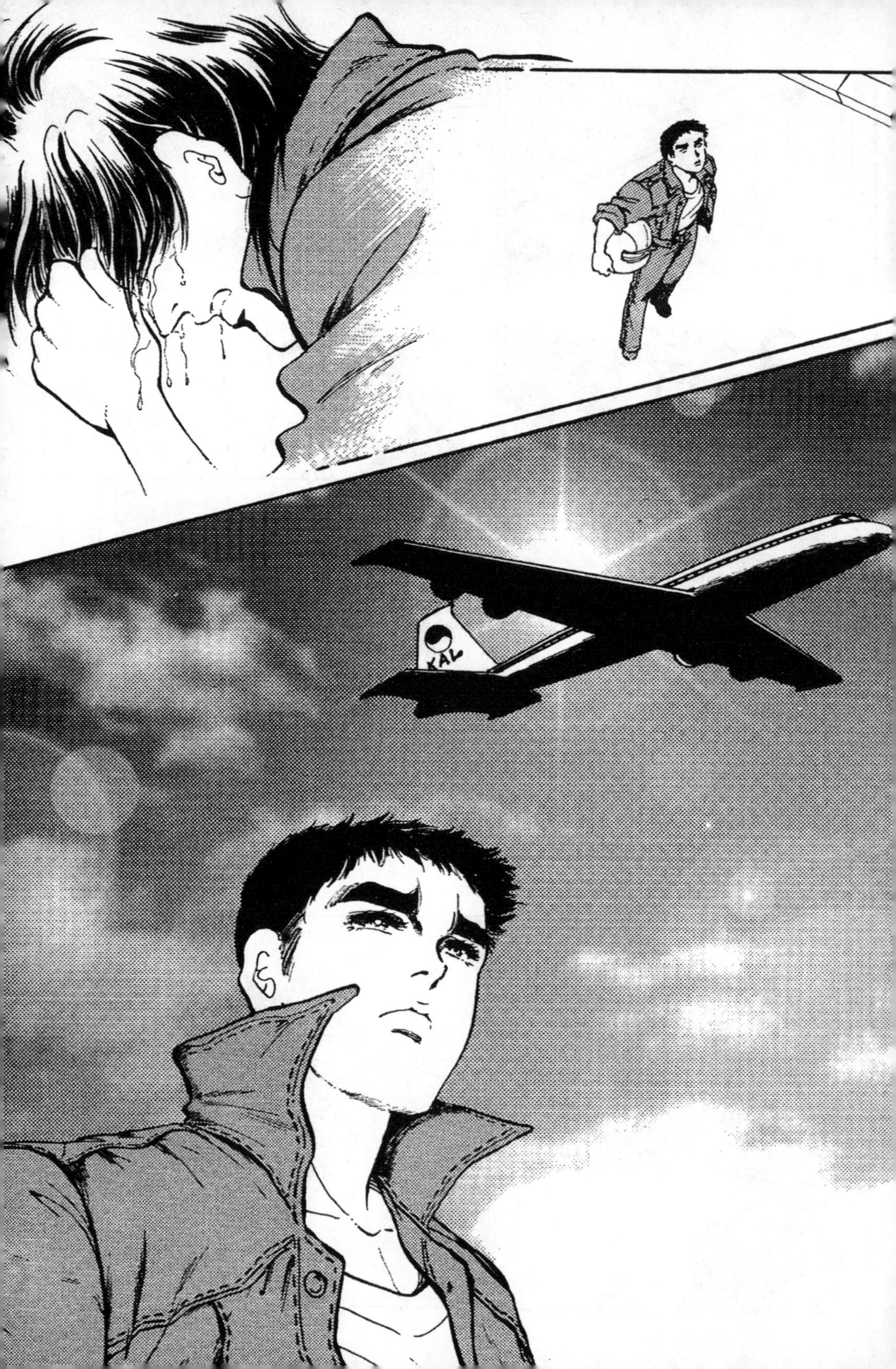
KAL

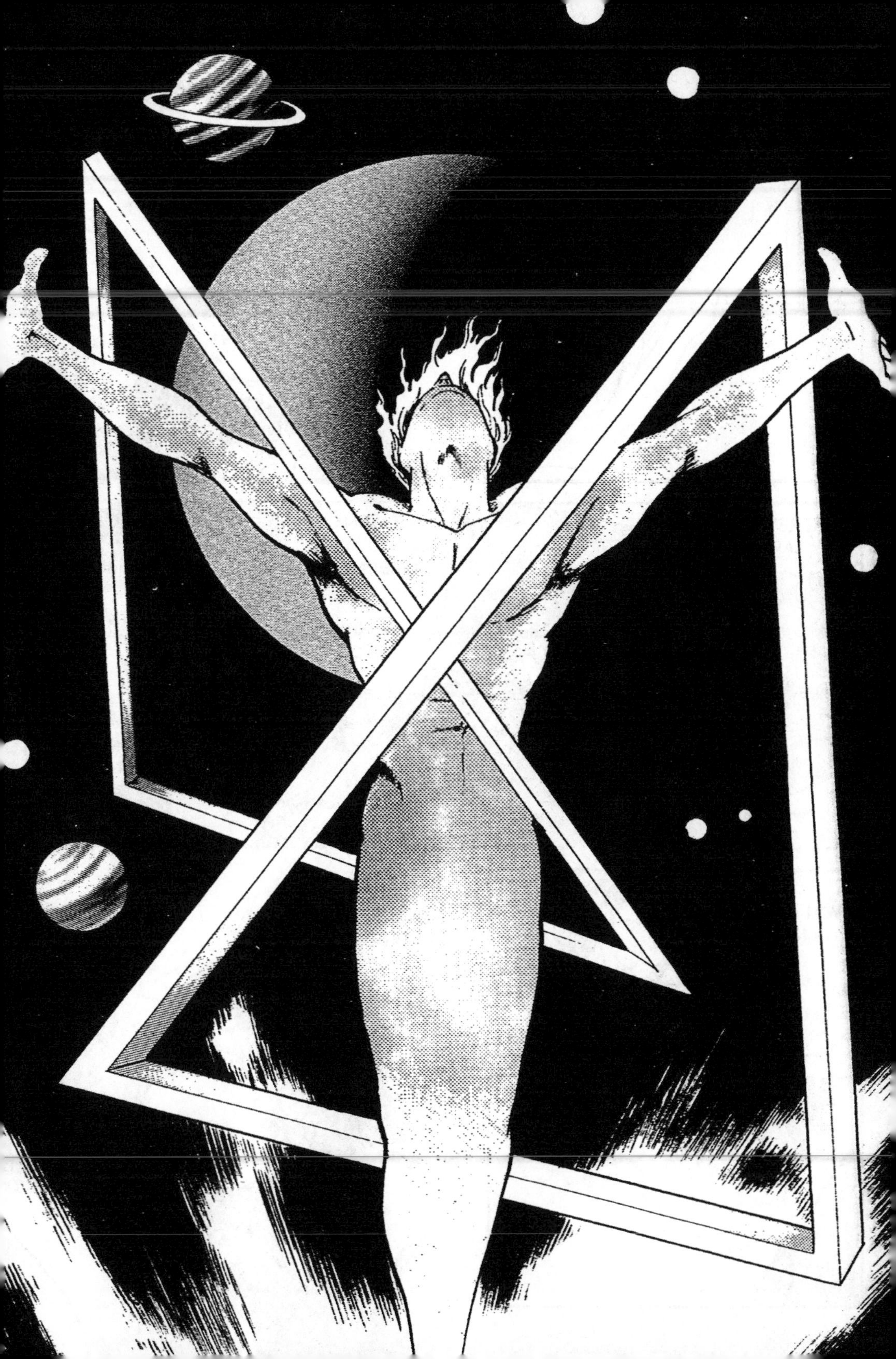

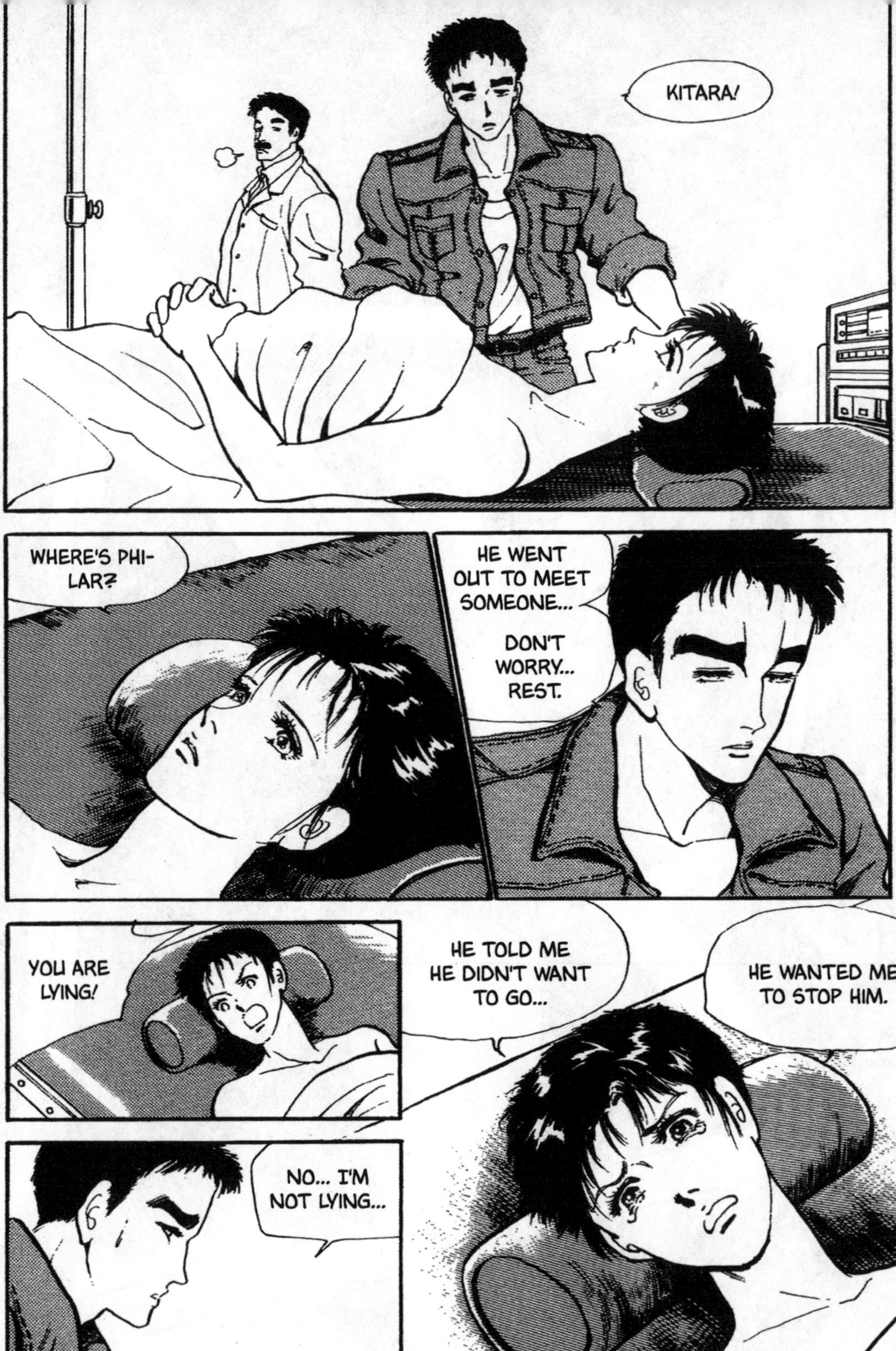
KITARA!
WHERE'S PHI-
LAR?
HE WENT
OUT TO MEET
SOMEONE...
DON'T
WORRY...
REST.
YOU ARE
LYING!
HE TOLD ME
HE DIDN'T WANT
TO GO...
HE WANTED ME
TO STOP HIM.
NO... I'M
NOT LYING...

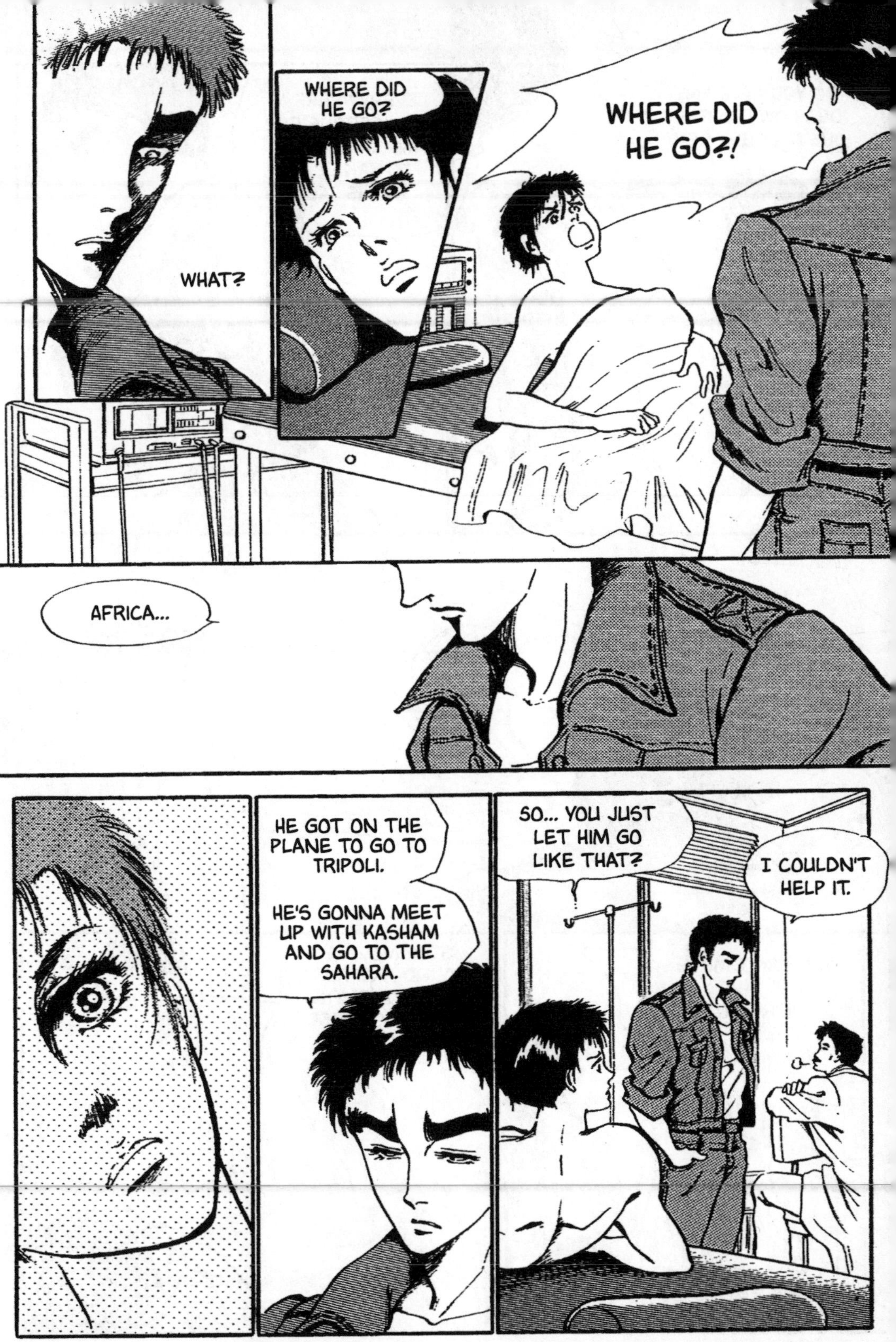
WHAT?
WHERE DID HE GO?
WHERE DID HE GO?!
AFRICA...
HE GOT ON THE PLANE TO GO TO TRIPOLI.
HE'S GONNA MEET UP WITH KASHAM AND GO TO THE SAHARA.
SO... YOU JUST LET HIM GO LIKE THAT?
I COULDN'T HELP IT.

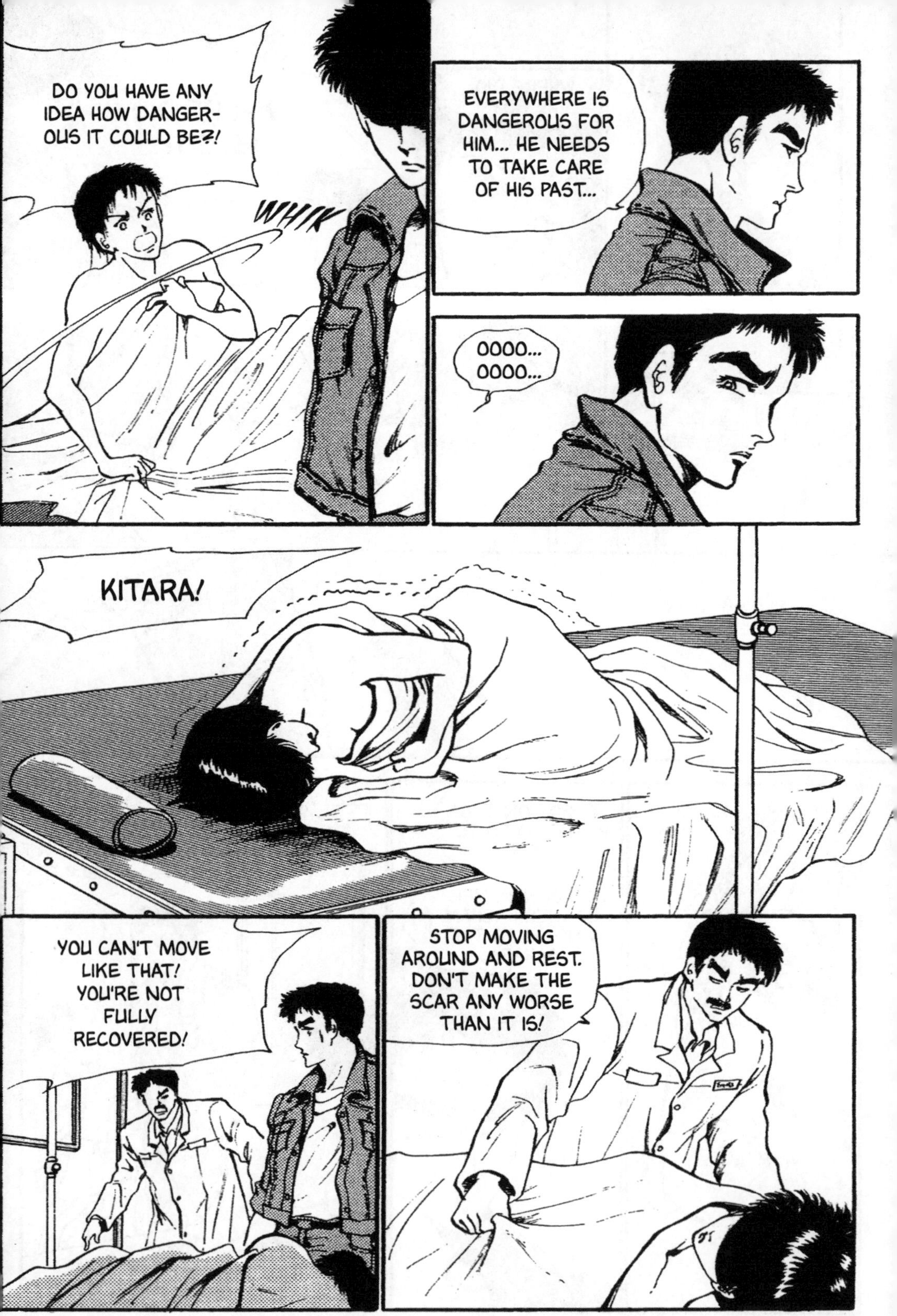
DO YOU HAVE ANY IDEA HOW DANGER-OUS IT COULD BE?!
WHIK
EVERYWHERE IS DANGEROUS FOR HIM... HE NEEDS TO TAKE CARE OF HIS PAST...
OOOO... OOOO...
KITARA!
YOU CAN'T MOVE LIKE THAT! YOU'RE NOT FULLY RECOVERED!
STOP MOVING AROUND AND REST. DON'T MAKE THE SCAR ANY WORSE THAN IT IS!

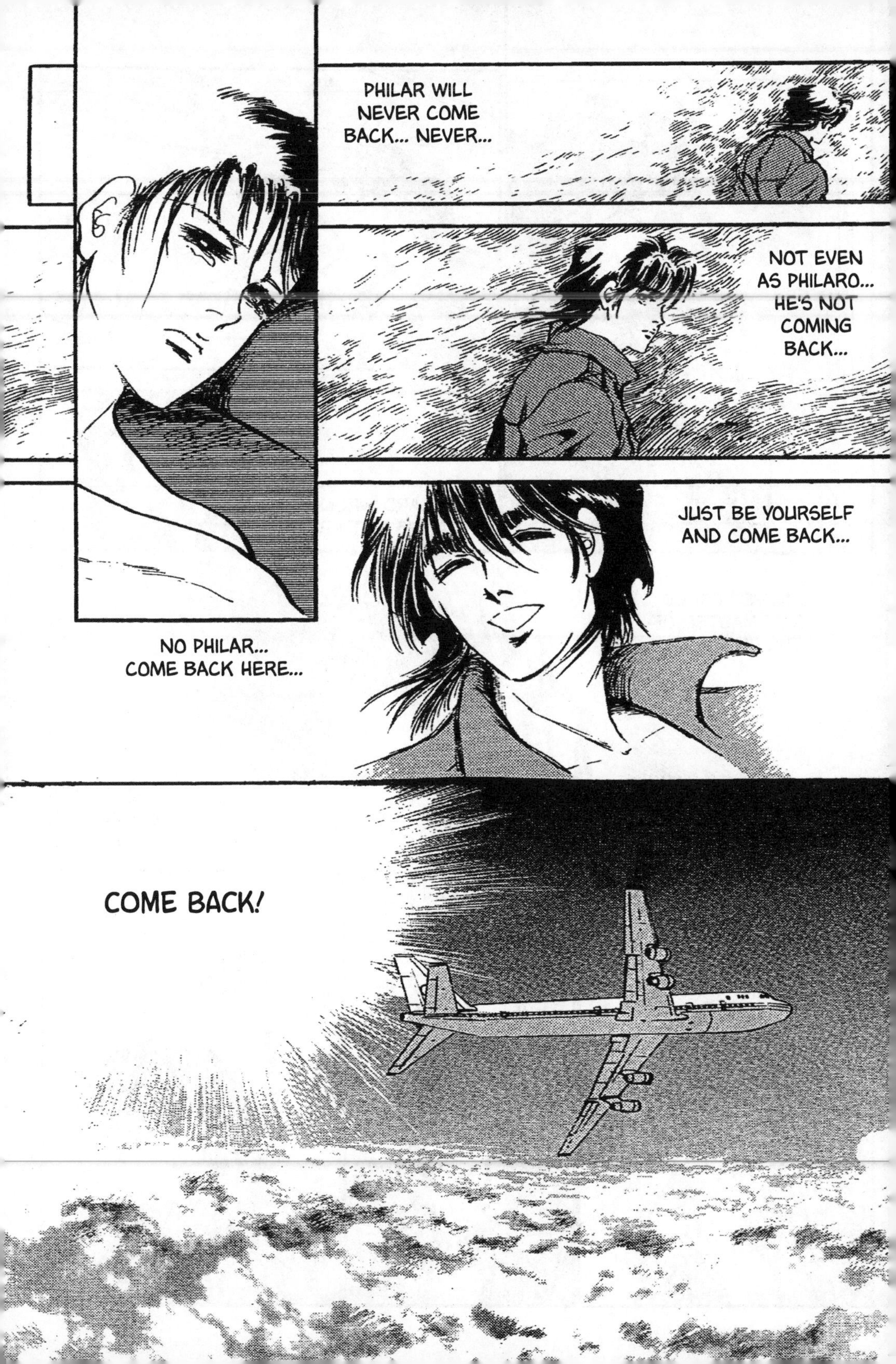
PHILAR WILL NEVER COME BACK... NEVER...
NOT EVEN AS PHILARO... HE'S NOT COMING BACK...
JUST BE YOURSELF AND COME BACK...
NO PHILAR... COME BACK HERE...
COME BACK!

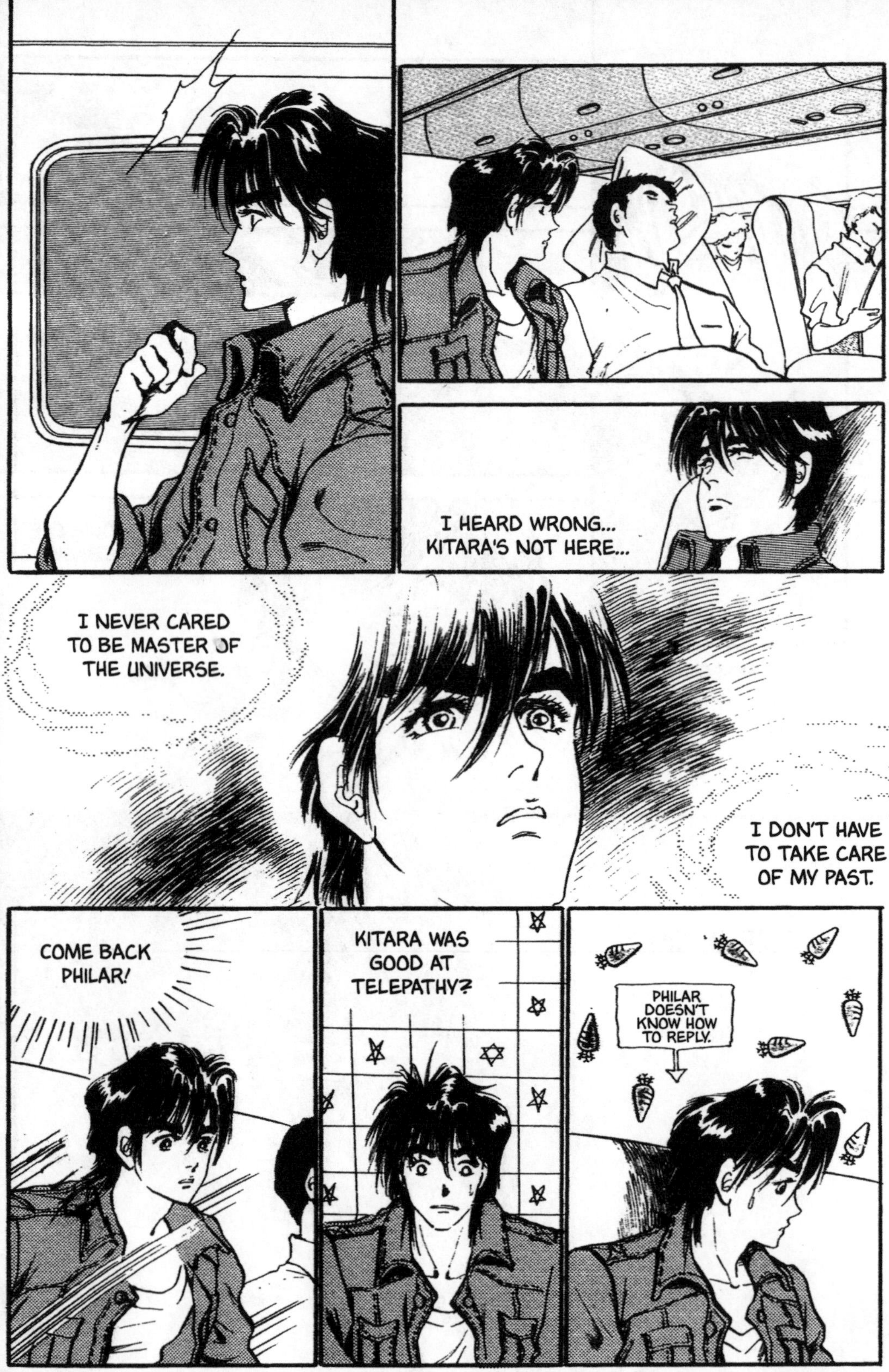
I HEARD WRONG... KITARA'S NOT HERE...
I NEVER CARED TO BE MASTER OF THE UNIVERSE.
I DON'T HAVE TO TAKE CARE OF MY PAST.
COME BACK PHILAR!
KITARA WAS GOOD AT TELEPATHY?
PHILAR DOESN'T KNOW HOW TO REPLY.

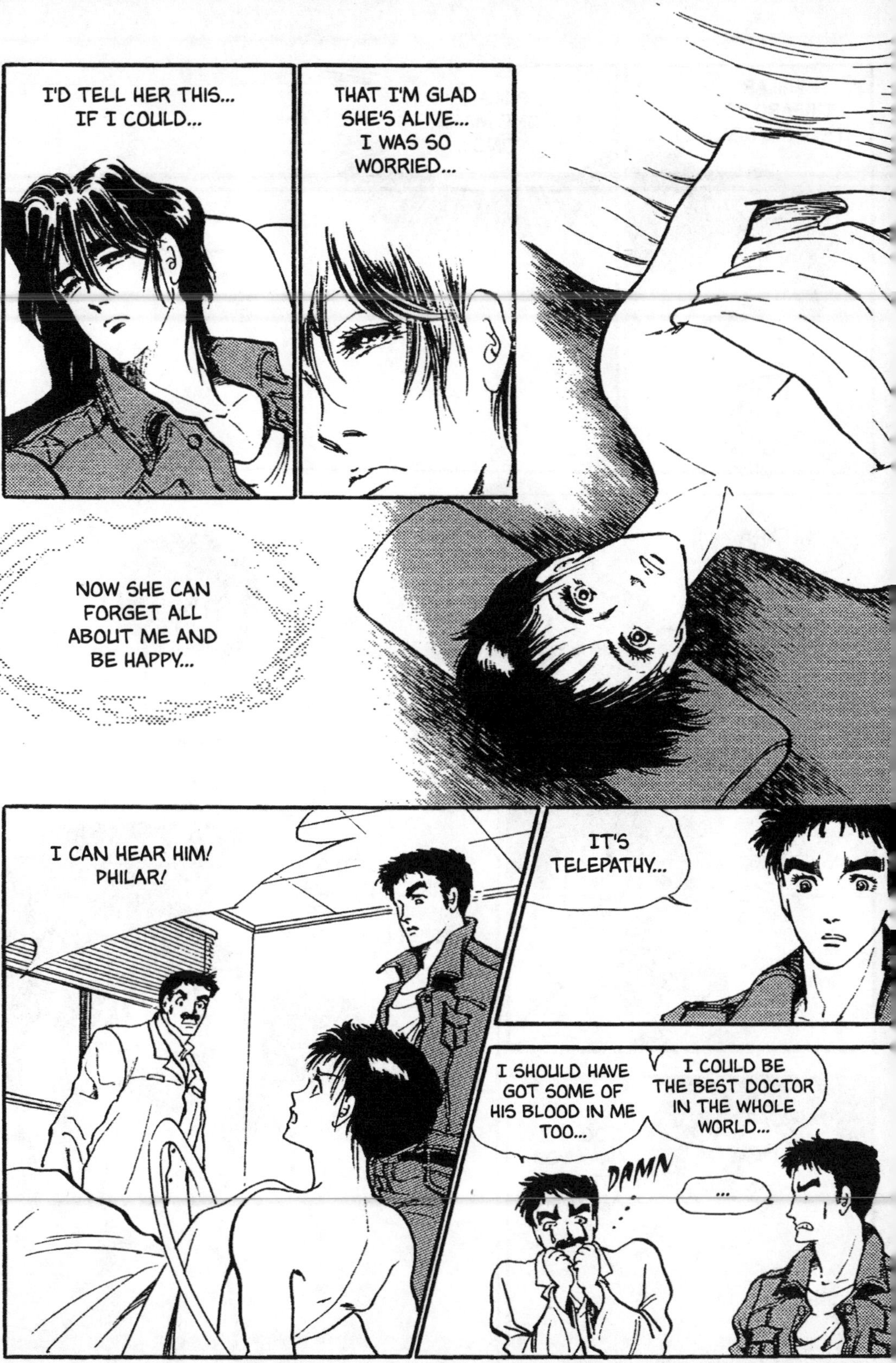

I'D TELL HER THIS... IF I COULD...
THAT I'M GLAD SHE'S ALIVE... I WAS SO WORRIED...
NOW SHE CAN FORGET ALL ABOUT ME AND BE HAPPY...
I CAN HEAR HIM! PHILAR!
IT'S TELEPATHY...
I COULD BE THE BEST DOCTOR IN THE WHOLE WORLD...
I SHOULD HAVE GOT SOME OF HIS BLOOD IN ME TOO...
DAMN
...

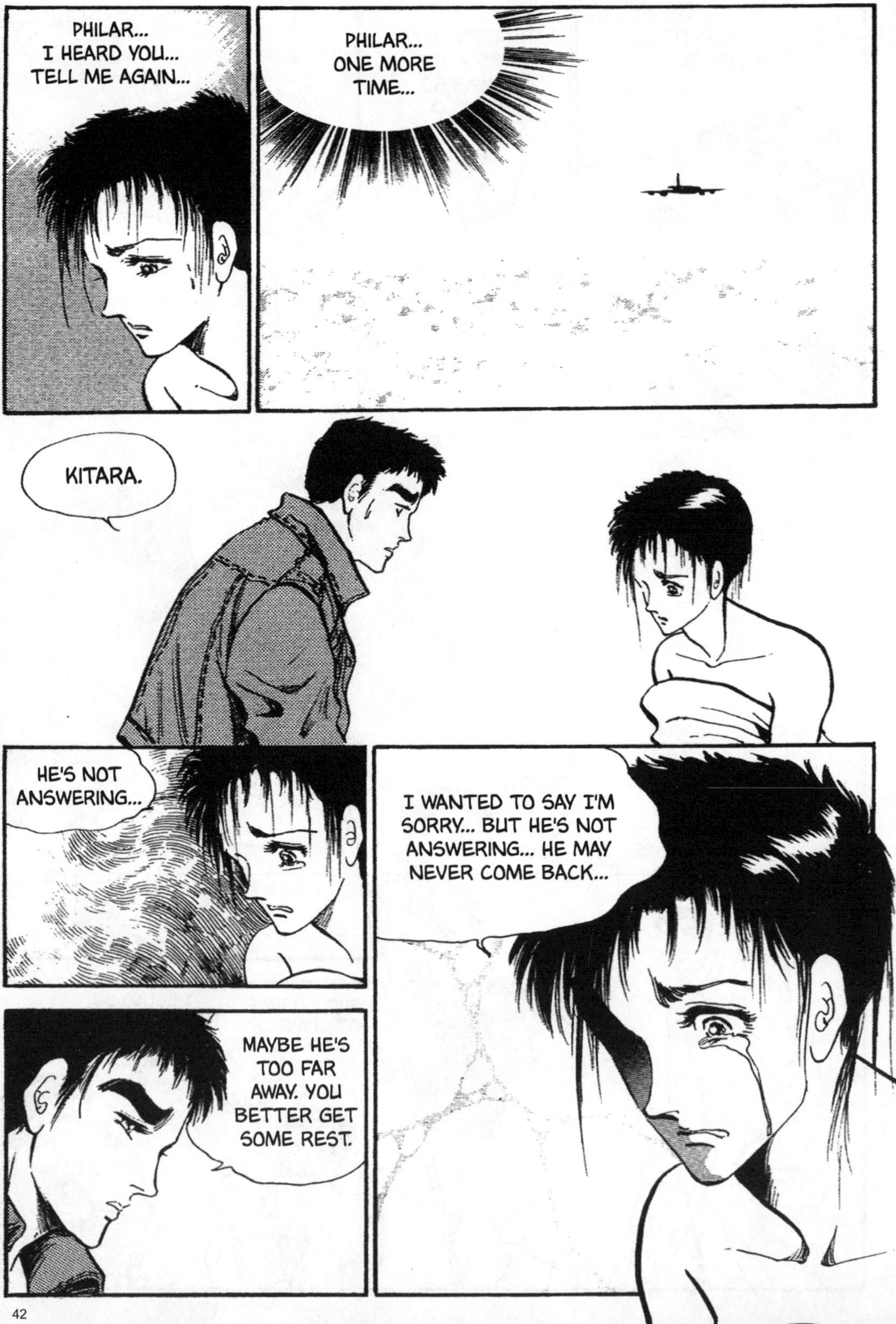

PHILAR... I HEARD YOU... TELL ME AGAIN...
PHILAR... ONE MORE TIME...
KITARA.
HE'S NOT ANSWERING...
I WANTED TO SAY I'M SORRY... BUT HE'S NOT ANSWERING... HE MAY NEVER COME BACK...
MAYBE HE'S TOO FAR AWAY. YOU BETTER GET SOME REST.

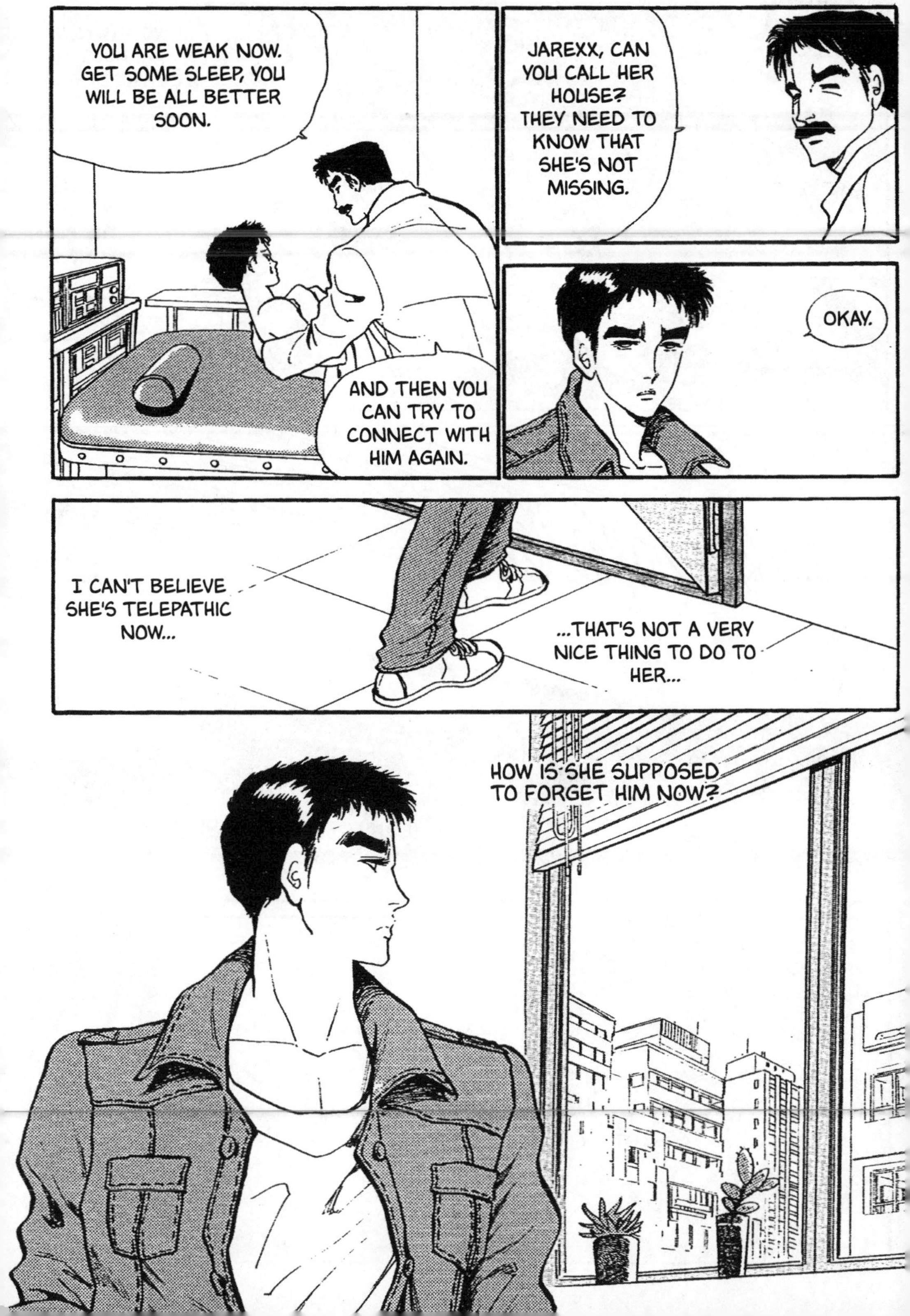
YOU ARE WEAK NOW. GET SOME SLEEP, YOU WILL BE ALL BETTER SOON.
AND THEN YOU CAN TRY TO CONNECT WITH HIM AGAIN.
JAREXX, CAN YOU CALL HER HOUSE? THEY NEED TO KNOW THAT SHE'S NOT MISSING.
OKAY.
I CAN'T BELIEVE SHE'S TELEPATHIC NOW...
...THAT'S NOT A VERY NICE THING TO DO TO HER...
HOW IS SHE SUPPOSED TO FORGET HIM NOW?

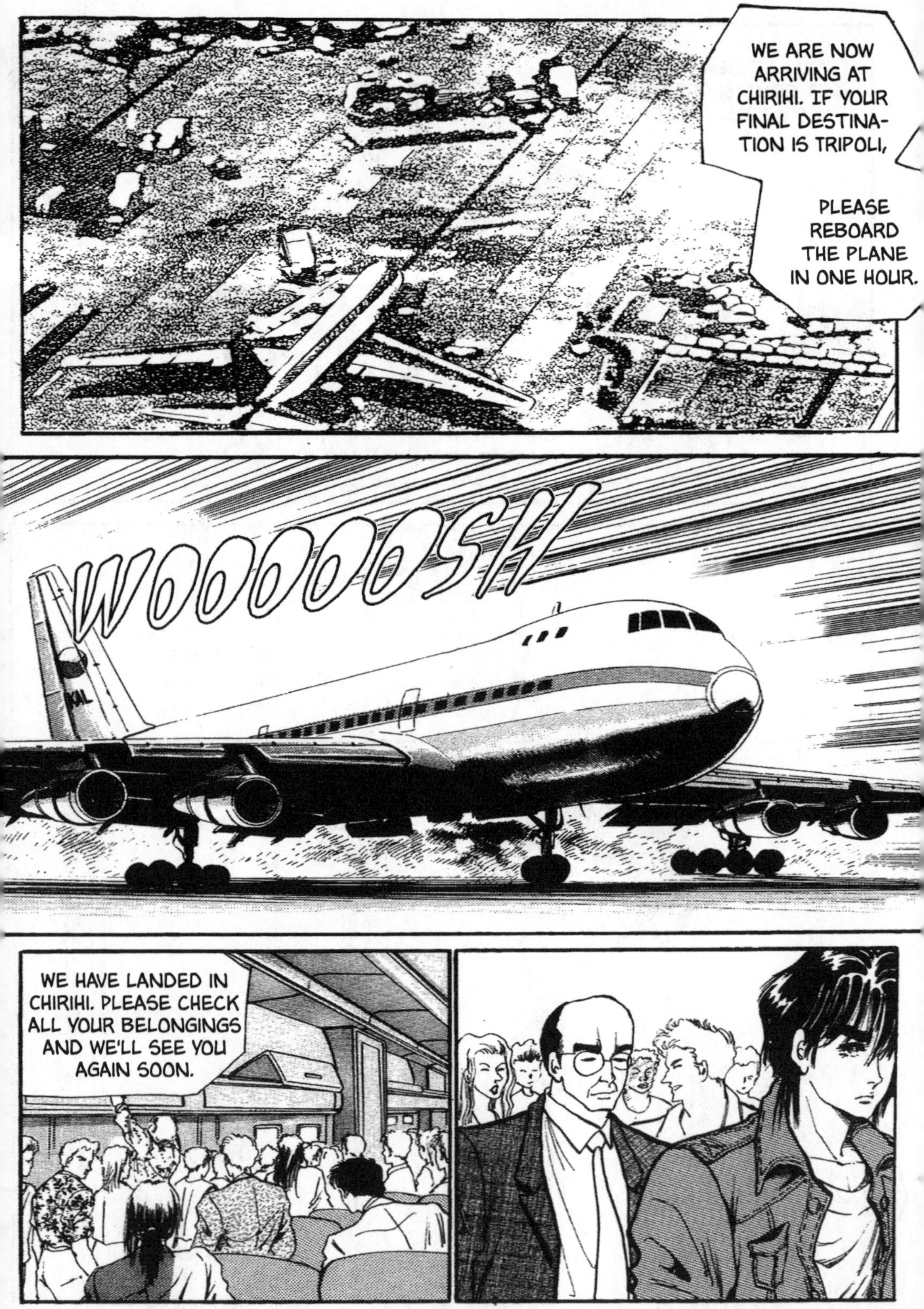
WE ARE NOW ARRIVING AT CHIRIHI. IF YOUR FINAL DESTINATION IS TRIPOLI,
PLEASE REBOARD THE PLANE IN ONE HOUR.
WOOOOOOSH
KAL
WE HAVE LANDED IN CHIRIHI. PLEASE CHECK ALL YOUR BELONGINGS AND WE'LL SEE YOU AGAIN SOON.

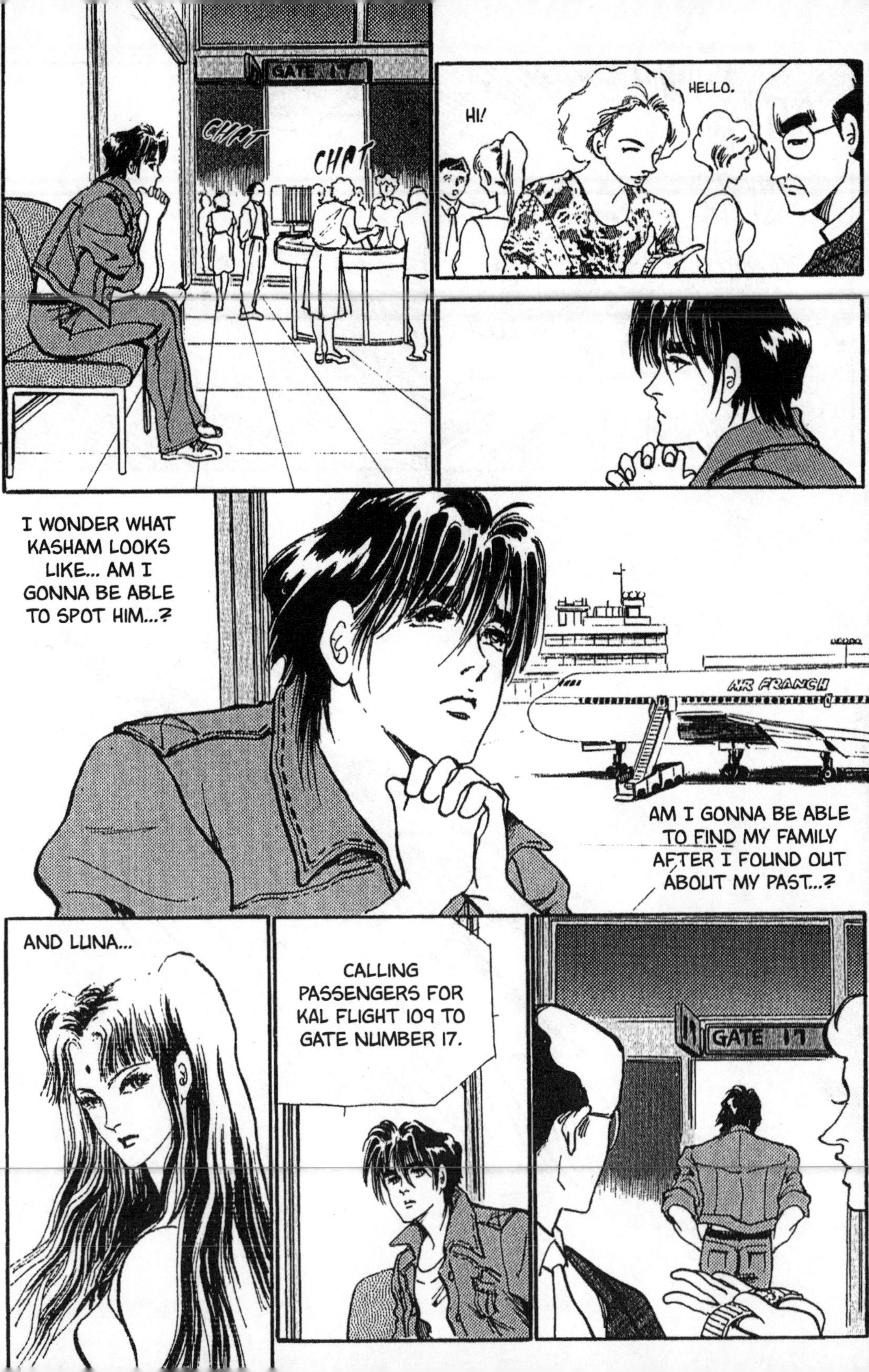
GATE 17
CHAT
CHAT
HI!
HELLO.
I WONDER WHAT KASHAM LOOKS LIKE... AM I GONNA BE ABLE TO SPOT HIM...?
AIR FRANCH
AM I GONNA BE ABLE TO FIND MY FAMILY AFTER I FOUND OUT ABOUT MY PAST...?
AND LUNA...
CALLING PASSENGERS FOR KAL FLIGHT 109 TO GATE NUMBER 17.
GATE 17

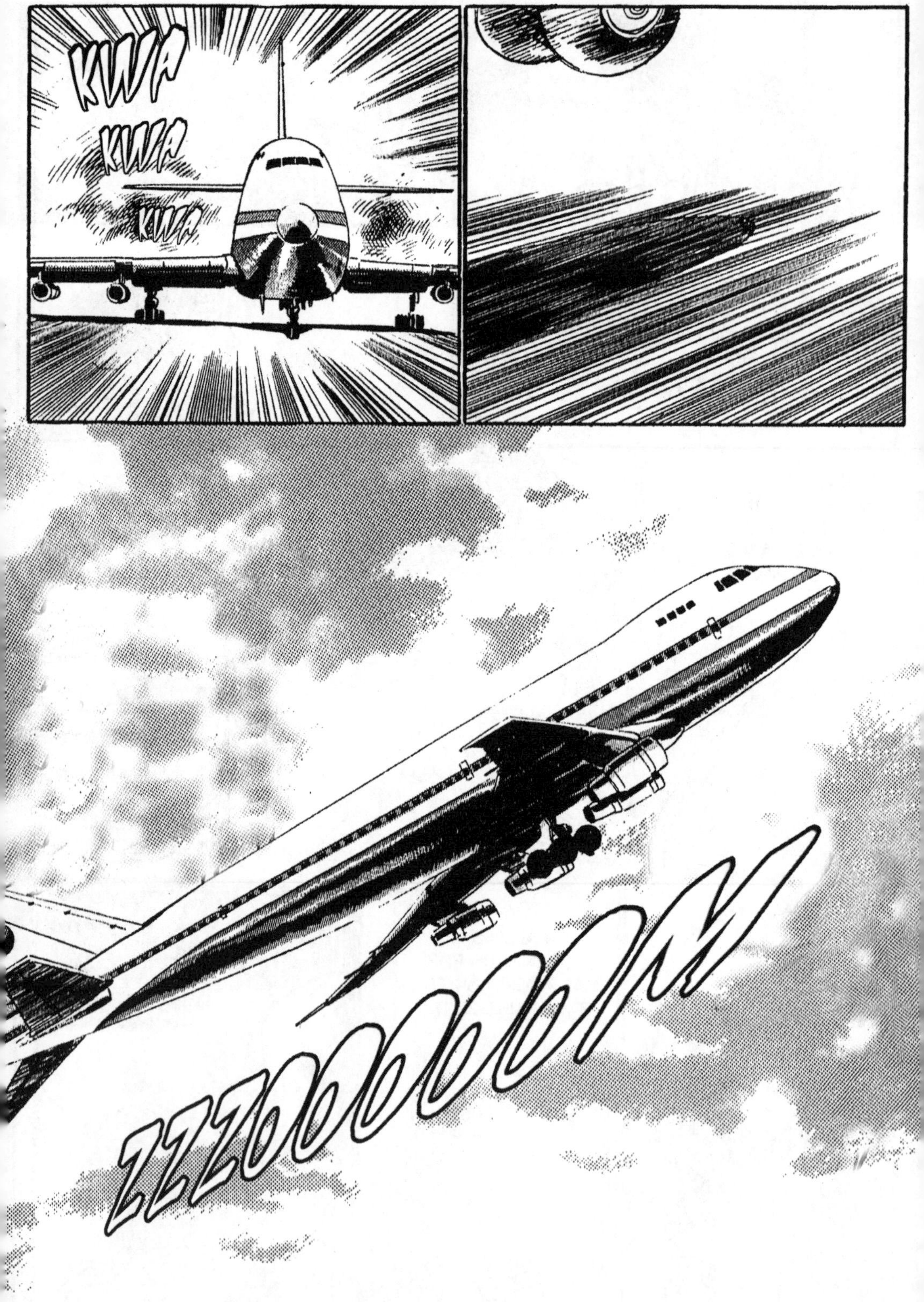
KWA
KWA
KWA
ZZZOOOOOM

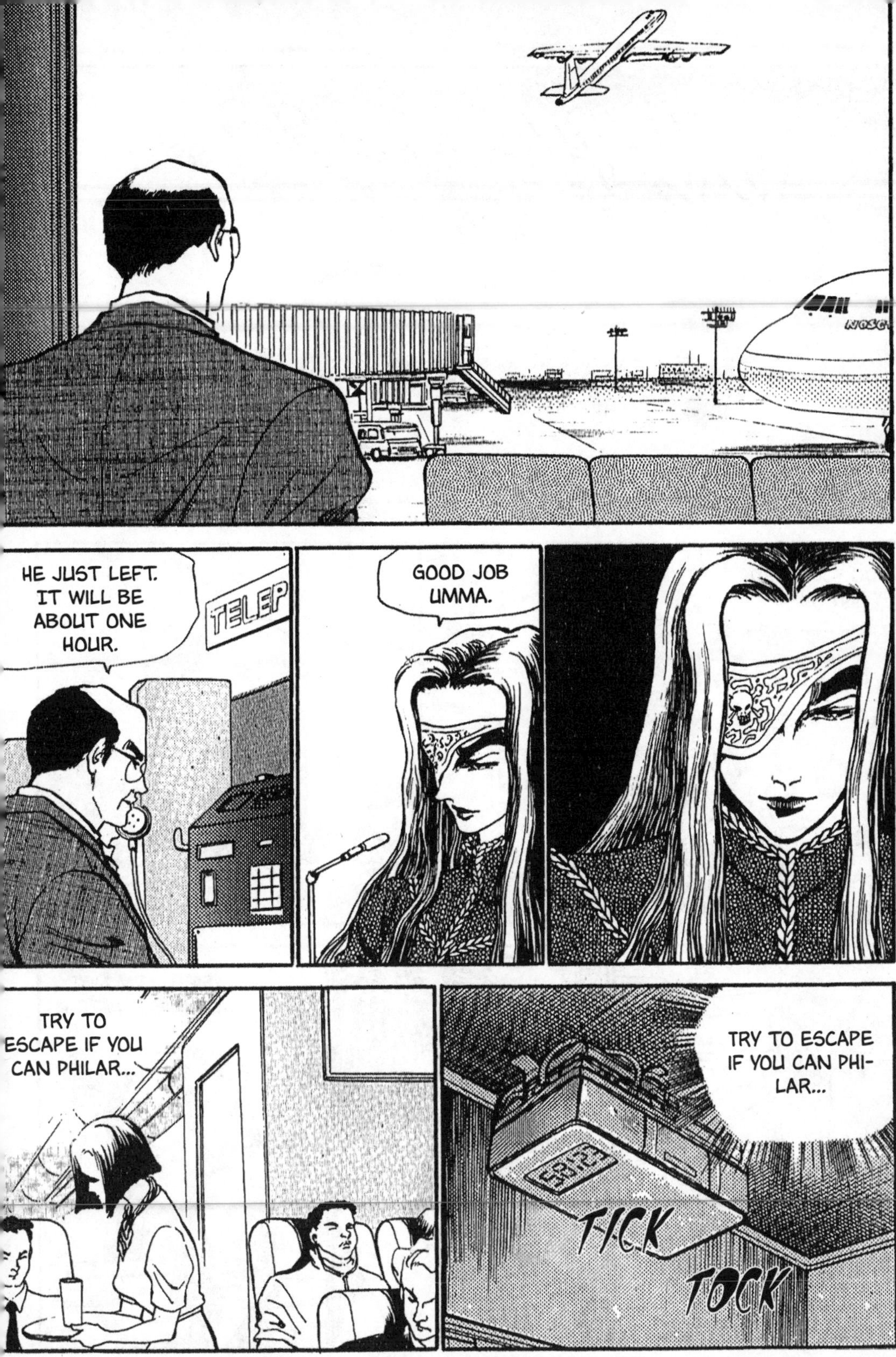
HE JUST LEFT. IT WILL BE ABOUT ONE HOUR.
TELEP
GOOD JOB UMMA.
TRY TO ESCAPE IF YOU CAN PHILAR...
TRY TO ESCAPE IF YOU CAN PHI-LAR...
TICK
TOCK

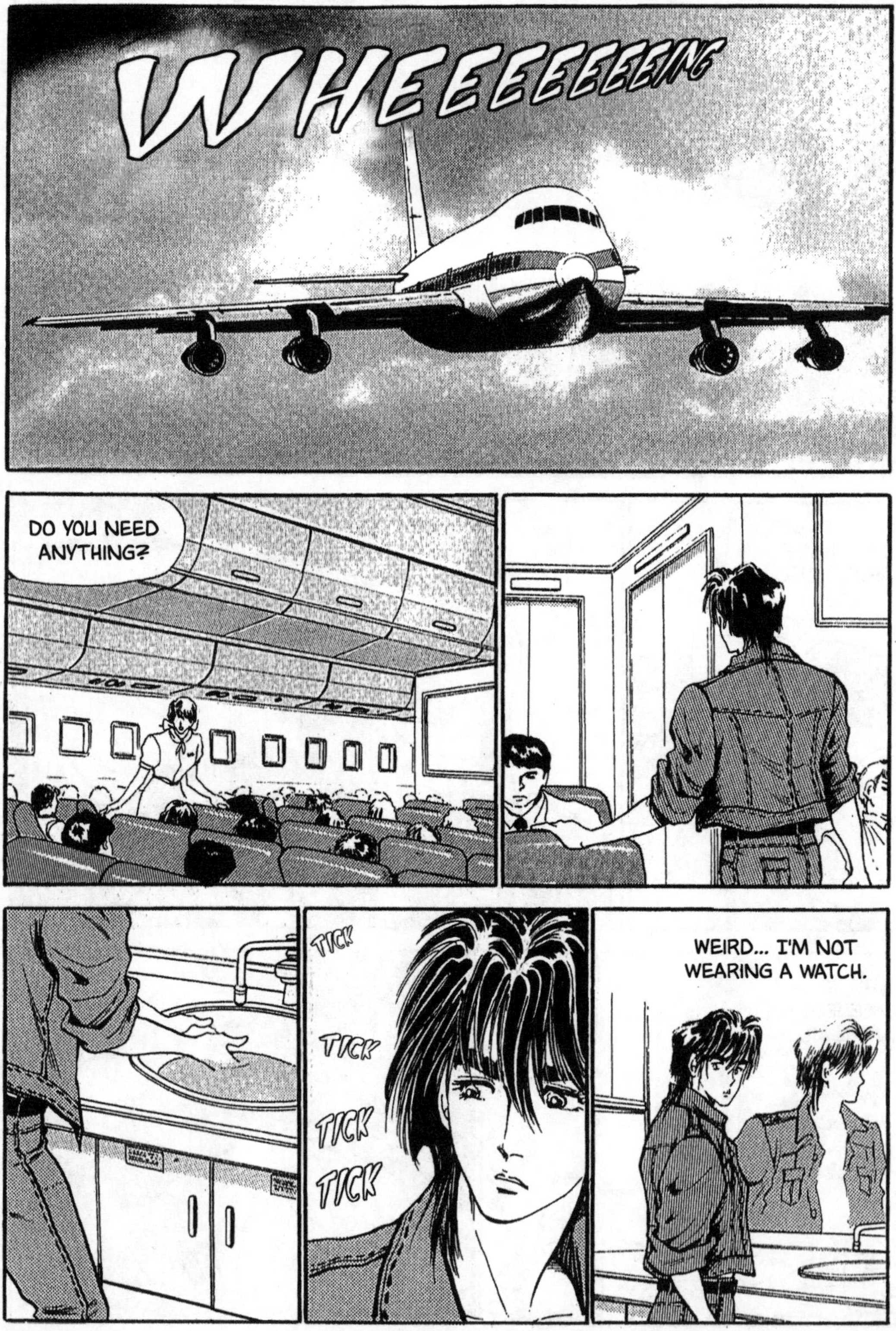
WHEEEEEEEEING
DO YOU NEED ANYTHING?
TICK
TICK
TICK
TICK
WEIRD... I'M NOT WEARING A WATCH.

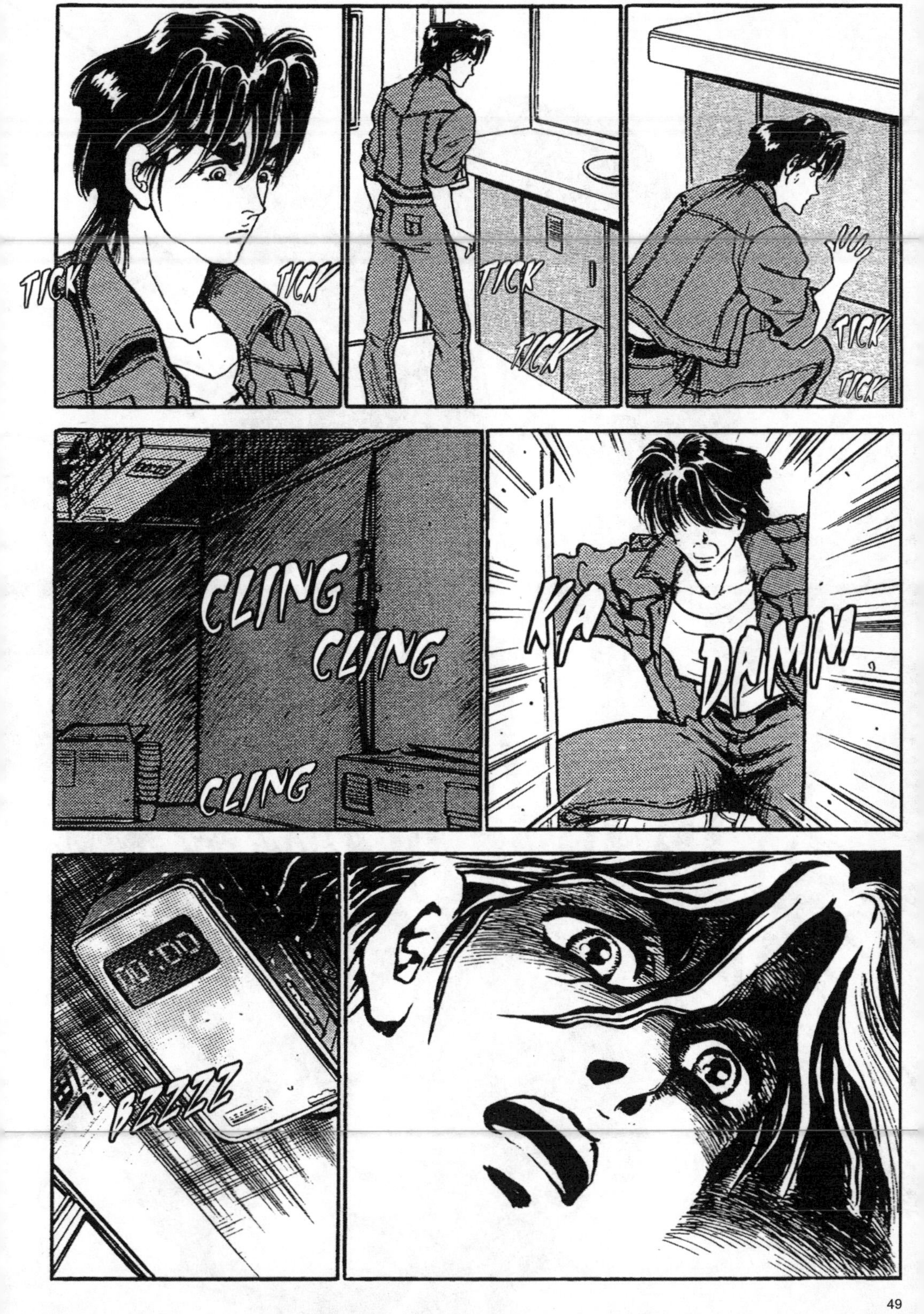
TICK
TICK
TICK
TICK
TICK
TICK
CLING
CLING
CLING
KA
DAMM
BZZZZ

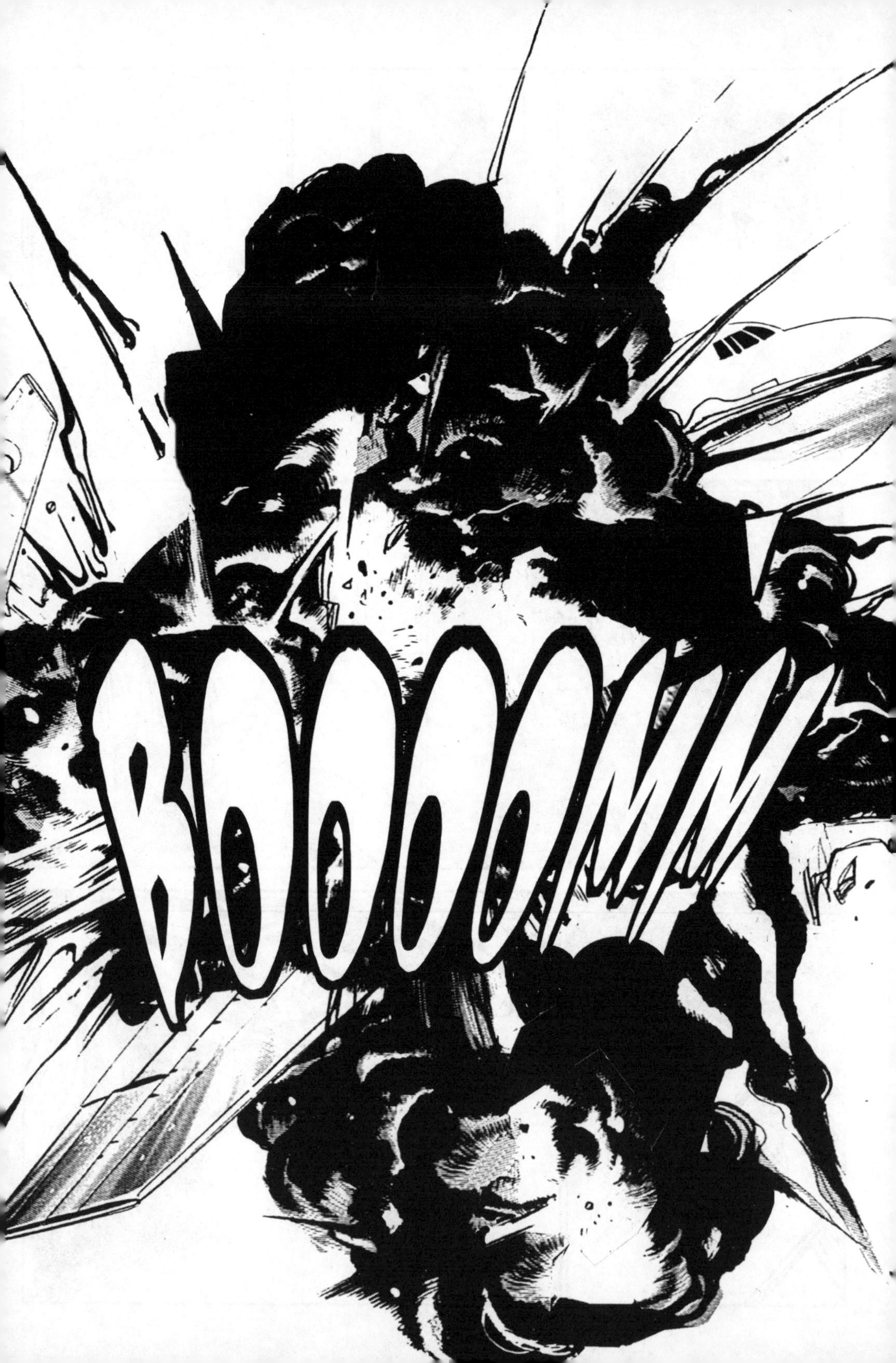
BOOOOMM

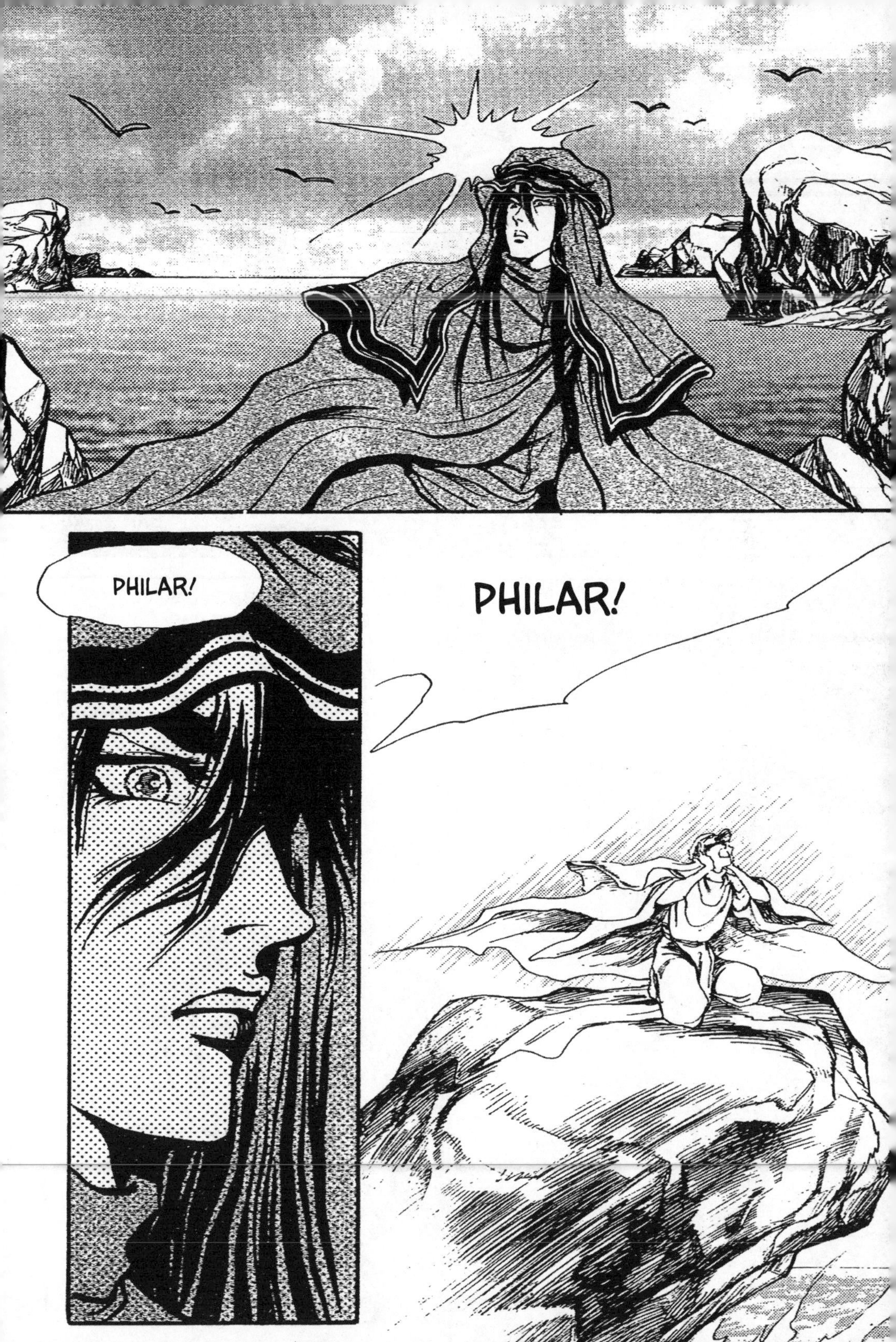
PHILAR!
PHILAR!

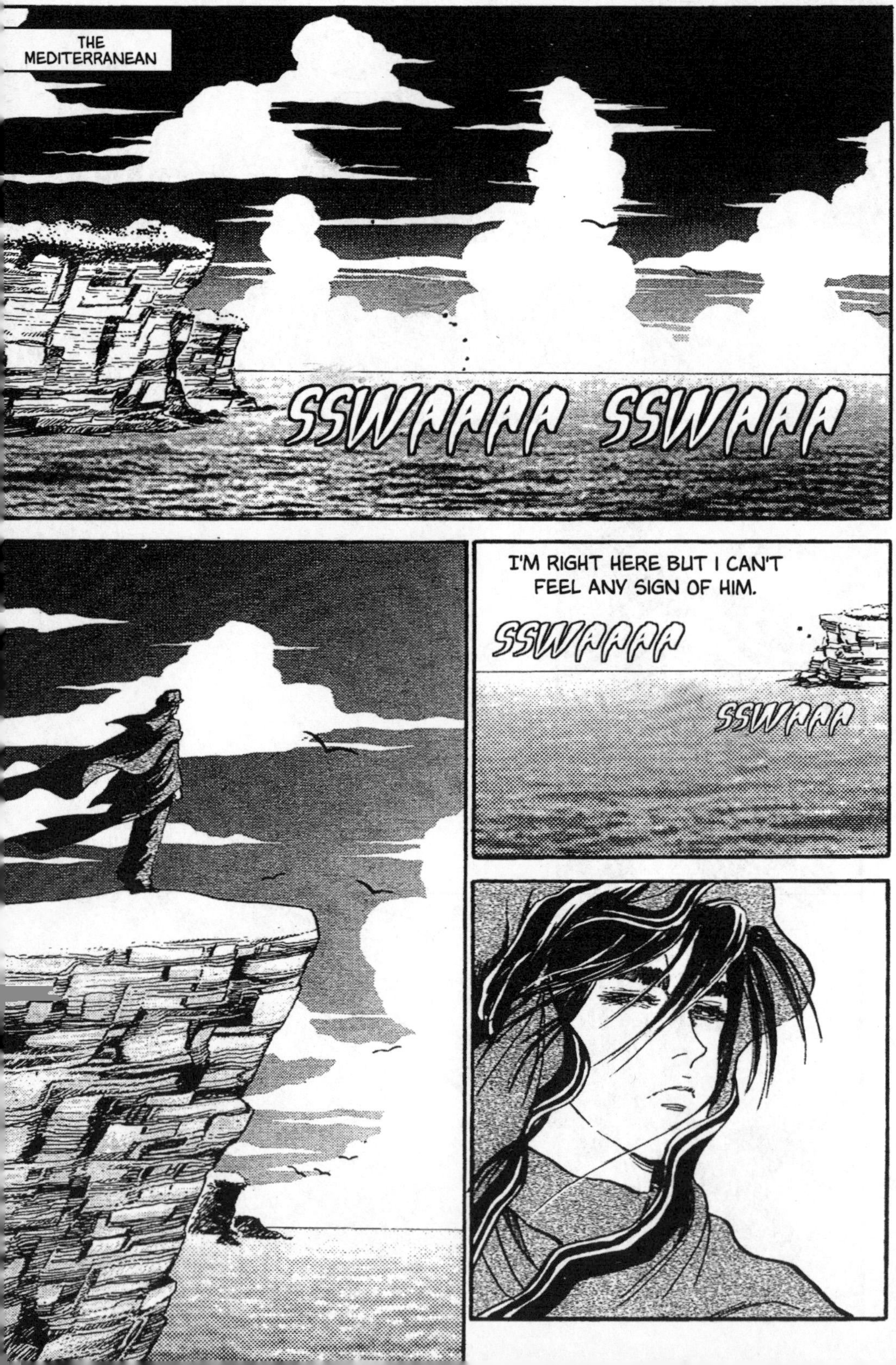
THE MEDITERRANEAN
SSWAAAA SSWAAA
I'M RIGHT HERE BUT I CAN'T FEEL ANY SIGN OF HIM.
SSWAAAA
SSWAAA

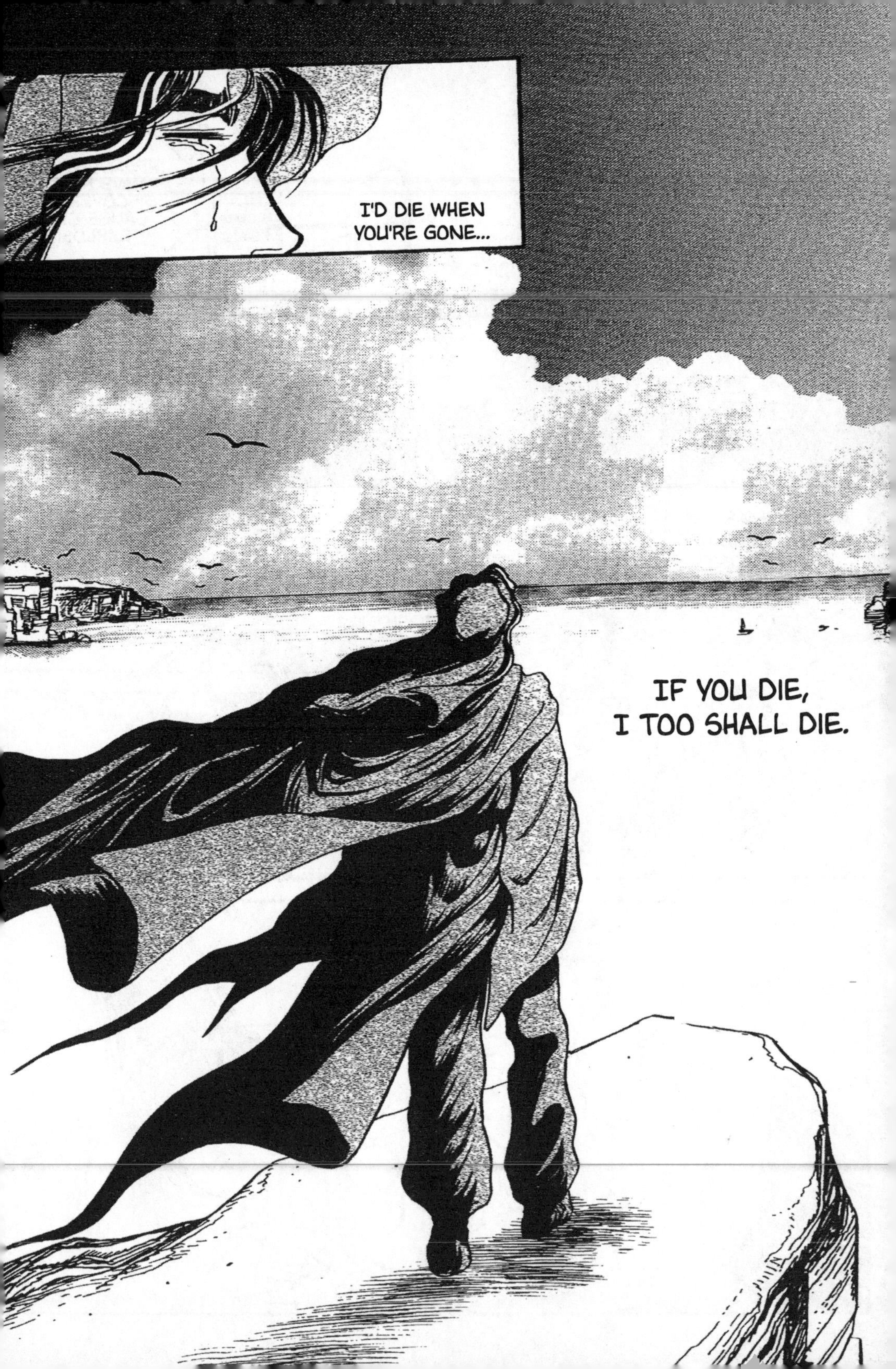
I'D DIE WHEN YOU'RE GONE...
IF YOU DIE, I TOO SHALL DIE.

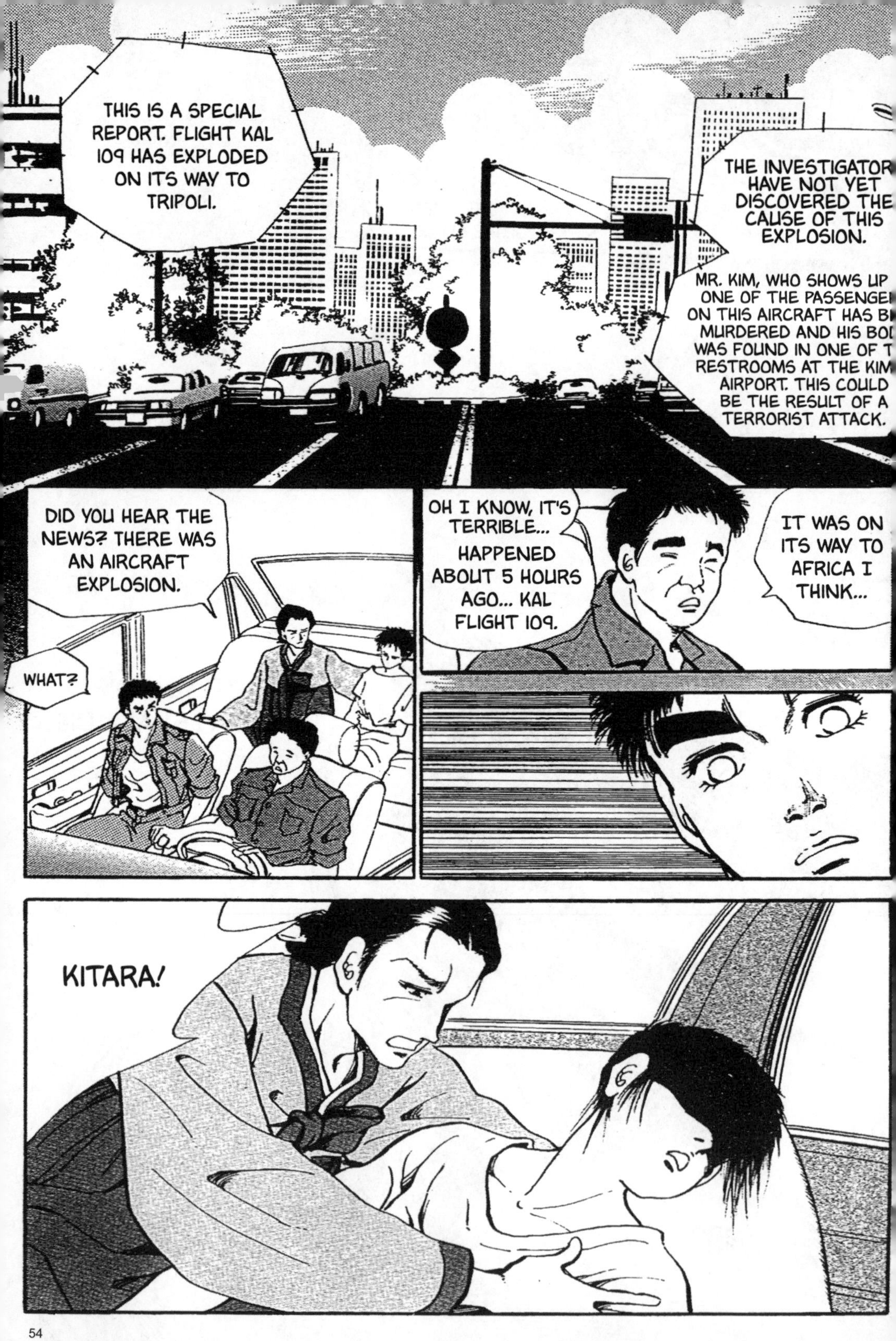
THIS IS A SPECIAL REPORT. FLIGHT KAL 109 HAS EXPLODED ON ITS WAY TO TRIPOLI.
THE INVESTIGATOR HAVE NOT YET DISCOVERED THE CAUSE OF THIS EXPLOSION.
MR. KIM, WHO SHOWS UP ONE OF THE PASSENGE ON THIS AIRCRAFT HAS B MURDERED AND HIS BOD WAS FOUND IN ONE OF T RESTROOMS AT THE KIM AIRPORT. THIS COULD BE THE RESULT OF A TERRORIST ATTACK.
DID YOU HEAR THE NEWS? THERE WAS AN AIRCRAFT EXPLOSION.
WHAT?
OH I KNOW, IT'S TERRIBLE...
HAPPENED ABOUT 5 HOURS AGO... KAL FLIGHT 109.
IT WAS ON ITS WAY TO AFRICA I THINK...
KITARA!

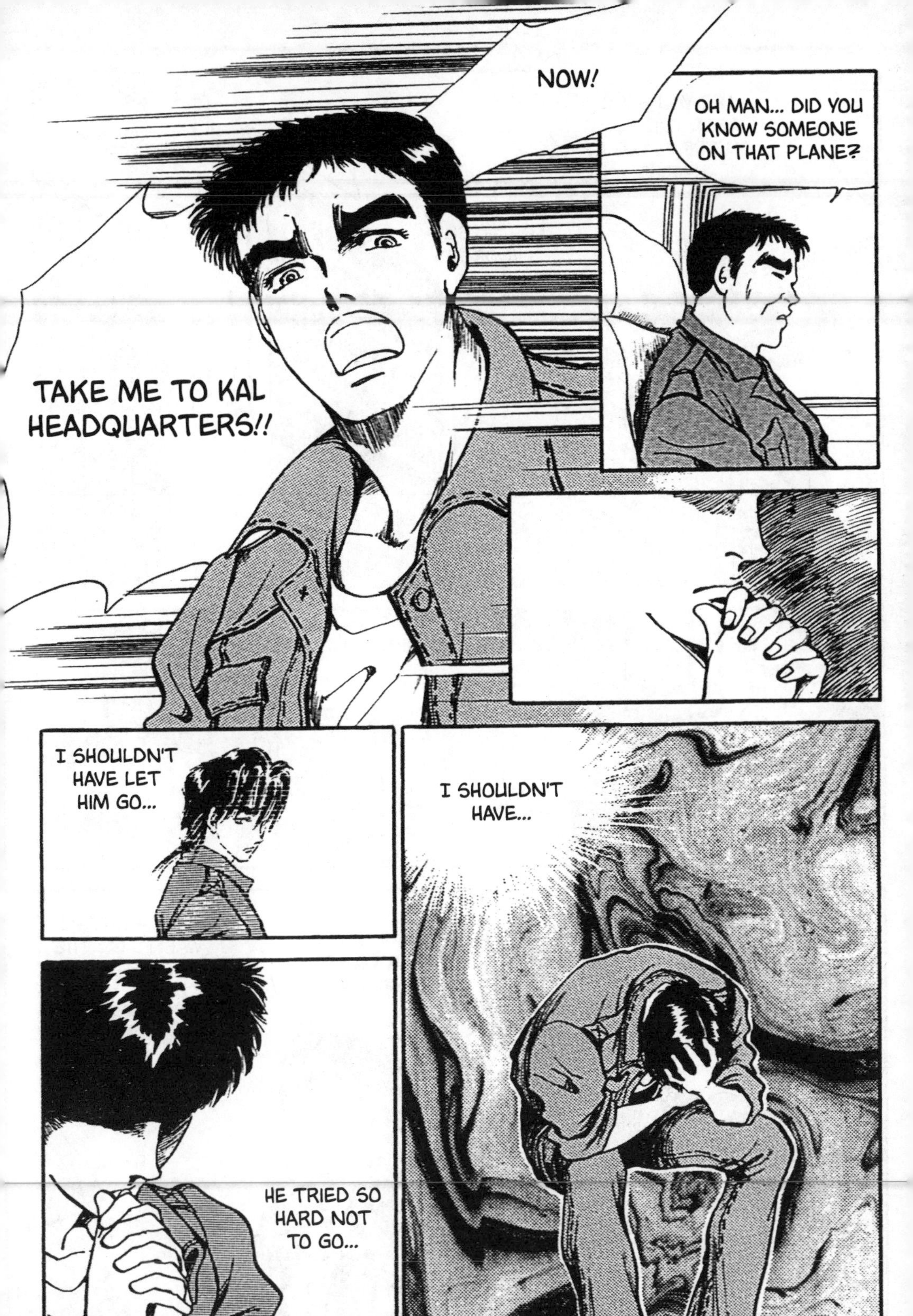
NOW!
OH MAN... DID YOU KNOW SOMEONE ON THAT PLANE?
TAKE ME TO KAL HEADQUARTERS!!
I SHOULDN'T HAVE LET HIM GO...
I SHOULDN'T HAVE...
HE TRIED SO HARD NOT TO GO...

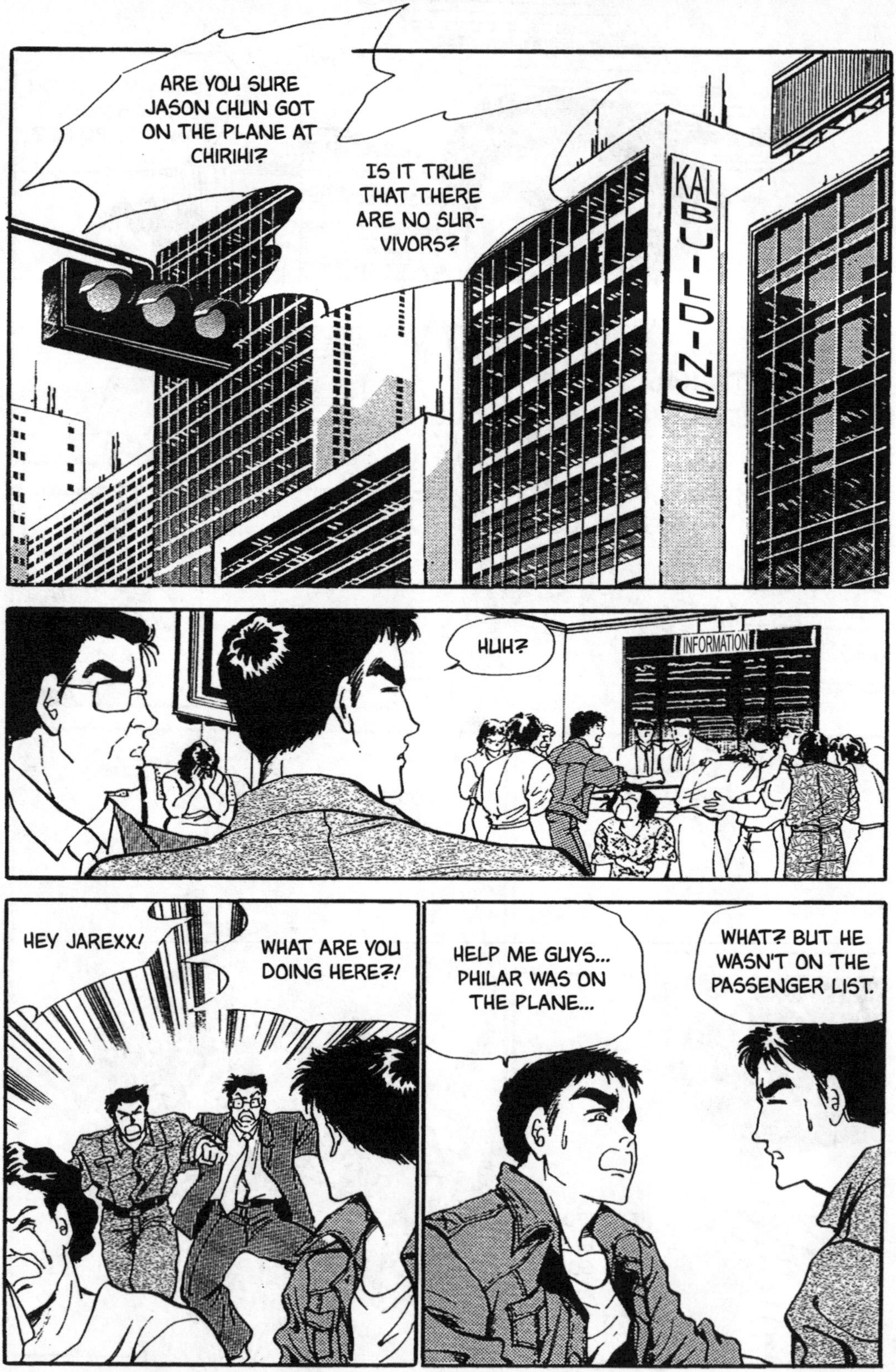
ARE YOU SURE JASON CHUN GOT ON THE PLANE AT CHIRIHI?
IS IT TRUE THAT THERE ARE NO SUR-VIVORS?
KAL BUILDING
HUH?
INFORMATION
HEY JAREXX!
WHAT ARE YOU DOING HERE?!
HELP ME GUYS... PHILAR WAS ON THE PLANE...
WHAT? BUT HE WASN'T ON THE PASSENGER LIST.

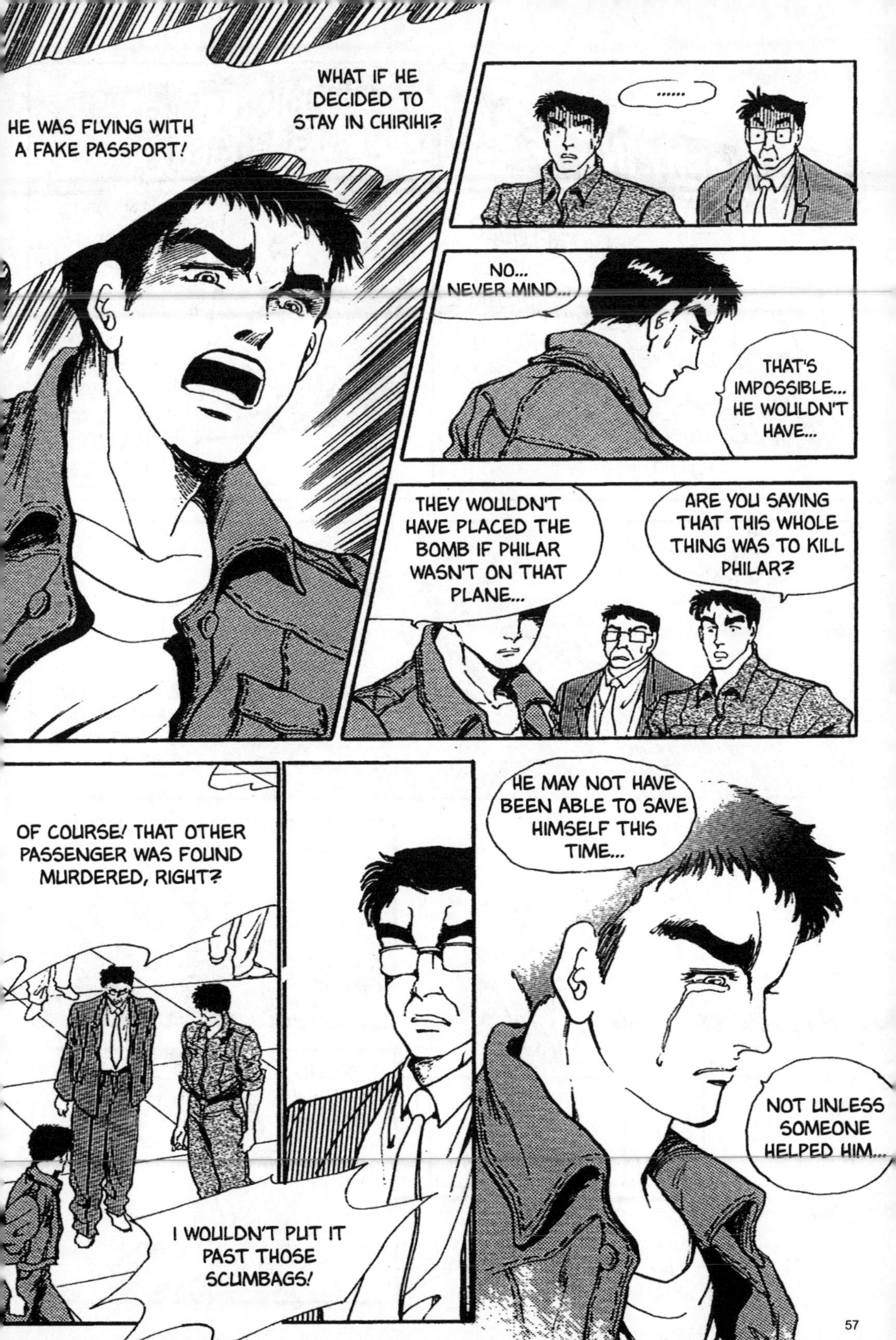
HE WAS FLYING WITH A FAKE PASSPORT!
WHAT IF HE DECIDED TO STAY IN CHIRIHI?
......
NO... NEVER MIND...
THAT'S IMPOSSIBLE... HE WOULDN'T HAVE...
THEY WOULDN'T HAVE PLACED THE BOMB IF PHILAR WASN'T ON THAT PLANE...
ARE YOU SAYING THAT THIS WHOLE THING WAS TO KILL PHILAR?
OF COURSE! THAT OTHER PASSENGER WAS FOUND MURDERED, RIGHT?
I WOULDN'T PUT IT PAST THOSE SCUMBAGS!
HE MAY NOT HAVE BEEN ABLE TO SAVE HIMSELF THIS TIME...
NOT UNLESS SOMEONE HELPED HIM...

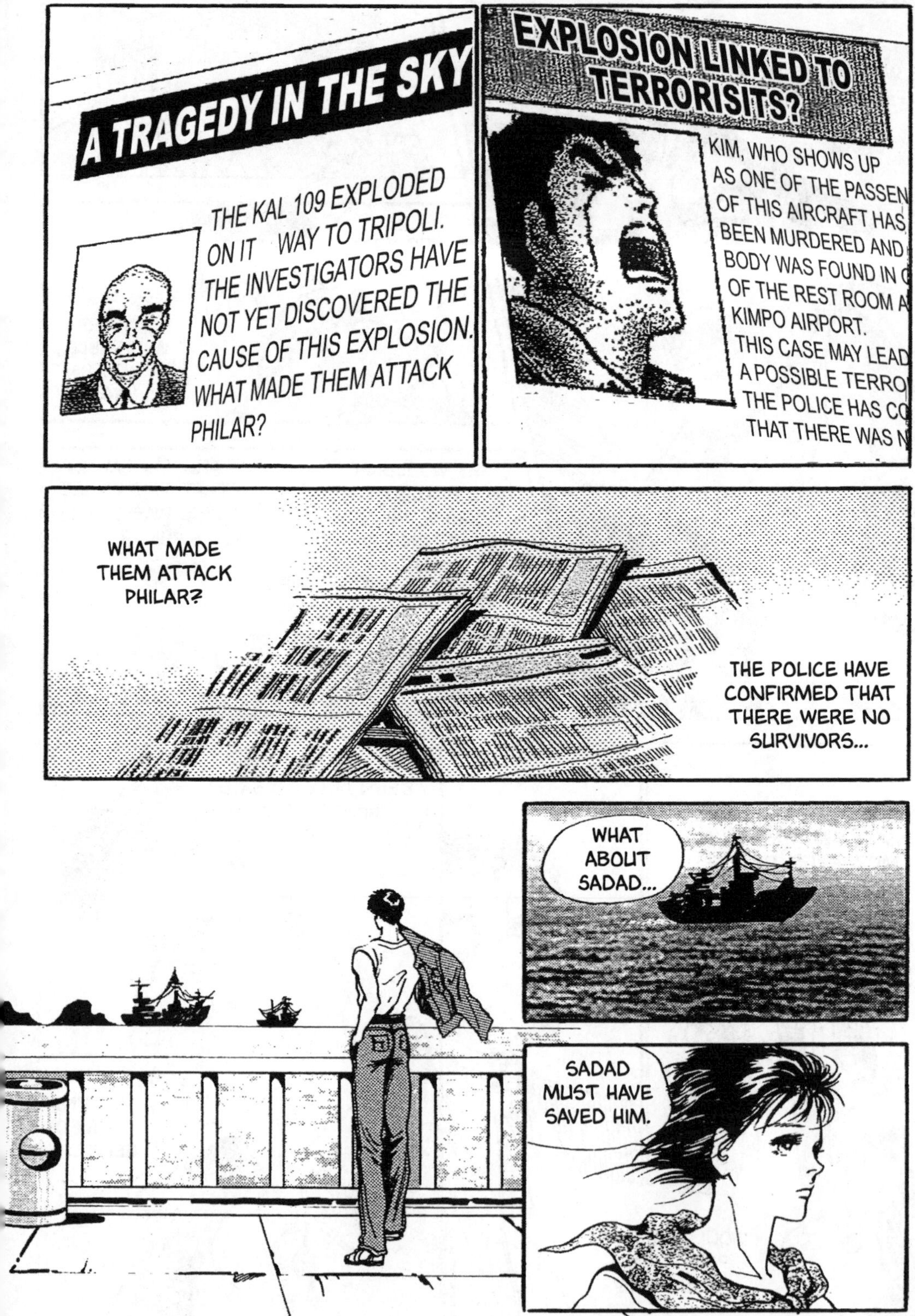
A TRAGEDY IN THE SKY
THE KAL 109 EXPLODED ON IT WAY TO TRIPOLI. THE INVESTIGATORS HAVE NOT YET DISCOVERED THE CAUSE OF THIS EXPLOSION. WHAT MADE THEM ATTACK PHILAR?
EXPLOSION LINKED TO TERRORISITS?
KIM, WHO SHOWS UP AS ONE OF THE PASSEN OF THIS AIRCRAFT HAS BEEN MURDERED AND BODY WAS FOUND IN OF THE REST ROOM A KIMPO AIRPORT. THIS CASE MAY LEAD A POSSIBLE TERRO THE POLICE HAS CO THAT THERE WAS N
WHAT MADE THEM ATTACK PHILAR?
THE POLICE HAVE CONFIRMED THAT THERE WERE NO SURVIVORS...
WHAT ABOUT SADAD...
SADAD MUST HAVE SAVED HIM.

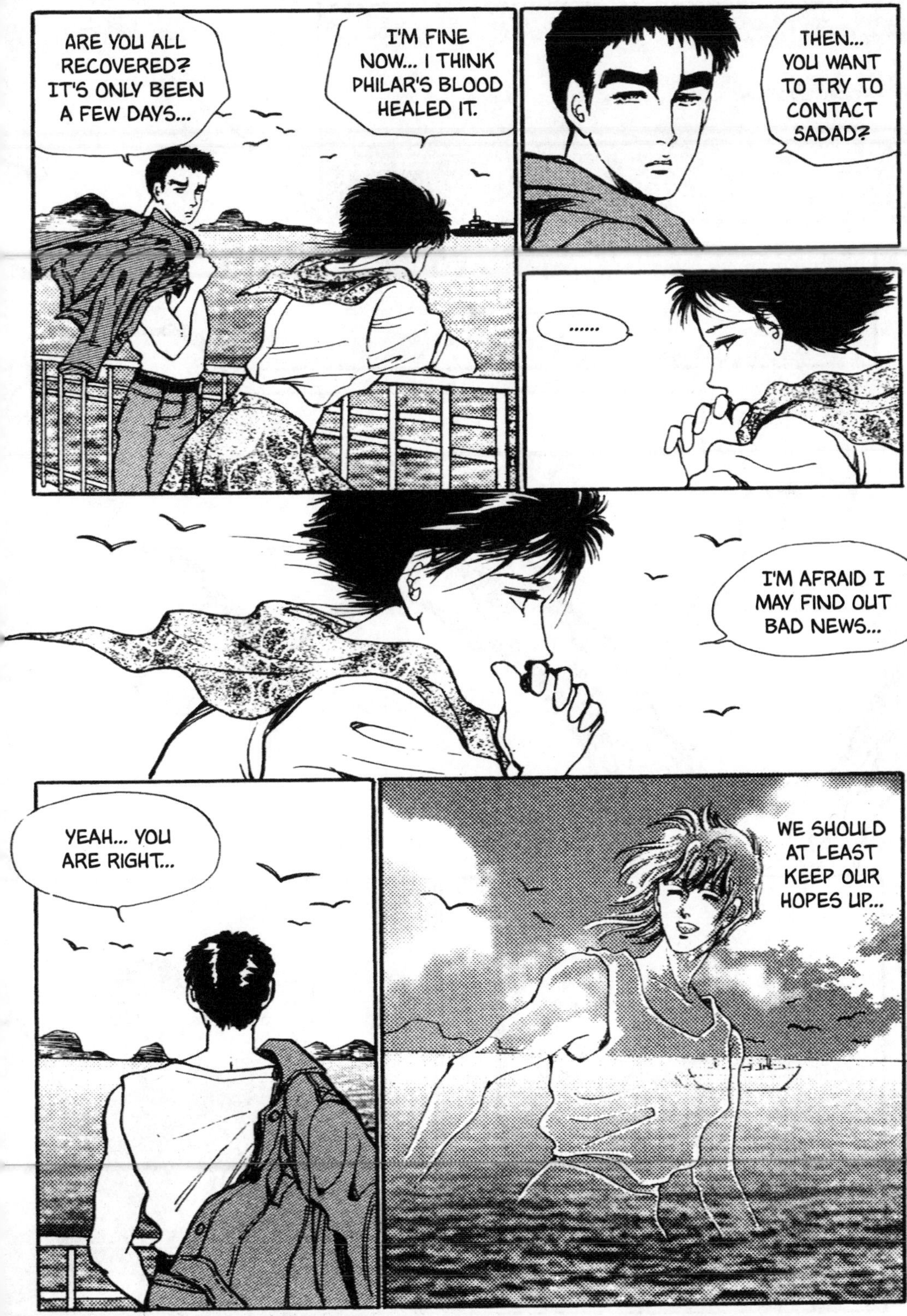
ARE YOU ALL RECOVERED? IT'S ONLY BEEN A FEW DAYS...
I'M FINE NOW... I THINK PHILAR'S BLOOD HEALED IT.
THEN... YOU WANT TO TRY TO CONTACT SADAD?
......
I'M AFRAID I MAY FIND OUT BAD NEWS...
YEAH... YOU ARE RIGHT...
WE SHOULD AT LEAST KEEP OUR HOPES UP...

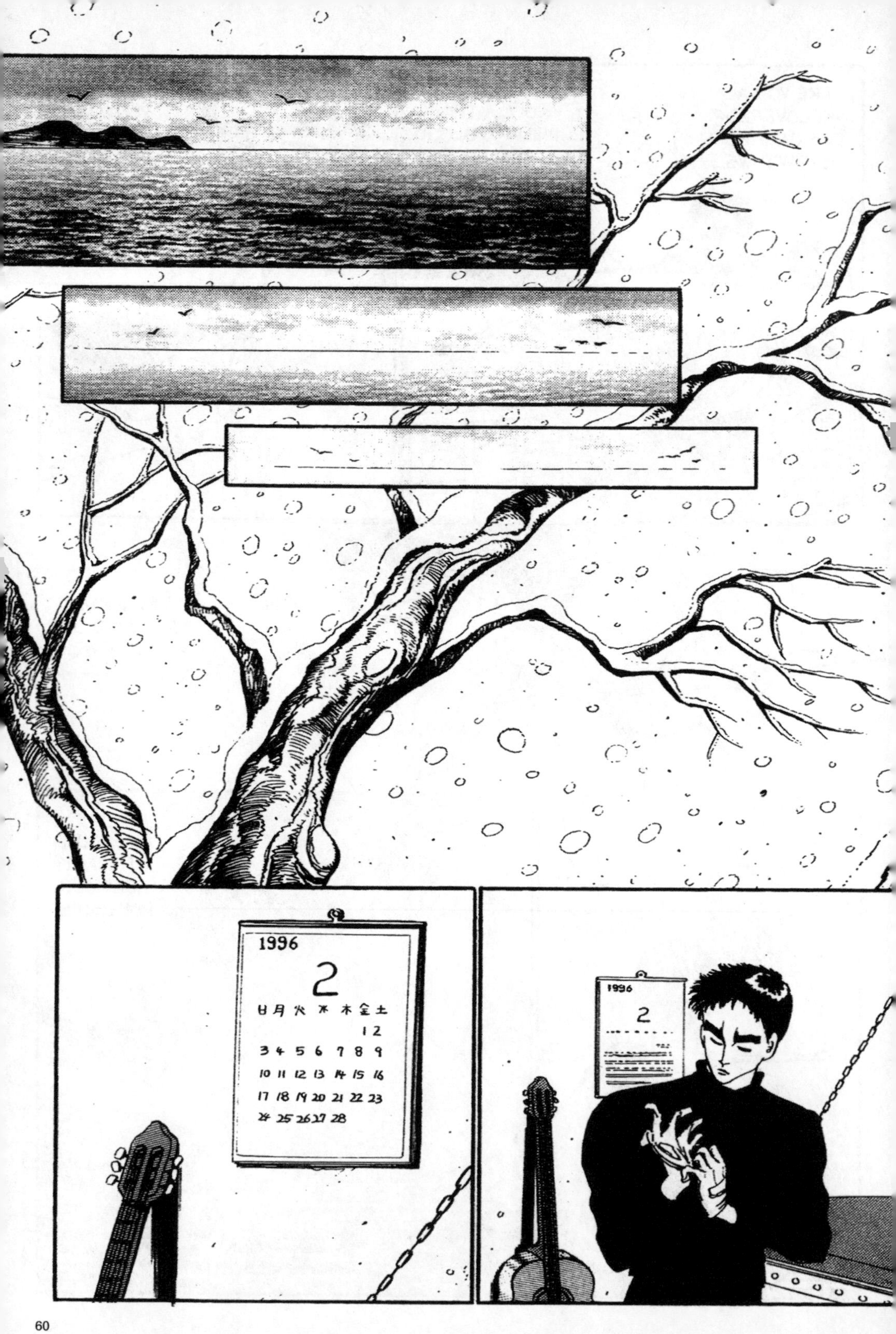
1996
2
日 月 火 水 木 金 土
1 2
3 4 5 6 7 8 9
10 11 12 13 14 15 16
17 18 19 20 21 22 23
24 25 26 27 28
1996
2

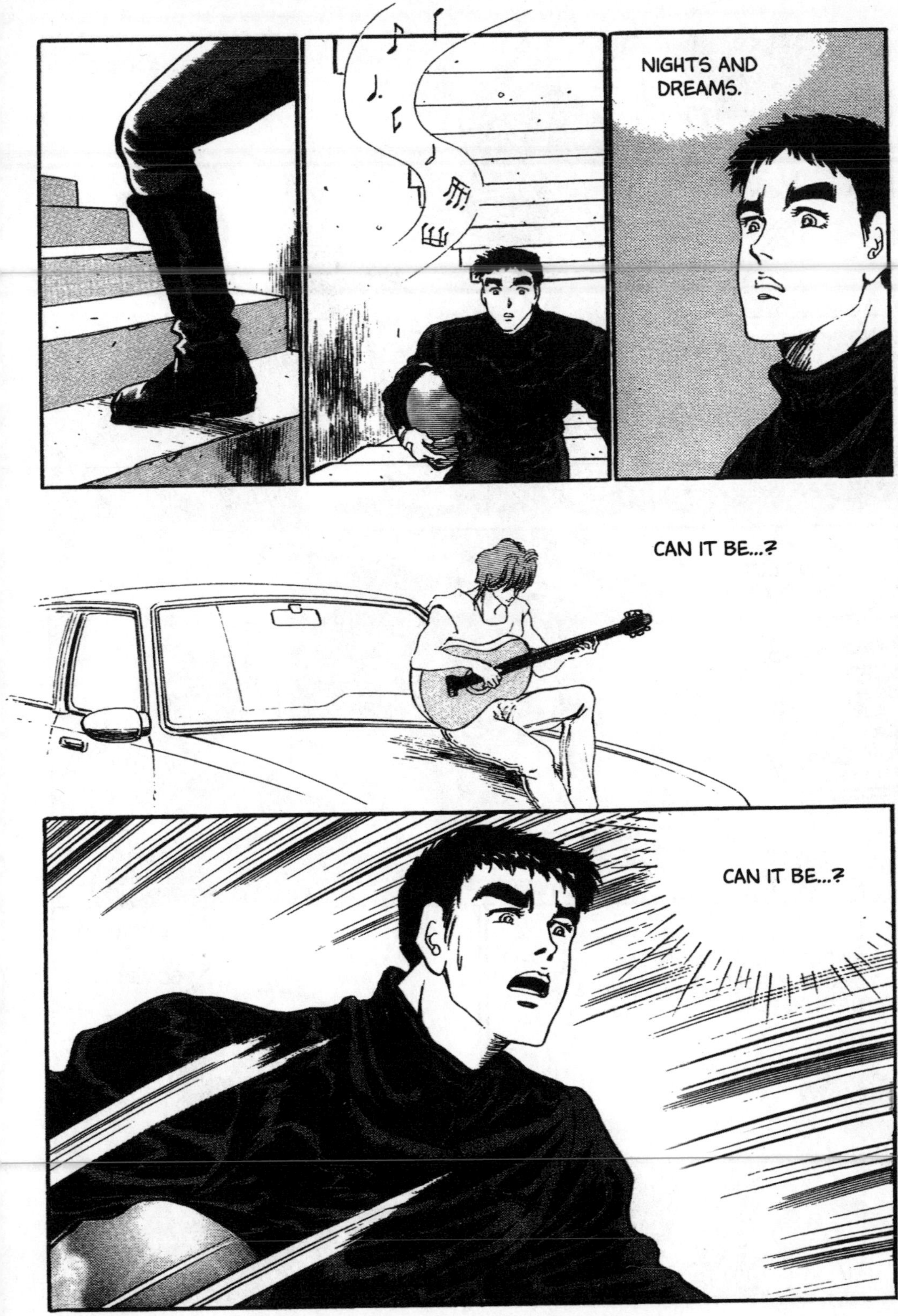
NIGHTS AND
DREAMS.
CAN IT BE...?
CAN IT BE...?

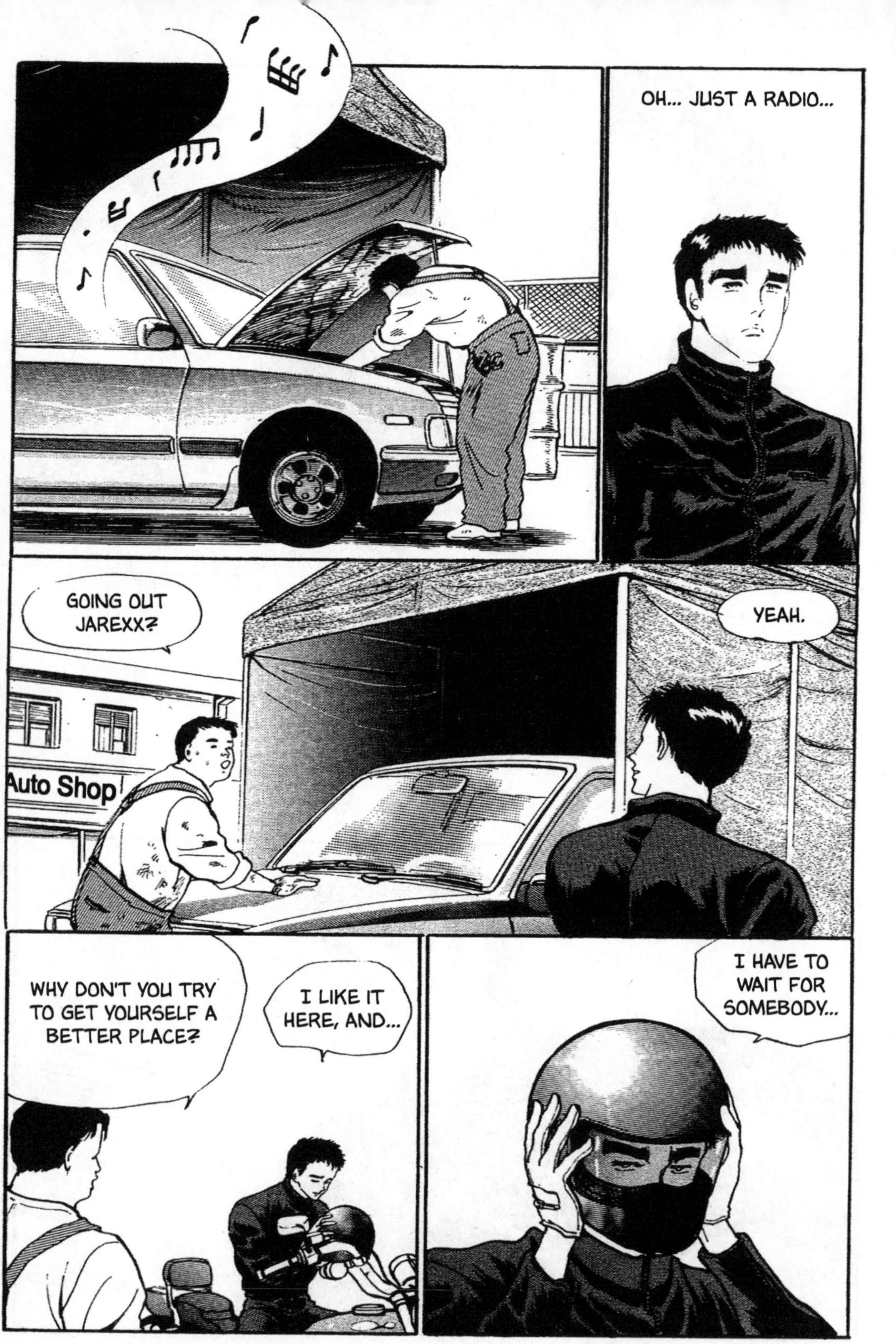
OH... JUST A RADIO...
GOING OUT JAREXX?
YEAH.
Auto Shop
WHY DON'T YOU TRY TO GET YOURSELF A BETTER PLACE?
I LIKE IT HERE, AND...
I HAVE TO WAIT FOR SOMEBODY...

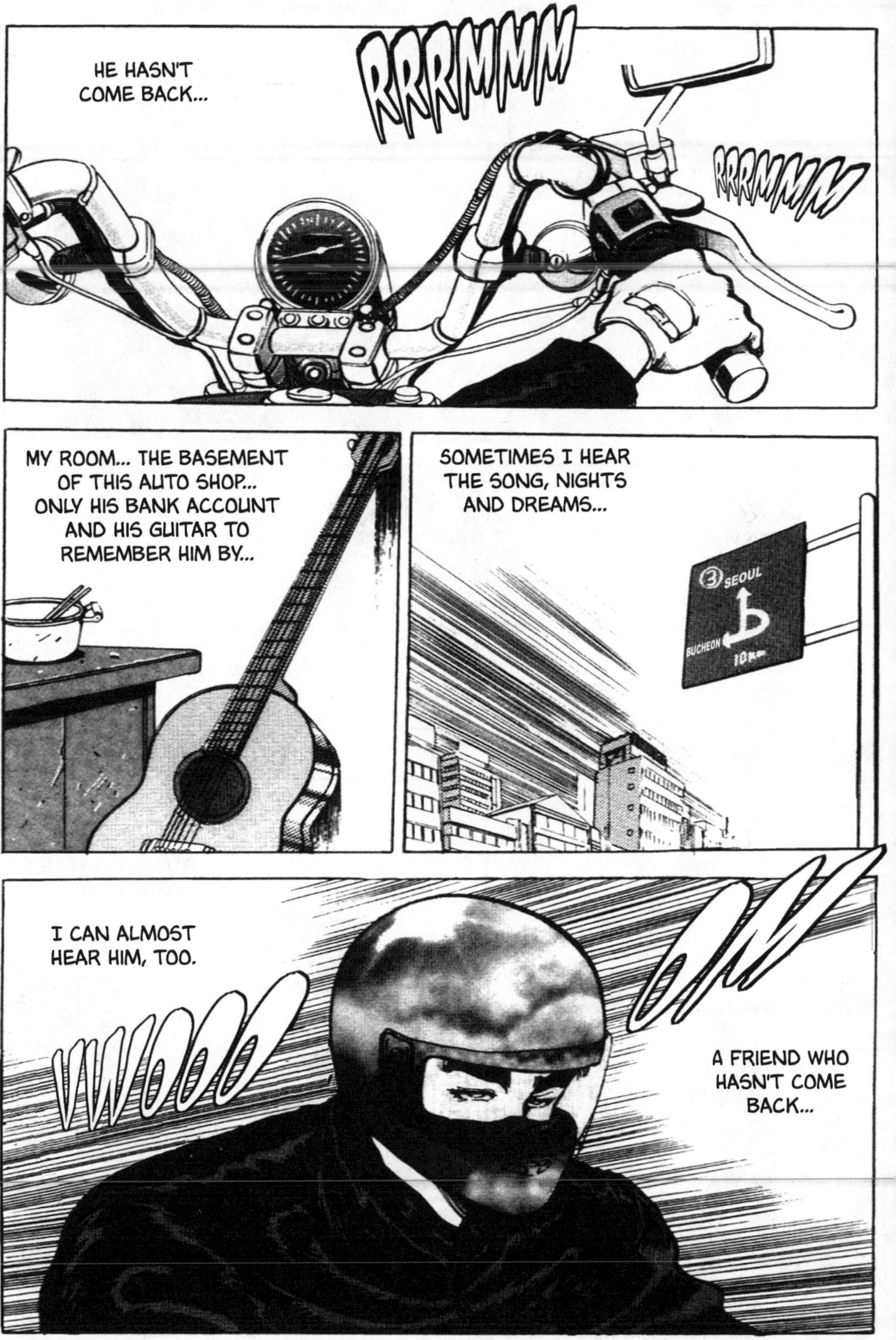
HE HASN'T COME BACK...
RRRMMMM
RRRMMMM
MY ROOM... THE BASEMENT OF THIS AUTO SHOP... ONLY HIS BANK ACCOUNT AND HIS GUITAR TO REMEMBER HIM BY...
SOMETIMES I HEAR THE SONG, NIGHTS AND DREAMS...
SEOUL
BUCHEON
I CAN ALMOST HEAR HIM, TOO.
VWOOOO
OM
A FRIEND WHO HASN'T COME BACK...

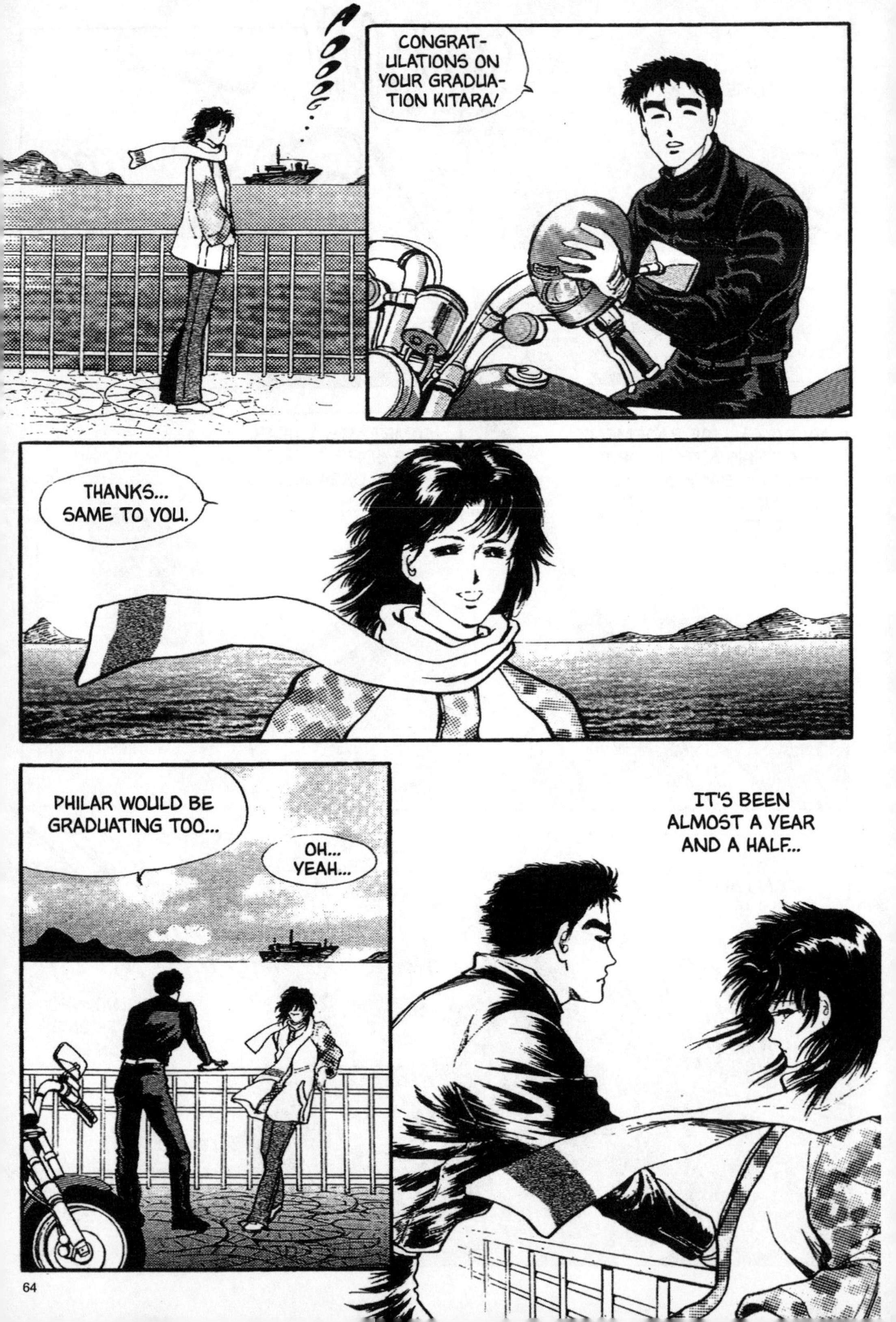
AOOOOG...
CONGRAT-ULATIONS ON YOUR GRADUA-TION KITARA!
THANKS... SAME TO YOU.
PHILAR WOULD BE GRADUATING TOO...
OH... YEAH...
IT'S BEEN ALMOST A YEAR AND A HALF...

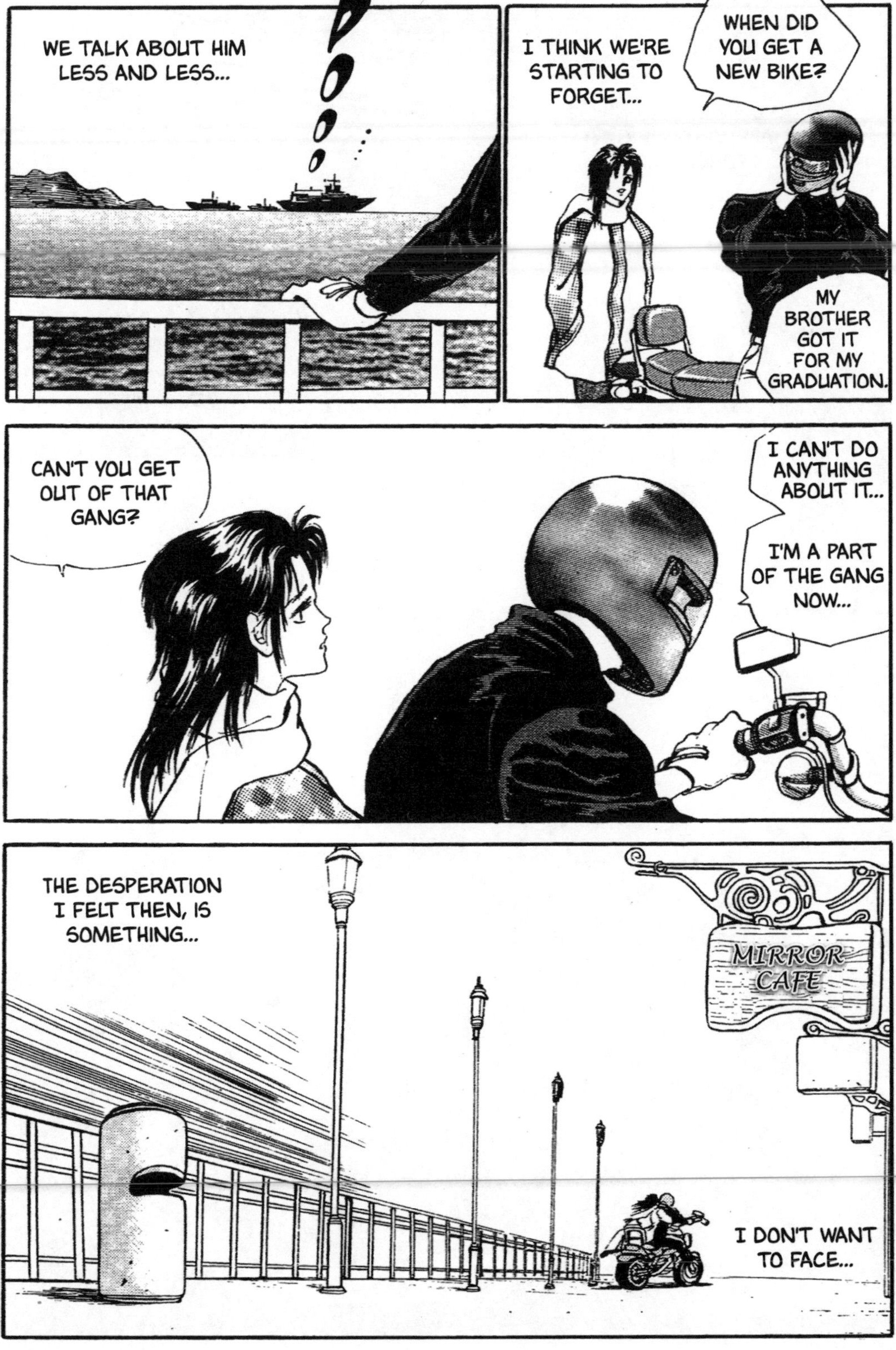
WE TALK ABOUT HIM LESS AND LESS...
BOOO...
I THINK WE'RE STARTING TO FORGET...
WHEN DID YOU GET A NEW BIKE?
MY BROTHER GOT IT FOR MY GRADUATION.
CAN'T YOU GET OUT OF THAT GANG?
I CAN'T DO ANYTHING ABOUT IT...
I'M A PART OF THE GANG NOW...
THE DESPERATION I FELT THEN, IS SOMETHING...
MIRROR CAFE
I DON'T WANT TO FACE...

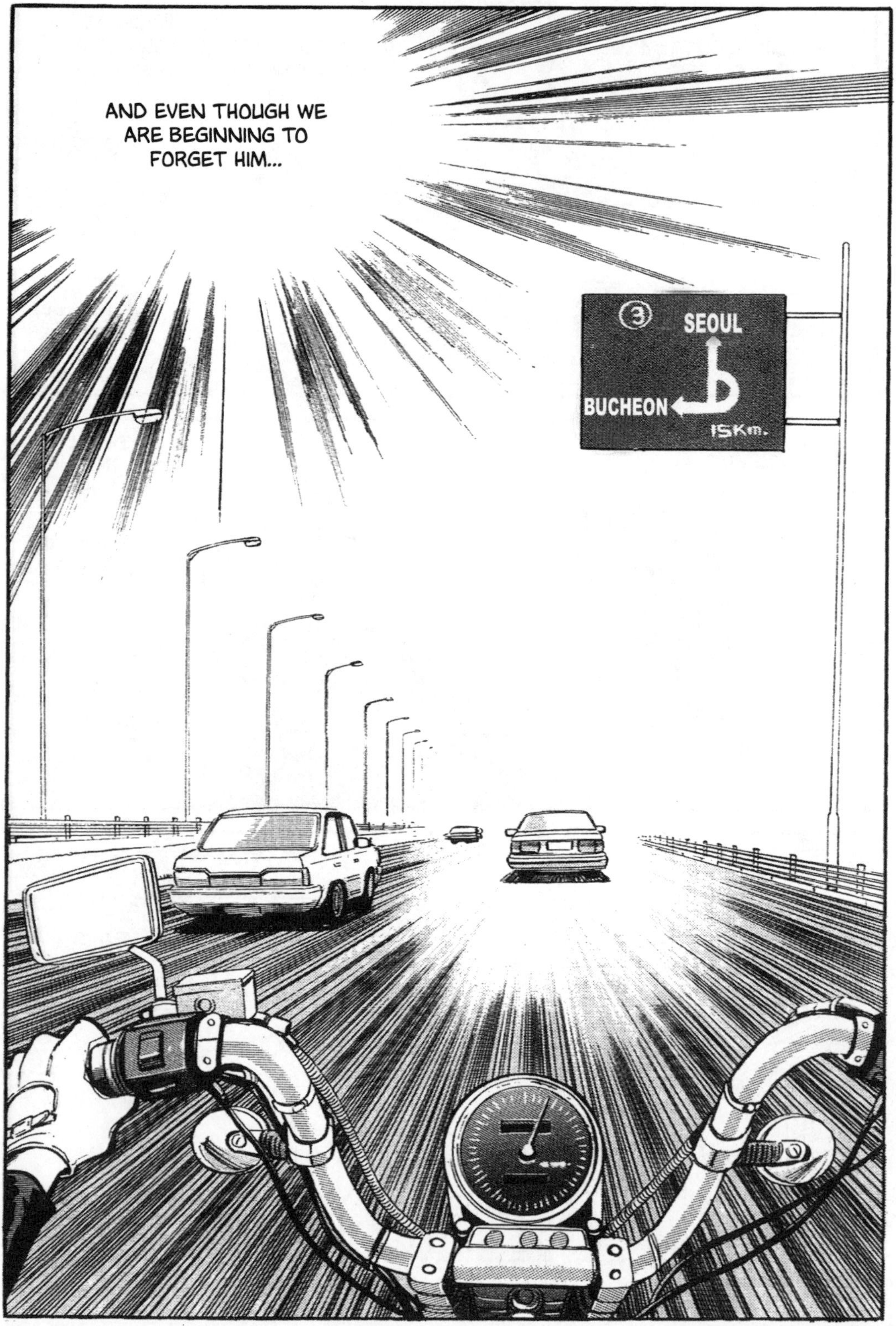
AND EVEN THOUGH WE ARE BEGINNING TO FORGET HIM...
③
SEOUL
BUCHEON
15Km.

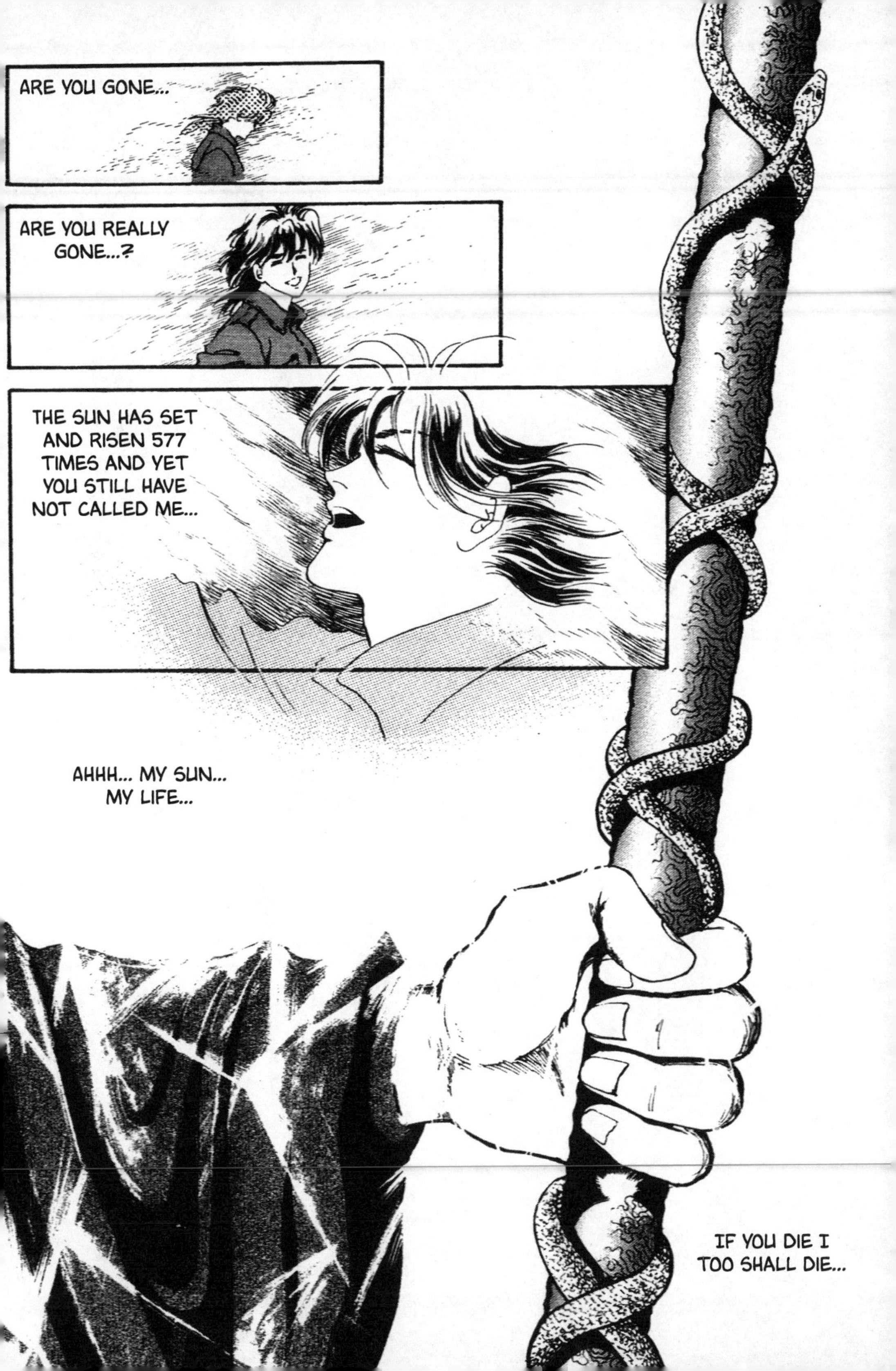
ARE YOU GONE...
ARE YOU REALLY GONE...?
THE SUN HAS SET AND RISEN 577 TIMES AND YET YOU STILL HAVE NOT CALLED ME...
AHHH... MY SUN... MY LIFE...
IF YOU DIE I TOO SHALL DIE...

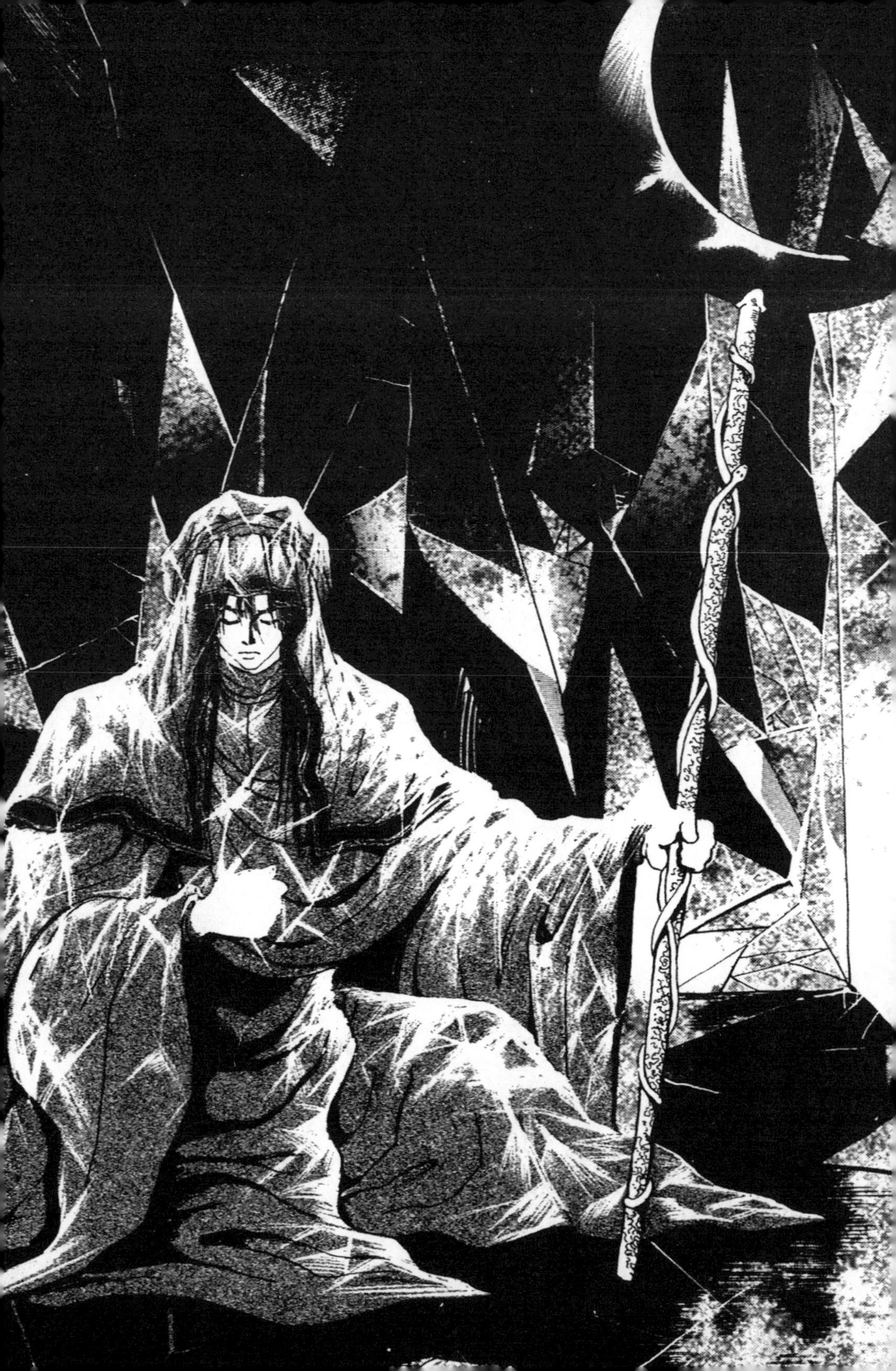

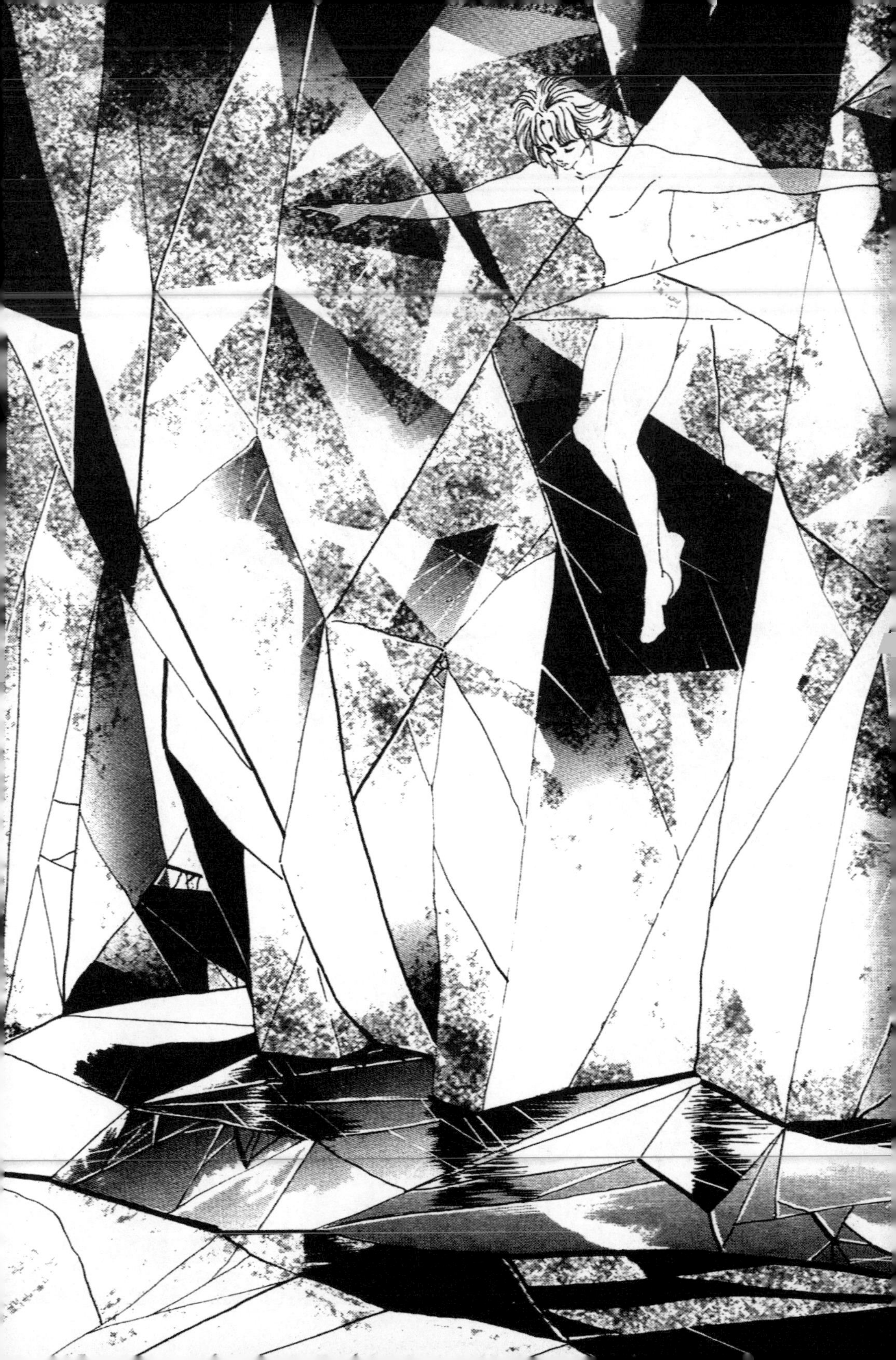

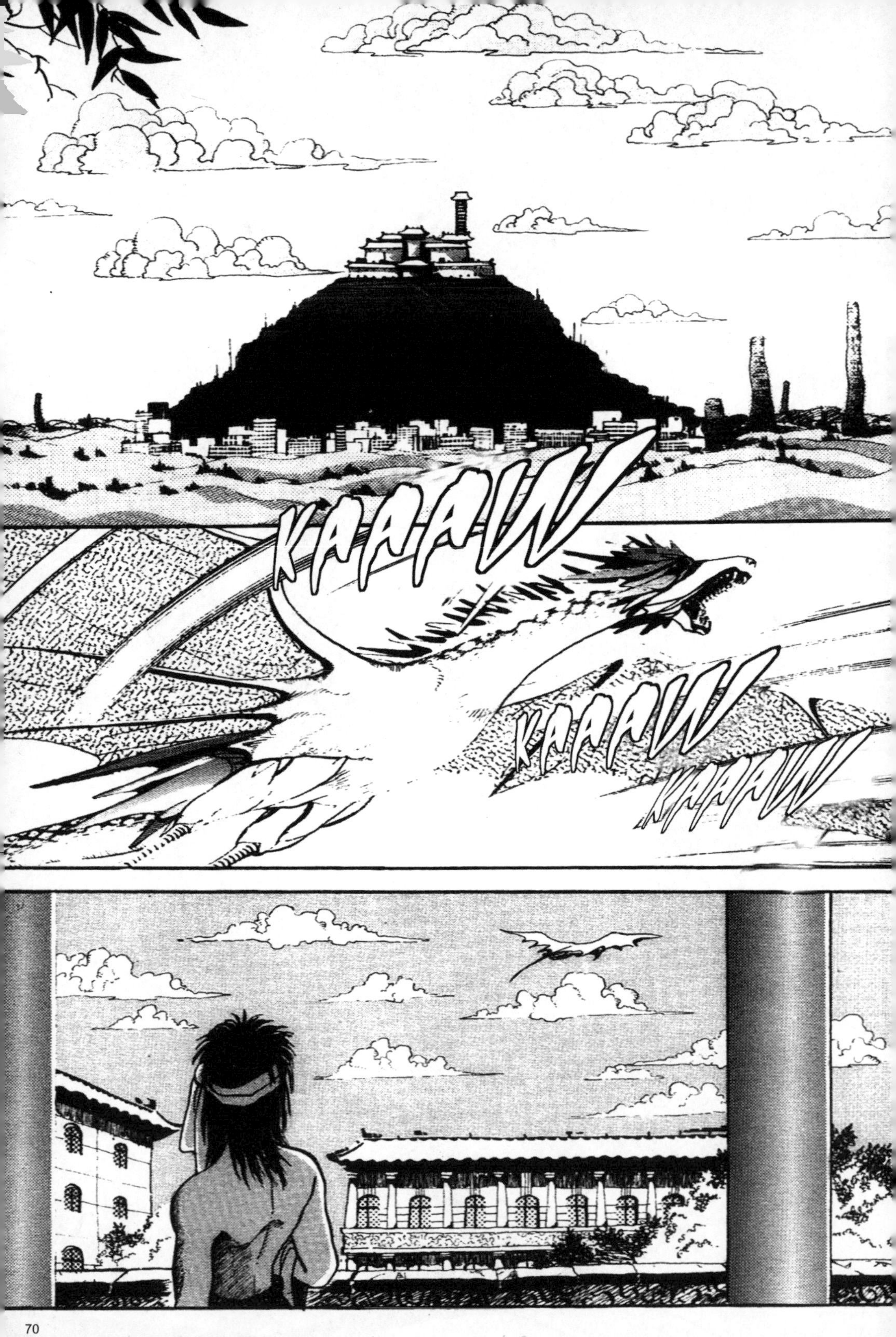
KAAAAW
KAAAAW
KAAAAW

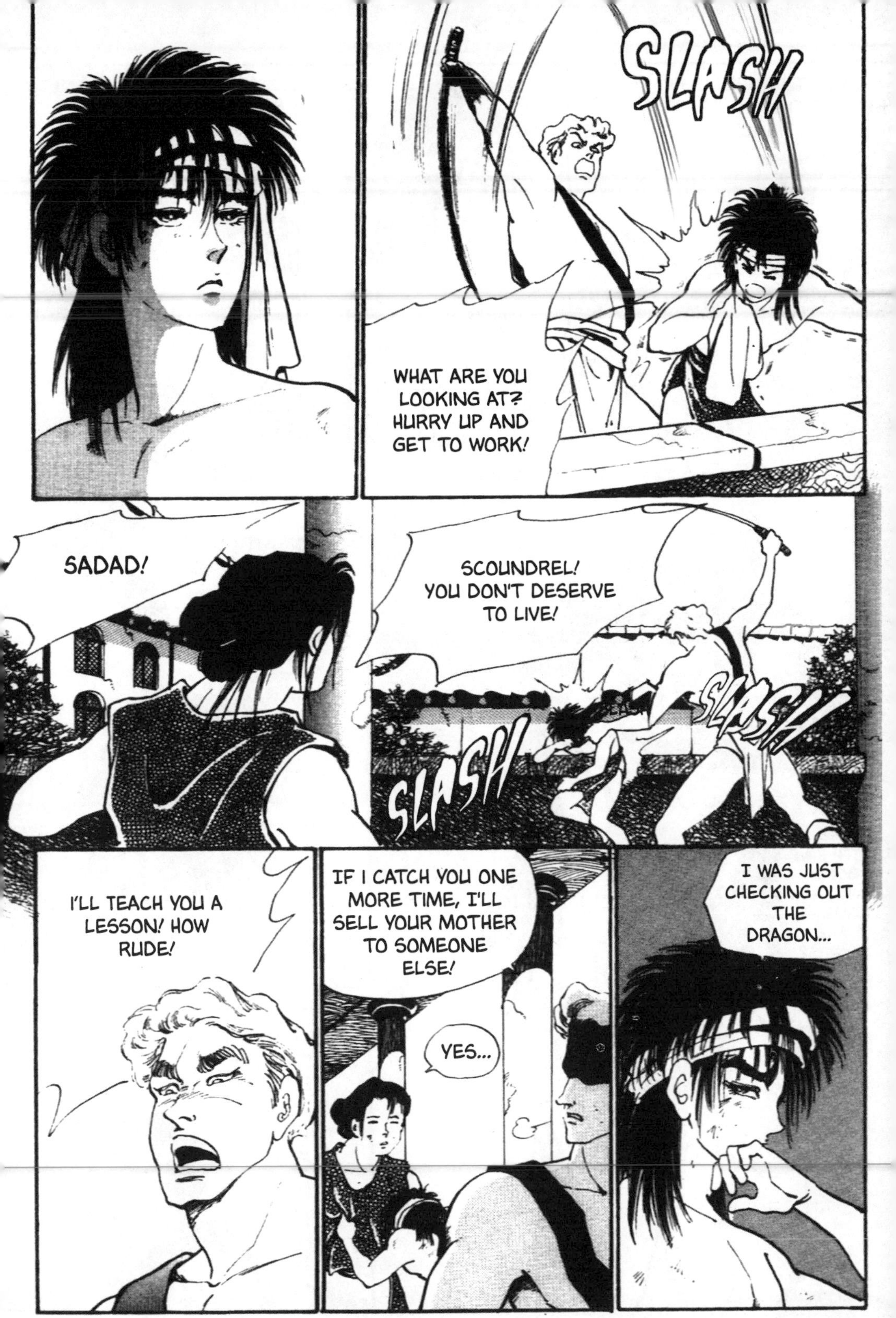
SLASH
WHAT ARE YOU LOOKING AT? HURRY UP AND GET TO WORK!
SADAD!
SCOUNDREL! YOU DON'T DESERVE TO LIVE!
SLASH
SLASH
I'LL TEACH YOU A LESSON! HOW RUDE!
IF I CATCH YOU ONE MORE TIME, I'LL SELL YOUR MOTHER TO SOMEONE ELSE!
YES...
I WAS JUST CHECKING OUT THE DRAGON...

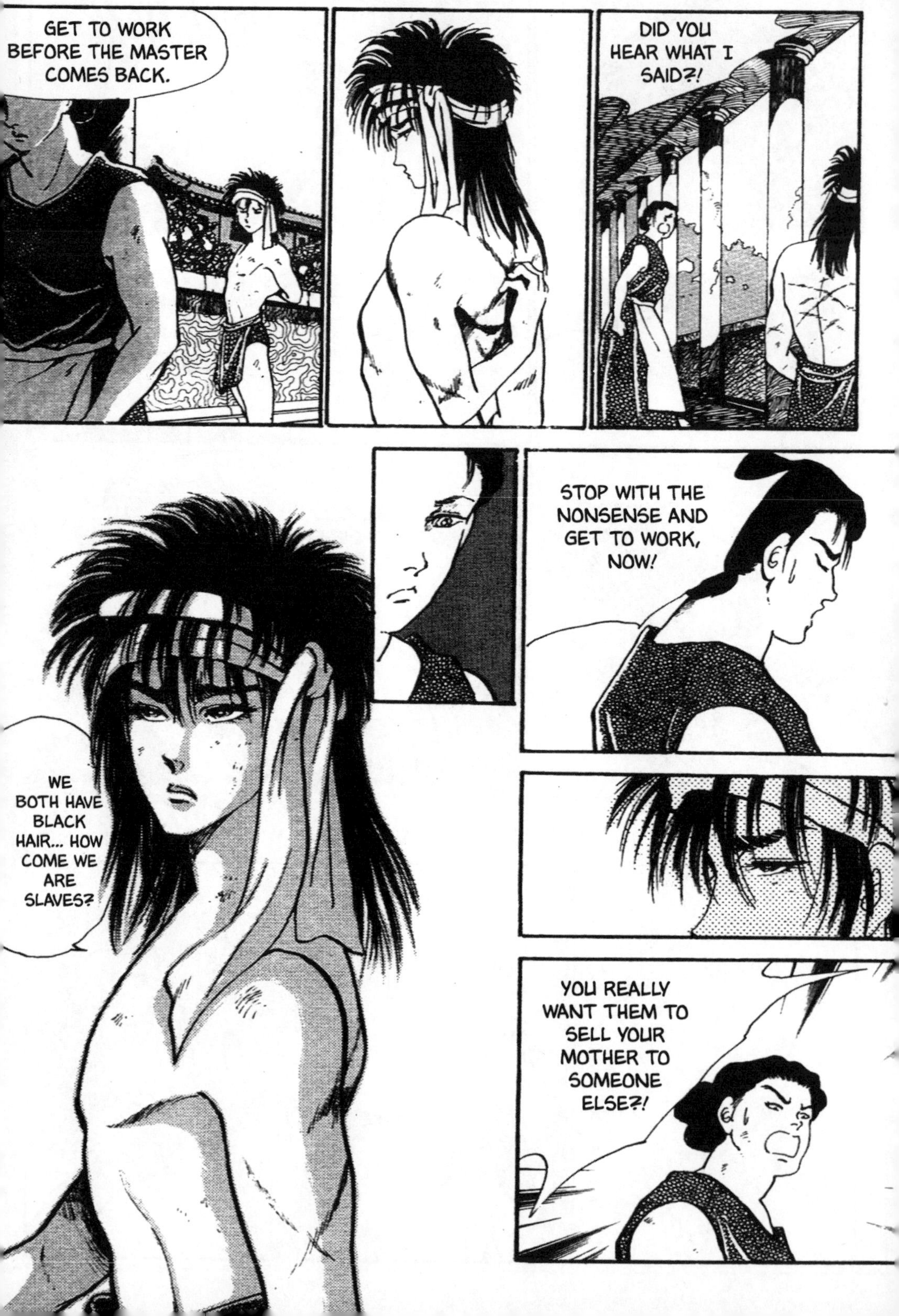
GET TO WORK BEFORE THE MASTER COMES BACK.
DID YOU HEAR WHAT I SAID?!
STOP WITH THE NONSENSE AND GET TO WORK, NOW!
WE BOTH HAVE BLACK HAIR... HOW COME WE ARE SLAVES?
YOU REALLY WANT THEM TO SELL YOUR MOTHER TO SOMEONE ELSE?!

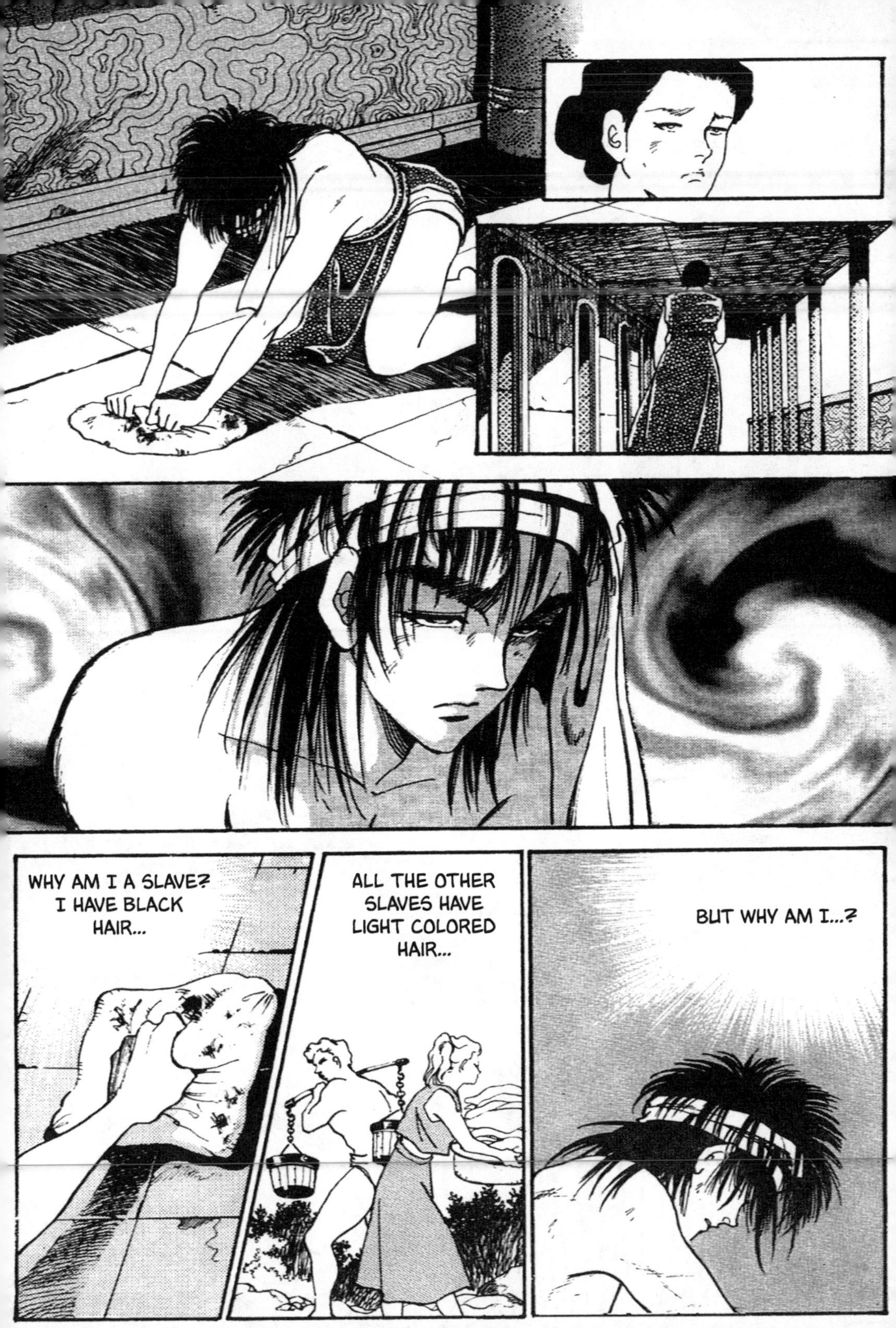
WHY AM I A SLAVE?
I HAVE BLACK
HAIR...
ALL THE OTHER
SLAVES HAVE
LIGHT COLORED
HAIR...
BUT WHY AM I...?

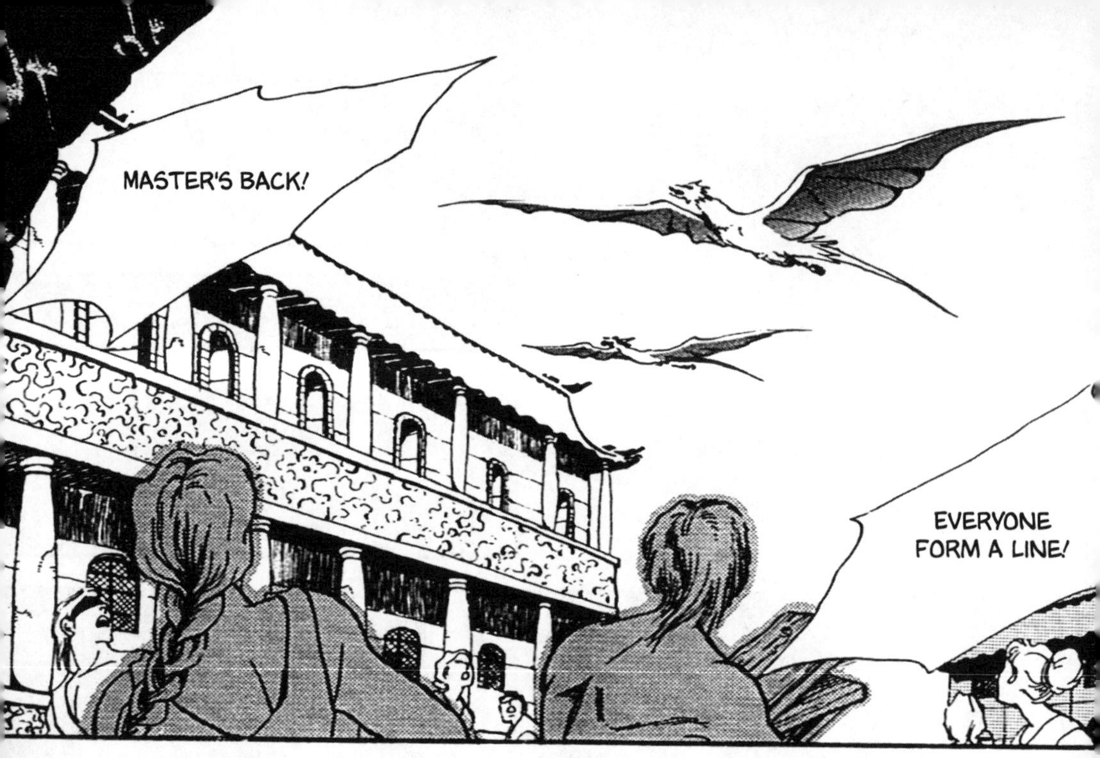
MASTER'S BACK!
EVERYONE FORM A LINE!

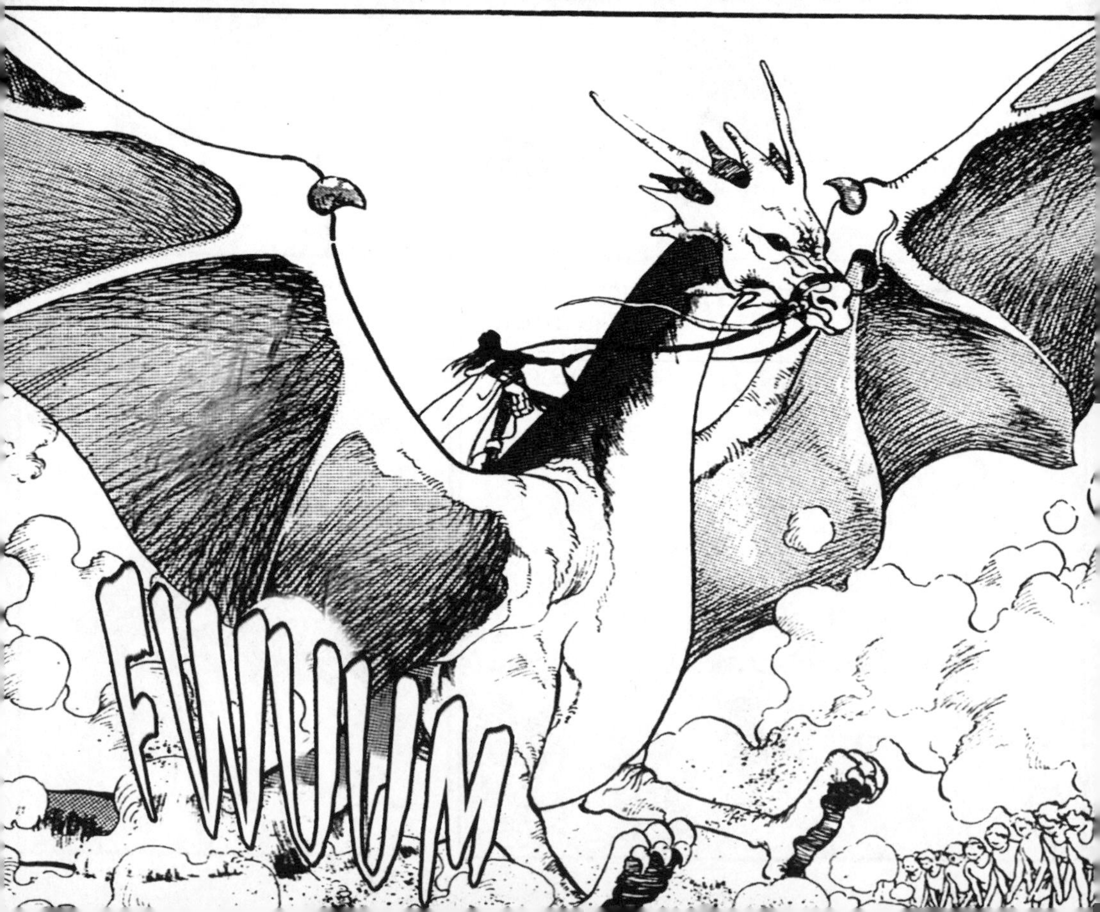
FWUUUM

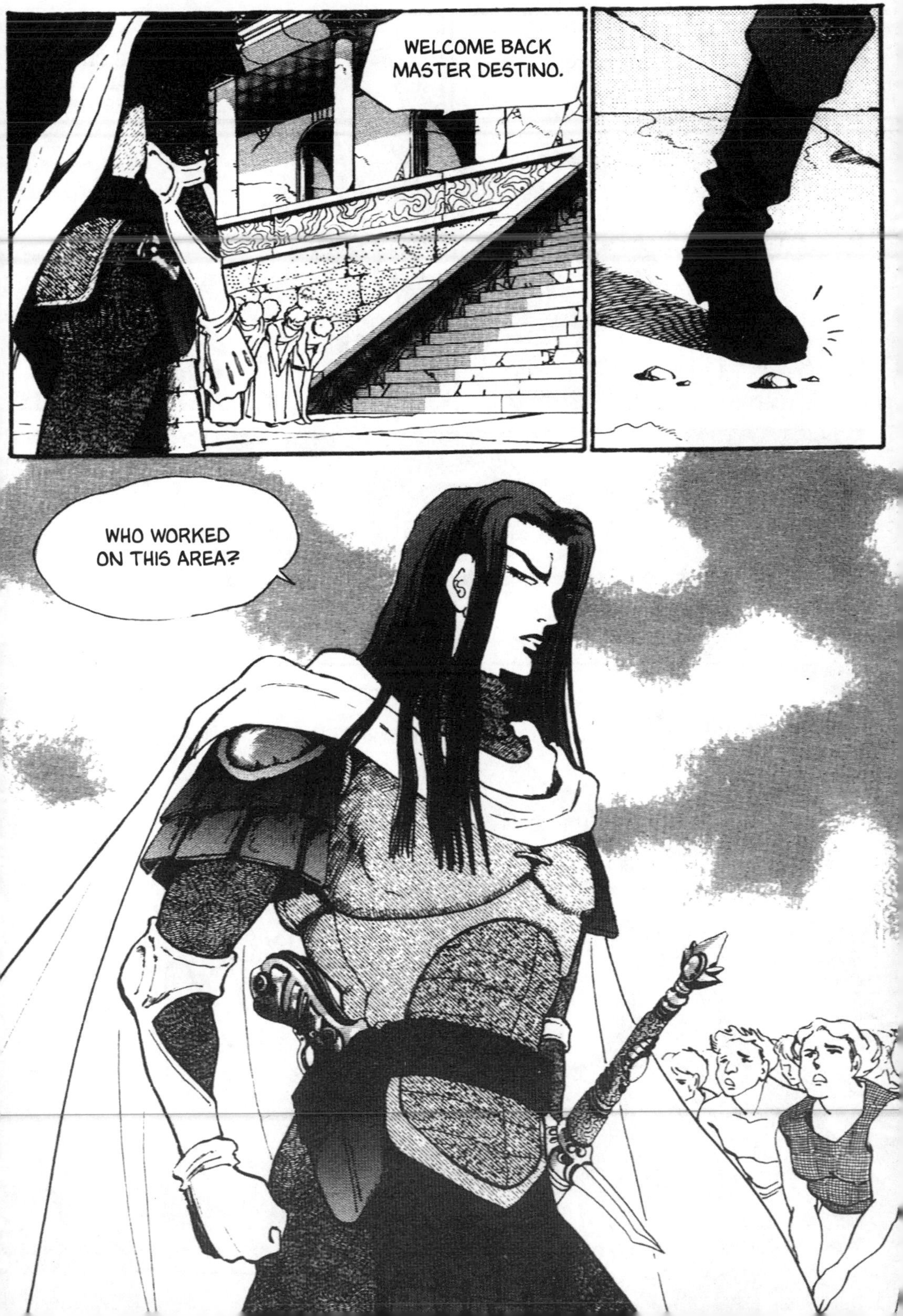
WELCOME BACK MASTER DESTINO.
WHO WORKED ON THIS AREA?

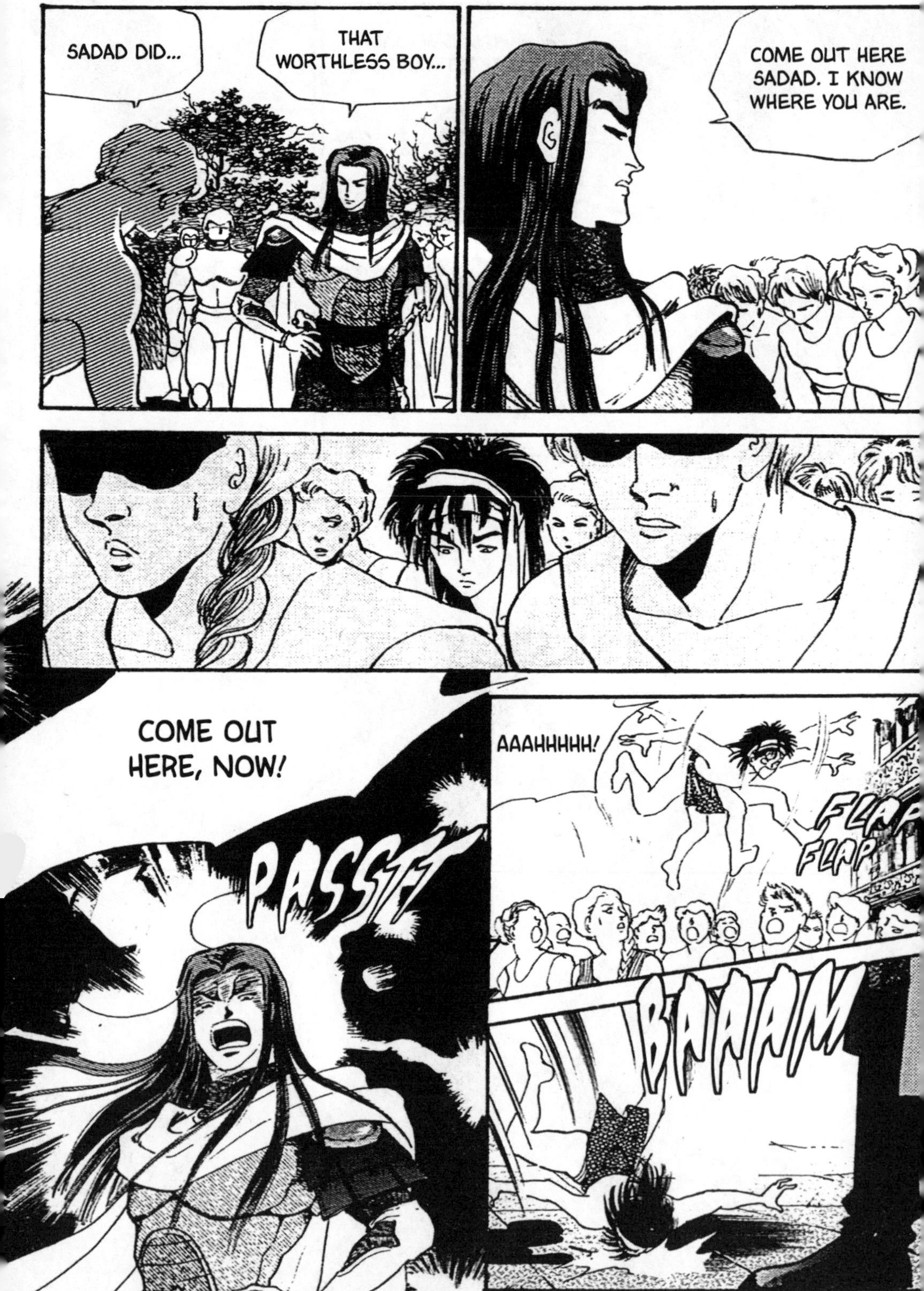
SADAD DID...
THAT WORTHLESS BOY...
COME OUT HERE SADAD. I KNOW WHERE YOU ARE.
COME OUT HERE, NOW!
PASSST
AAAHHHHH!
FLAP
FLAP
BAAAM

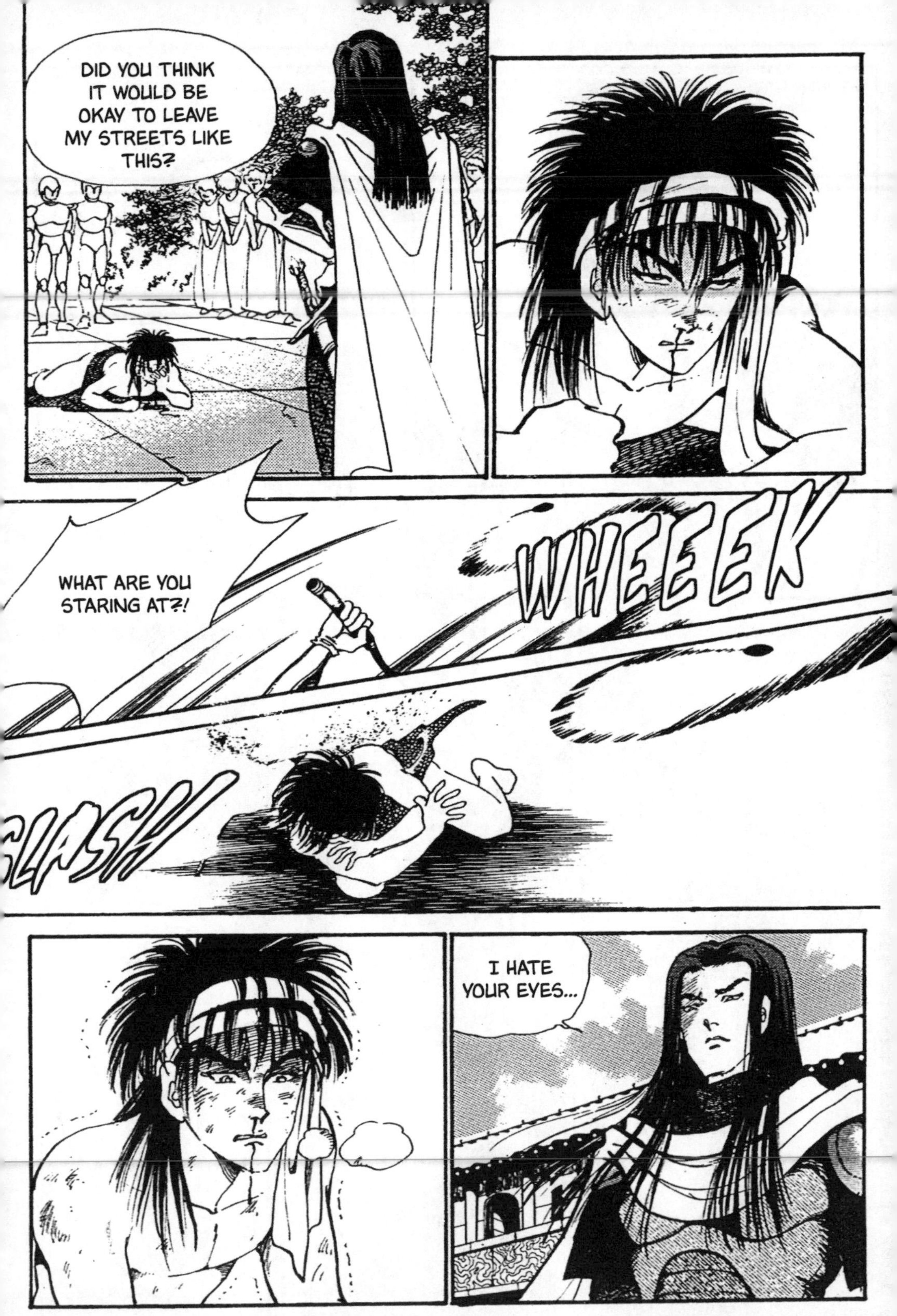
DID YOU THINK IT WOULD BE OKAY TO LEAVE MY STREETS LIKE THIS?
WHAT ARE YOU STARING AT?!
WHEEEK
SLASH
I HATE YOUR EYES...

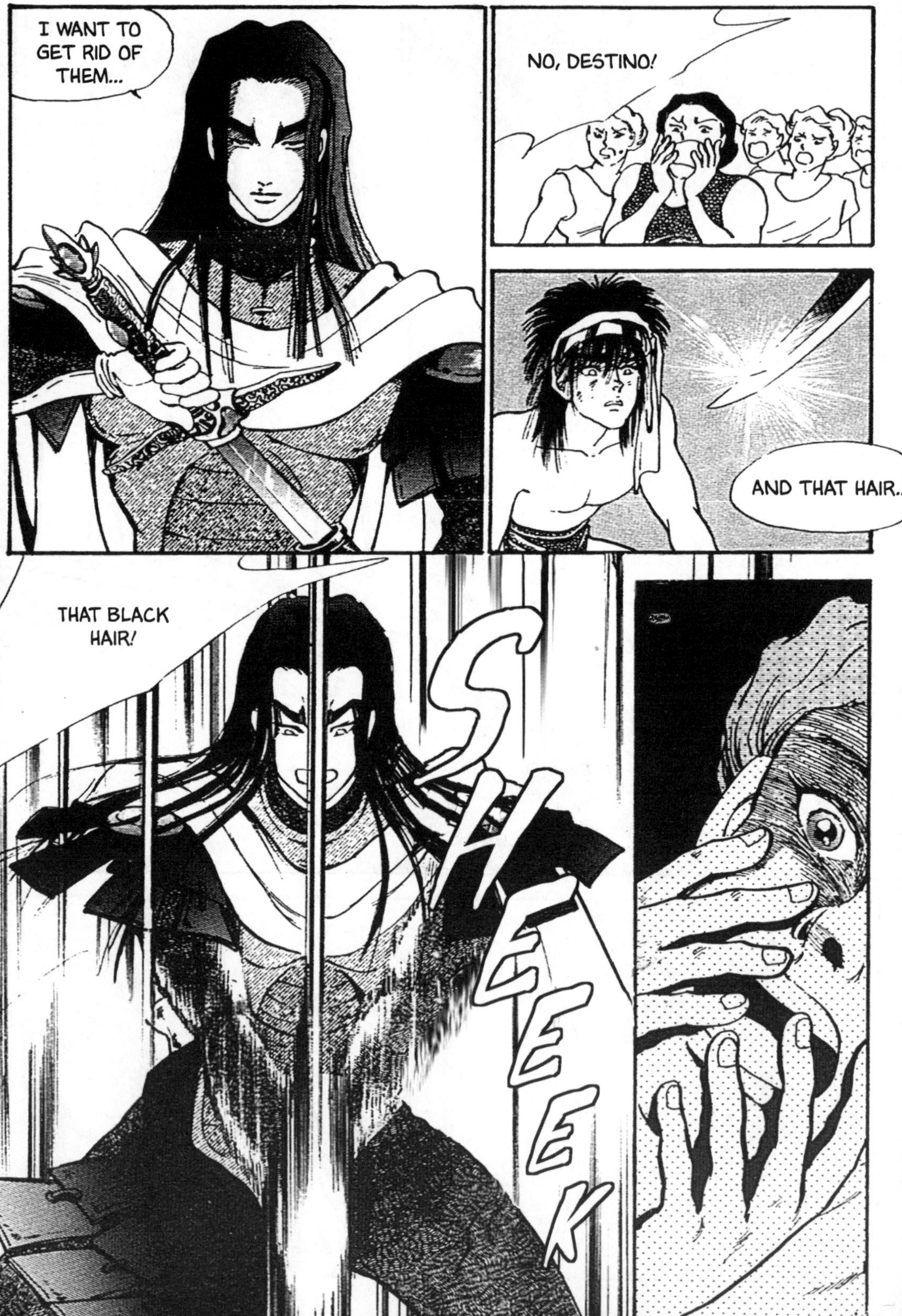
I WANT TO GET RID OF THEM...
NO, DESTINO!
AND THAT HAIR..
THAT BLACK HAIR!
SHEEEK

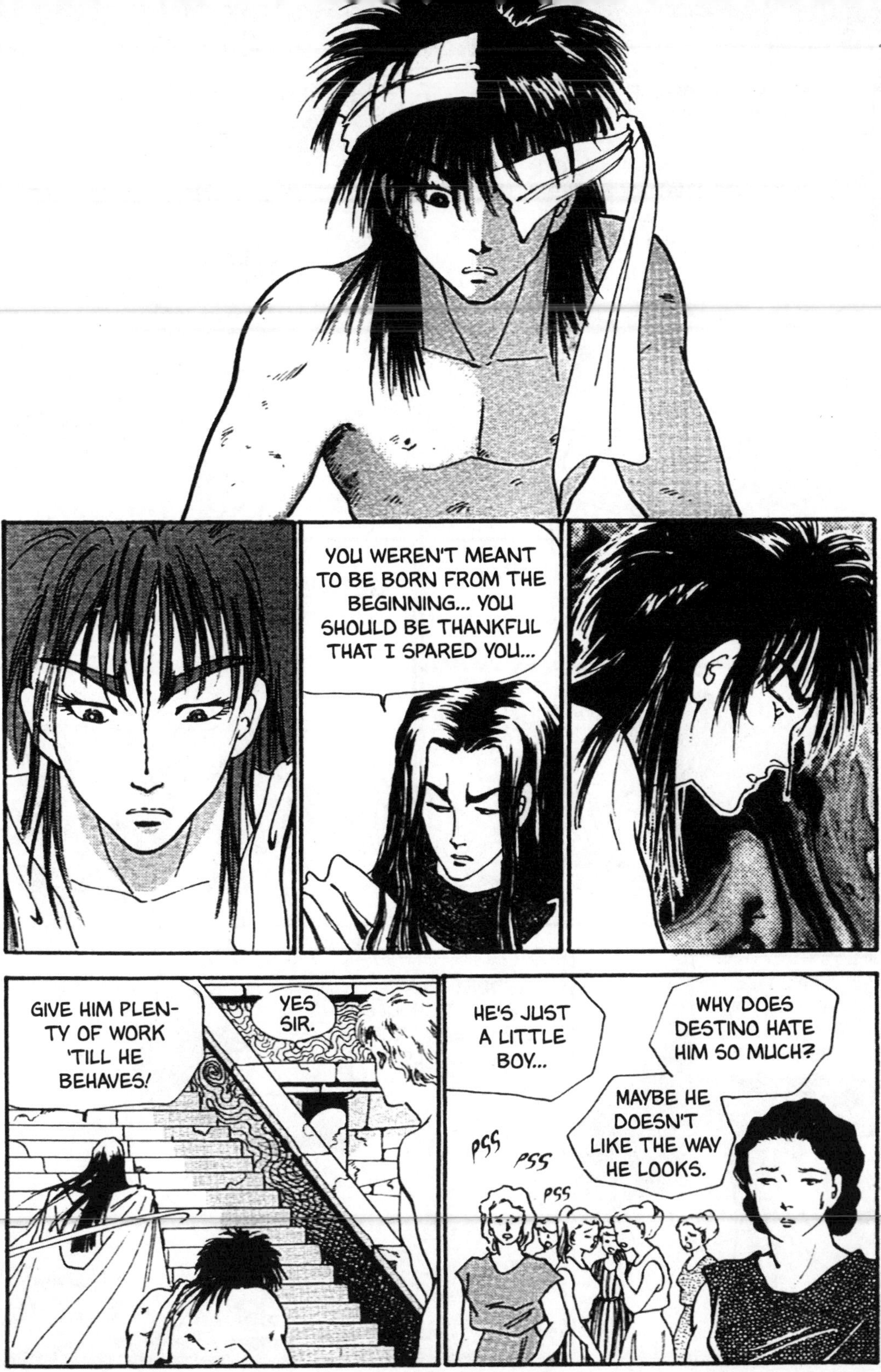
YOU WEREN'T MEANT TO BE BORN FROM THE BEGINNING... YOU SHOULD BE THANKFUL THAT I SPARED YOU...
GIVE HIM PLENTY OF WORK 'TILL HE BEHAVES!
YES SIR.
WHY DOES DESTINO HATE HIM SO MUCH?
HE'S JUST A LITTLE BOY...
MAYBE HE DOESN'T LIKE THE WAY HE LOOKS.
PSS
PSS
PSS

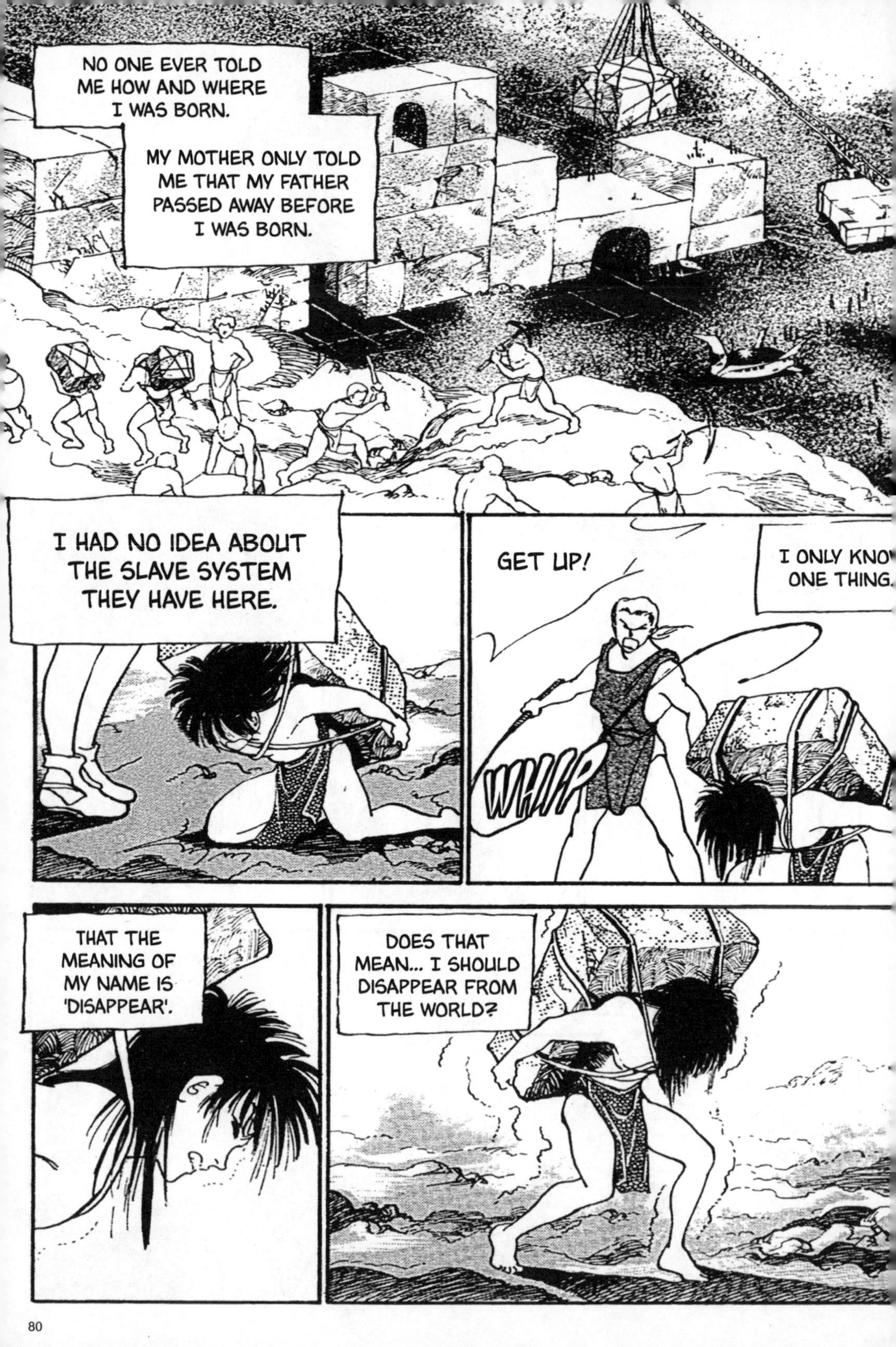
NO ONE EVER TOLD ME HOW AND WHERE I WAS BORN.
MY MOTHER ONLY TOLD ME THAT MY FATHER PASSED AWAY BEFORE I WAS BORN.
I HAD NO IDEA ABOUT THE SLAVE SYSTEM THEY HAVE HERE.
GET UP!
WHIP
I ONLY KNOW ONE THING.
THAT THE MEANING OF MY NAME IS 'DISAPPEAR'.
DOES THAT MEAN... I SHOULD DISAPPEAR FROM THE WORLD?

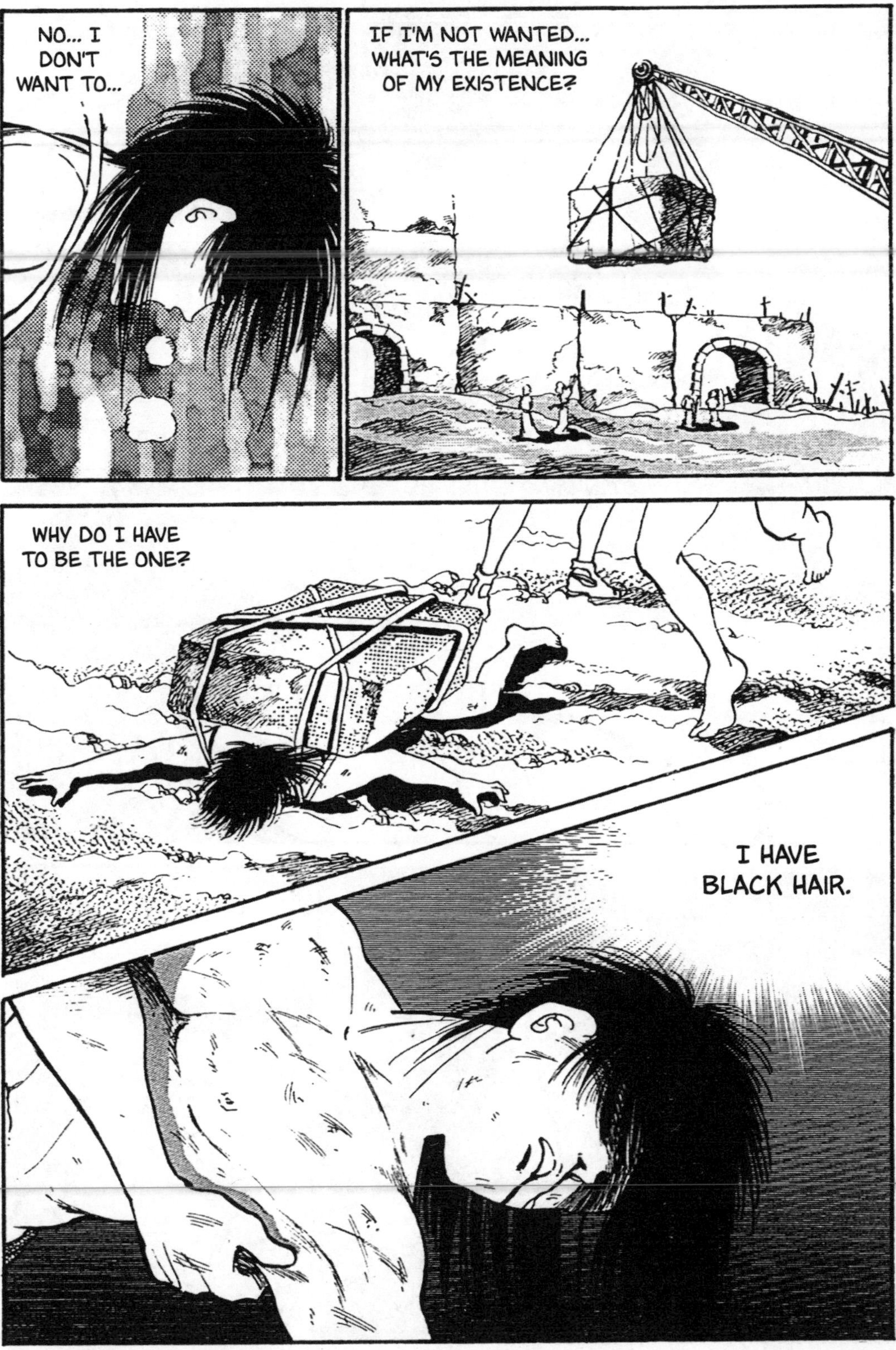

NO... I DON'T WANT TO...
IF I'M NOT WANTED... WHAT'S THE MEANING OF MY EXISTENCE?
WHY DO I HAVE TO BE THE ONE?
I HAVE BLACK HAIR.

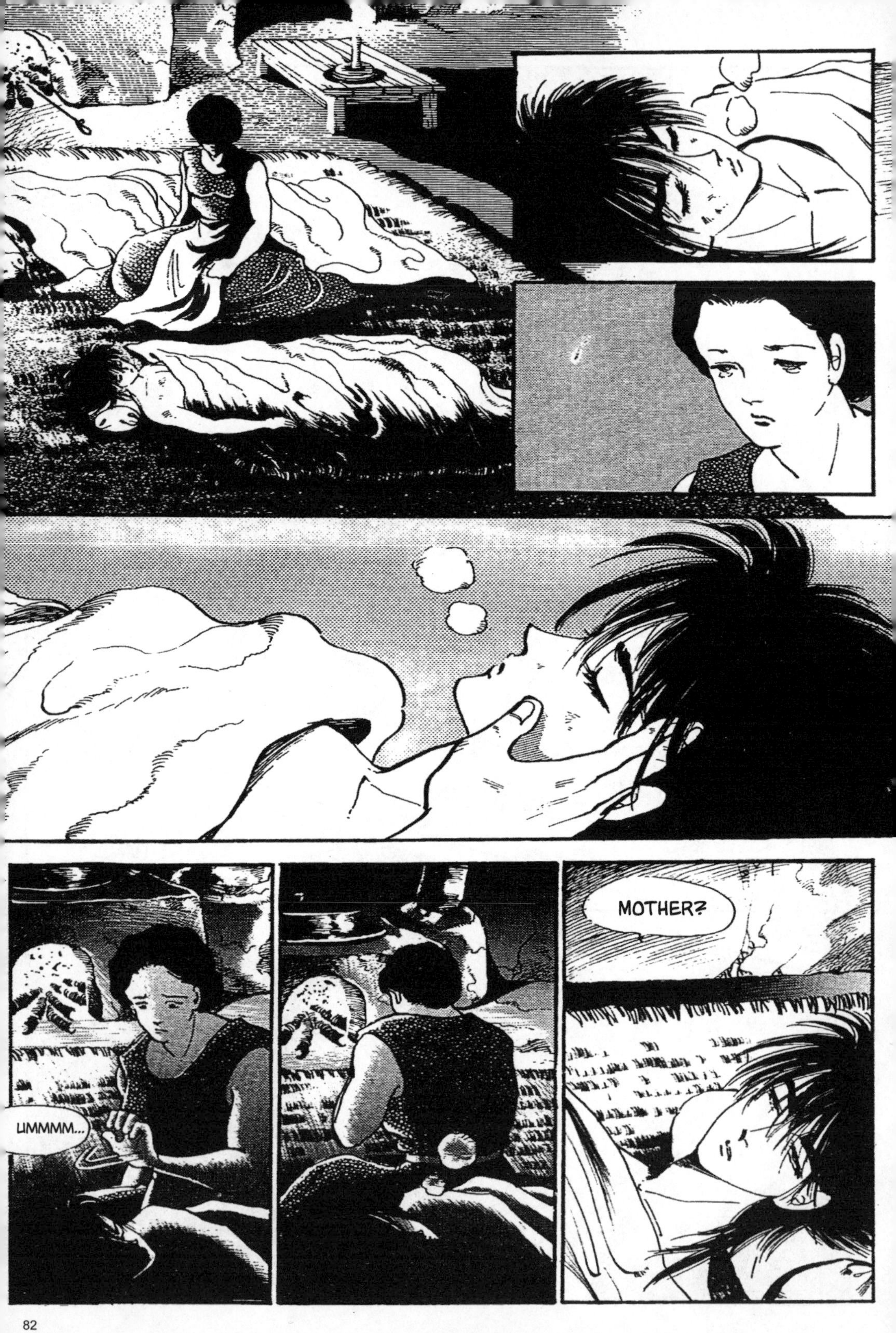
MOTHER?
UMMMM...

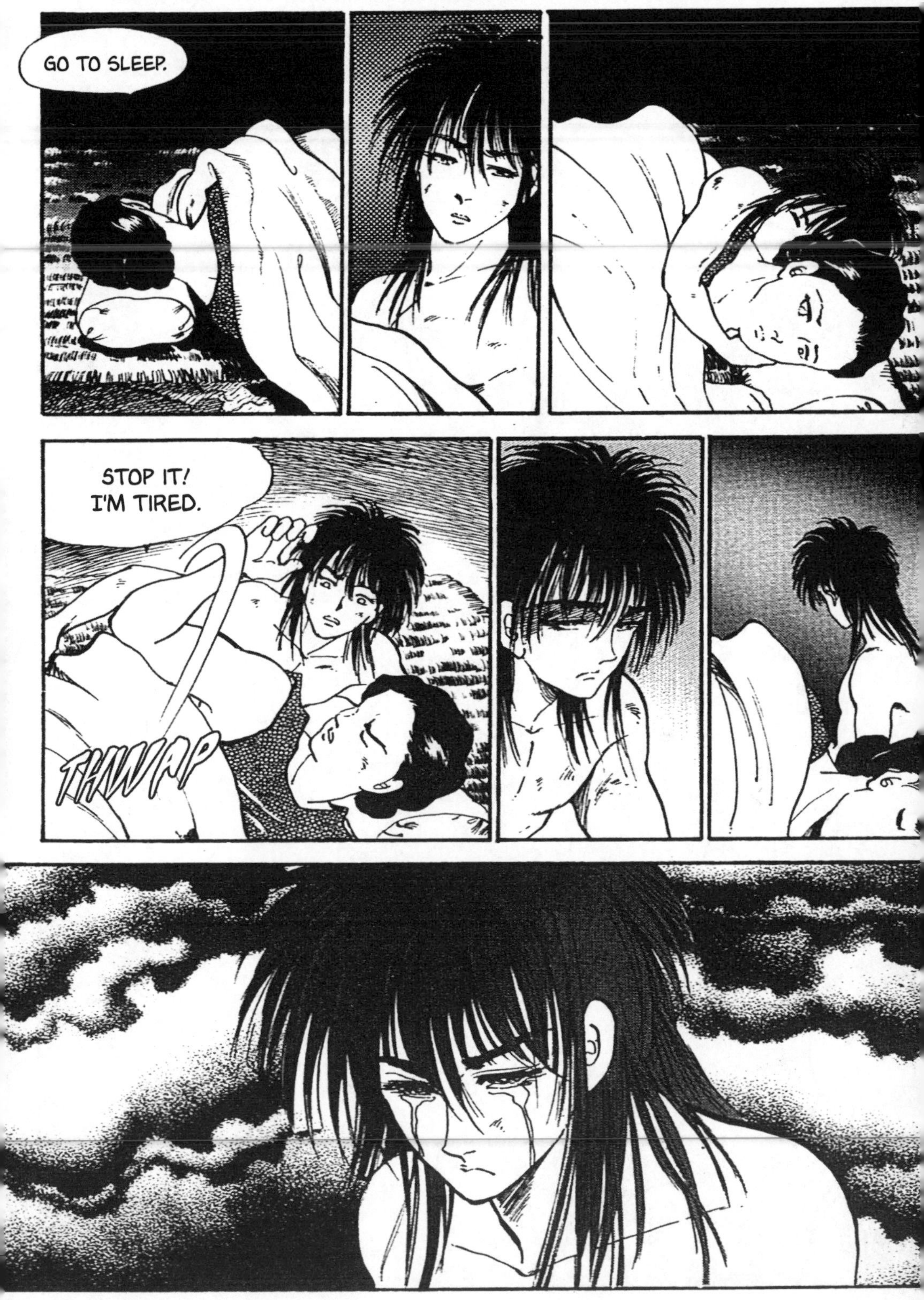
GO TO SLEEP.
STOP IT! I'M TIRED.
THWAP

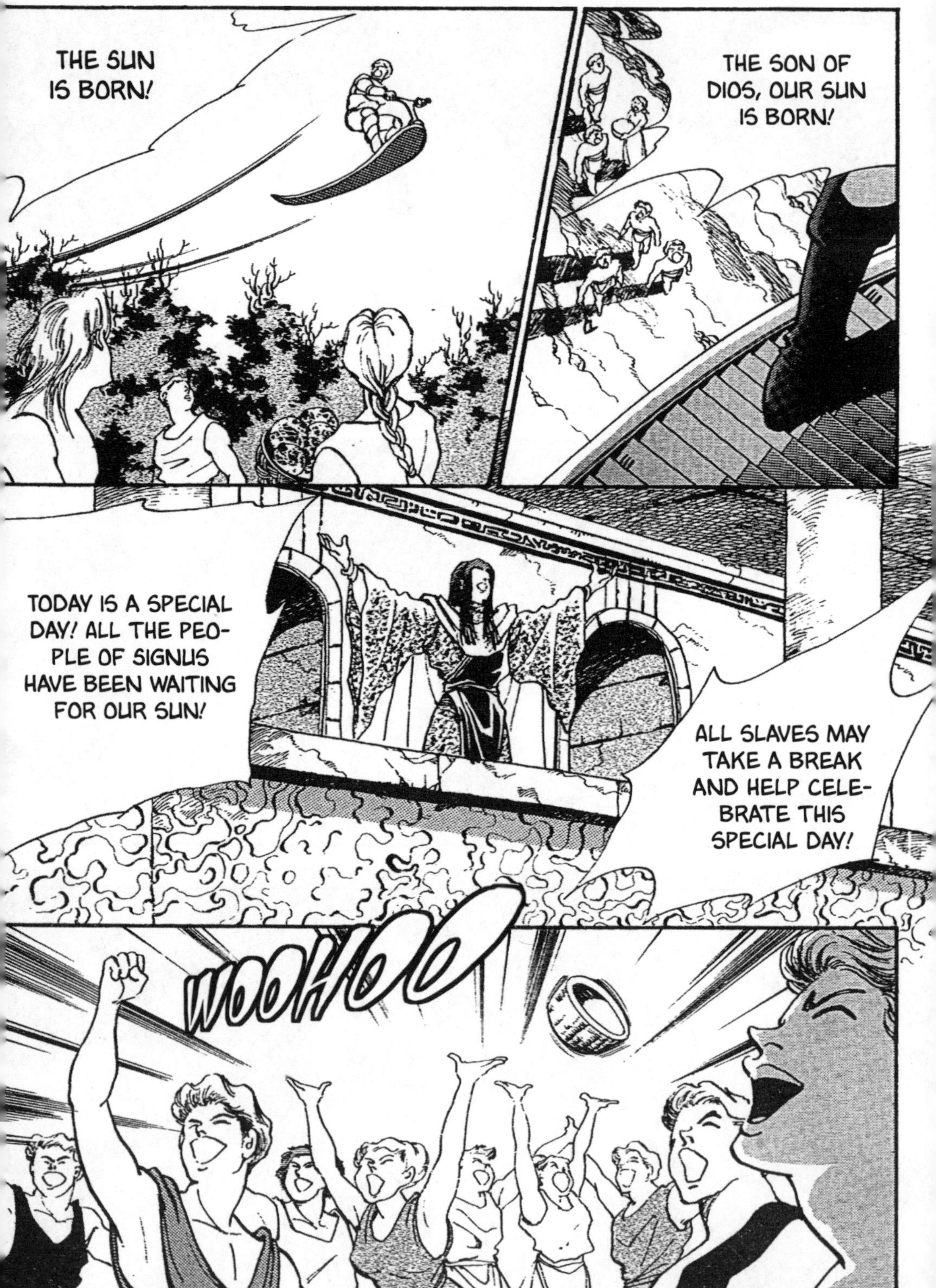
THE SUN IS BORN!
THE SON OF DIOS, OUR SUN IS BORN!
TODAY IS A SPECIAL DAY! ALL THE PEO-PLE OF SIGNUS HAVE BEEN WAITING FOR OUR SUN!
ALL SLAVES MAY TAKE A BREAK AND HELP CELE-BRATE THIS SPECIAL DAY!
WOOHOO

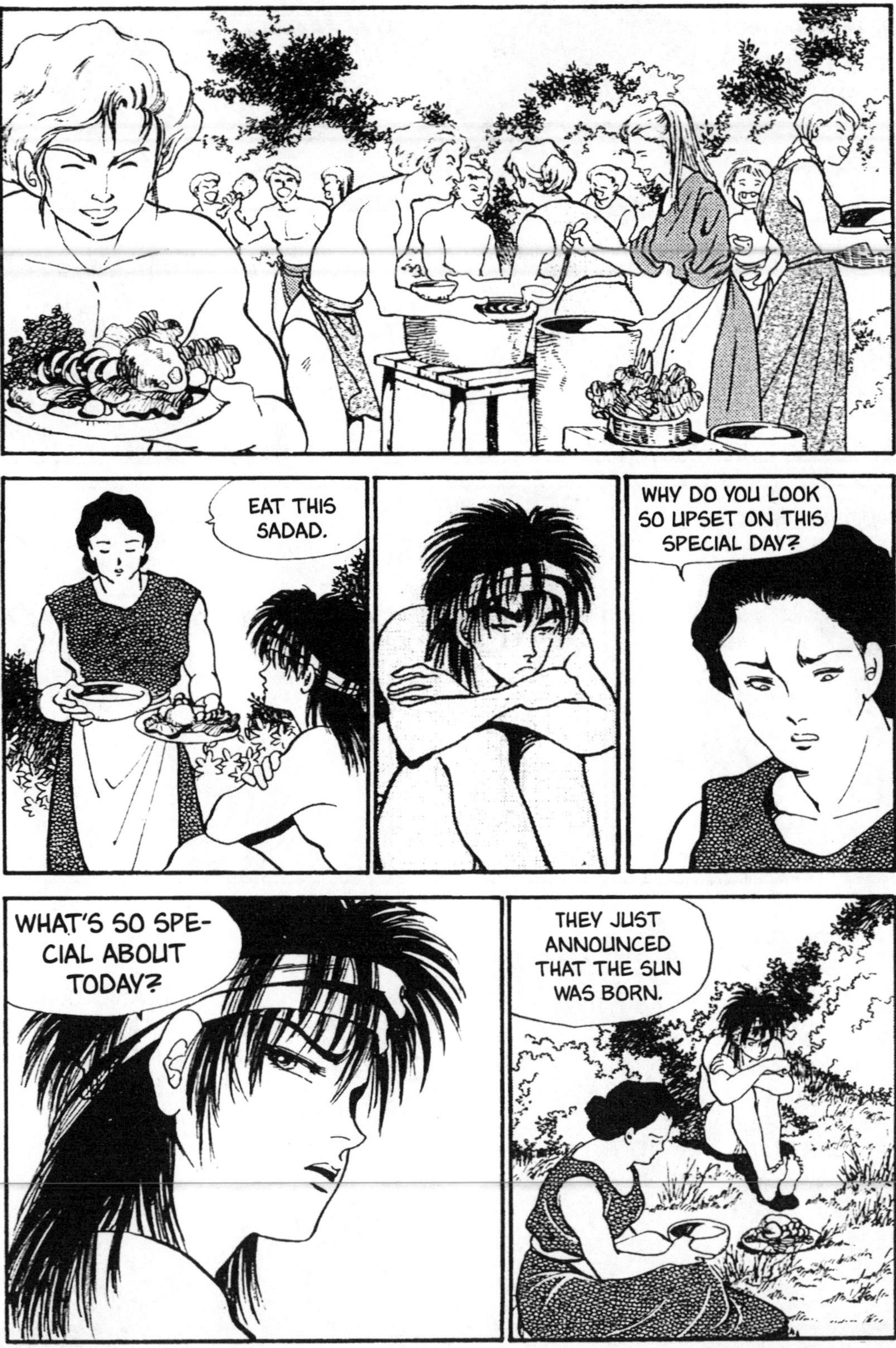
EAT THIS SADAD.
WHY DO YOU LOOK SO UPSET ON THIS SPECIAL DAY?
WHAT'S SO SPECIAL ABOUT TODAY?
THEY JUST ANNOUNCED THAT THE SUN WAS BORN.

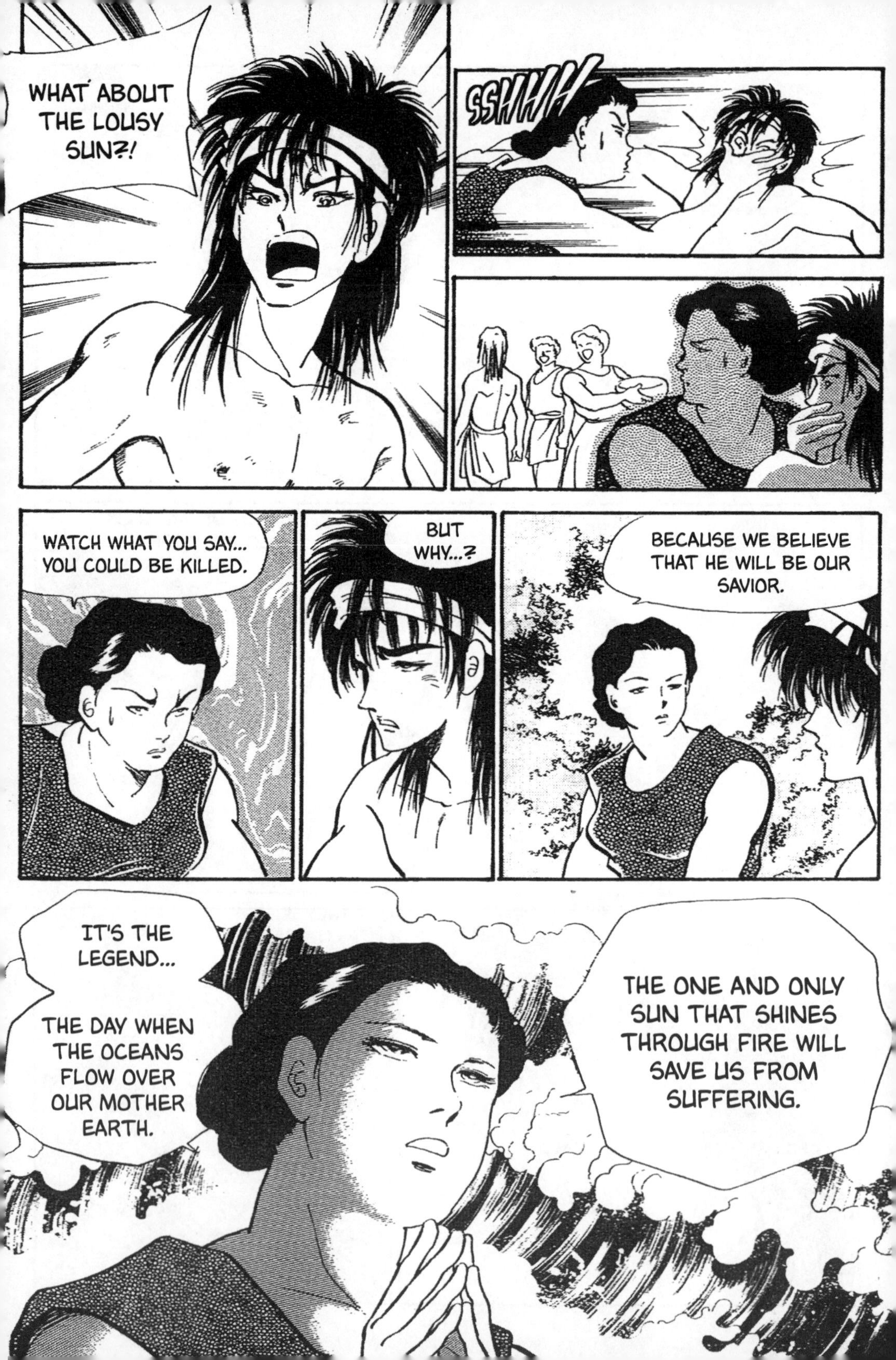
WHAT ABOUT THE LOUSY SUN?!
SSHHHH
WATCH WHAT YOU SAY... YOU COULD BE KILLED.
BUT WHY...?
BECAUSE WE BELIEVE THAT HE WILL BE OUR SAVIOR.
IT'S THE LEGEND...
THE DAY WHEN THE OCEANS FLOW OVER OUR MOTHER EARTH.
THE ONE AND ONLY SUN THAT SHINES THROUGH FIRE WILL SAVE US FROM SUFFERING.

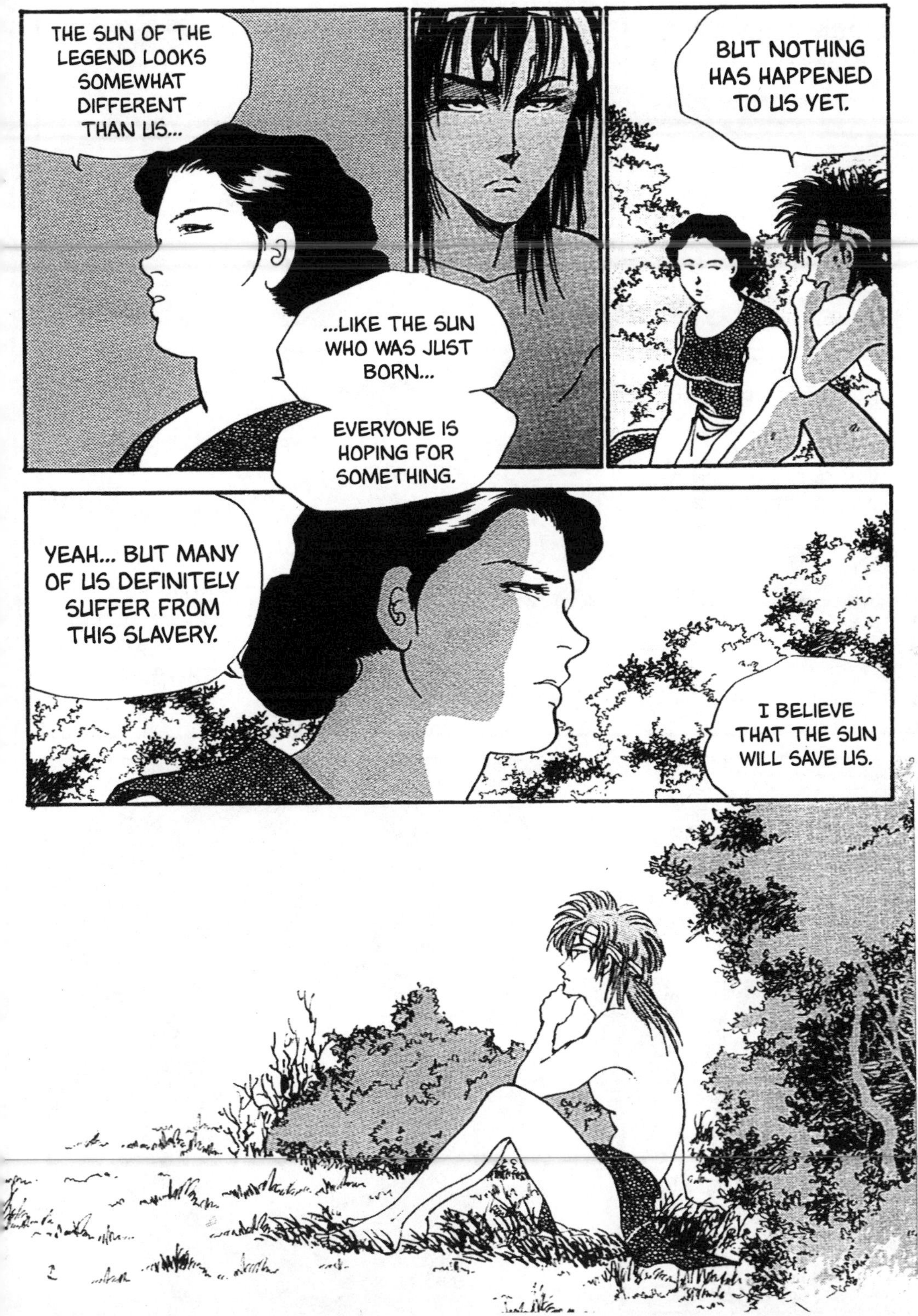
THE SUN OF THE LEGEND LOOKS SOMEWHAT DIFFERENT THAN US...
...LIKE THE SUN WHO WAS JUST BORN...
EVERYONE IS HOPING FOR SOMETHING.
BUT NOTHING HAS HAPPENED TO US YET.
YEAH... BUT MANY OF US DEFINITELY SUFFER FROM THIS SLAVERY.
I BELIEVE THAT THE SUN WILL SAVE US.

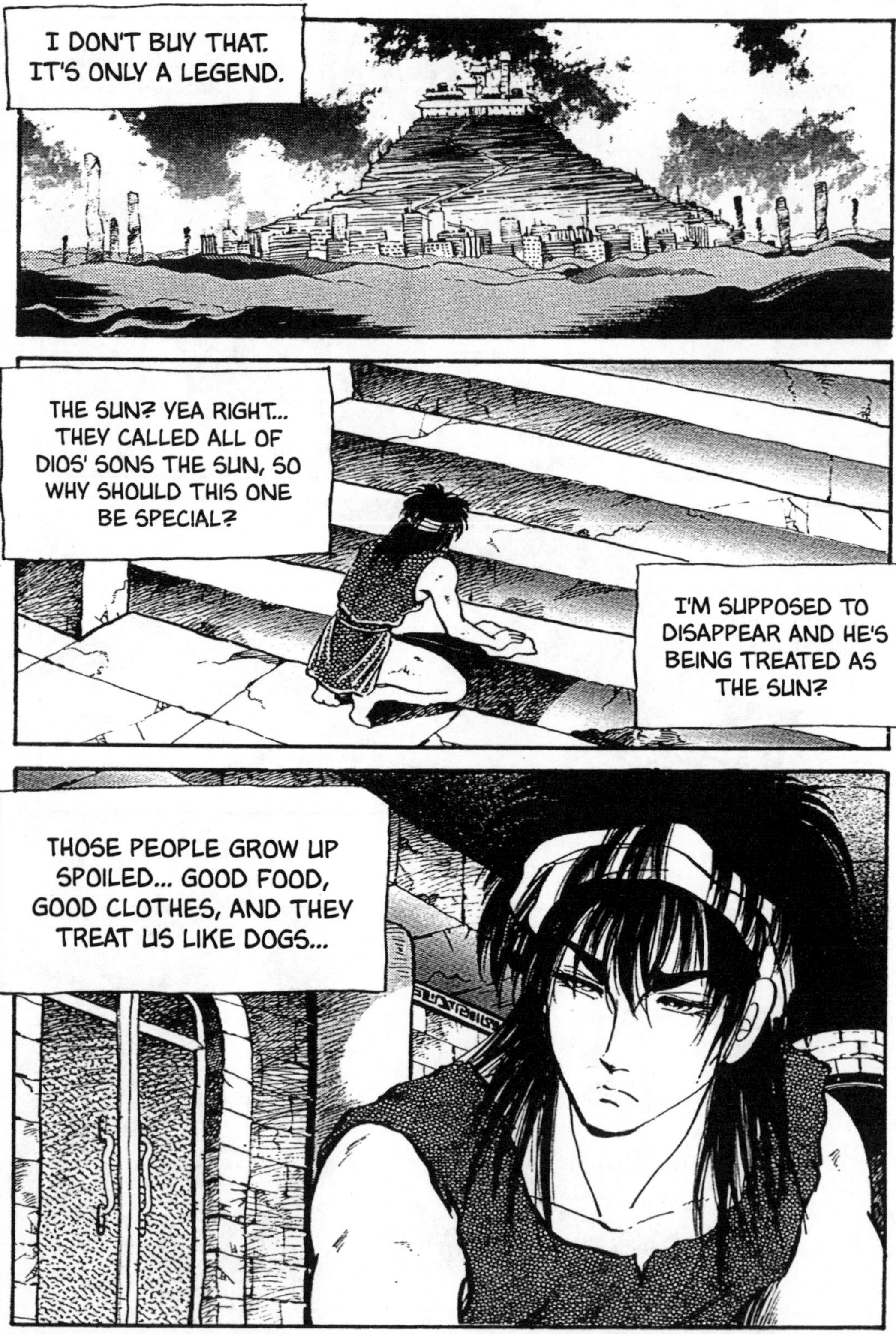
I DON'T BUY THAT. IT'S ONLY A LEGEND.
THE SUN? YEA RIGHT... THEY CALLED ALL OF DIOS' SONS THE SUN, SO WHY SHOULD THIS ONE BE SPECIAL?
I'M SUPPOSED TO DISAPPEAR AND HE'S BEING TREATED AS THE SUN?
THOSE PEOPLE GROW UP SPOILED... GOOD FOOD, GOOD CLOTHES, AND THEY TREAT US LIKE DOGS...

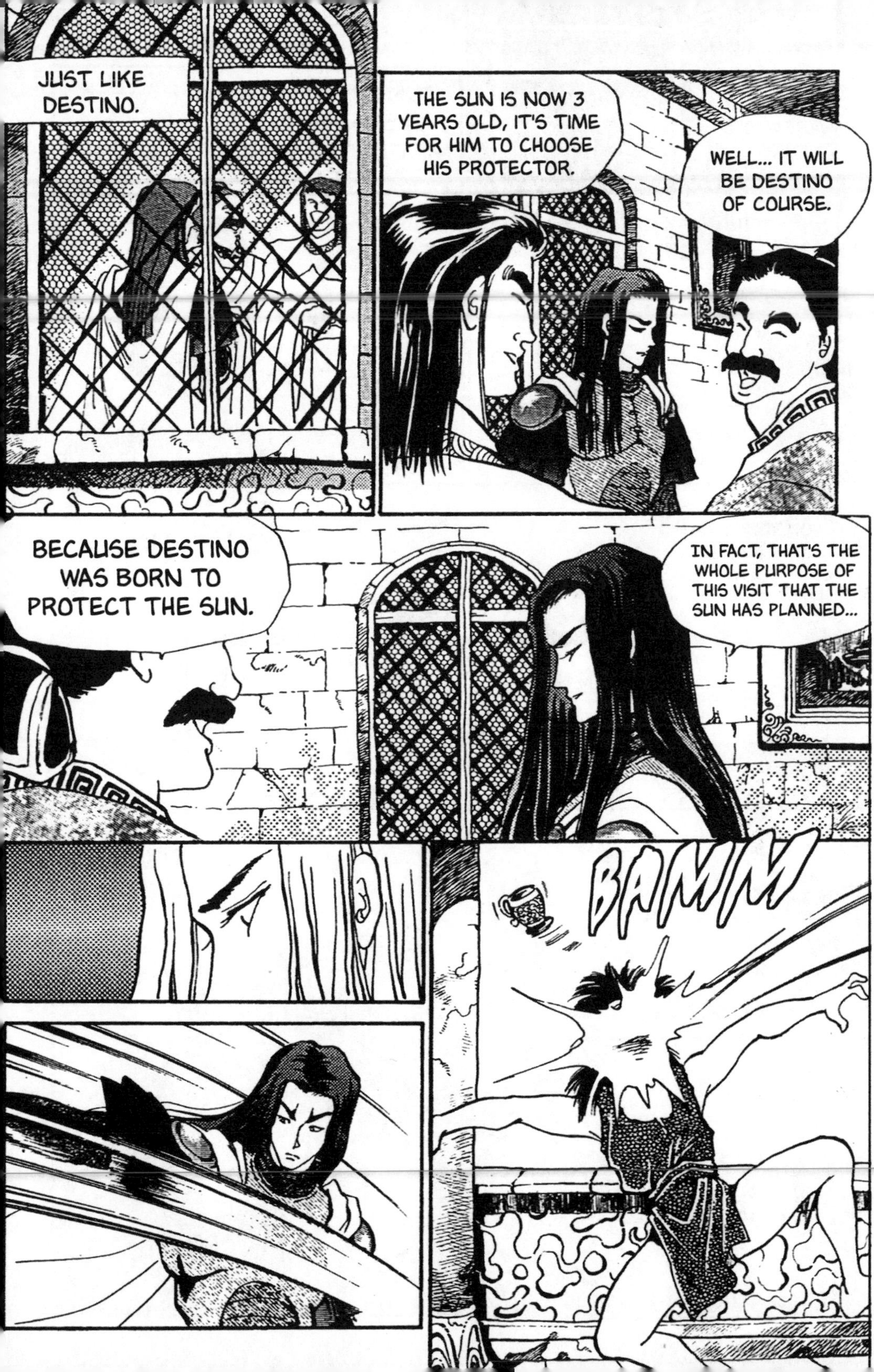
JUST LIKE DESTINO.
THE SUN IS NOW 3 YEARS OLD, IT'S TIME FOR HIM TO CHOOSE HIS PROTECTOR.
WELL... IT WILL BE DESTINO OF COURSE.
BECAUSE DESTINO WAS BORN TO PROTECT THE SUN.
IN FACT, THAT'S THE WHOLE PURPOSE OF THIS VISIT THAT THE SUN HAS PLANNED...
BAMM

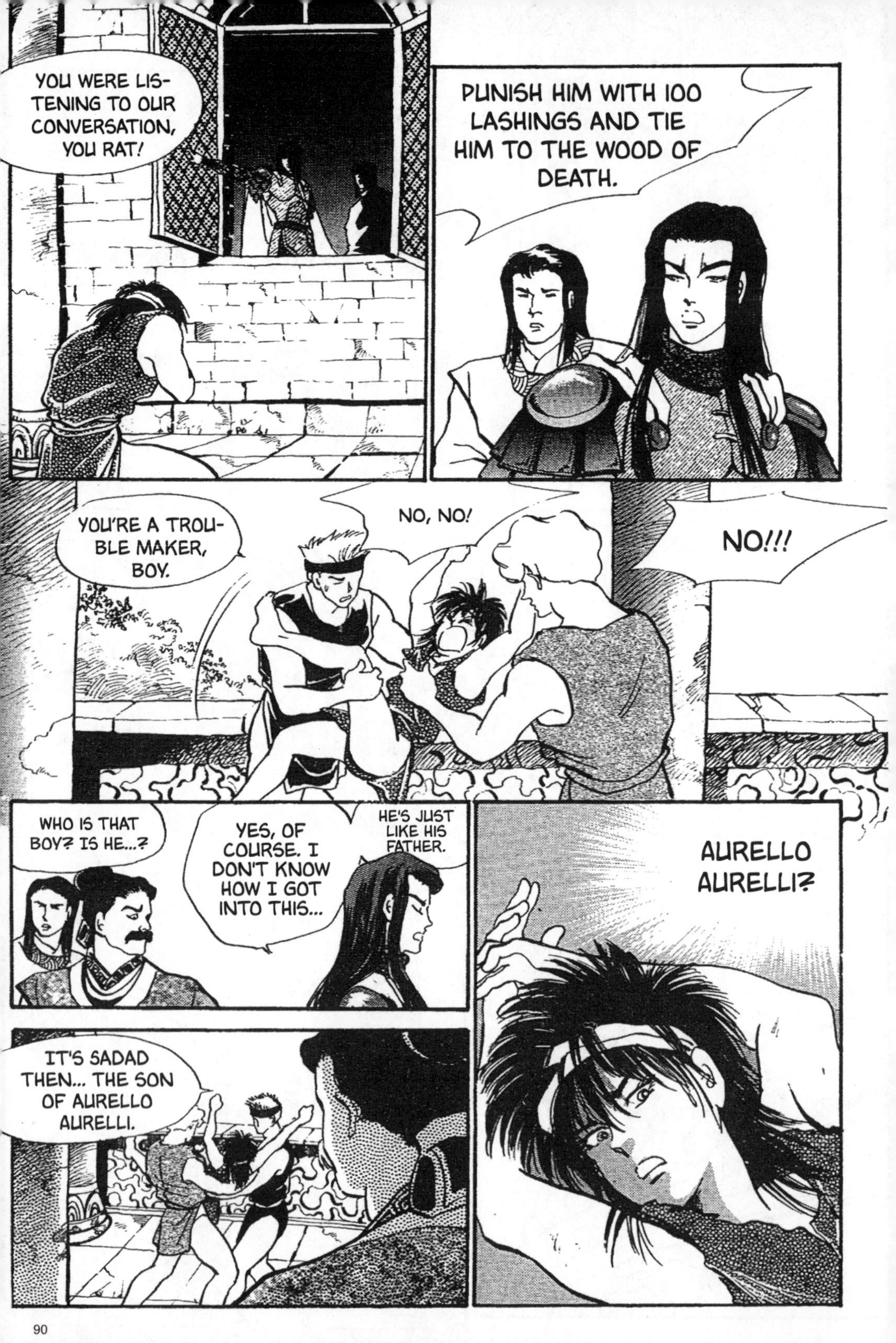
YOU WERE LISTENING TO OUR CONVERSATION, YOU RAT!
PUNISH HIM WITH 100 LASHINGS AND TIE HIM TO THE WOOD OF DEATH.
YOU'RE A TROUBLE MAKER, BOY.
NO, NO!
NO!!!
WHO IS THAT BOY? IS HE...?
YES, OF COURSE. I DON'T KNOW HOW I GOT INTO THIS...
HE'S JUST LIKE HIS FATHER.
AURELLO AURELLI?
IT'S SADAD THEN... THE SON OF AURELLO AURELLI.

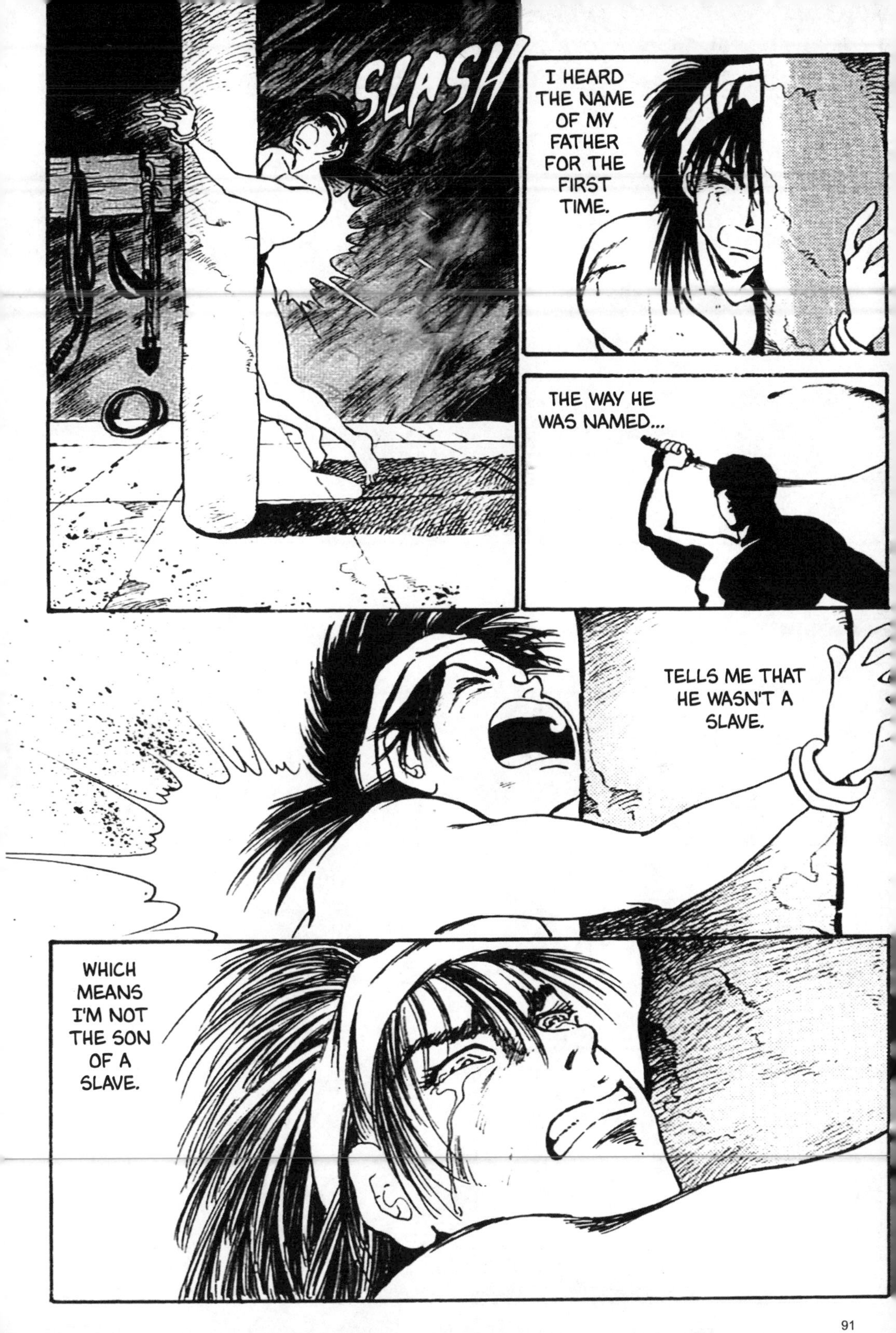
SLASH
I HEARD THE NAME OF MY FATHER FOR THE FIRST TIME.
THE WAY HE WAS NAMED...
TELLS ME THAT HE WASN'T A SLAVE.
WHICH MEANS I'M NOT THE SON OF A SLAVE.

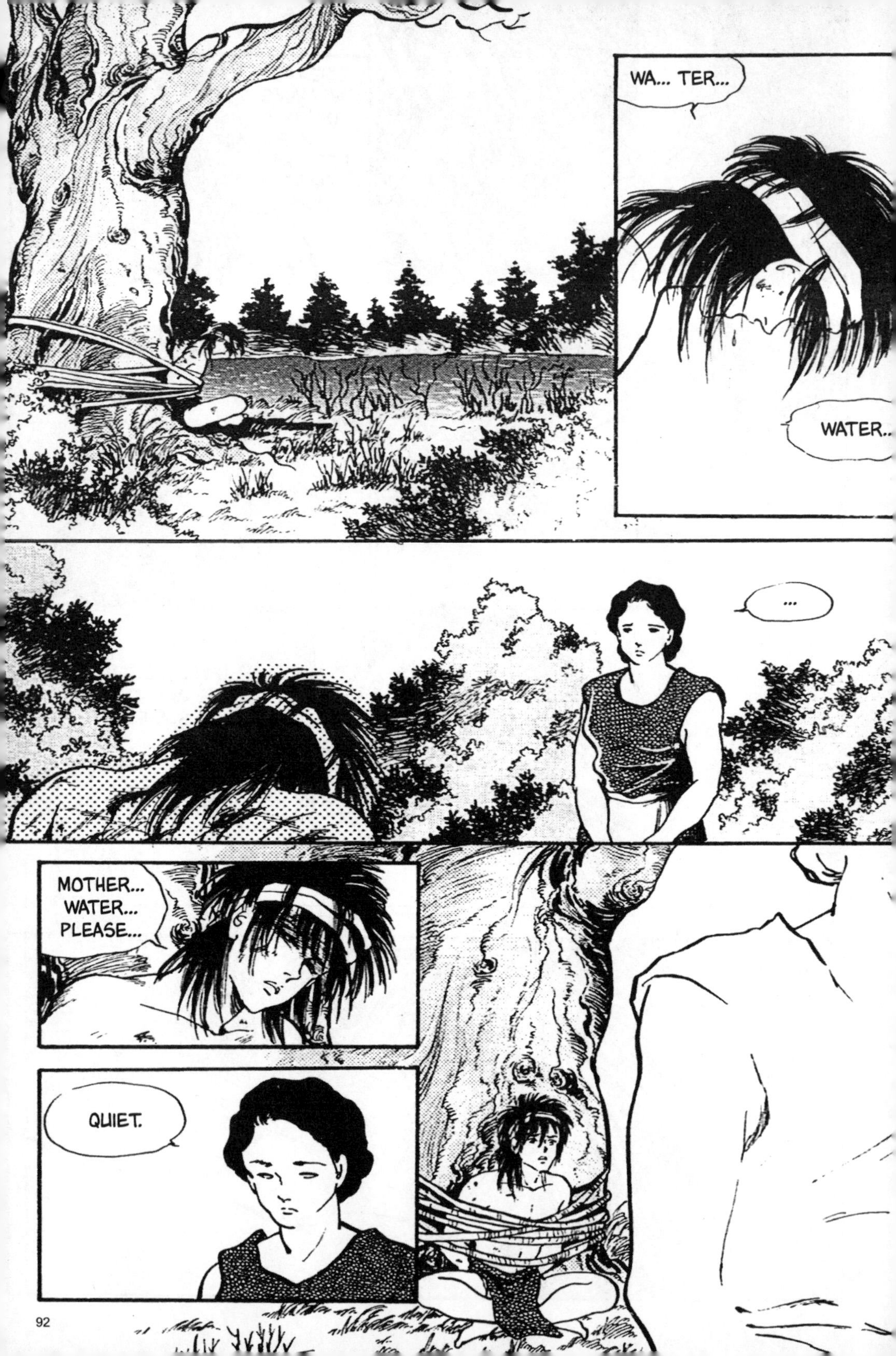
WA... TER...
WATER...
...
MOTHER... WATER... PLEASE...
QUIET.

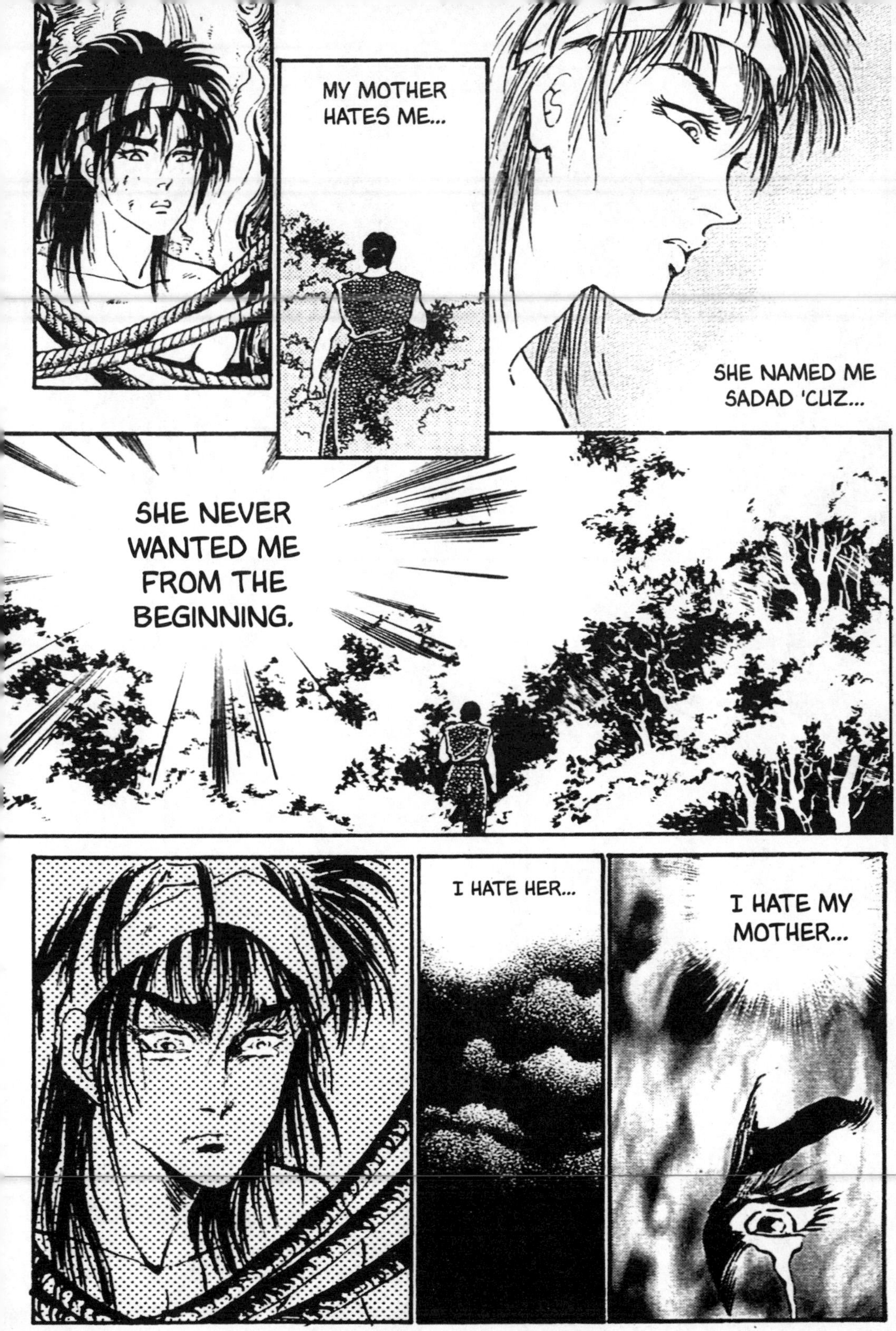
MY MOTHER HATES ME...
SHE NAMED ME SADAD 'CUZ...
SHE NEVER WANTED ME FROM THE BEGINNING.
I HATE HER...
I HATE MY MOTHER...

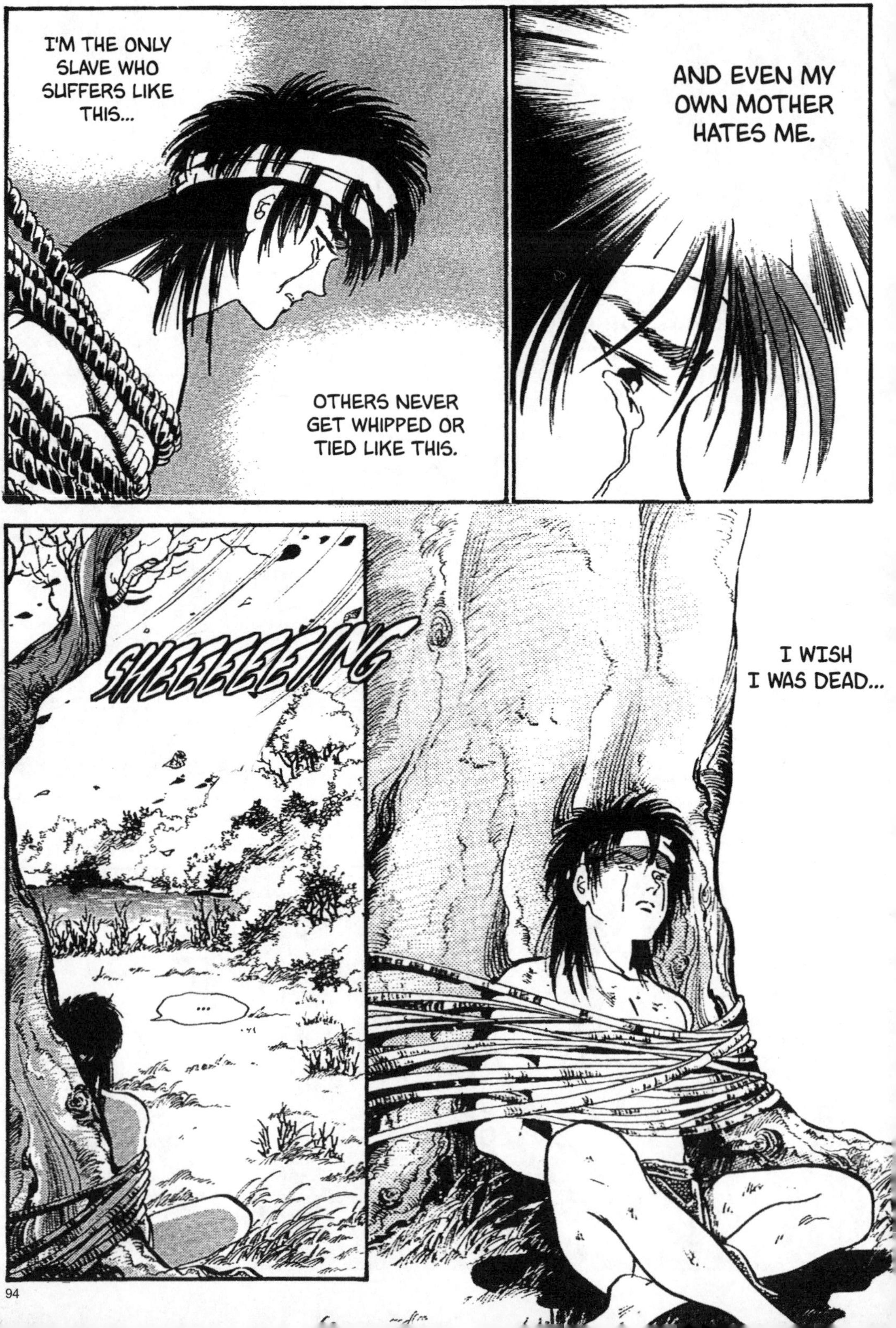
I'M THE ONLY SLAVE WHO SUFFERS LIKE THIS...
OTHERS NEVER GET WHIPPED OR TIED LIKE THIS.
AND EVEN MY OWN MOTHER HATES ME.
SHEEEEEING
...
I WISH I WAS DEAD...

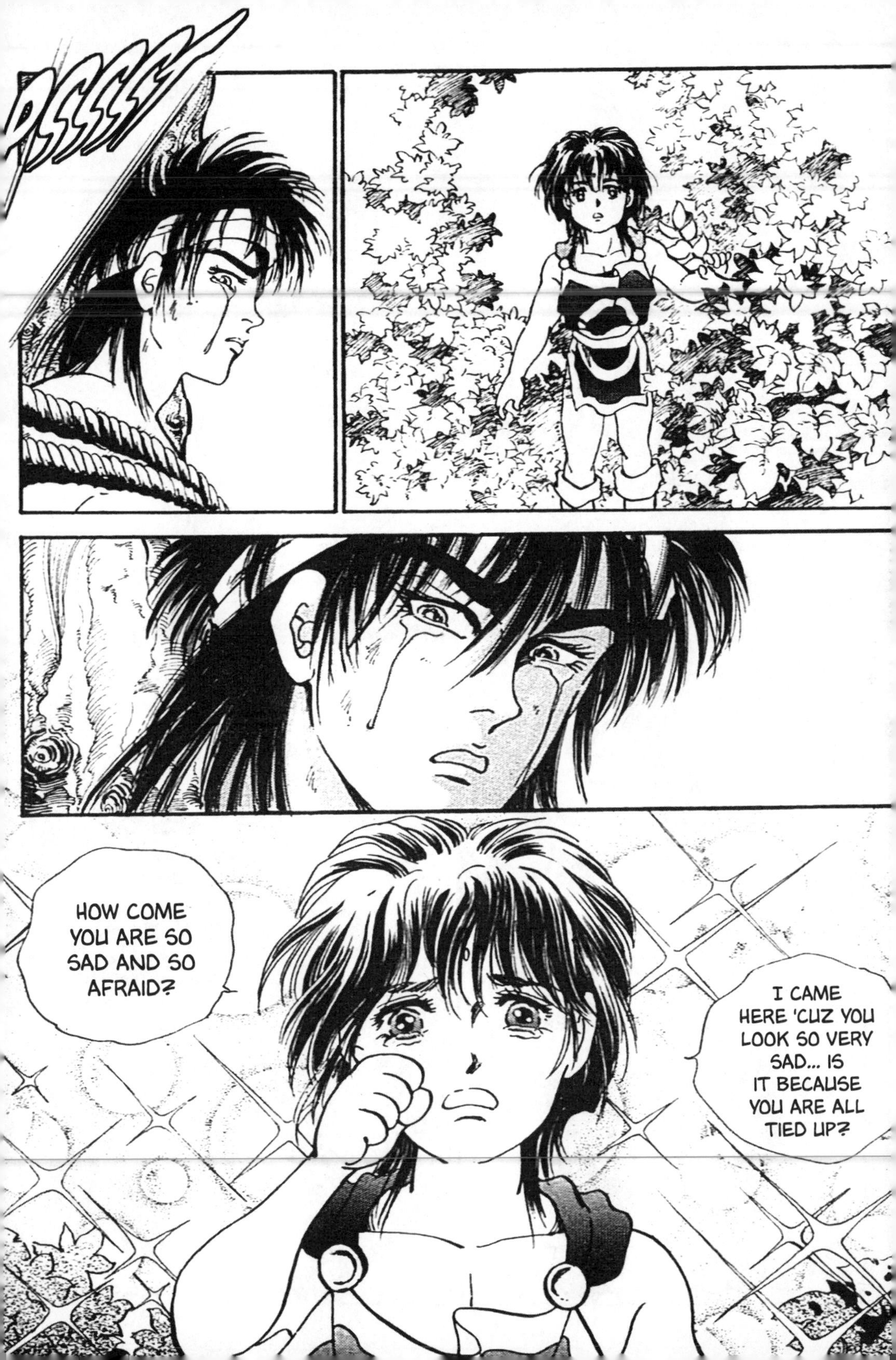
I CAME HERE 'CUZ YOU LOOK SO VERY SAD... IS IT BECAUSE YOU ARE ALL TIED UP?
HOW COME YOU ARE SO SAD AND SO AFRAID?

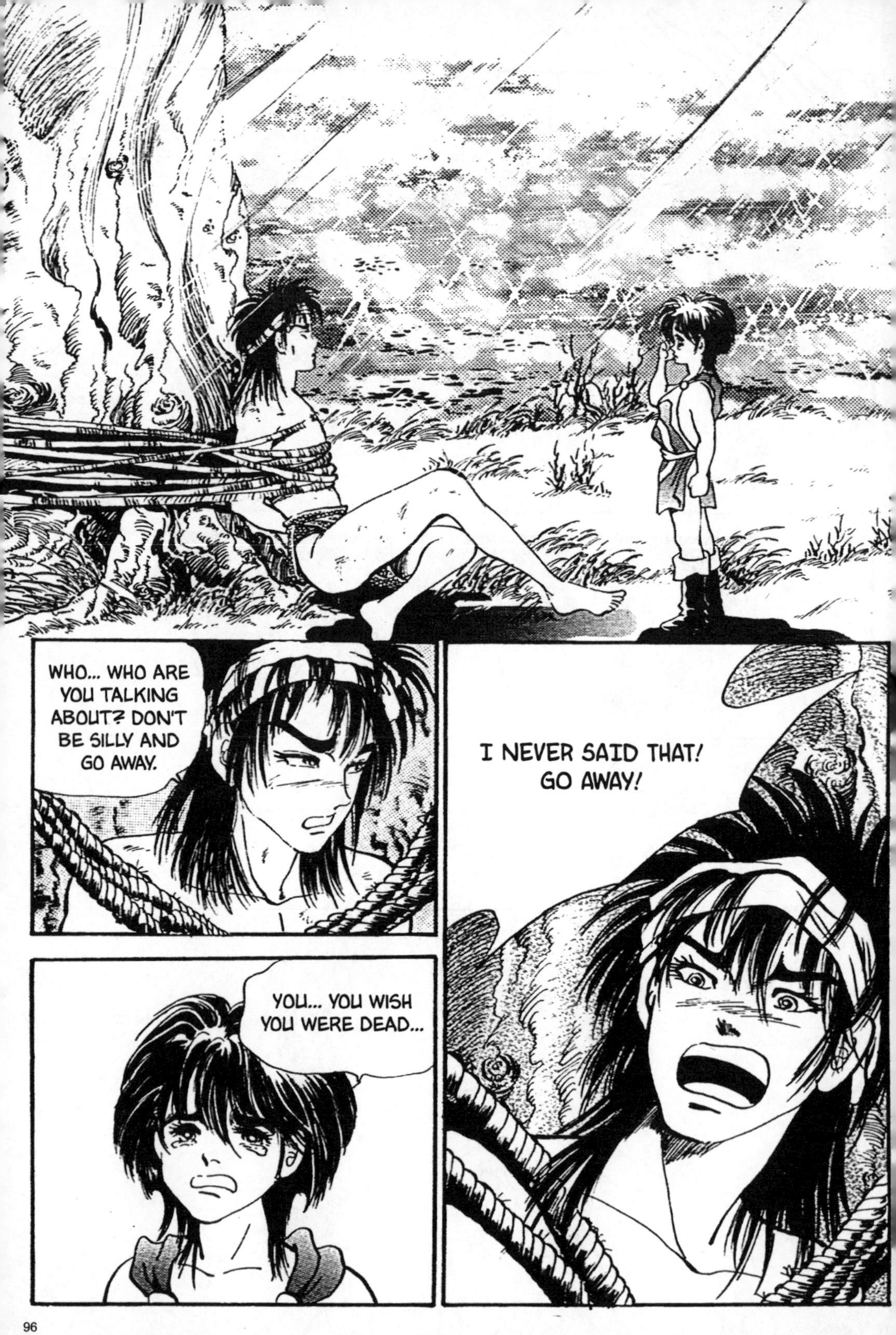
WHO... WHO ARE YOU TALKING ABOUT? DON'T BE SILLY AND GO AWAY.
YOU... YOU WISH YOU WERE DEAD...
I NEVER SAID THAT! GO AWAY!

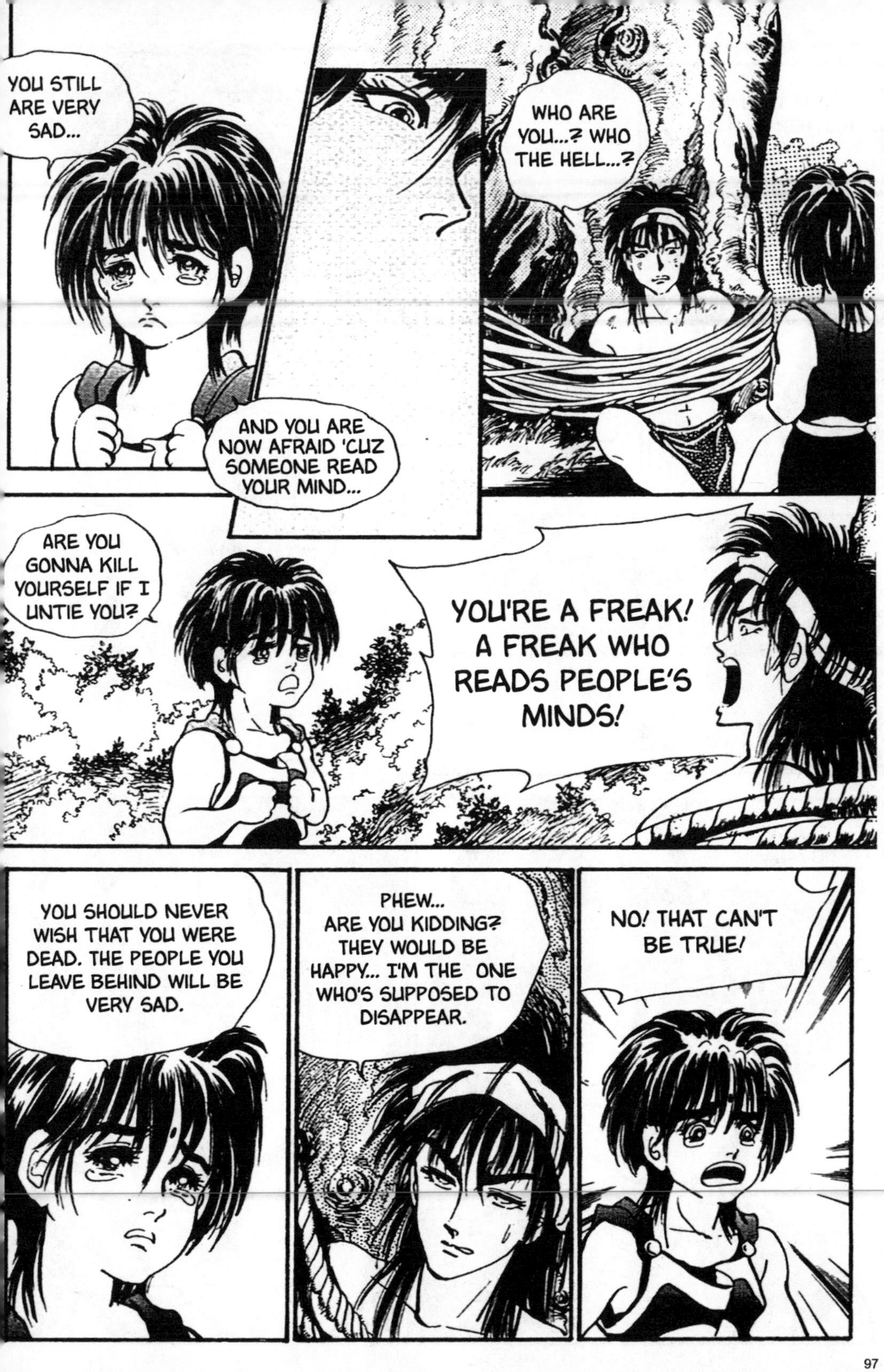
YOU STILL ARE VERY SAD...
WHO ARE YOU...? WHO THE HELL...?
AND YOU ARE NOW AFRAID 'CUZ SOMEONE READ YOUR MIND...
ARE YOU GONNA KILL YOURSELF IF I UNTIE YOU?
YOU'RE A FREAK! A FREAK WHO READS PEOPLE'S MINDS!
YOU SHOULD NEVER WISH THAT YOU WERE DEAD. THE PEOPLE YOU LEAVE BEHIND WILL BE VERY SAD.
PHEW... ARE YOU KIDDING? THEY WOULD BE HAPPY... I'M THE ONE WHO'S SUPPOSED TO DISAPPEAR.
NO! THAT CAN'T BE TRUE!

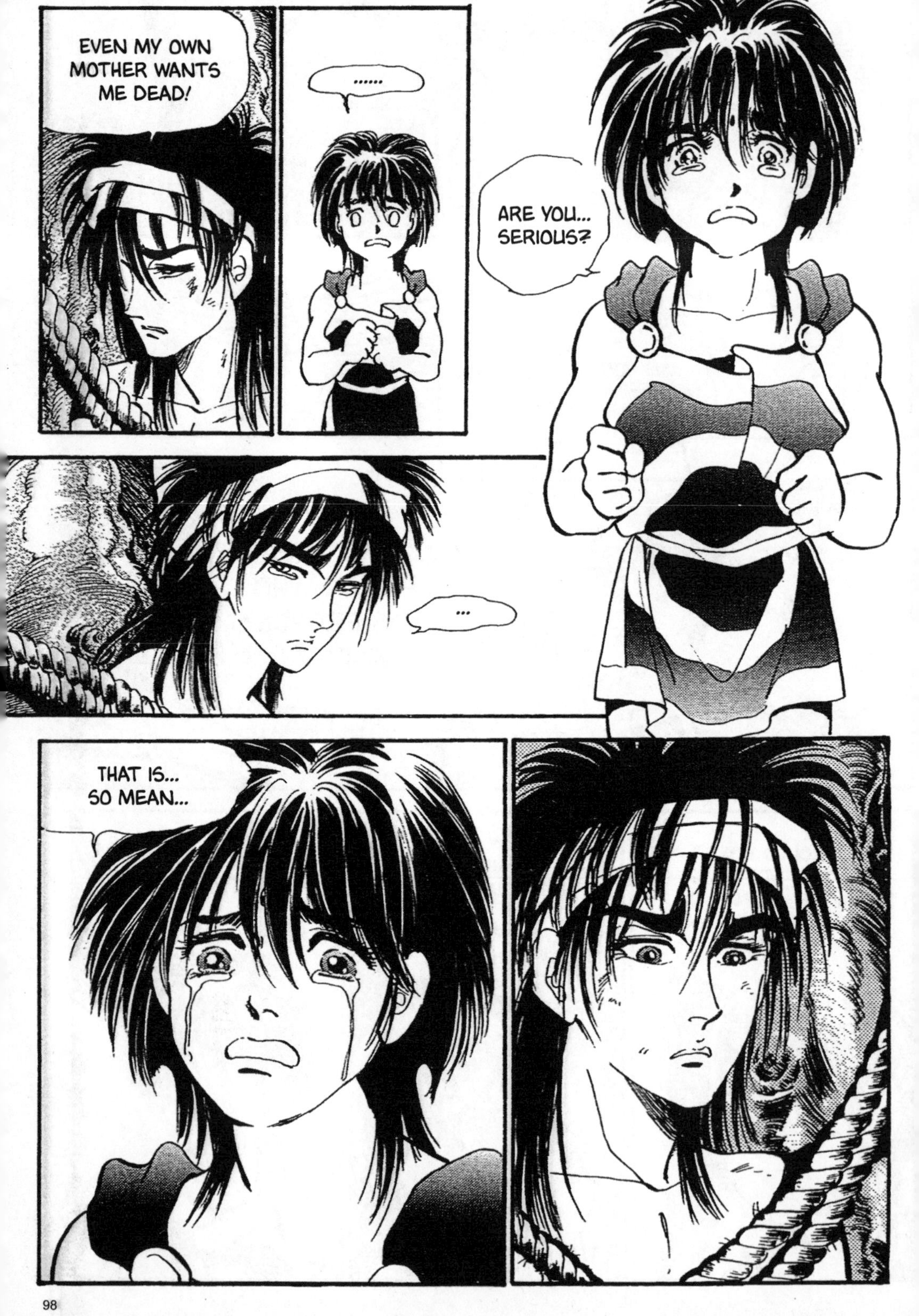
EVEN MY OWN MOTHER WANTS ME DEAD!
......
ARE YOU... SERIOUS?
...
THAT IS... SO MEAN...

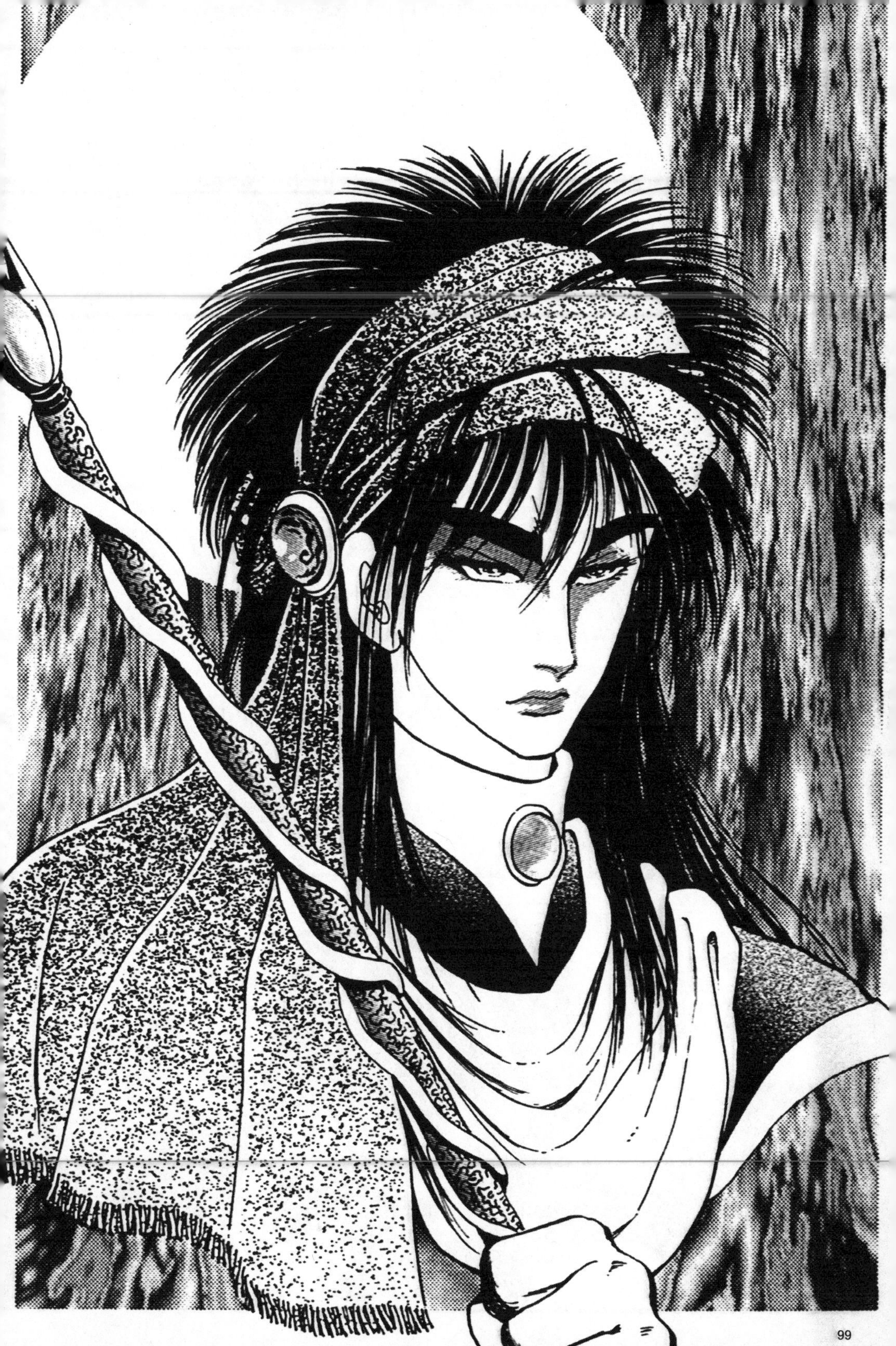

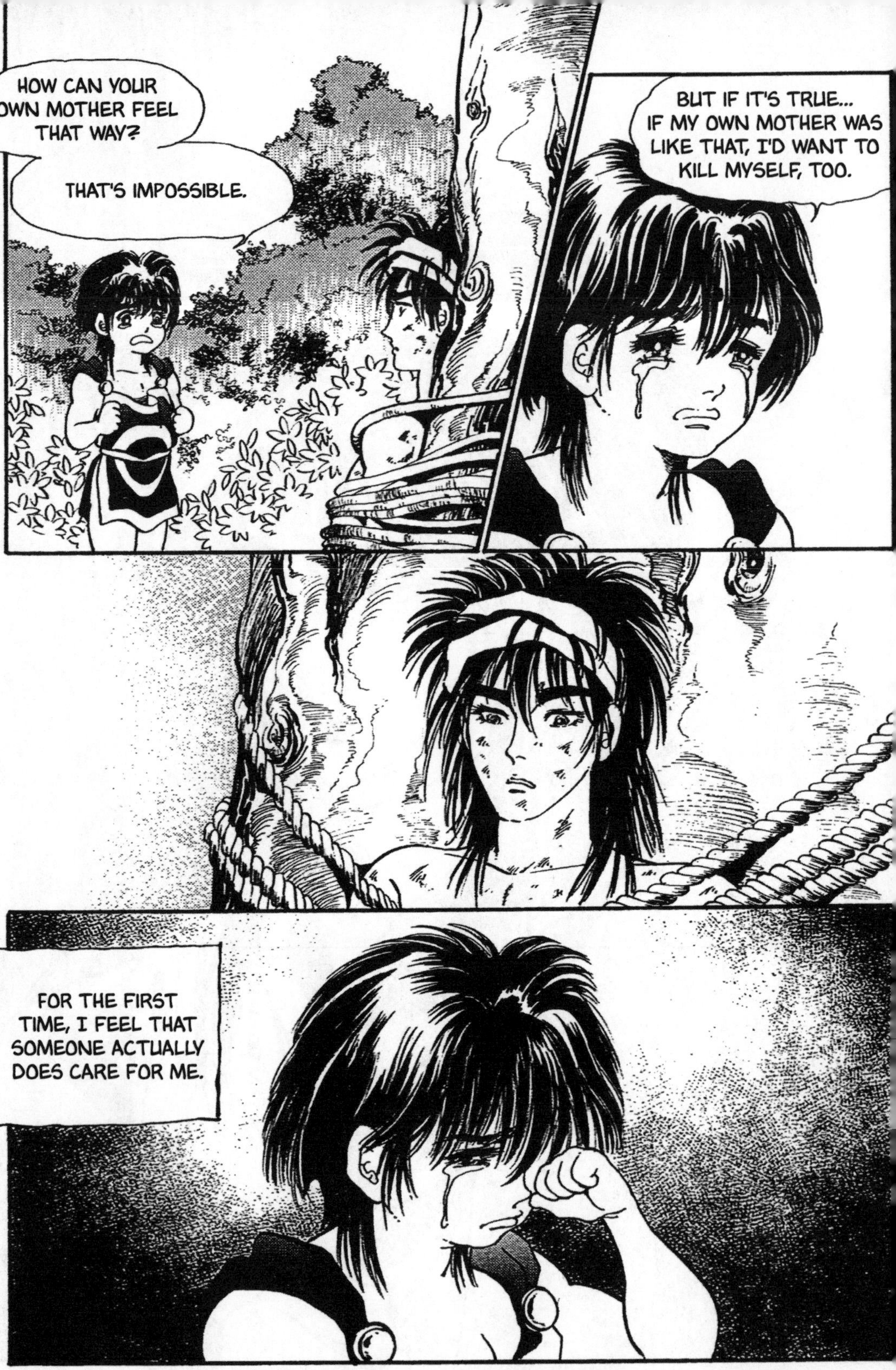
HOW CAN YOUR OWN MOTHER FEEL THAT WAY?
THAT'S IMPOSSIBLE.
BUT IF IT'S TRUE... IF MY OWN MOTHER WAS LIKE THAT, I'D WANT TO KILL MYSELF, TOO.
FOR THE FIRST TIME, I FEEL THAT SOMEONE ACTUALLY DOES CARE FOR ME.

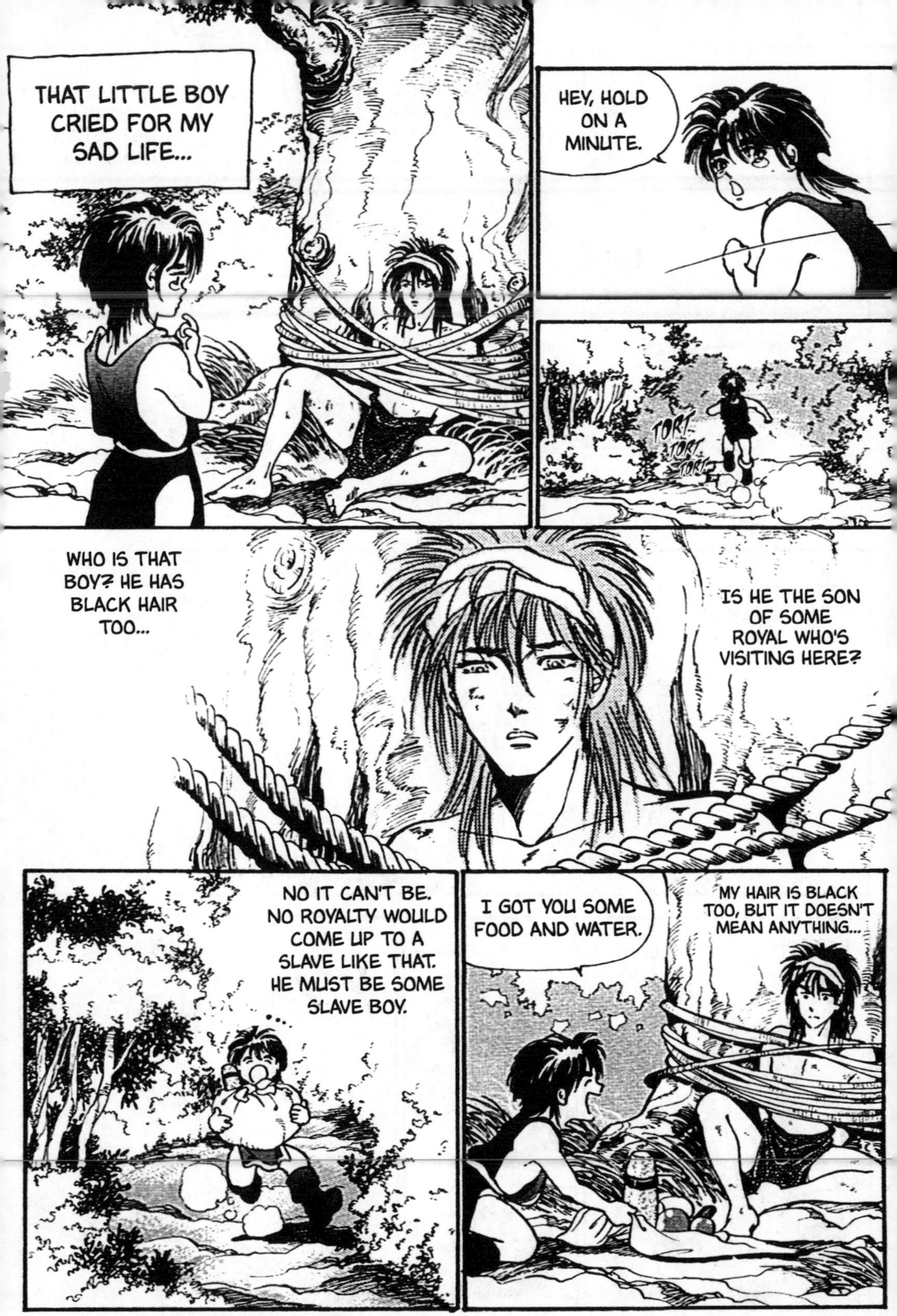

THAT LITTLE BOY CRIED FOR MY SAD LIFE...
HEY, HOLD ON A MINUTE.
TORI TORI TORI
WHO IS THAT BOY? HE HAS BLACK HAIR TOO...
IS HE THE SON OF SOME ROYAL WHO'S VISITING HERE?
NO IT CAN'T BE. NO ROYALTY WOULD COME UP TO A SLAVE LIKE THAT. HE MUST BE SOME SLAVE BOY.
...
I GOT YOU SOME FOOD AND WATER.
MY HAIR IS BLACK TOO, BUT IT DOESN'T MEAN ANYTHING...

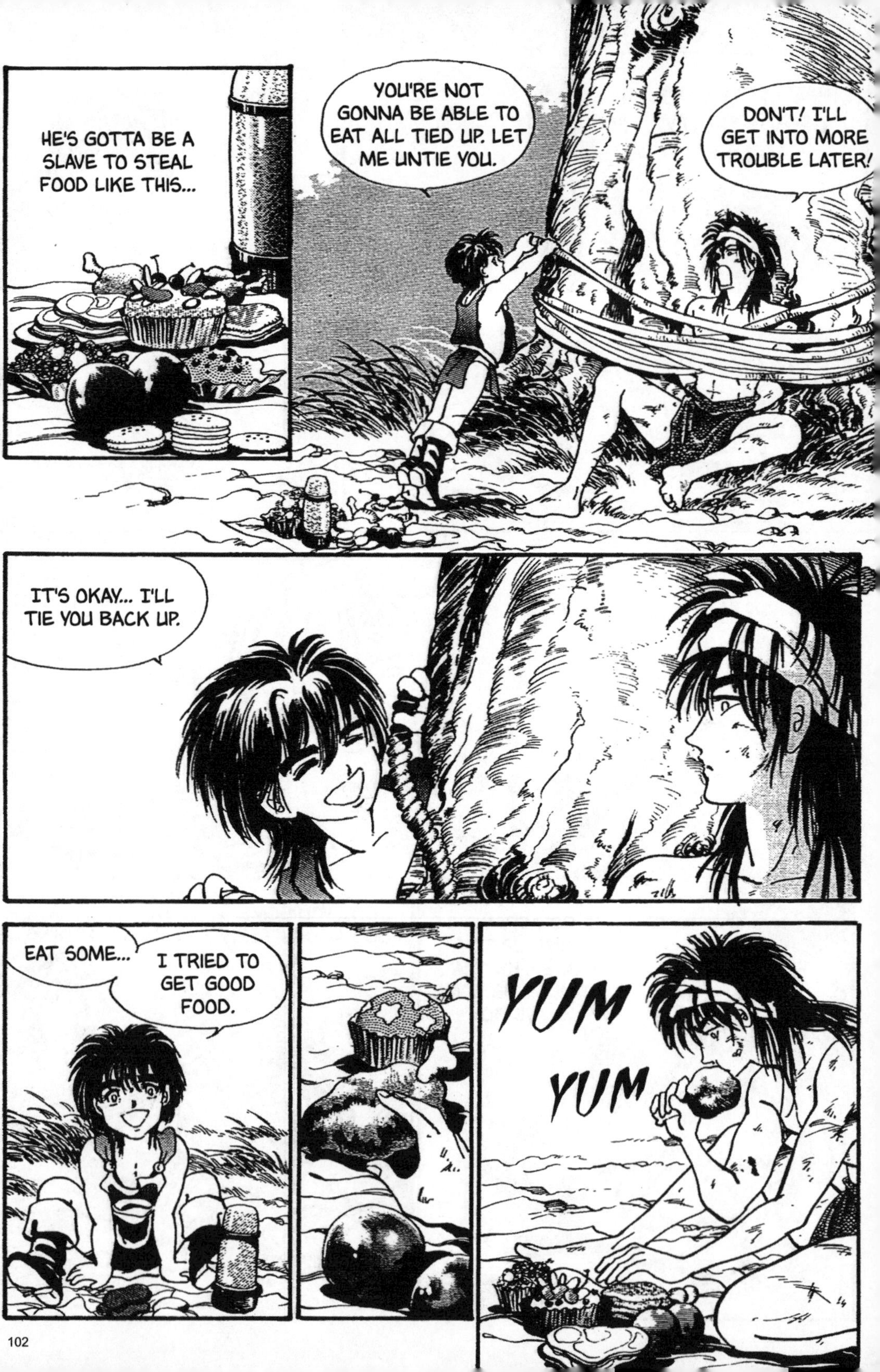
HE'S GOTTA BE A SLAVE TO STEAL FOOD LIKE THIS...
YOU'RE NOT GONNA BE ABLE TO EAT ALL TIED UP. LET ME UNTIE YOU.
DON'T! I'LL GET INTO MORE TROUBLE LATER!
IT'S OKAY... I'LL TIE YOU BACK UP.
EAT SOME...
I TRIED TO GET GOOD FOOD.
YUM
YUM

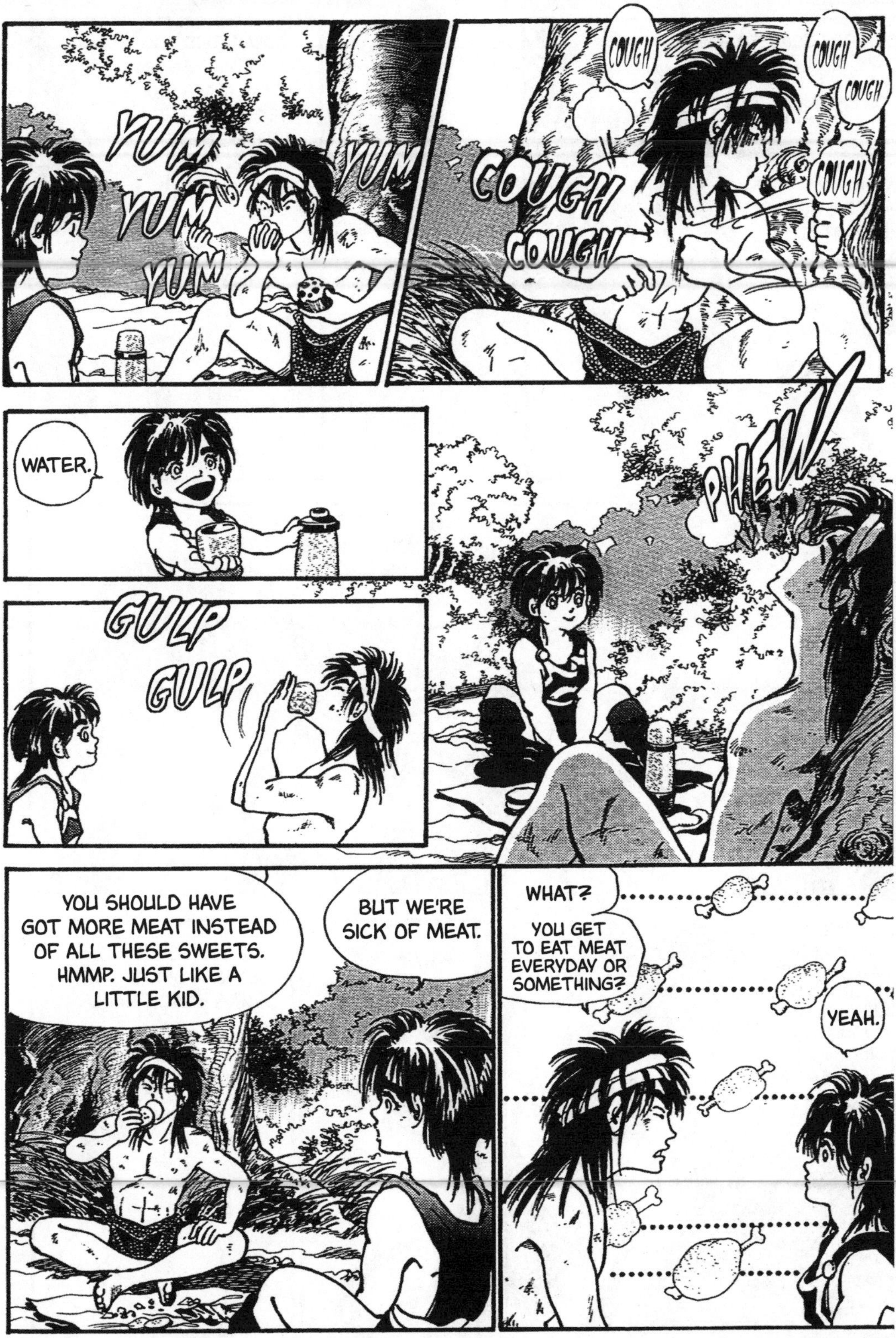
YUM
YUM
YUM
YUM
COUGH
COUGH
COUGH
COUGH
COUGH
COUGH
WATER.
PHEW
GULP
GULP
YOU SHOULD HAVE GOT MORE MEAT INSTEAD OF ALL THESE SWEETS. HMMP. JUST LIKE A LITTLE KID.
BUT WE'RE SICK OF MEAT.
WHAT?
YOU GET TO EAT MEAT EVERYDAY OR SOMETHING?
YEAH.

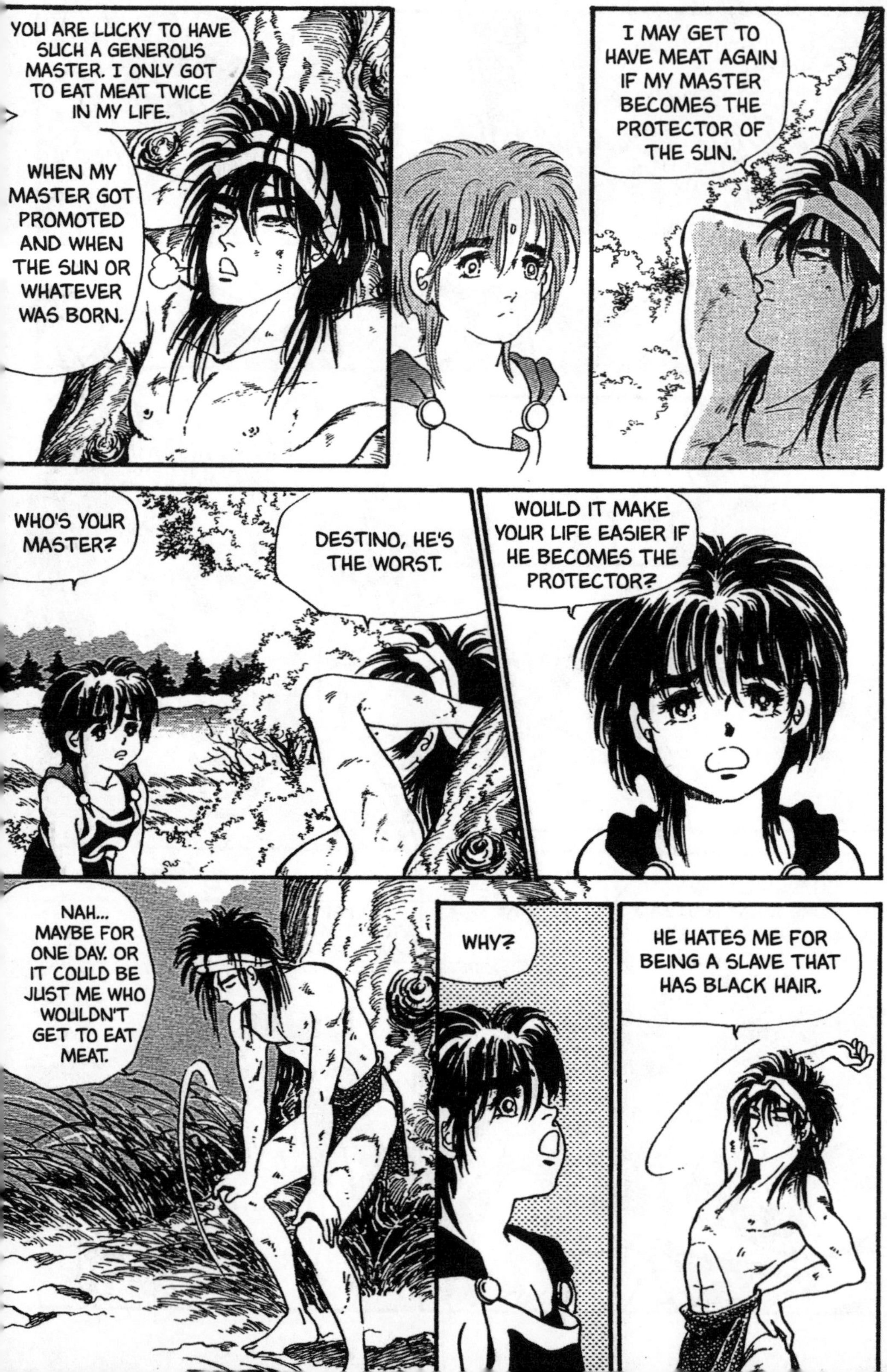
YOU ARE LUCKY TO HAVE SUCH A GENEROUS MASTER. I ONLY GOT TO EAT MEAT TWICE IN MY LIFE.
WHEN MY MASTER GOT PROMOTED AND WHEN THE SUN OR WHATEVER WAS BORN.
I MAY GET TO HAVE MEAT AGAIN IF MY MASTER BECOMES THE PROTECTOR OF THE SUN.
WHO'S YOUR MASTER?
DESTINO, HE'S THE WORST.
WOULD IT MAKE YOUR LIFE EASIER IF HE BECOMES THE PROTECTOR?
NAH... MAYBE FOR ONE DAY. OR IT COULD BE JUST ME WHO WOULDN'T GET TO EAT MEAT.
WHY?
HE HATES ME FOR BEING A SLAVE THAT HAS BLACK HAIR.

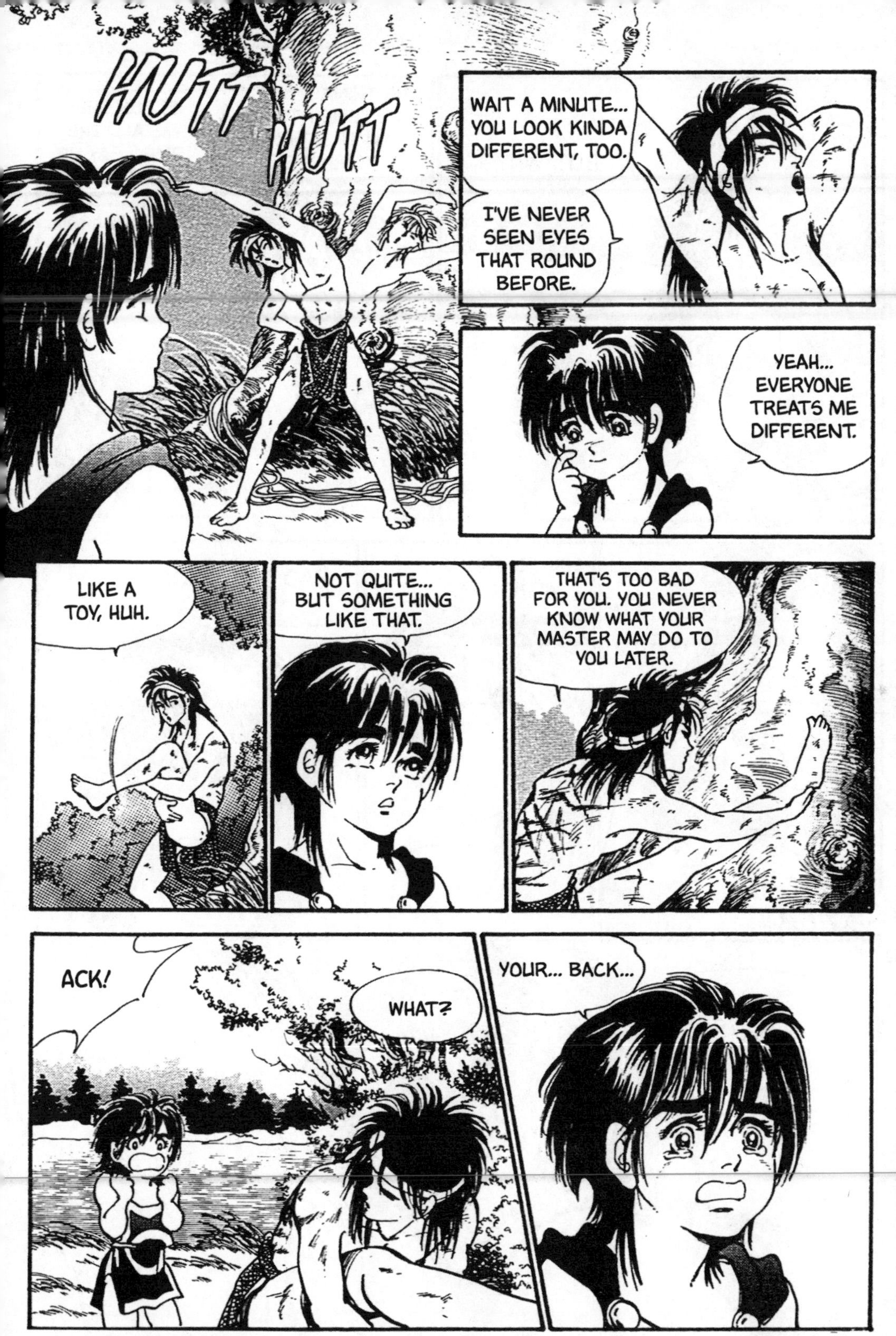
HUTT HUTT
WAIT A MINUTE... YOU LOOK KINDA DIFFERENT, TOO.
I'VE NEVER SEEN EYES THAT ROUND BEFORE.
YEAH... EVERYONE TREATS ME DIFFERENT.
LIKE A TOY, HUH.
NOT QUITE... BUT SOMETHING LIKE THAT.
THAT'S TOO BAD FOR YOU. YOU NEVER KNOW WHAT YOUR MASTER MAY DO TO YOU LATER.
ACK!
WHAT?
YOUR... BACK...

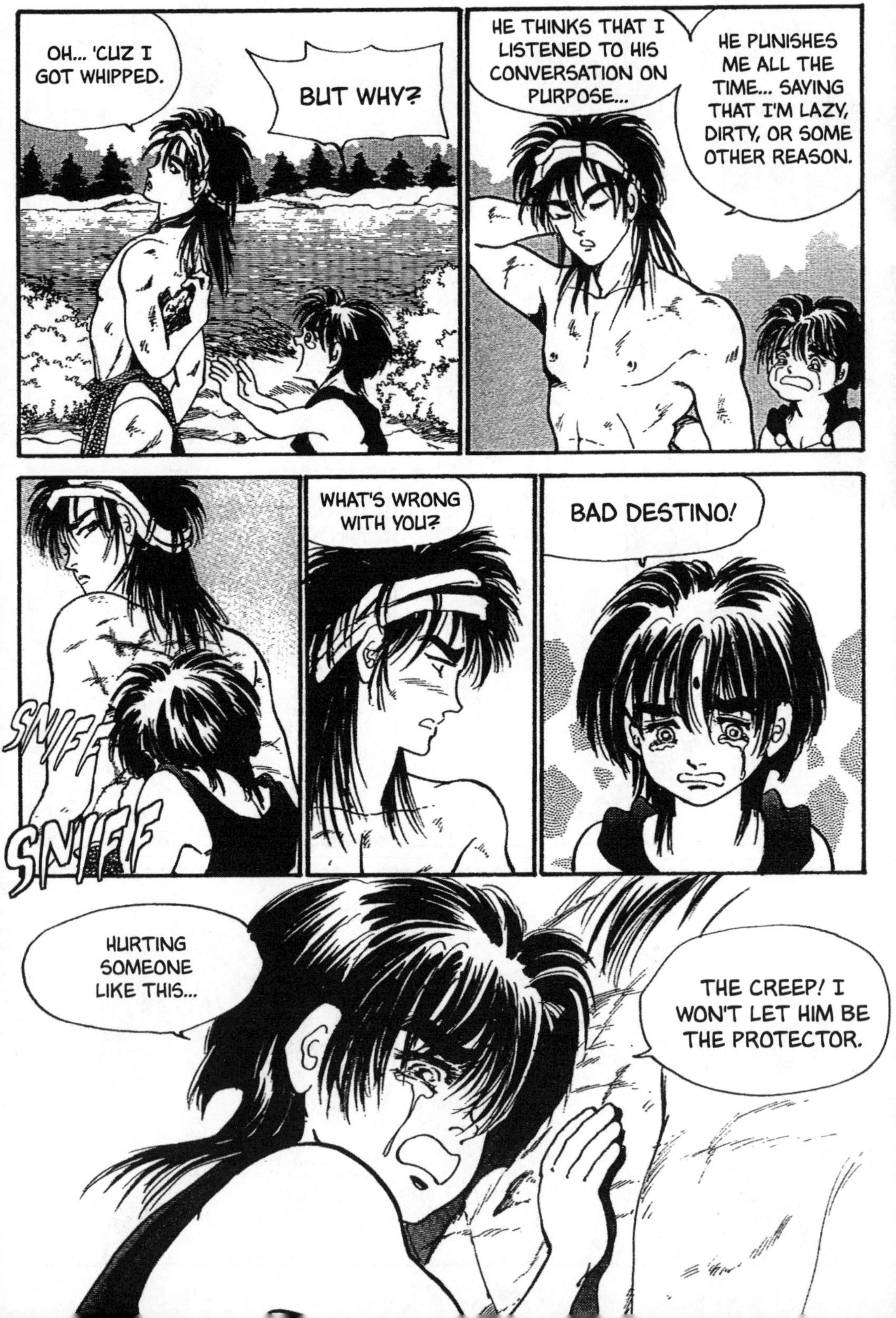
OH... 'CUZ I GOT WHIPPED.
BUT WHY?
HE THINKS THAT I LISTENED TO HIS CONVERSATION ON PURPOSE...
HE PUNISHES ME ALL THE TIME... SAYING THAT I'M LAZY, DIRTY, OR SOME OTHER REASON.
SNIFF
SNIFF
WHAT'S WRONG WITH YOU?
BAD DESTINO!
HURTING SOMEONE LIKE THIS...
THE CREEP! I WON'T LET HIM BE THE PROTECTOR.

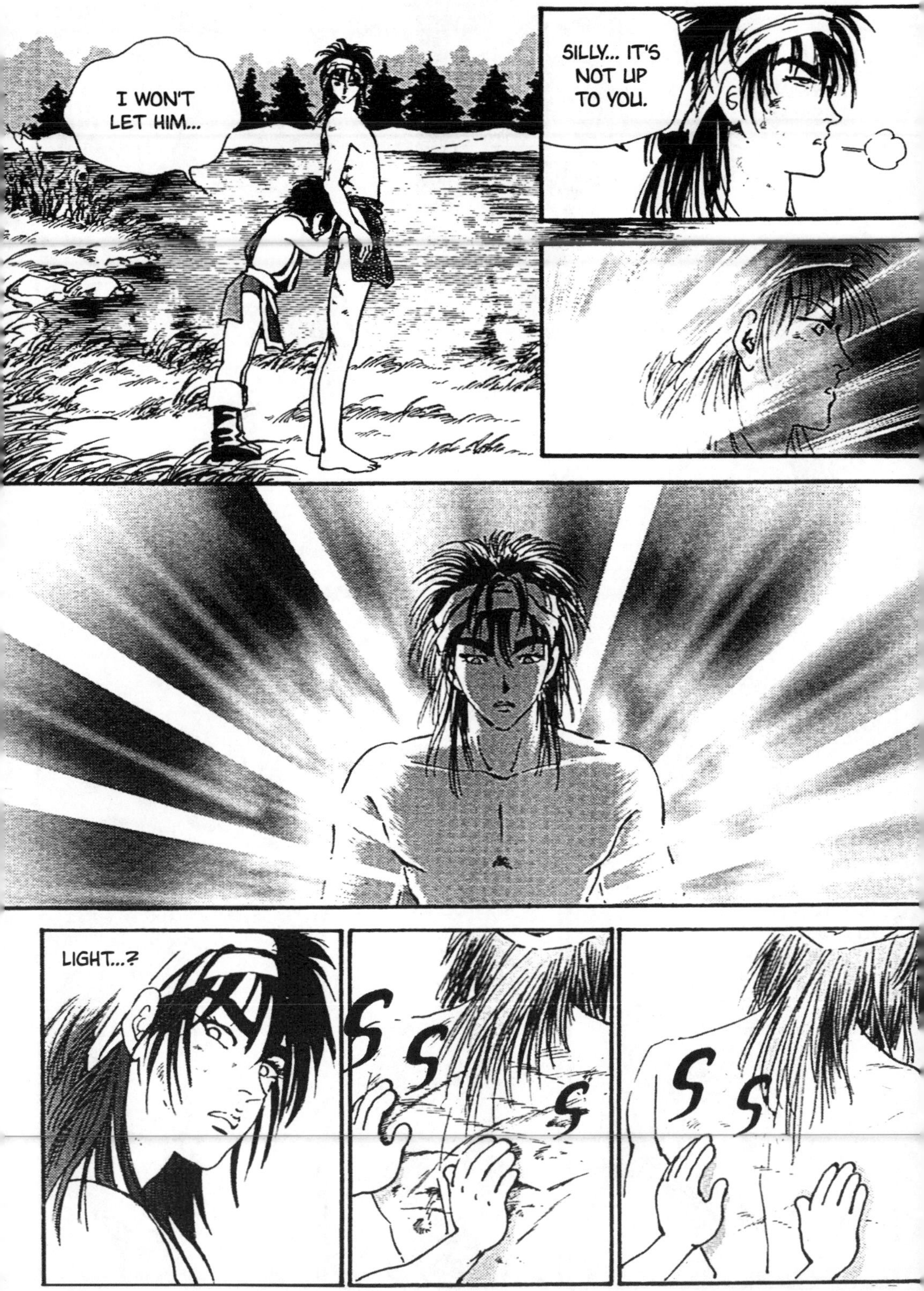
SILLY... IT'S NOT UP TO YOU.
I WON'T LET HIM...
LIGHT...?

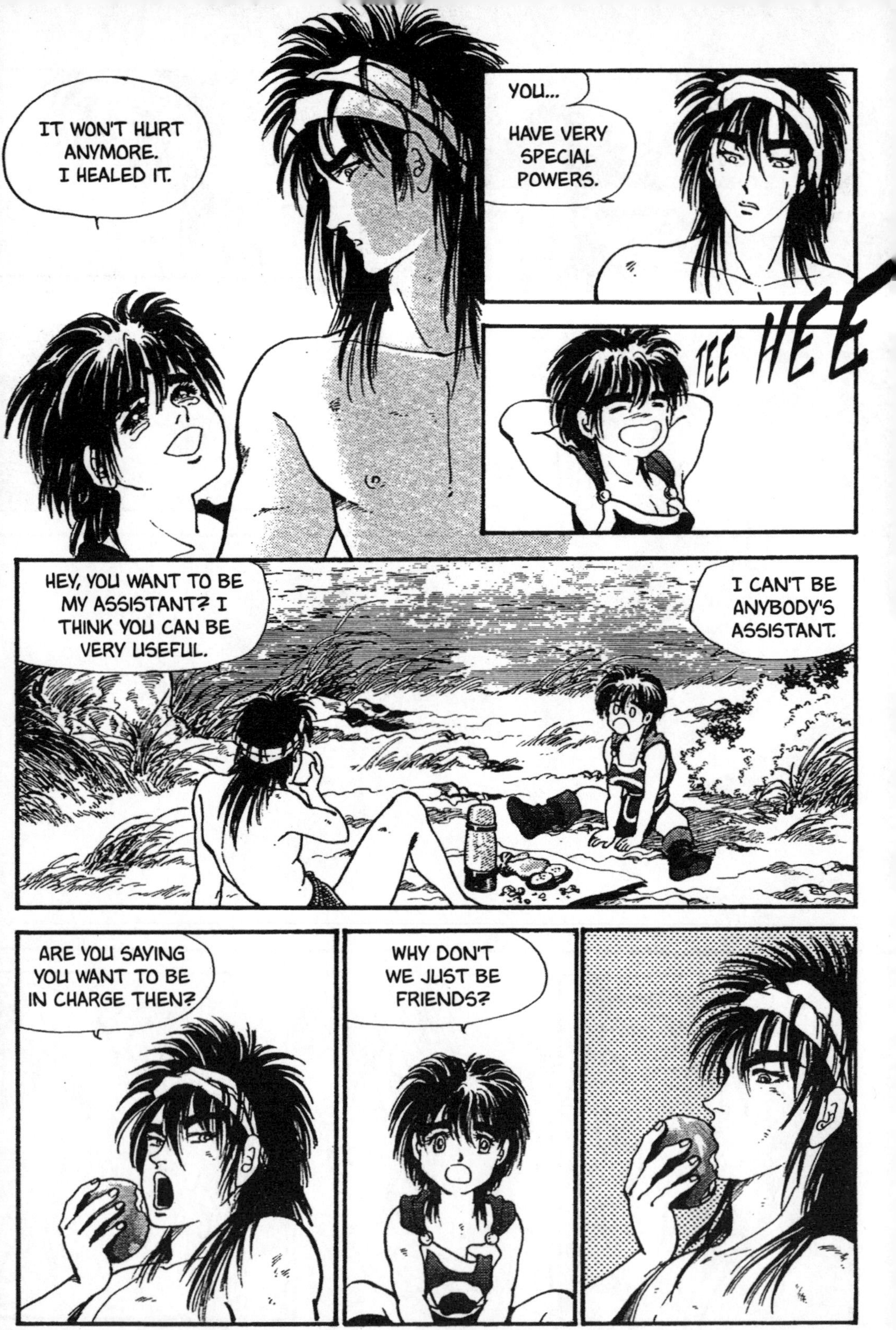
IT WON'T HURT ANYMORE. I HEALED IT.
YOU...
HAVE VERY SPECIAL POWERS.
TEE HEE
HEY, YOU WANT TO BE MY ASSISTANT? I THINK YOU CAN BE VERY USEFUL.
I CAN'T BE ANYBODY'S ASSISTANT.
ARE YOU SAYING YOU WANT TO BE IN CHARGE THEN?
WHY DON'T WE JUST BE FRIENDS?

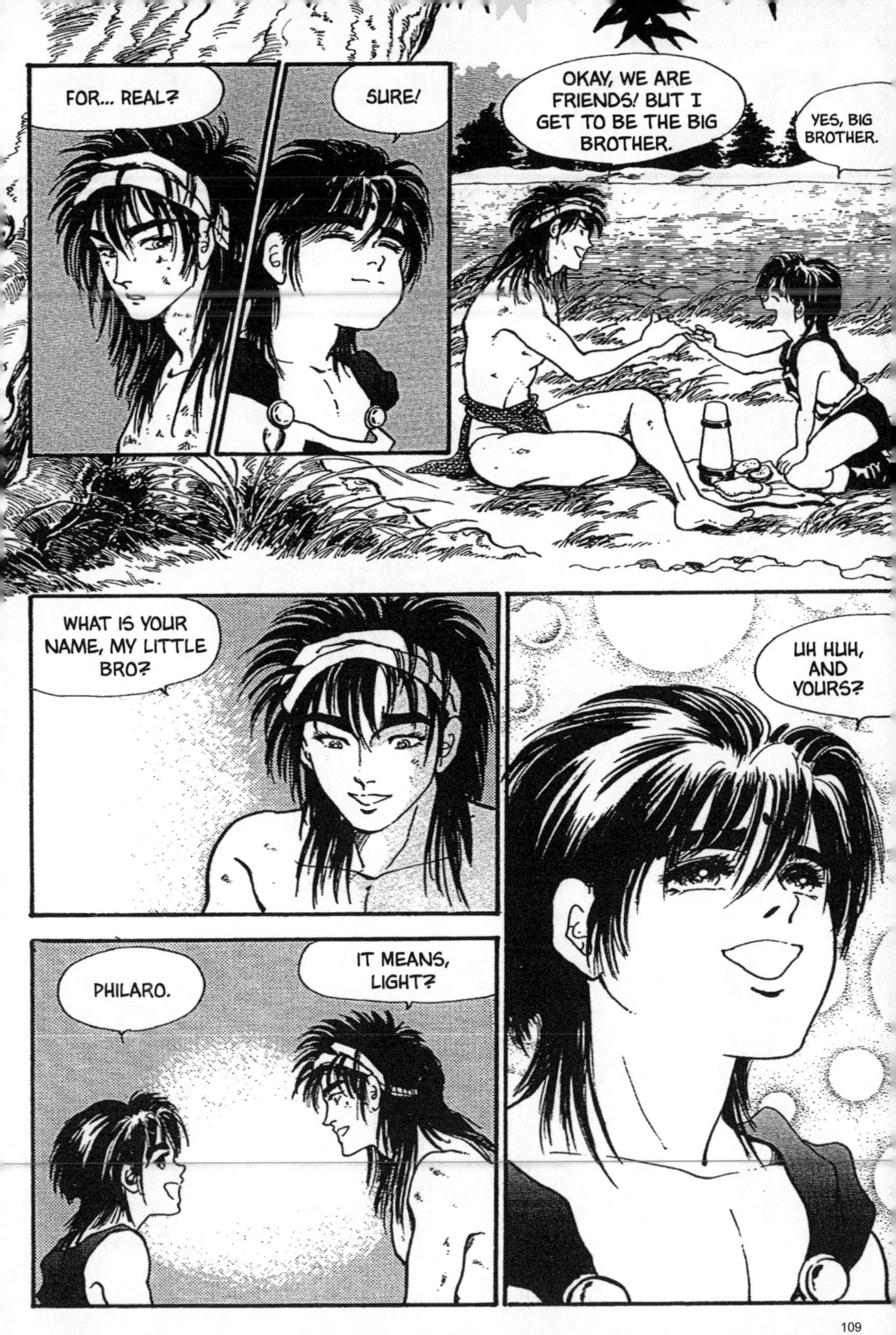
FOR... REAL?
SURE!
OKAY, WE ARE FRIENDS! BUT I GET TO BE THE BIG BROTHER.
YES, BIG BROTHER.
WHAT IS YOUR NAME, MY LITTLE BRO?
UH HUH, AND YOURS?
PHILARO.
IT MEANS, LIGHT?

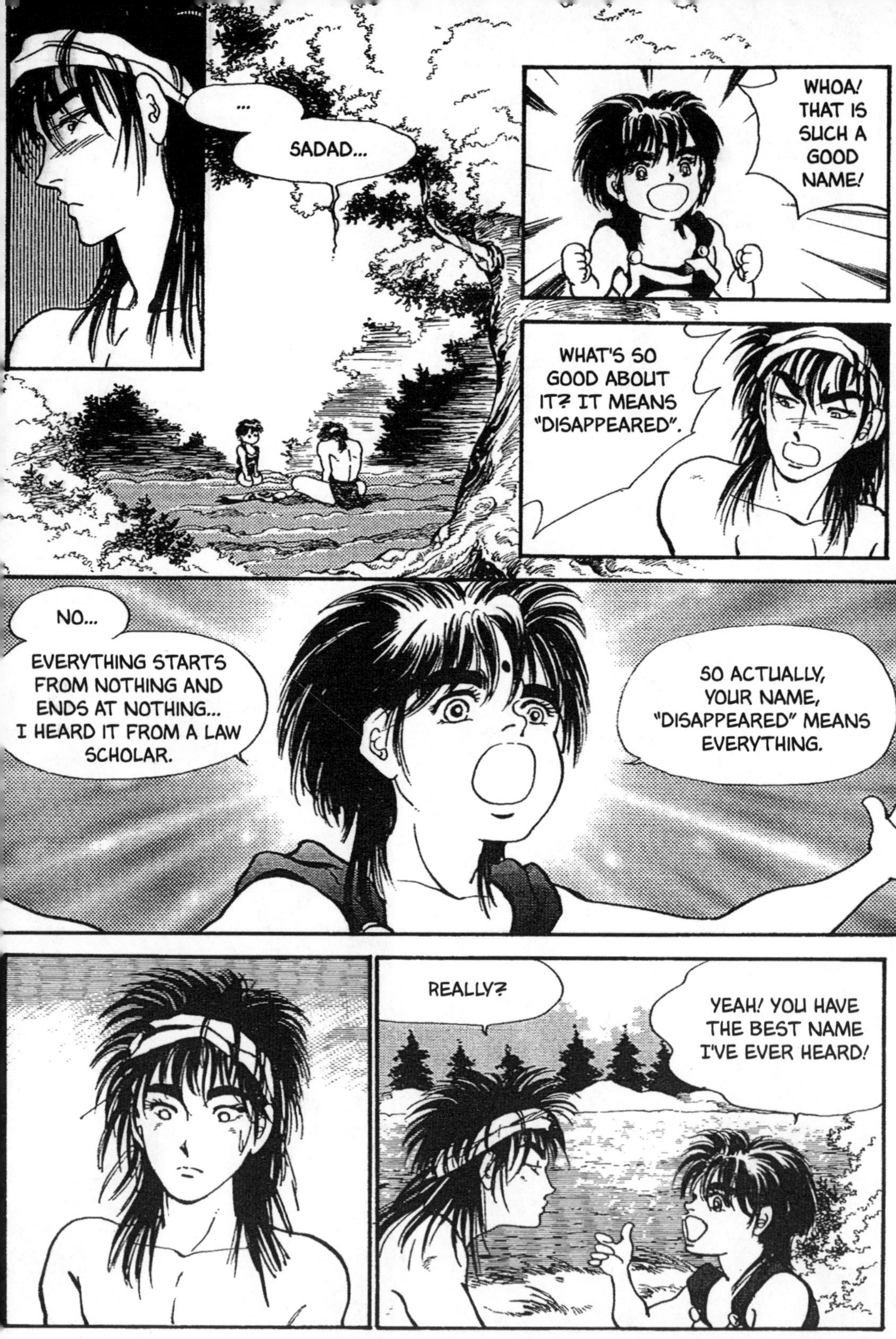
...
SADAD...
WHOA! THAT IS SUCH A GOOD NAME!
WHAT'S SO GOOD ABOUT IT? IT MEANS "DISAPPEARED".
NO...
EVERYTHING STARTS FROM NOTHING AND ENDS AT NOTHING... I HEARD IT FROM A LAW SCHOLAR.
SO ACTUALLY, YOUR NAME, "DISAPPEARED" MEANS EVERYTHING.
REALLY?
YEAH! YOU HAVE THE BEST NAME I'VE EVER HEARD!

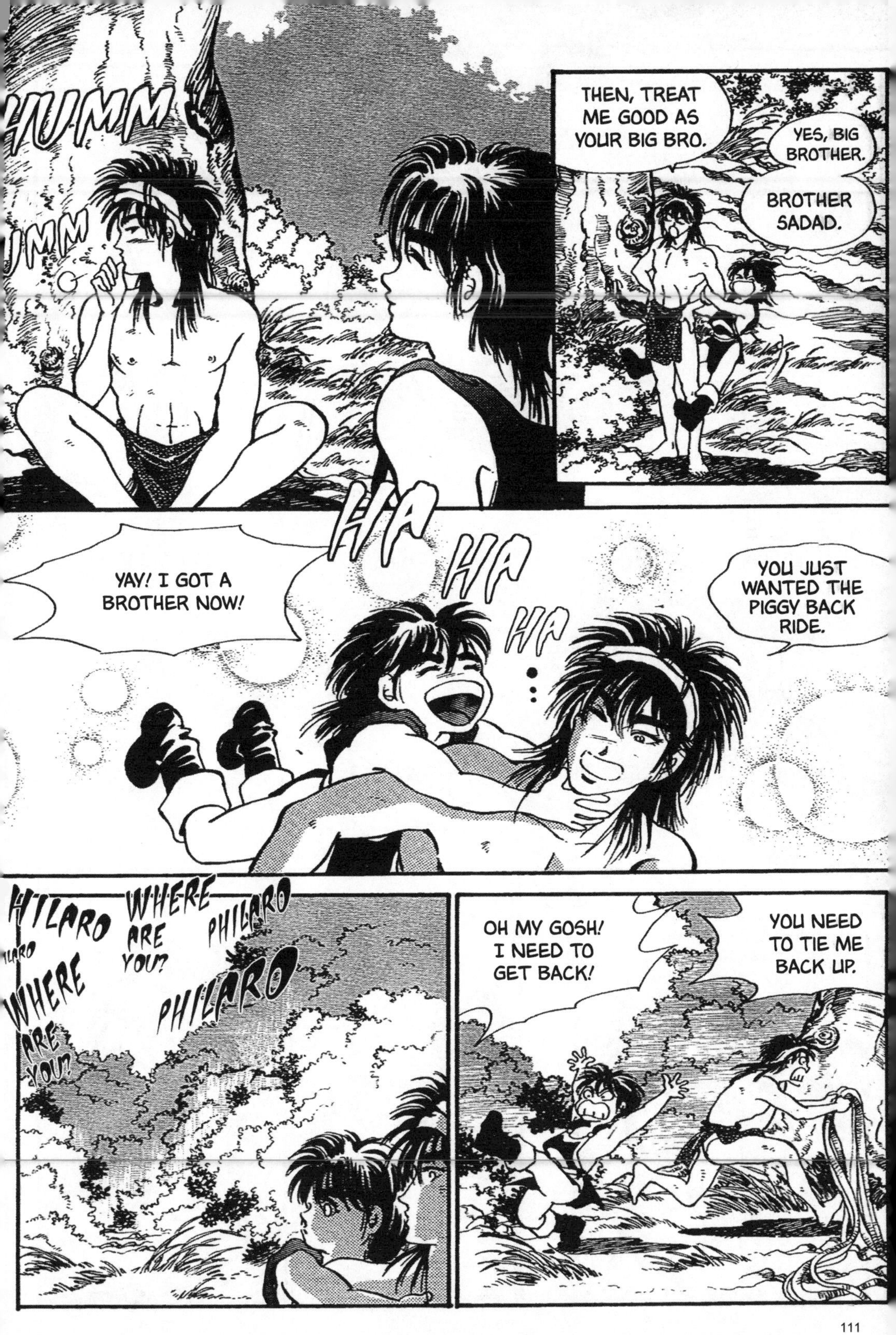
HUMM
UMM
THEN, TREAT ME GOOD AS YOUR BIG BRO.
YES, BIG BROTHER.
BROTHER SADAD.
HA
HA
HA
YAY! I GOT A BROTHER NOW!
YOU JUST WANTED THE PIGGY BACK RIDE.
...
HILARO
ILARO
WHERE ARE YOU?
WHERE ARE YOU?
PHILARO
PHILARO
OH MY GOSH! I NEED TO GET BACK!
YOU NEED TO TIE ME BACK UP.

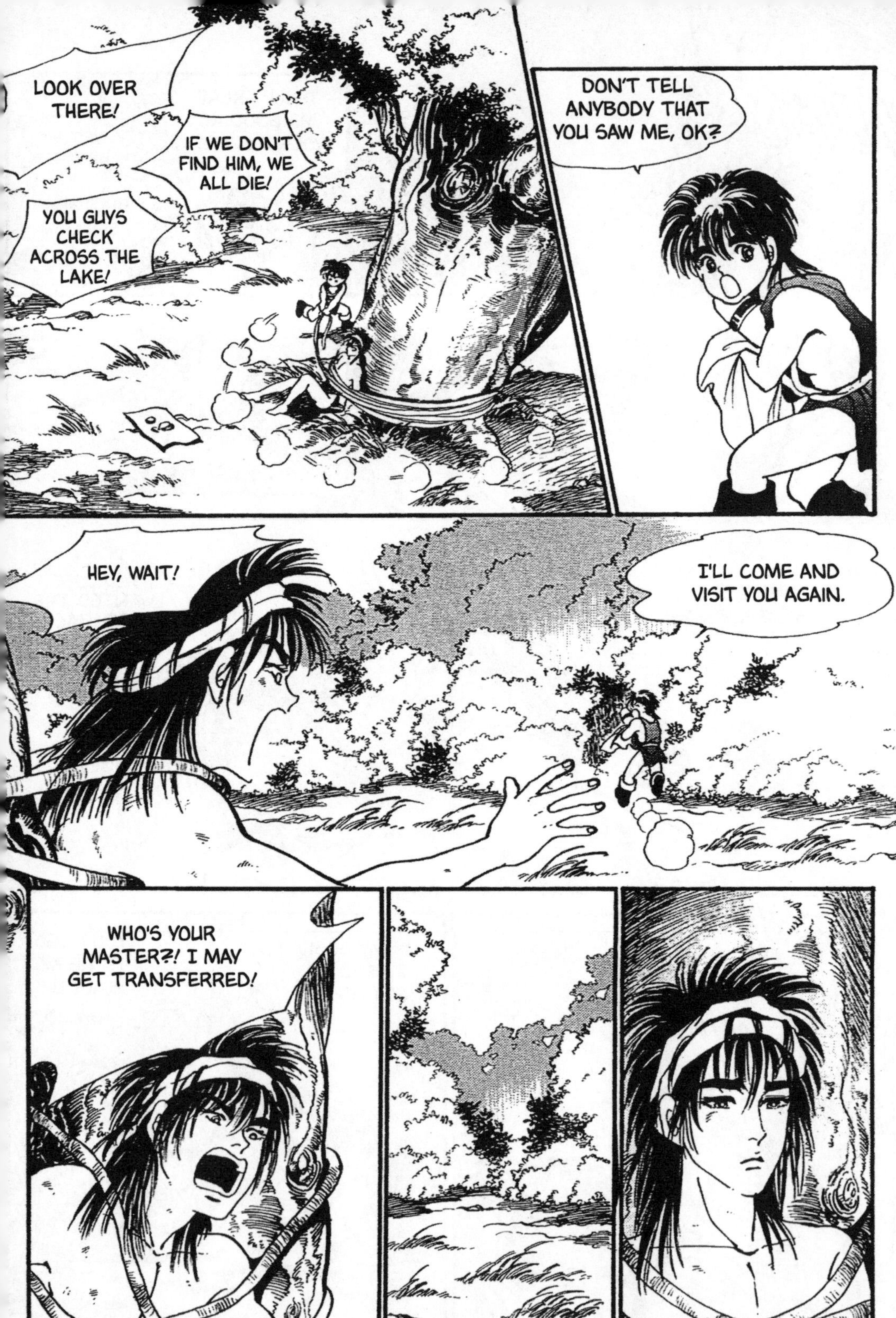

LOOK OVER THERE!
IF WE DON'T FIND HIM, WE ALL DIE!
YOU GUYS CHECK ACROSS THE LAKE!
DON'T TELL ANYBODY THAT YOU SAW ME, OK?
HEY, WAIT!
I'LL COME AND VISIT YOU AGAIN.
WHO'S YOUR MASTER?! I MAY GET TRANSFERRED!

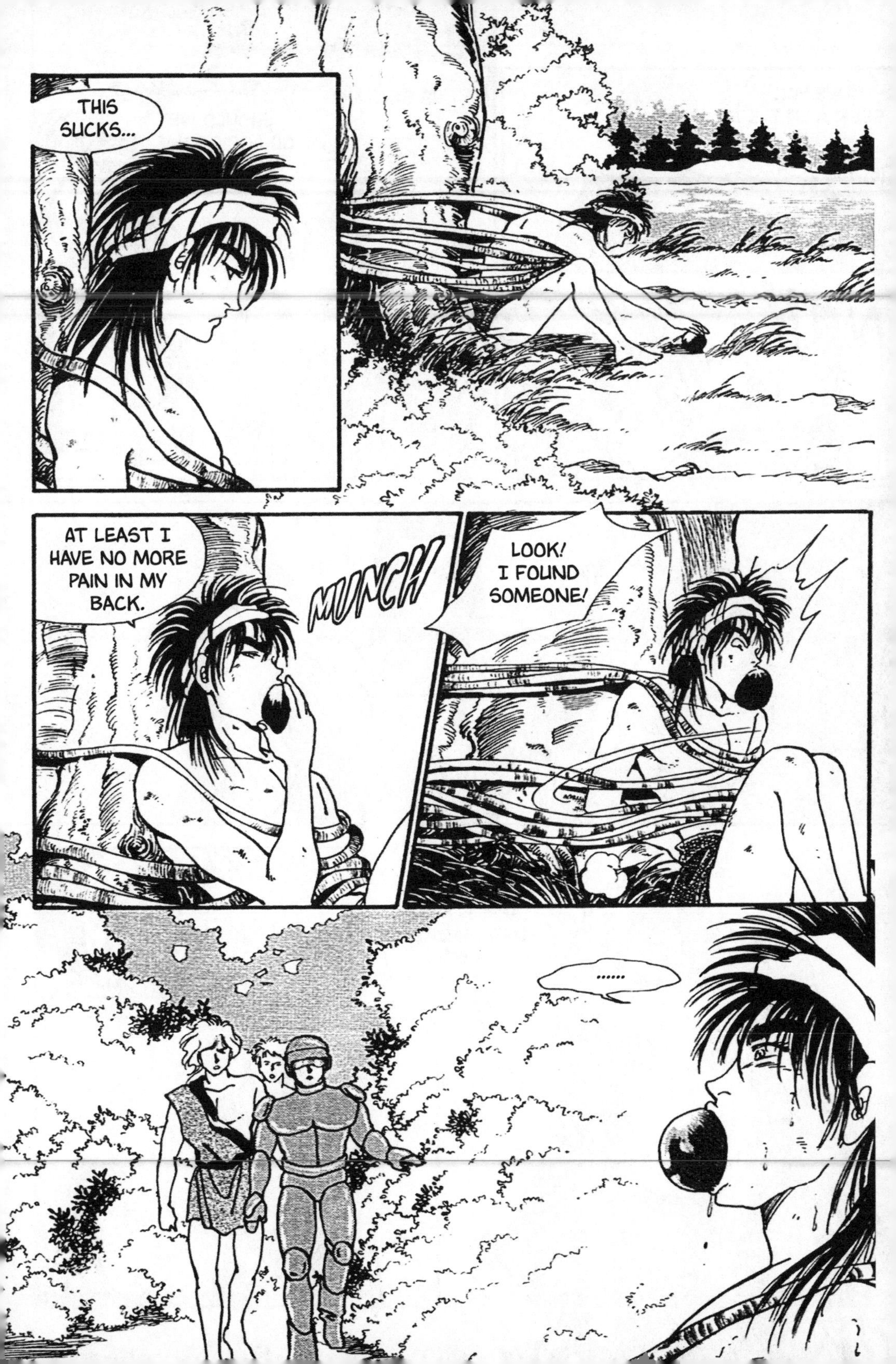

THIS SUCKS...
AT LEAST I HAVE NO MORE PAIN IN MY BACK.
MUNCH
LOOK! I FOUND SOMEONE!
......

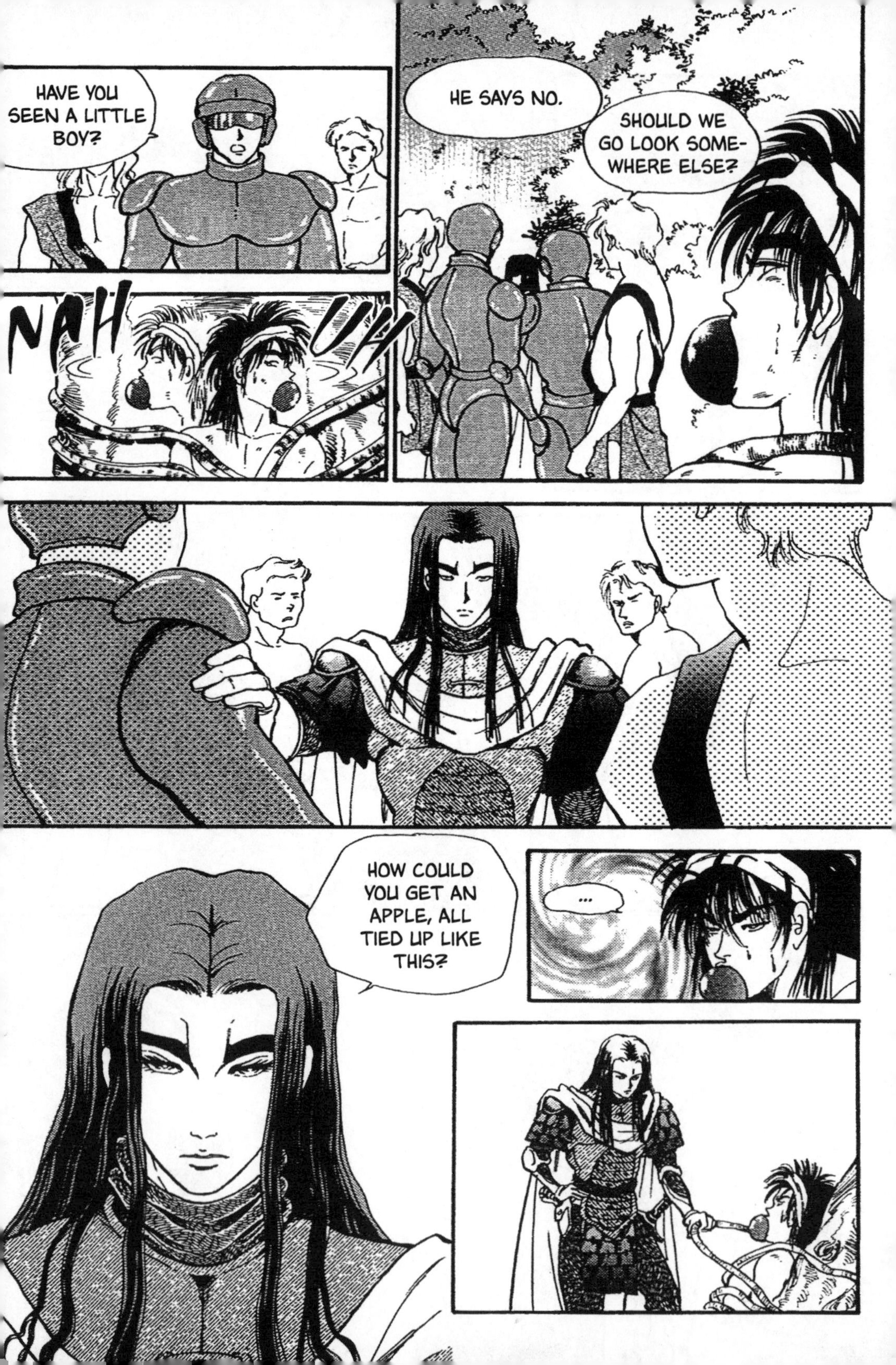
HE SAYS NO.
SHOULD WE GO LOOK SOME-WHERE ELSE?
HAVE YOU SEEN A LITTLE BOY?
NAH
UH
HOW COULD YOU GET AN APPLE, ALL TIED UP LIKE THIS?
...

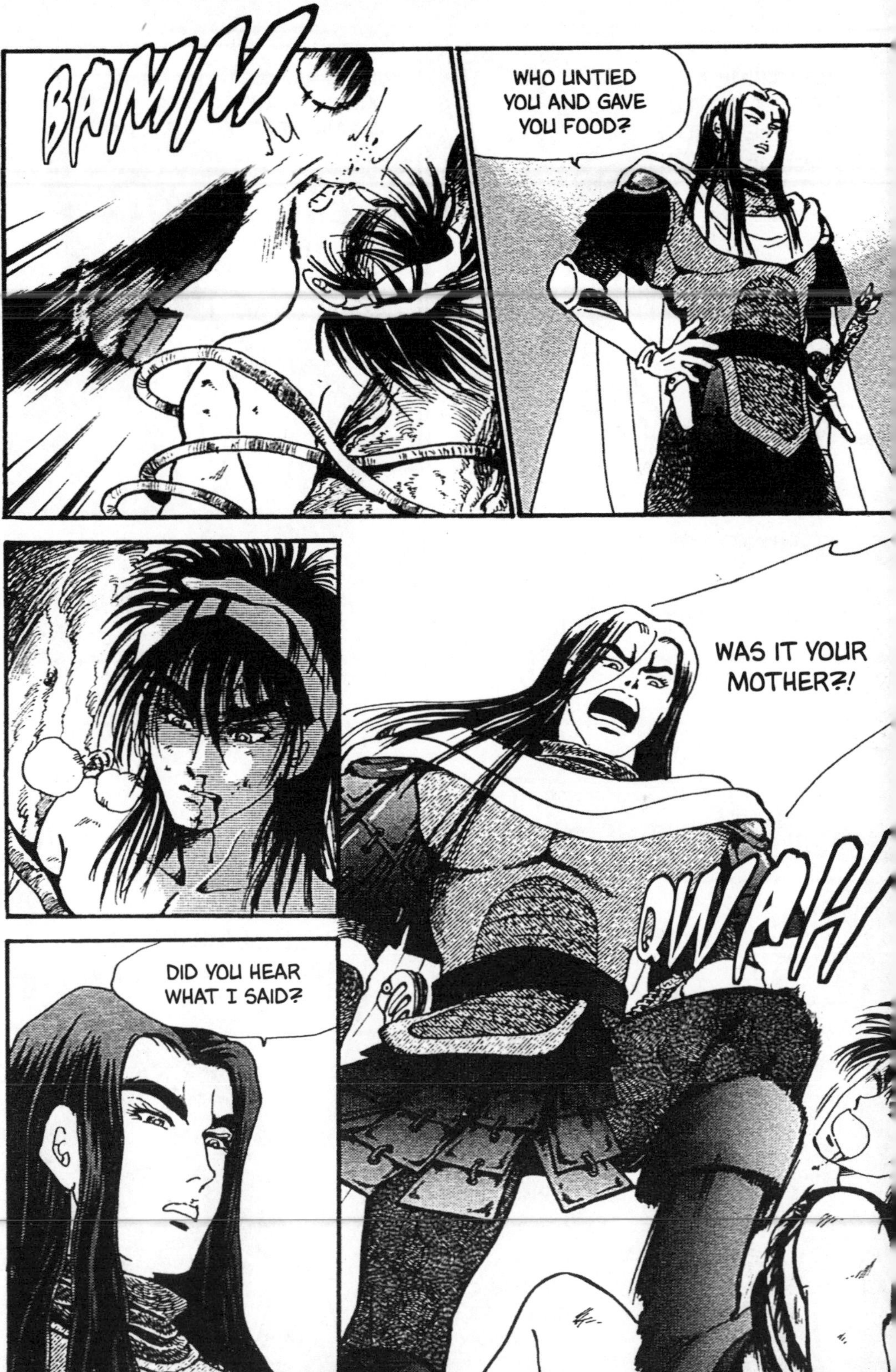
BAMM
WHO UNTIED YOU AND GAVE YOU FOOD?
WAS IT YOUR MOTHER?!
QWAH
DID YOU HEAR WHAT I SAID?

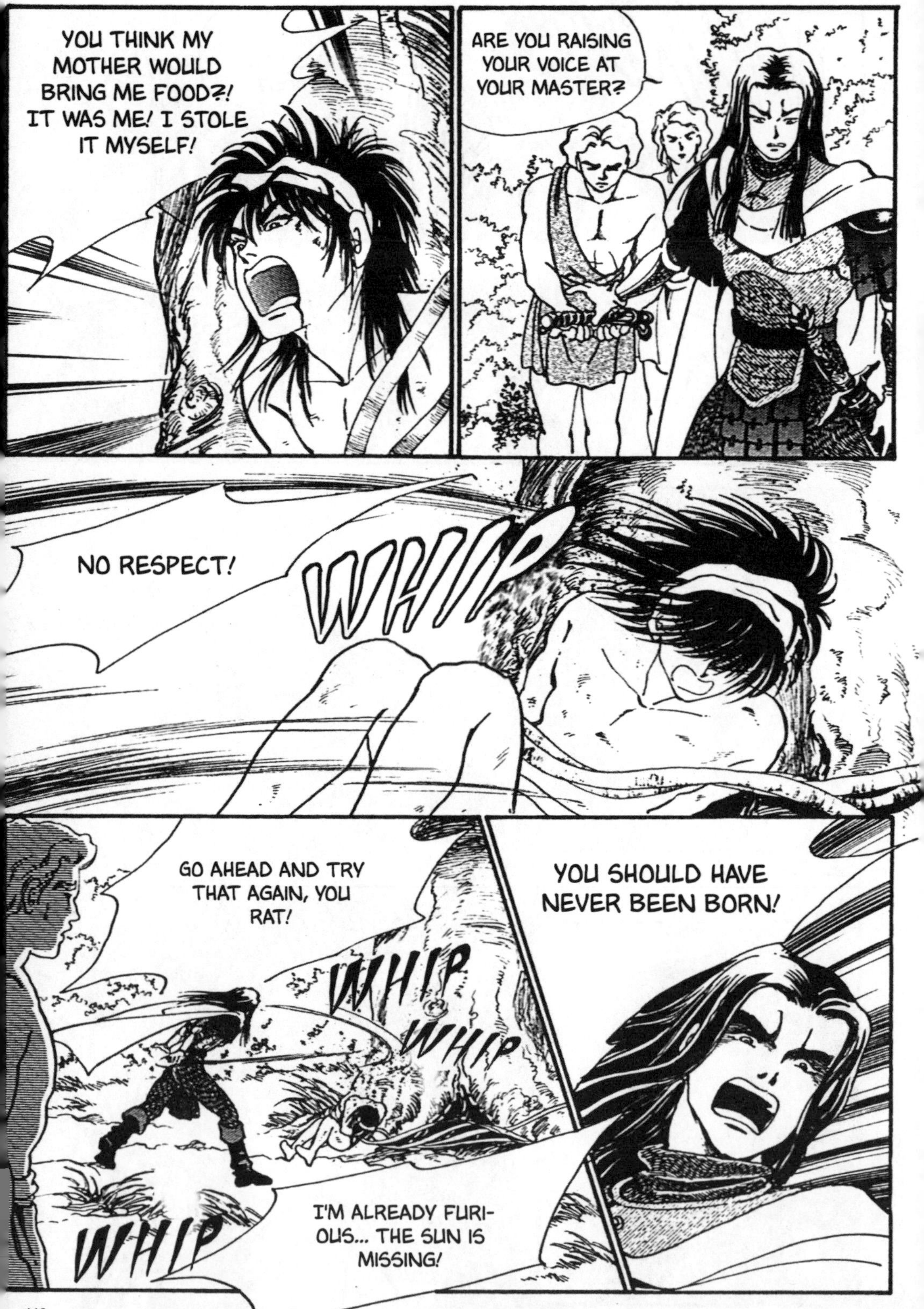
YOU THINK MY MOTHER WOULD BRING ME FOOD?! IT WAS ME! I STOLE IT MYSELF!
ARE YOU RAISING YOUR VOICE AT YOUR MASTER?
NO RESPECT!
WHIP
GO AHEAD AND TRY THAT AGAIN, YOU RAT!
WHIP
WHIP
WHIP
I'M ALREADY FURI-OUS... THE SUN IS MISSING!
YOU SHOULD HAVE NEVER BEEN BORN!

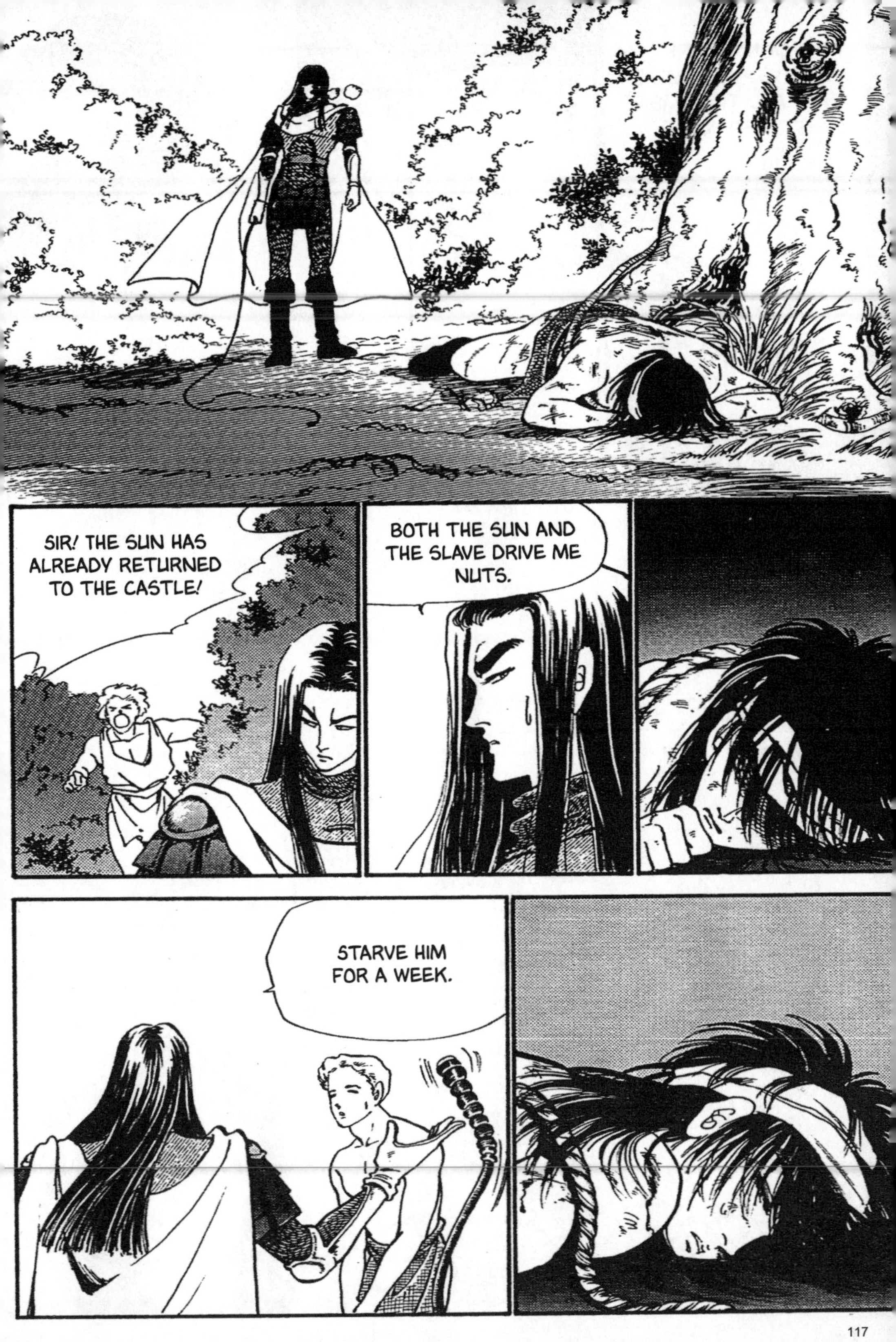
SIR! THE SUN HAS ALREADY RETURNED TO THE CASTLE!
BOTH THE SUN AND THE SLAVE DRIVE ME NUTS.
STARVE HIM FOR A WEEK.

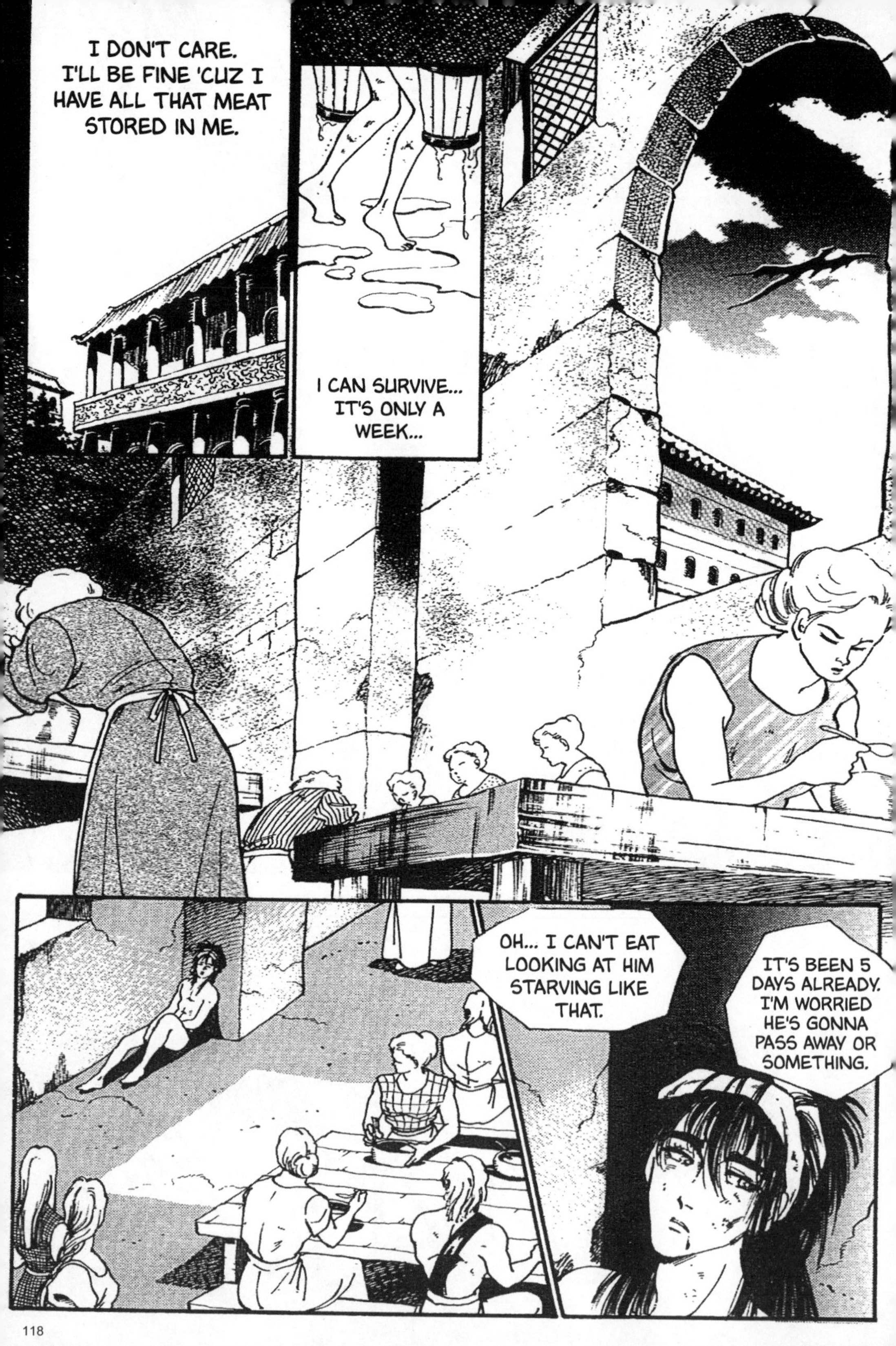
I DON'T CARE. I'LL BE FINE 'CUZ I HAVE ALL THAT MEAT STORED IN ME.
I CAN SURVIVE... IT'S ONLY A WEEK...
OH... I CAN'T EAT LOOKING AT HIM STARVING LIKE THAT.
IT'S BEEN 5 DAYS ALREADY. I'M WORRIED HE'S GONNA PASS AWAY OR SOMETHING.

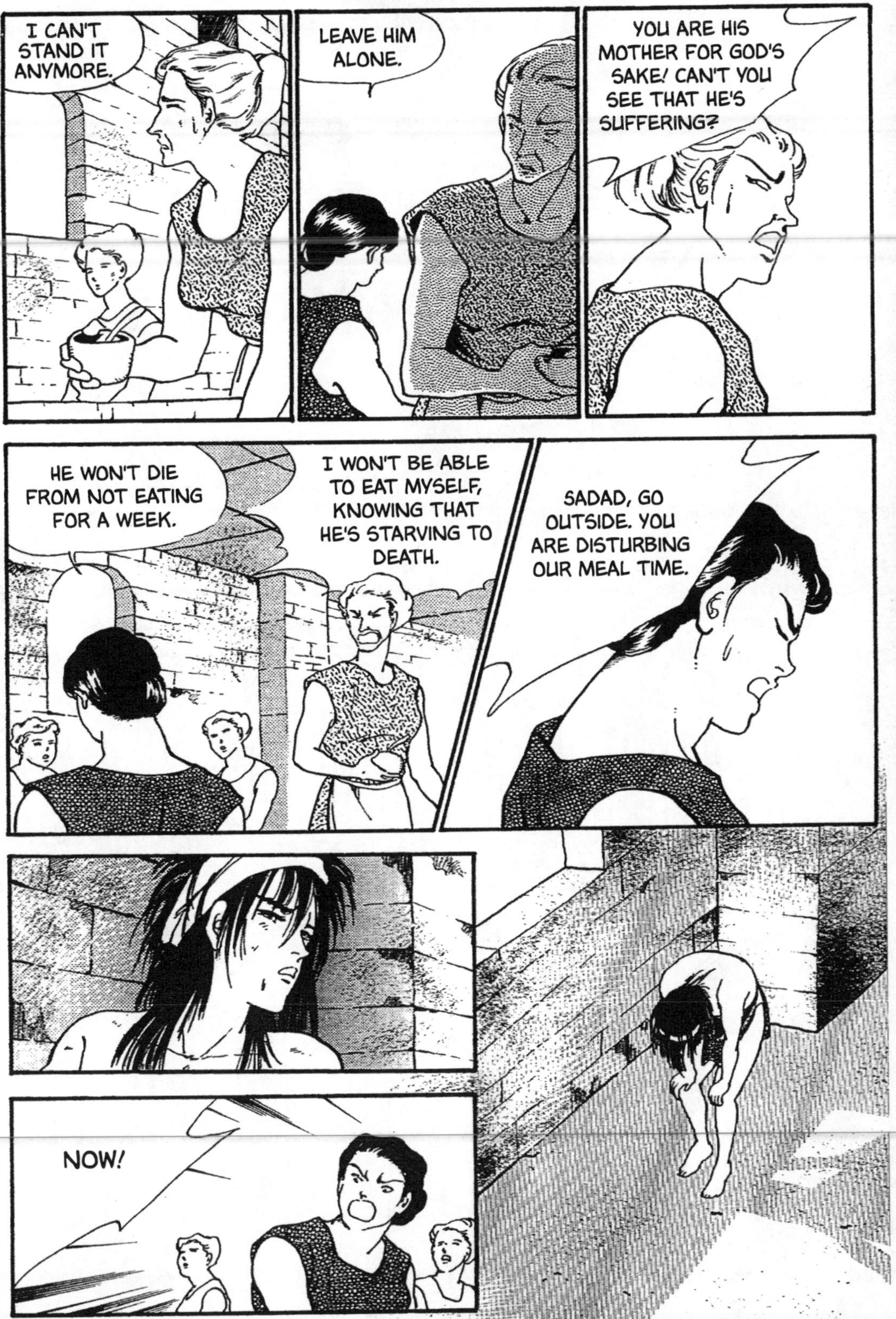

I CAN'T STAND IT ANYMORE.
LEAVE HIM ALONE.
YOU ARE HIS MOTHER FOR GOD'S SAKE! CAN'T YOU SEE THAT HE'S SUFFERING?
HE WON'T DIE FROM NOT EATING FOR A WEEK.
I WON'T BE ABLE TO EAT MYSELF, KNOWING THAT HE'S STARVING TO DEATH.
SADAD, GO OUTSIDE. YOU ARE DISTURBING OUR MEAL TIME.
NOW!

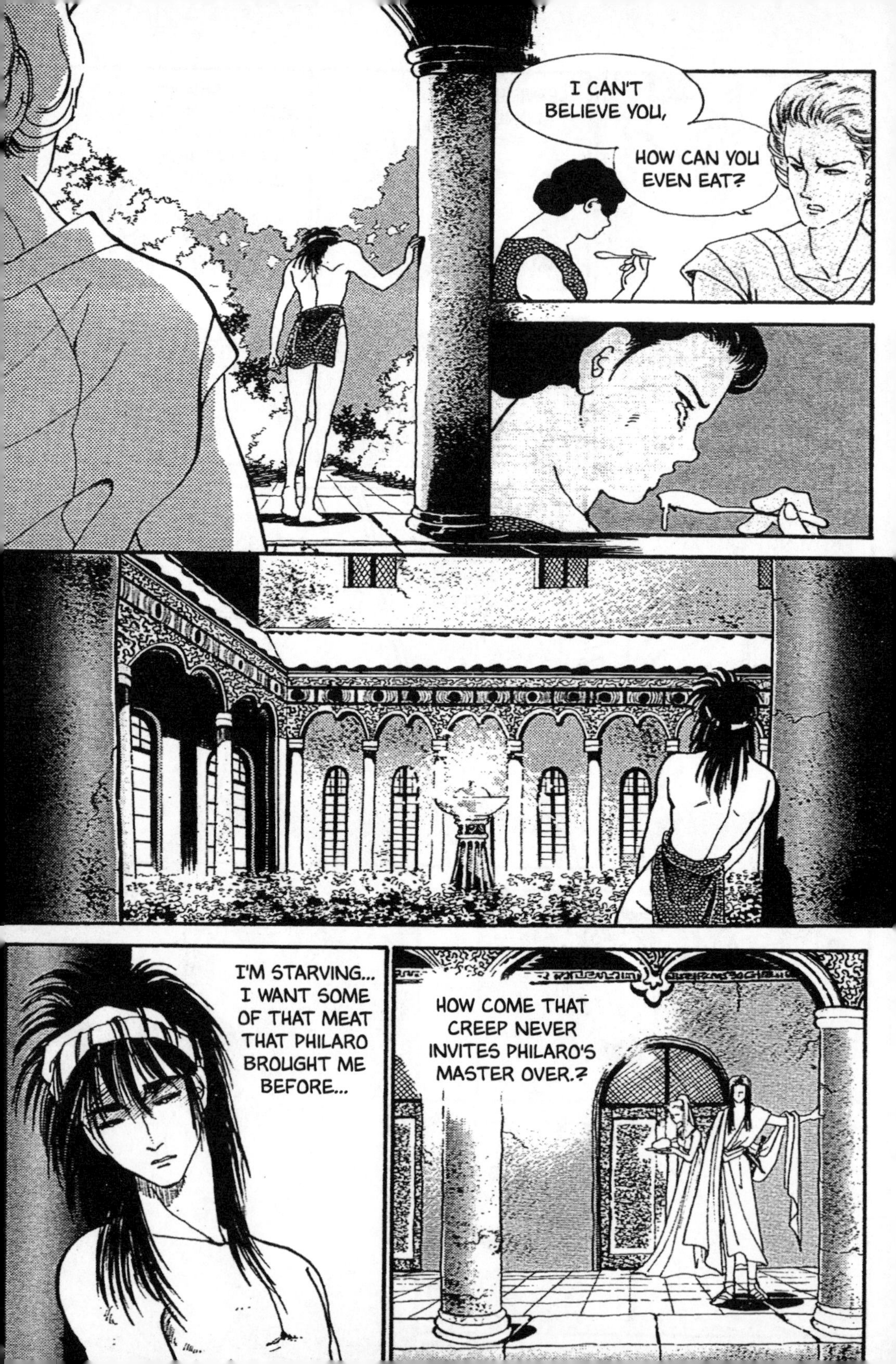
I CAN'T BELIEVE YOU,
HOW CAN YOU EVEN EAT?
I'M STARVING... I WANT SOME OF THAT MEAT THAT PHILARO BROUGHT ME BEFORE...
HOW COME THAT CREEP NEVER INVITES PHILARO'S MASTER OVER.?

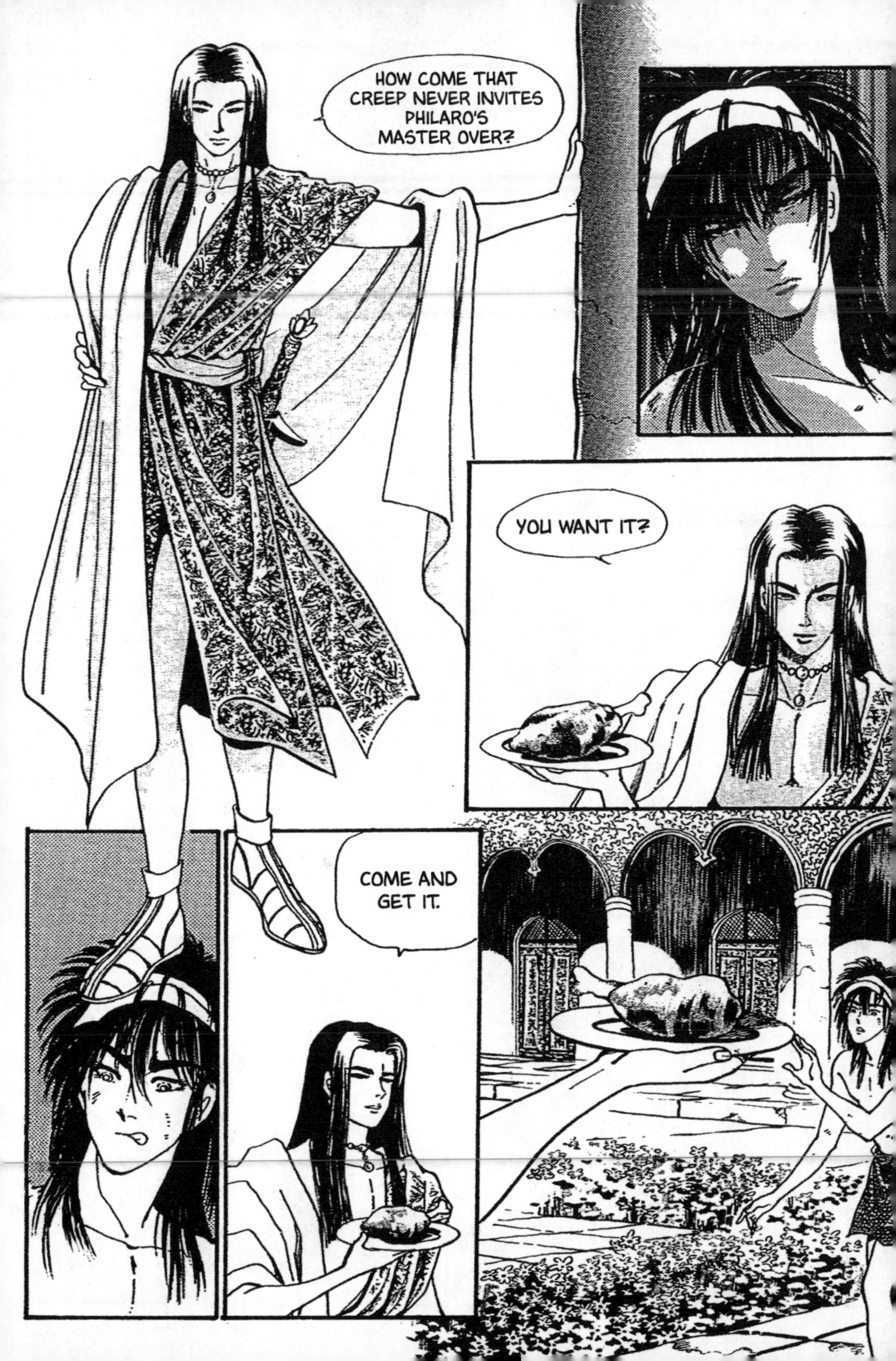
HOW COME THAT CREEP NEVER INVITES PHILARO'S MASTER OVER?
YOU WANT IT?
COME AND GET IT.

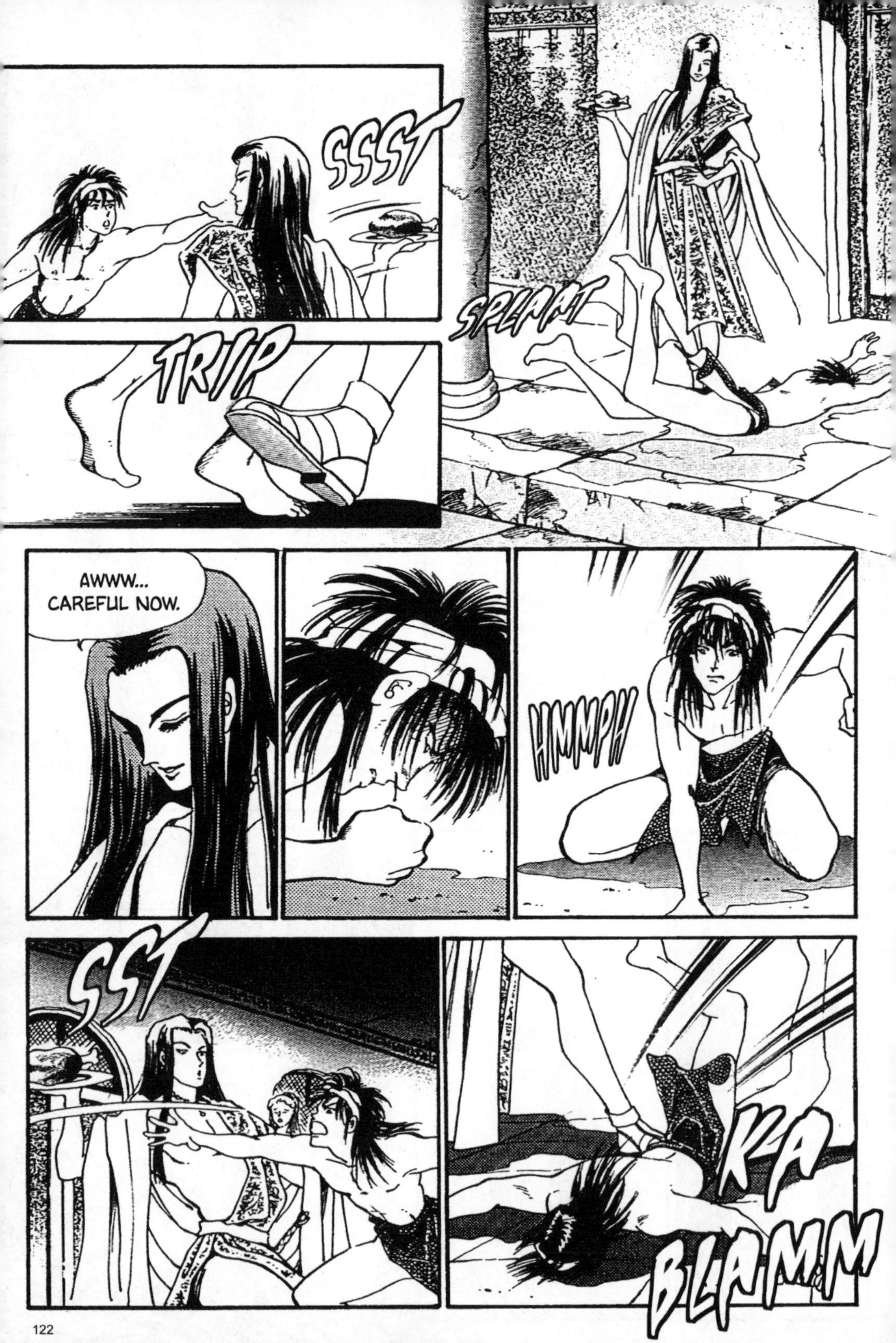
SSST
SPLAAT
TRIP
AWWW... CAREFUL NOW.
HMMPH
SST
KA
BLAMM

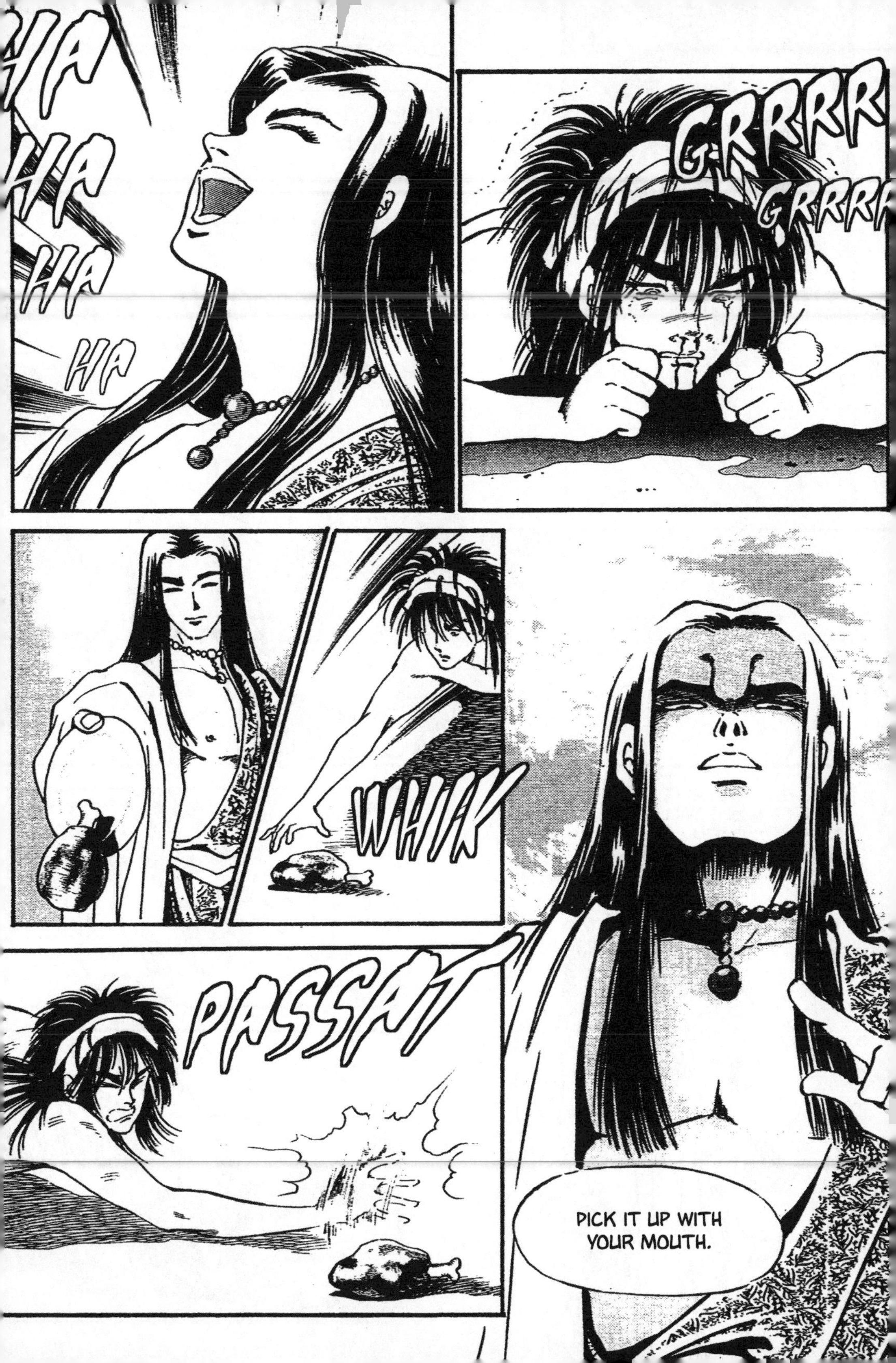
HA
HA
HA
HA
GRRRR
GRRRR
...
WHIK
PASSAT
PICK IT UP WITH YOUR MOUTH.

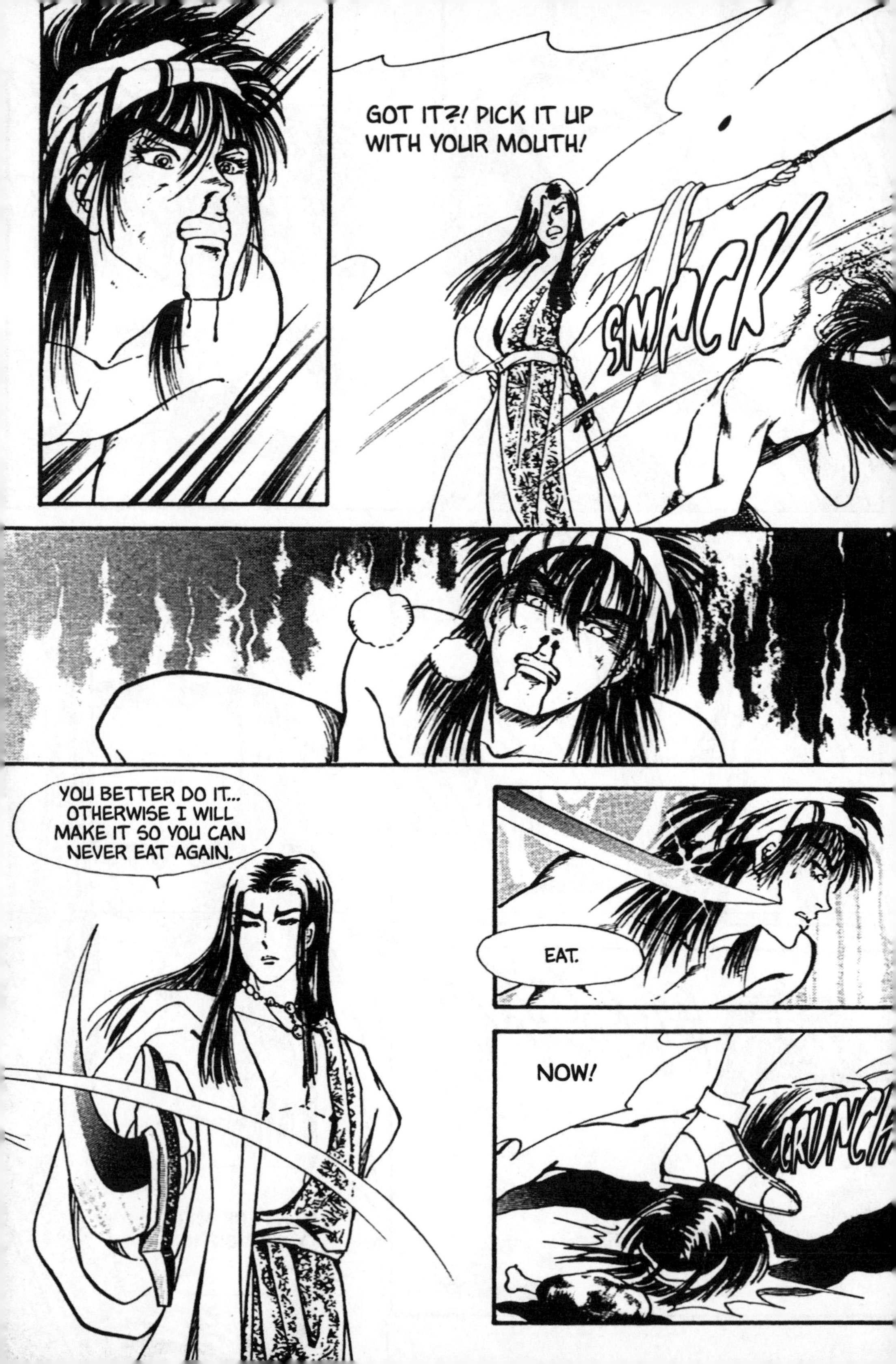
GOT IT?! PICK IT UP WITH YOUR MOUTH!
SMACK
YOU BETTER DO IT... OTHERWISE I WILL MAKE IT SO YOU CAN NEVER EAT AGAIN.
EAT.
NOW!
CRUNCH

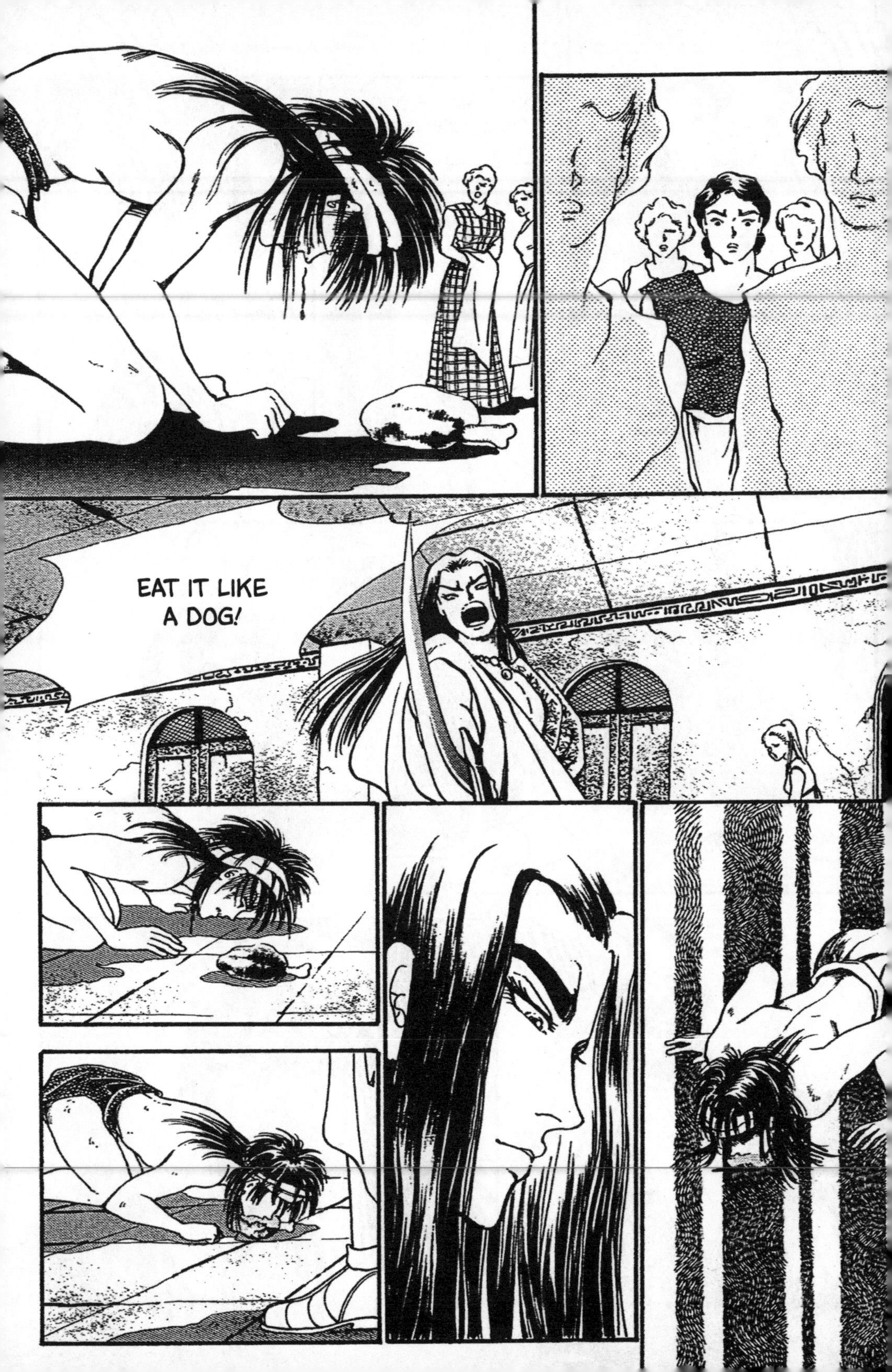
EAT IT LIKE
A DOG!

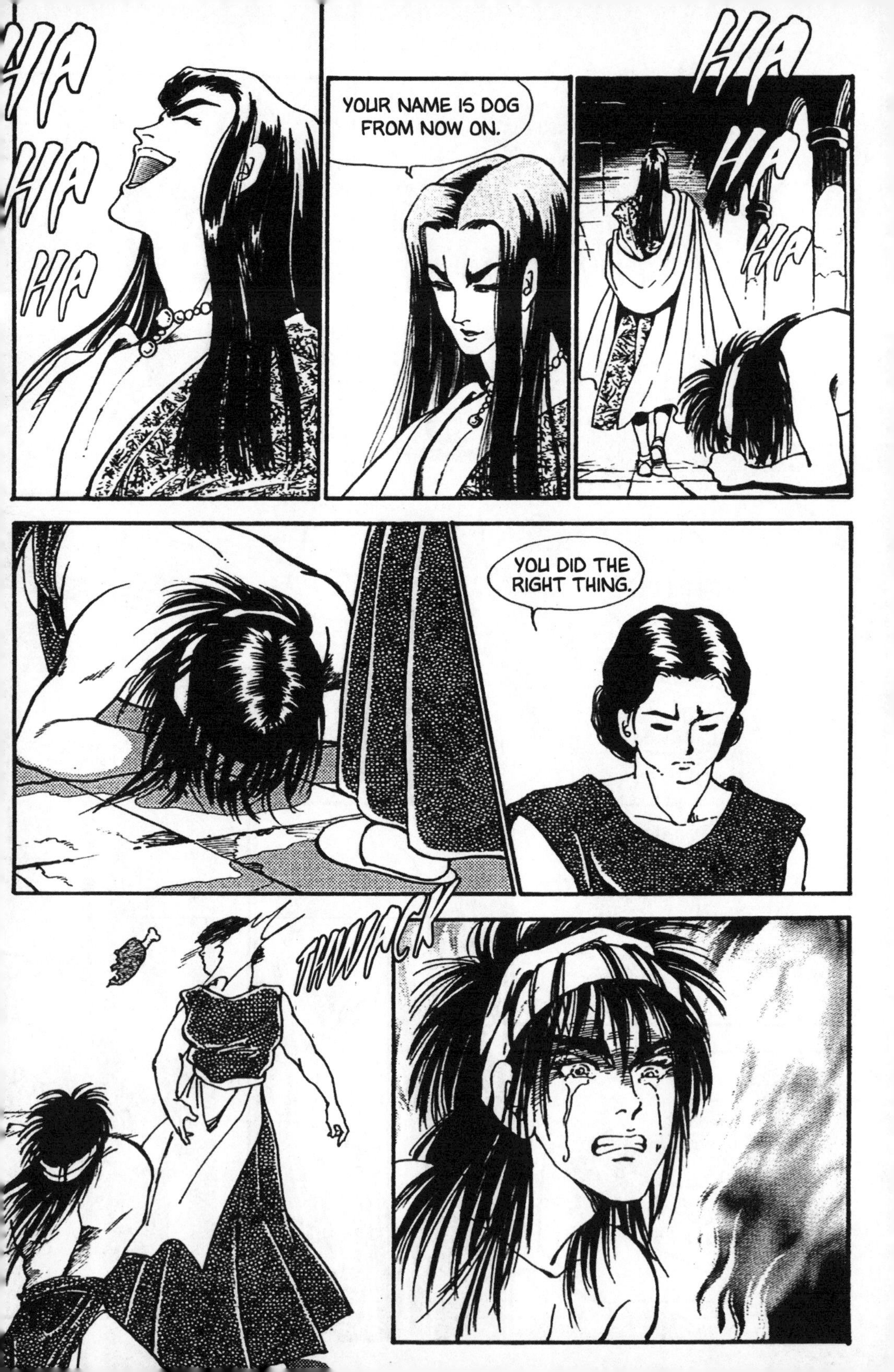

HA
HA
HA
YOUR NAME IS DOG FROM NOW ON.
HA
HA
HA
YOU DID THE RIGHT THING.
THWACK

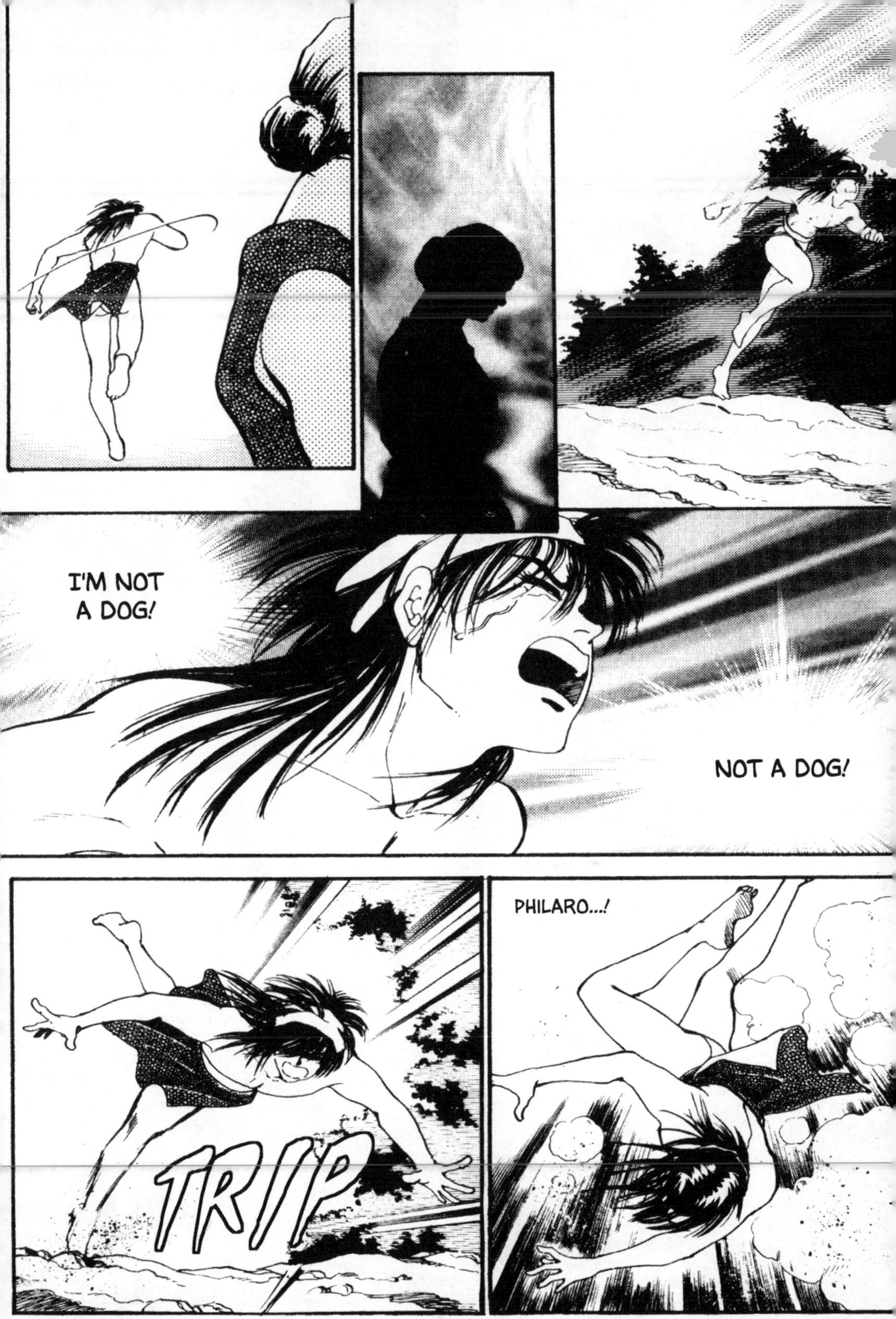
I'M NOT A DOG!
NOT A DOG!
TRIP
PHILARO...!

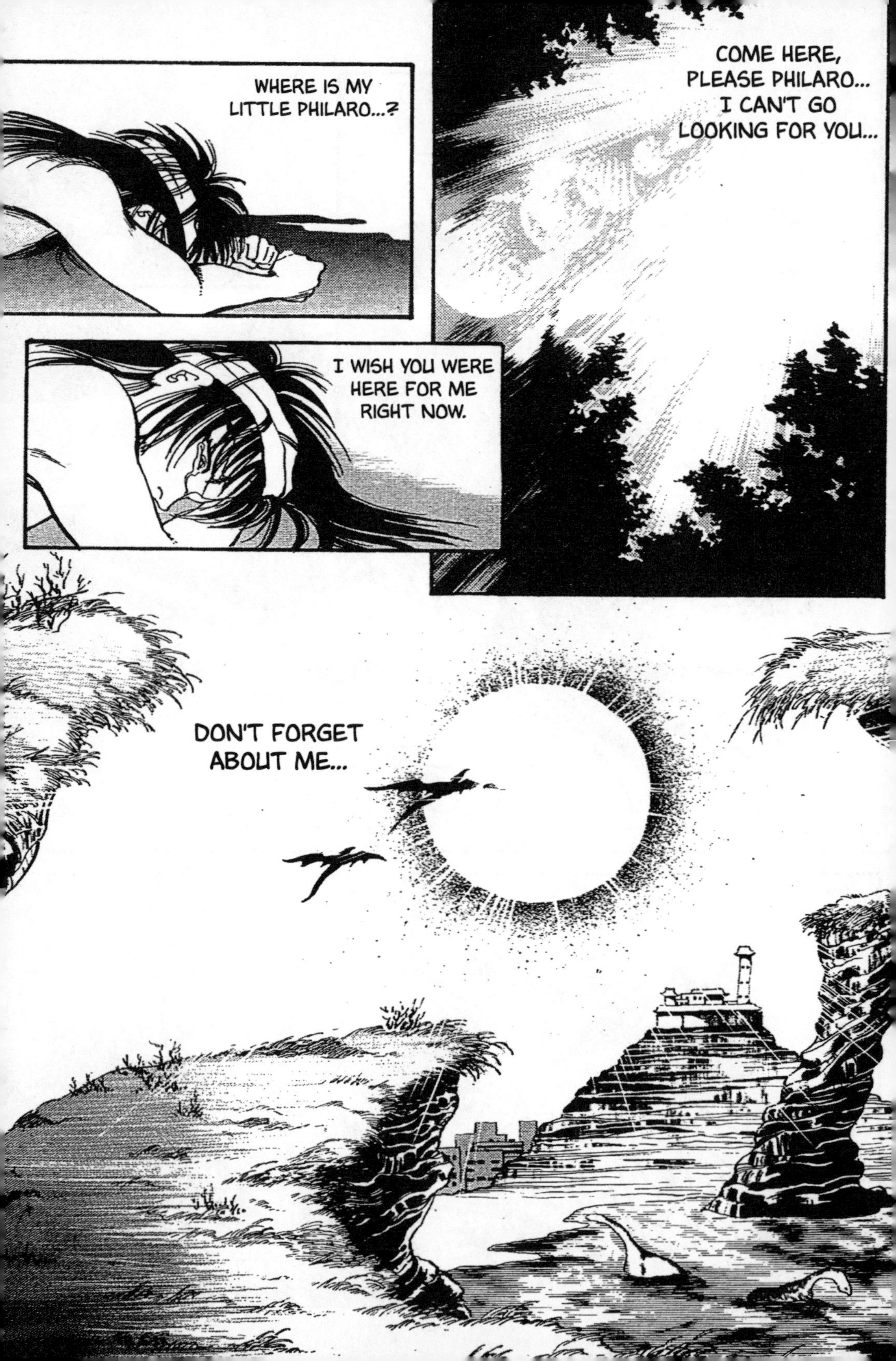
COME HERE, PLEASE PHILARO... I CAN'T GO LOOKING FOR YOU...
WHERE IS MY LITTLE PHILARO...?
I WISH YOU WERE HERE FOR ME RIGHT NOW.
DON'T FORGET ABOUT ME...

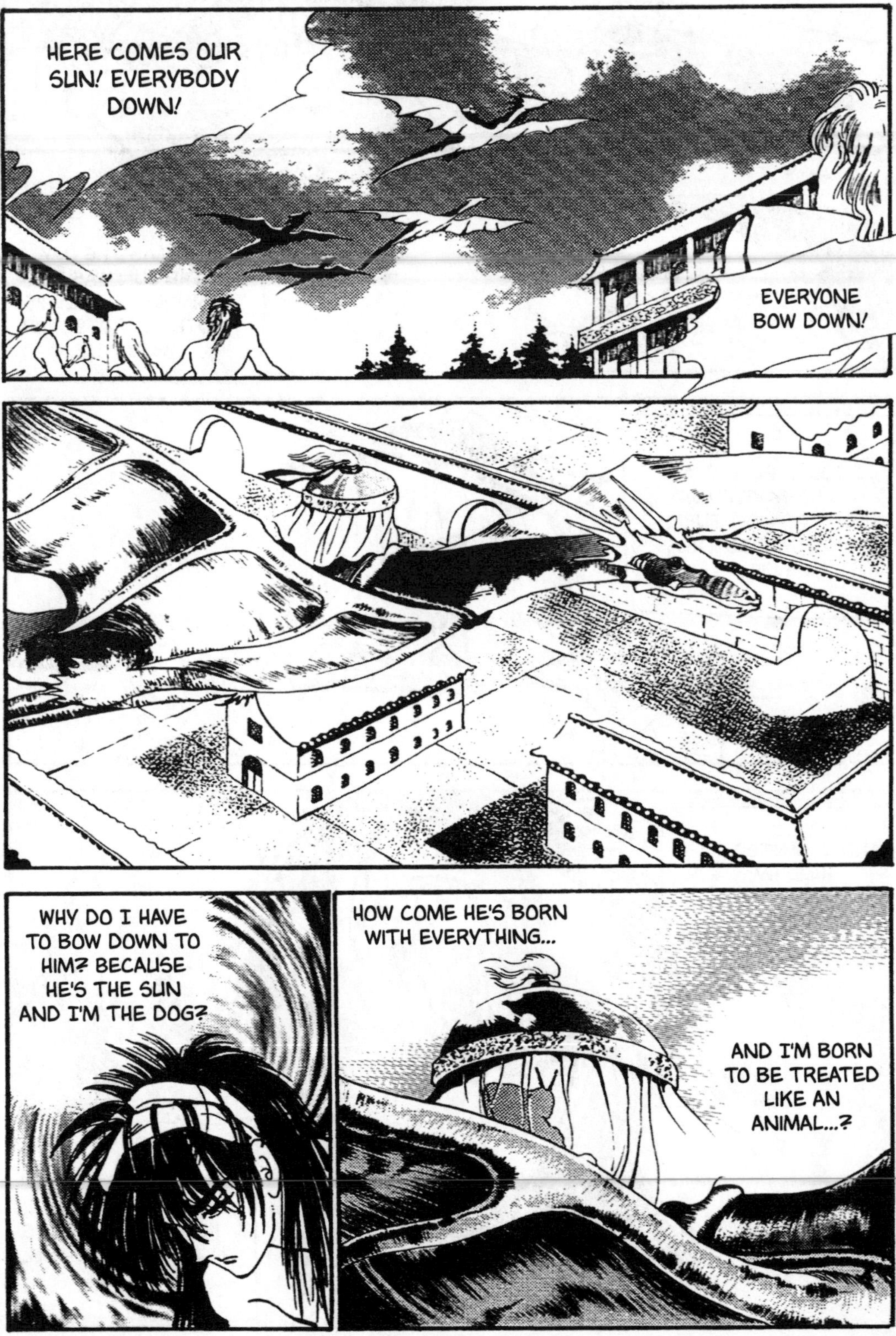
HERE COMES OUR SUN! EVERYBODY DOWN!
EVERYONE BOW DOWN!
WHY DO I HAVE TO BOW DOWN TO HIM? BECAUSE HE'S THE SUN AND I'M THE DOG?
HOW COME HE'S BORN WITH EVERYTHING...
AND I'M BORN TO BE TREATED LIKE AN ANIMAL...?

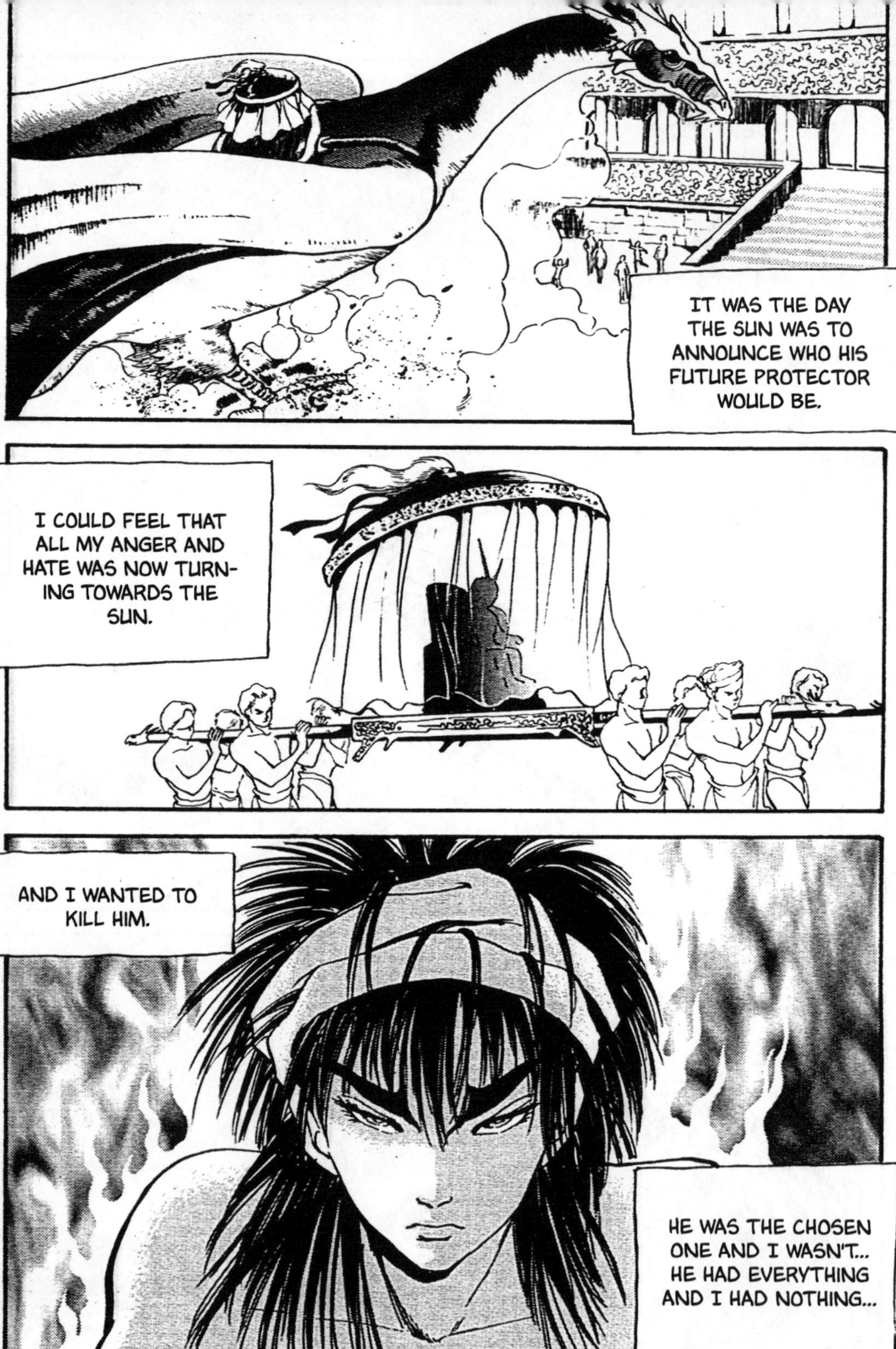
IT WAS THE DAY THE SUN WAS TO ANNOUNCE WHO HIS FUTURE PROTECTOR WOULD BE.
I COULD FEEL THAT ALL MY ANGER AND HATE WAS NOW TURNING TOWARDS THE SUN.
AND I WANTED TO KILL HIM.
HE WAS THE CHOSEN ONE AND I WASN'T... HE HAD EVERYTHING AND I HAD NOTHING...

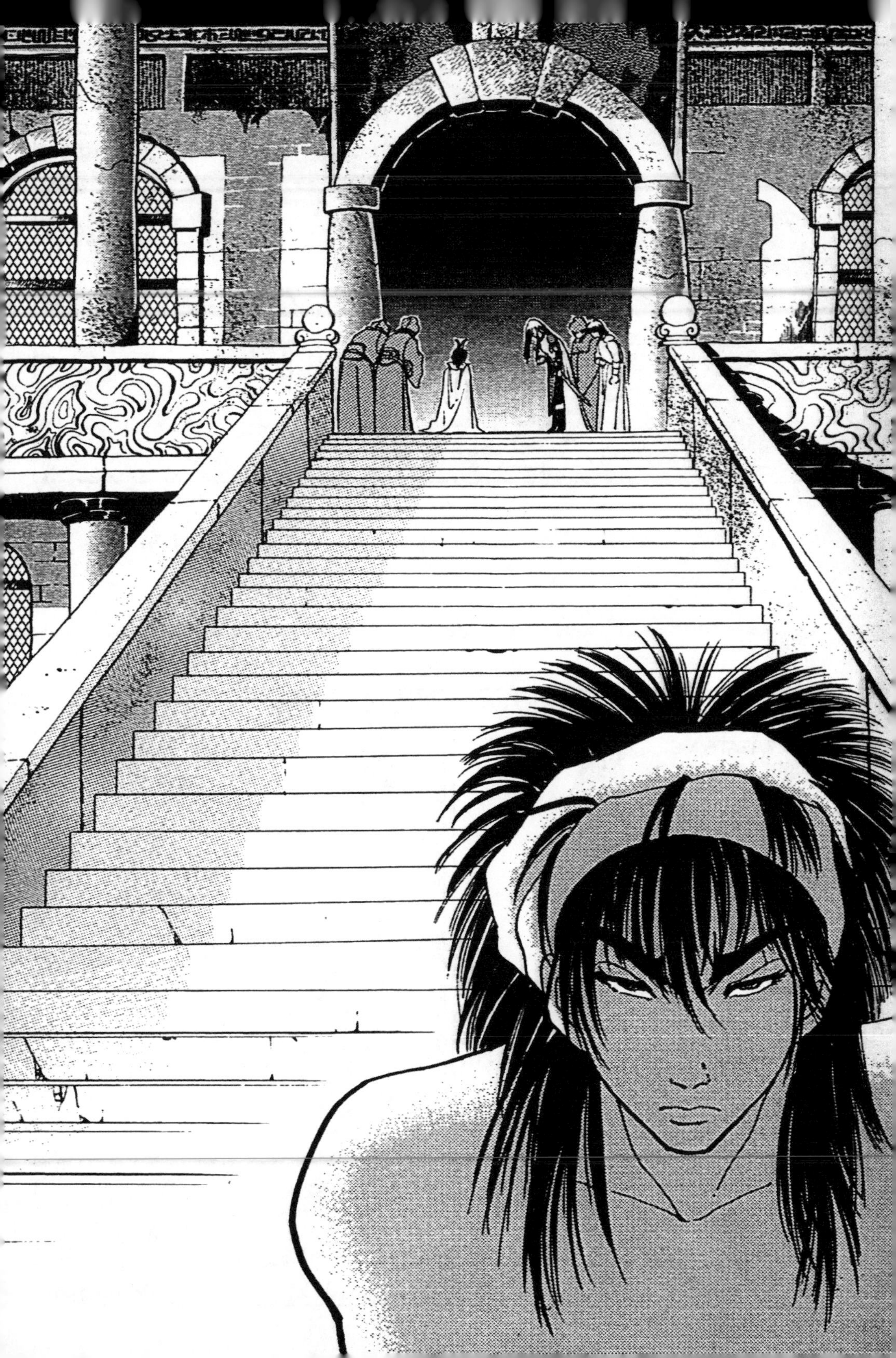

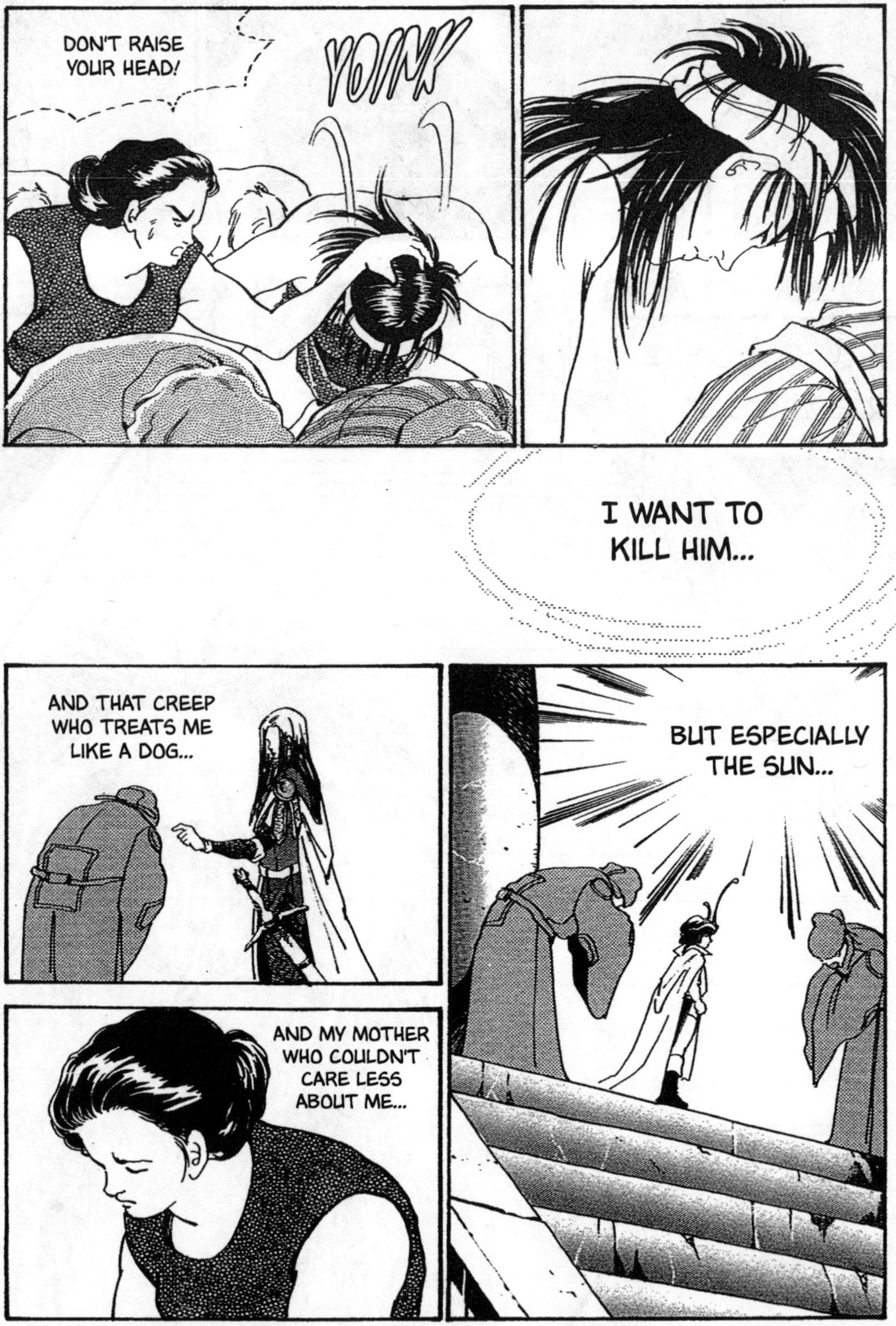
DON'T RAISE YOUR HEAD!
YOINK
I WANT TO KILL HIM...
AND THAT CREEP WHO TREATS ME LIKE A DOG...
AND MY MOTHER WHO COULDN'T CARE LESS ABOUT ME...
BUT ESPECIALLY THE SUN...

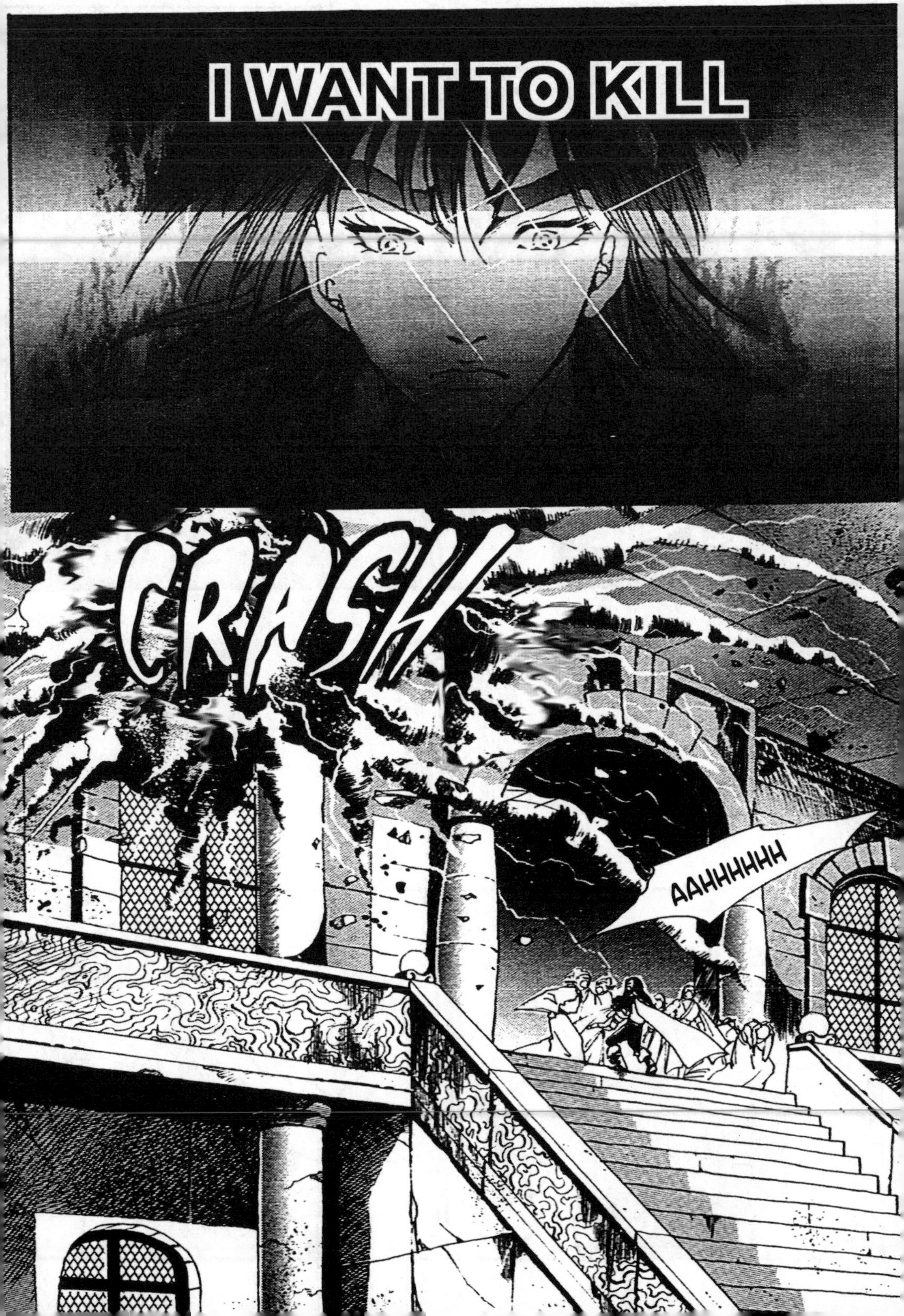
I WANT TO KILL
CRASH
AAHHHHHH

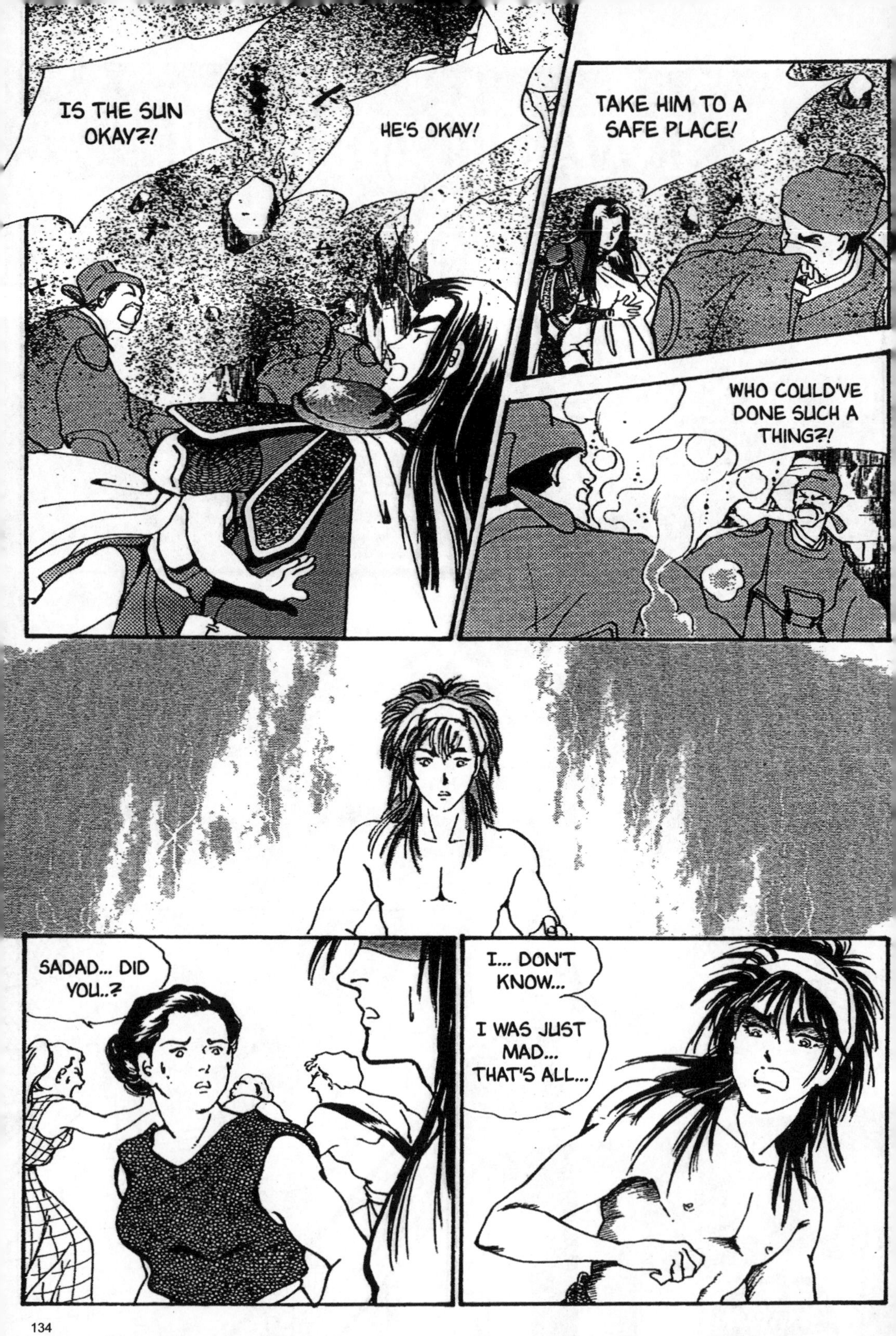

IS THE SUN OKAY?!
HE'S OKAY!
TAKE HIM TO A SAFE PLACE!
WHO COULD'VE DONE SUCH A THING?!
SADAD... DID YOU..?
I... DON'T KNOW...
I WAS JUST MAD... THAT'S ALL...

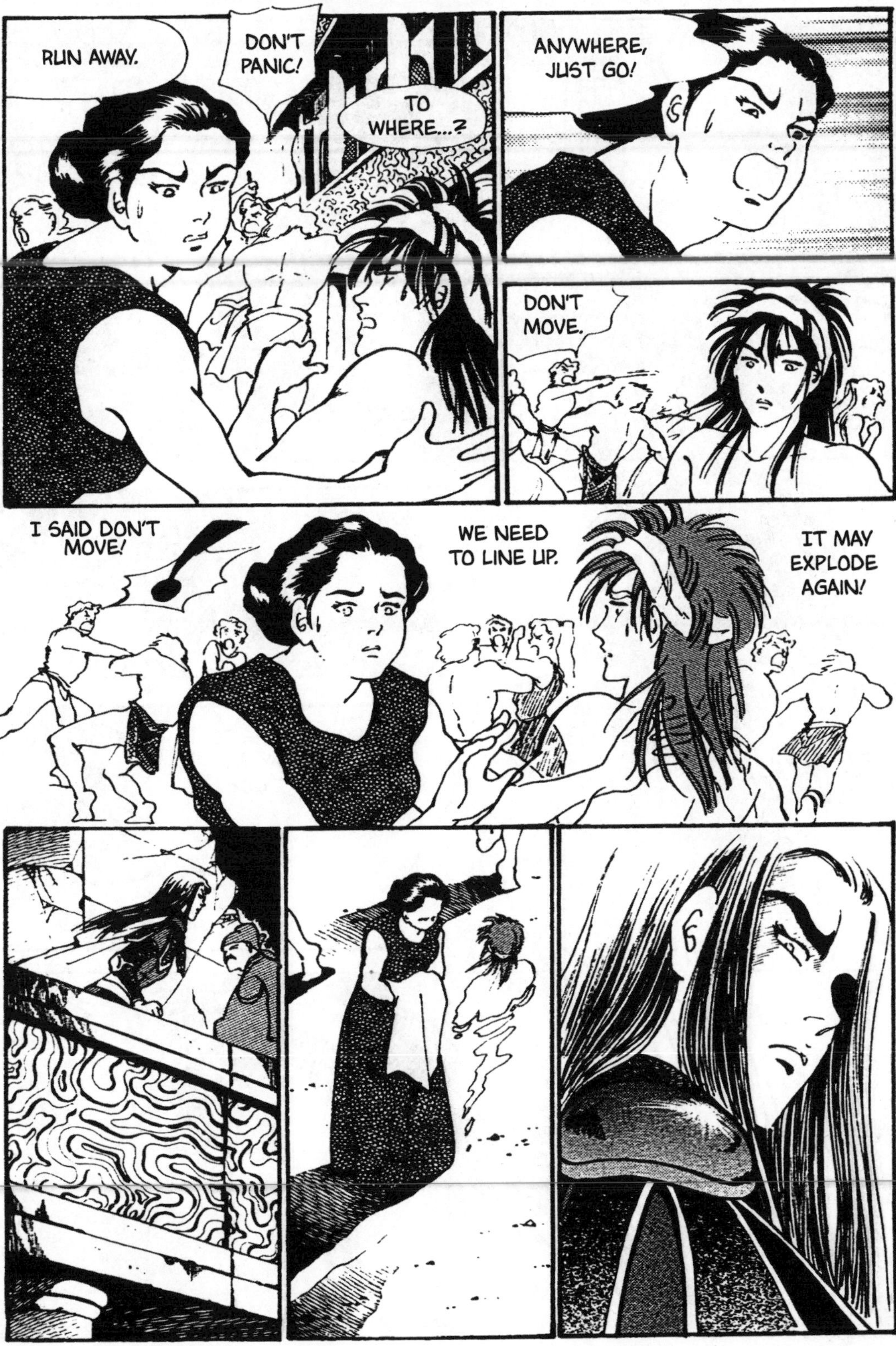
RUN AWAY.
DON'T PANIC!
TO WHERE...?
ANYWHERE, JUST GO!
DON'T MOVE.
I SAID DON'T MOVE!
WE NEED TO LINE UP.
IT MAY EXPLODE AGAIN!

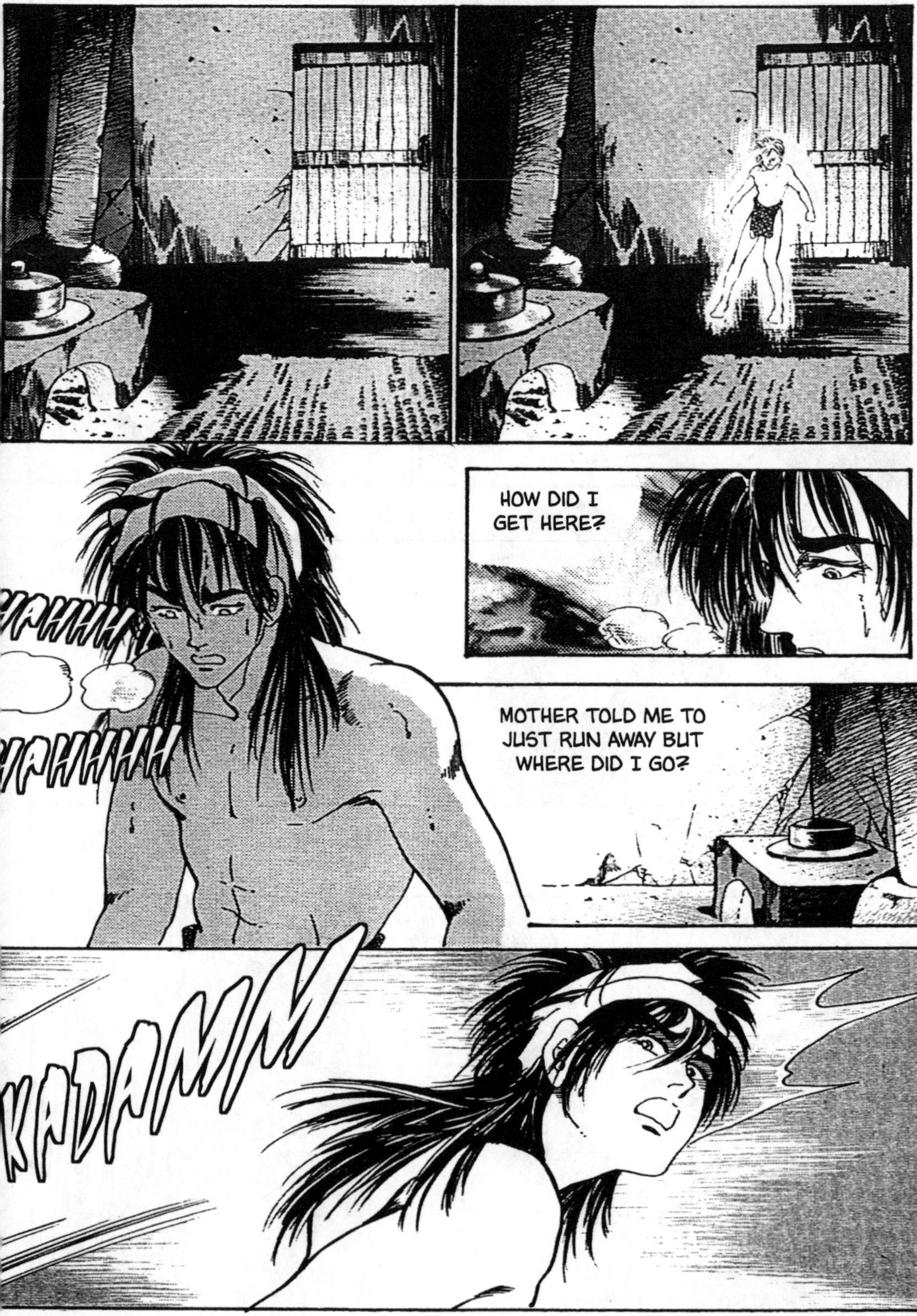
HOW DID I
GET HERE?
MOTHER TOLD ME TO
JUST RUN AWAY BUT
WHERE DID I GO?
KADAMM

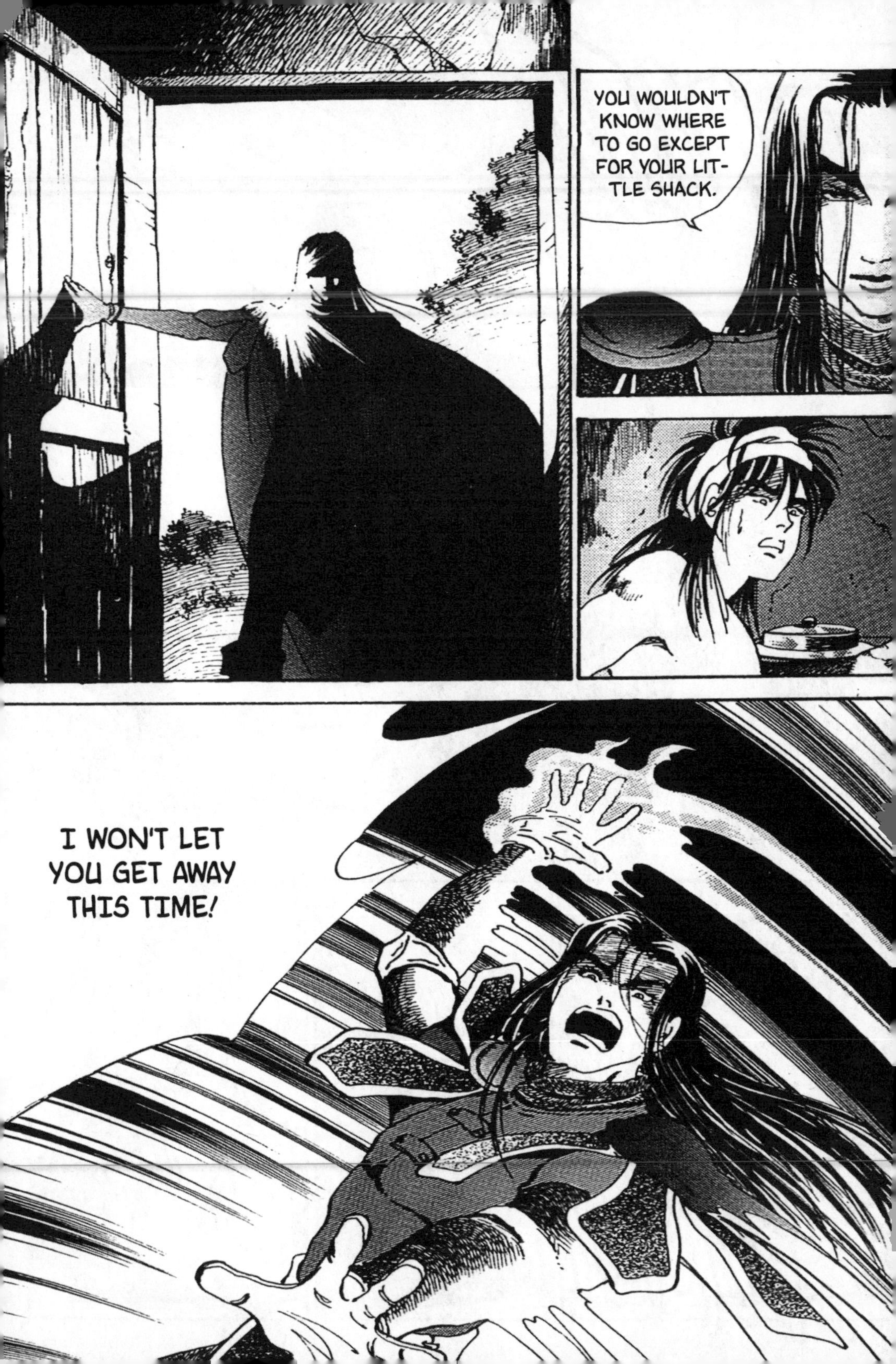
YOU WOULDN'T KNOW WHERE TO GO EXCEPT FOR YOUR LIT-TLE SHACK.
I WON'T LET YOU GET AWAY THIS TIME!

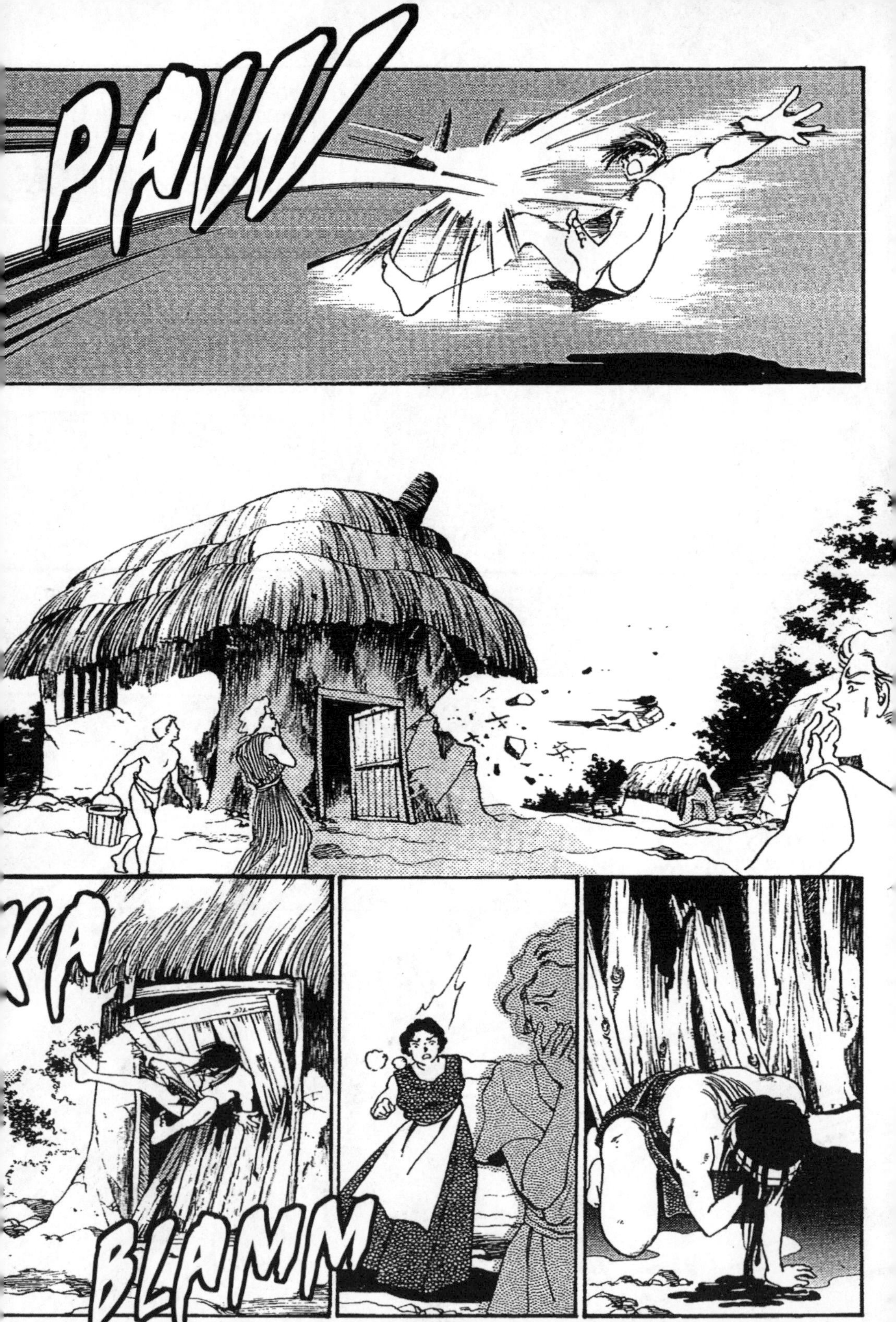
PAW
KA
BLAMM

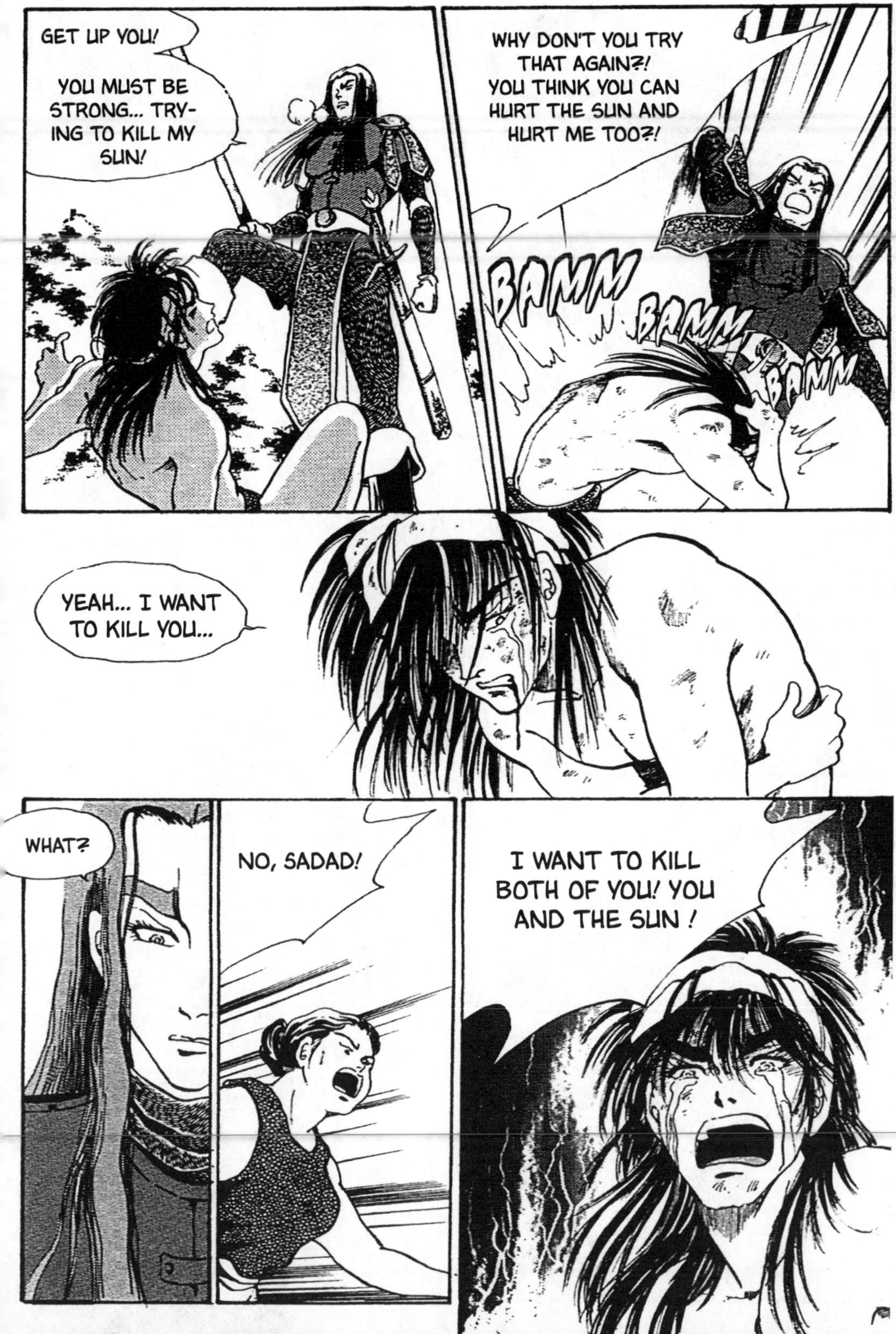
GET UP YOU!
YOU MUST BE STRONG... TRY- ING TO KILL MY SUN!
WHY DON'T YOU TRY THAT AGAIN?! YOU THINK YOU CAN HURT THE SUN AND HURT ME TOO?!
BAMM
BAMM
BAMM
YEAH... I WANT TO KILL YOU...
WHAT?
NO, SADAD!
I WANT TO KILL BOTH OF YOU! YOU AND THE SUN !

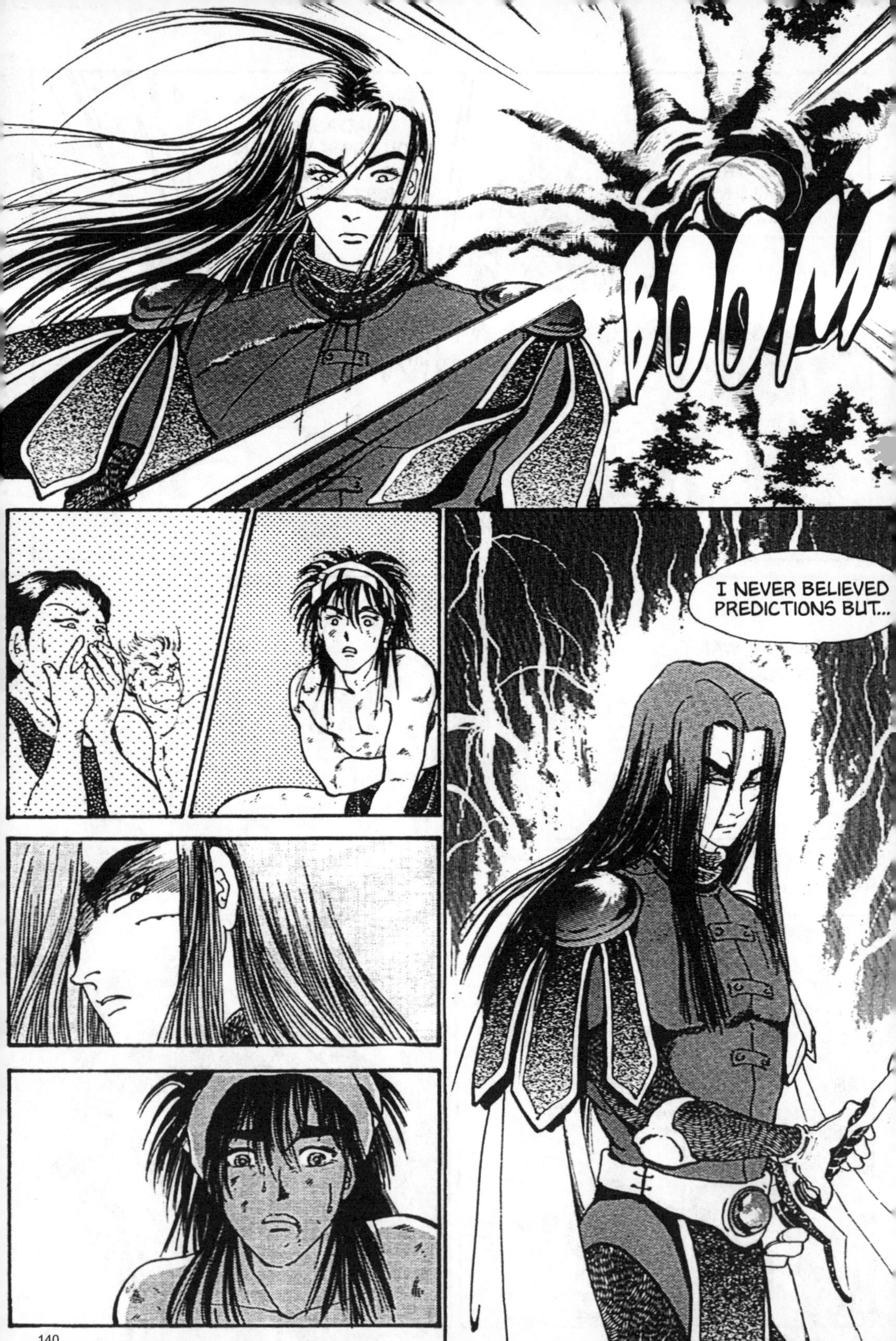
BOOM
I NEVER BELIEVED PREDICTIONS BUT...

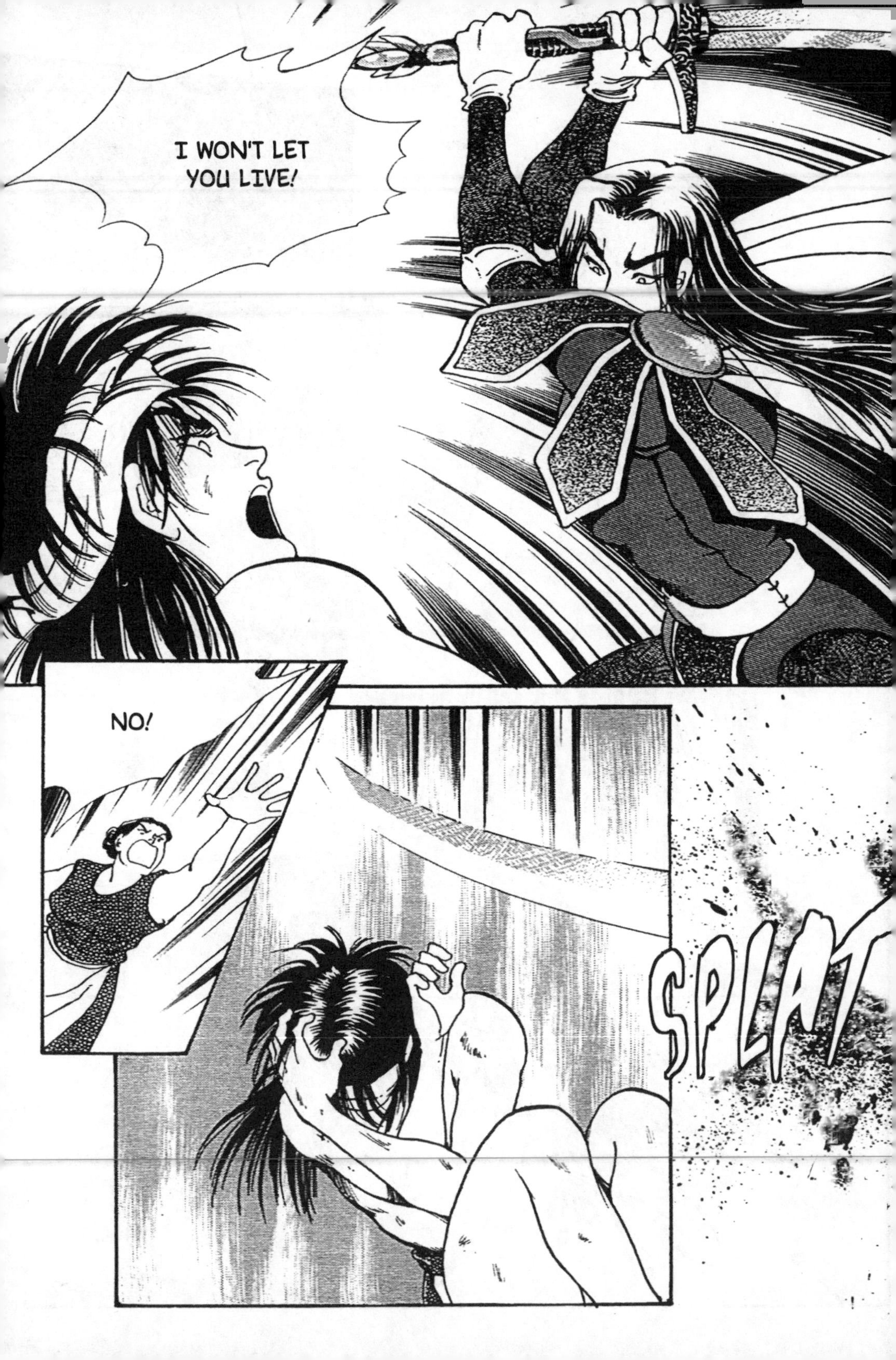
I WON'T LET YOU LIVE!
NO!
SPLAT

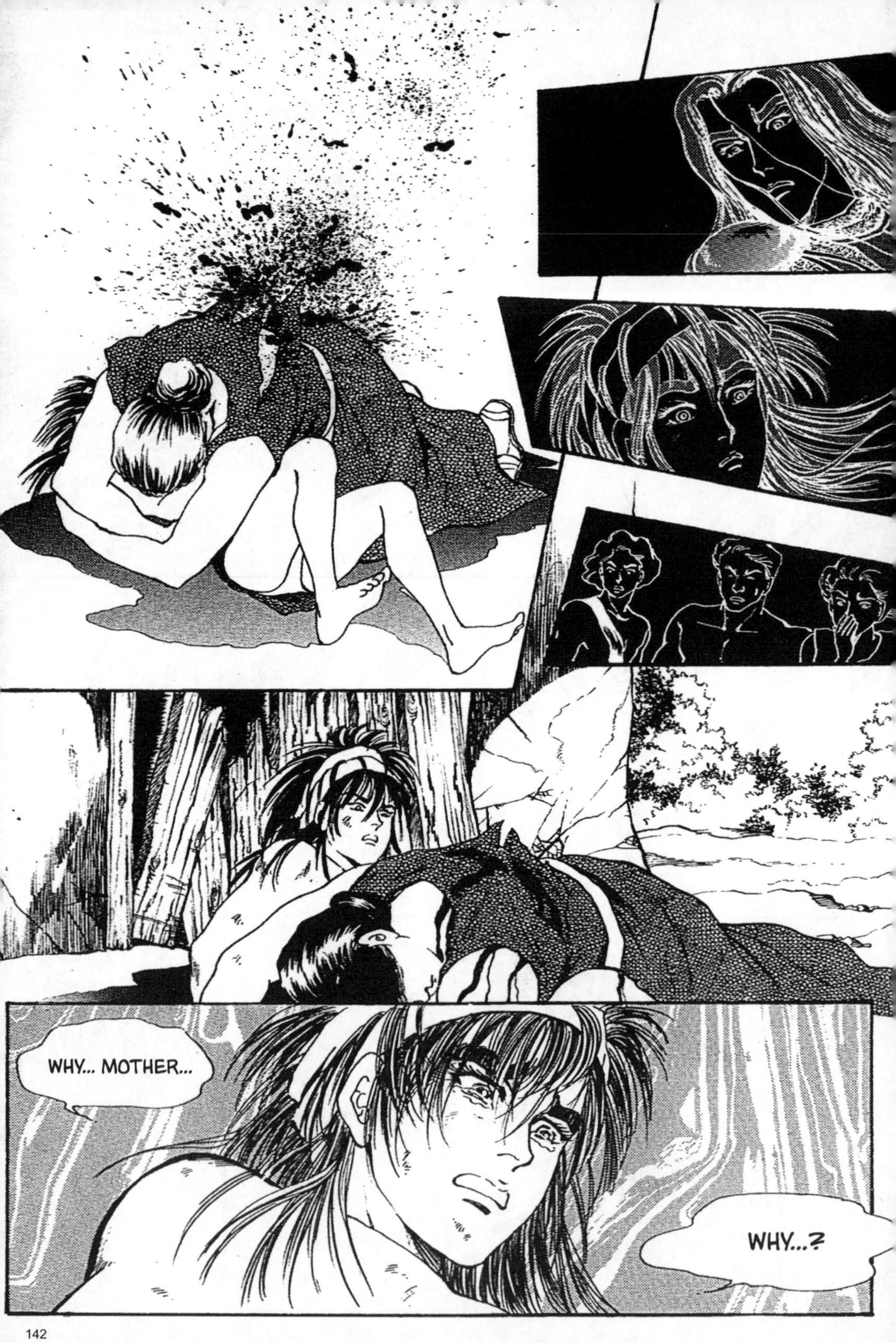
WHY... MOTHER...
WHY...?

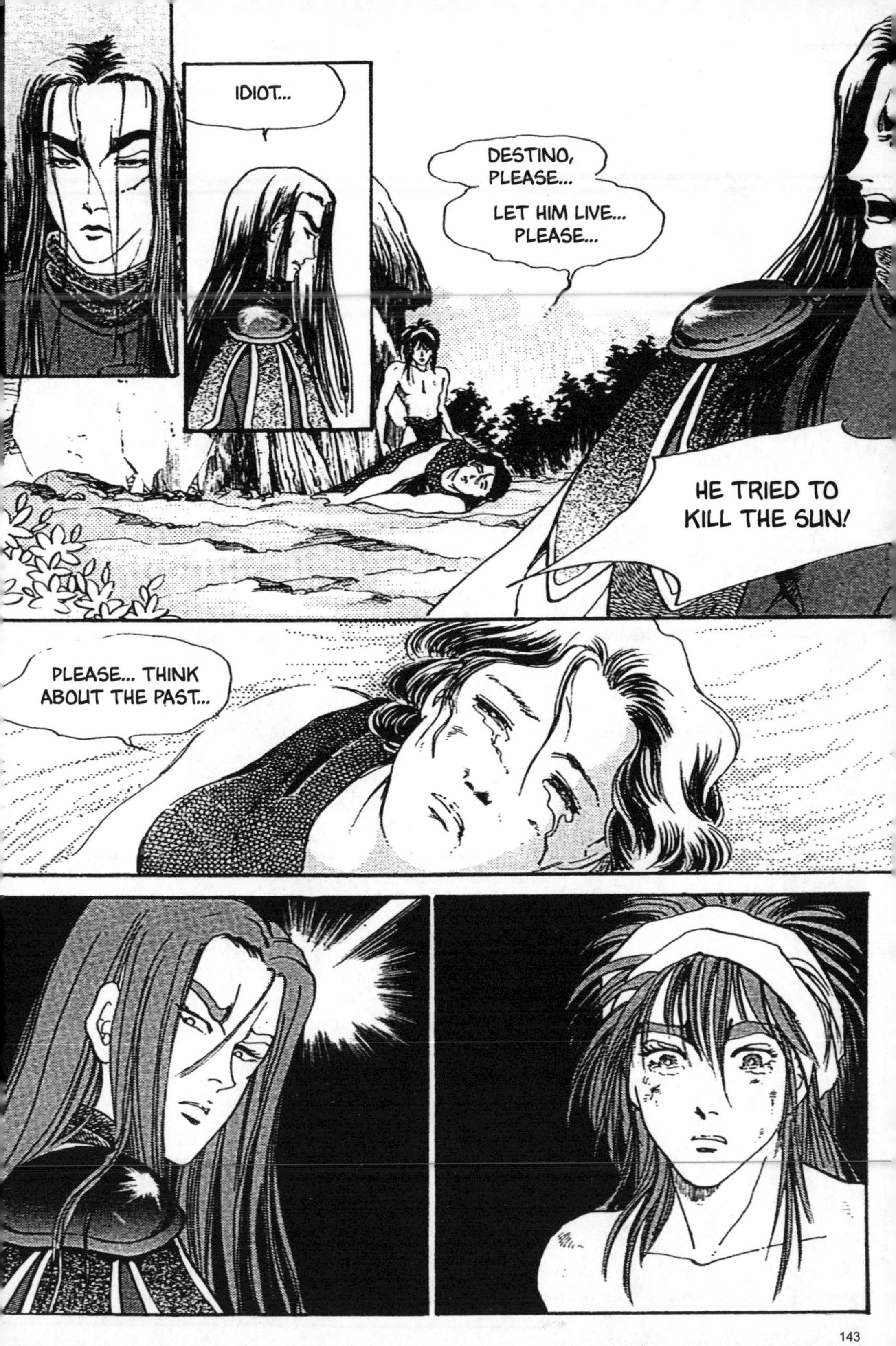

IDIOT...
DESTINO, PLEASE...
LET HIM LIVE... PLEASE...
HE TRIED TO KILL THE SUN!
PLEASE... THINK ABOUT THE PAST...

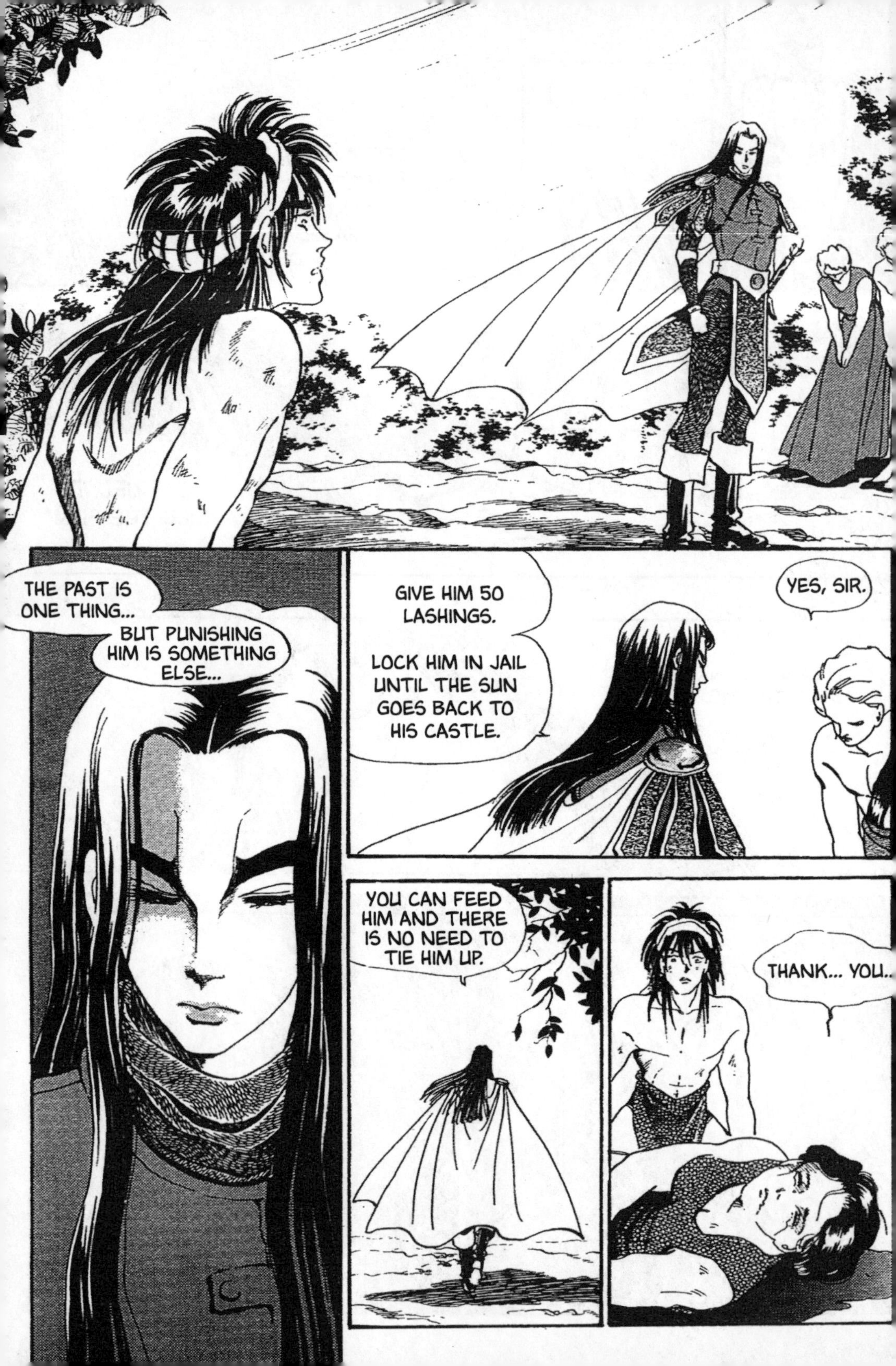
THE PAST IS ONE THING...
BUT PUNISHING HIM IS SOMETHING ELSE...
GIVE HIM 50 LASHINGS.
LOCK HIM IN JAIL UNTIL THE SUN GOES BACK TO HIS CASTLE.
YES, SIR.
YOU CAN FEED HIM AND THERE IS NO NEED TO TIE HIM UP.
THANK... YOU...

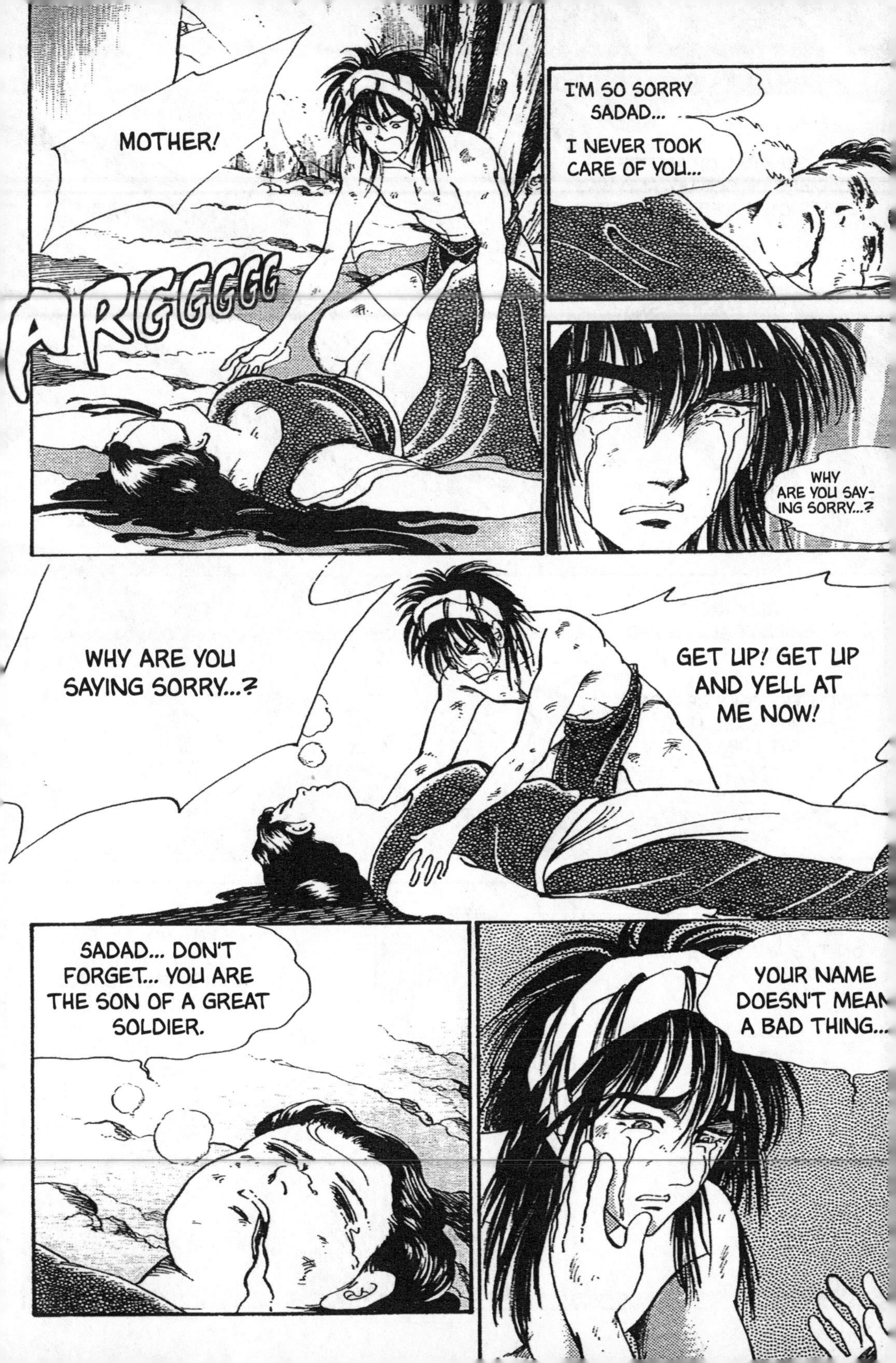
MOTHER!
ARGGGGG
I'M SO SORRY SADAD...
I NEVER TOOK CARE OF YOU...
WHY ARE YOU SAYING SORRY...?
WHY ARE YOU SAYING SORRY...?
GET UP! GET UP AND YELL AT ME NOW!
SADAD... DON'T FORGET... YOU ARE THE SON OF A GREAT SOLDIER.
YOUR NAME DOESN'T MEAN A BAD THING...

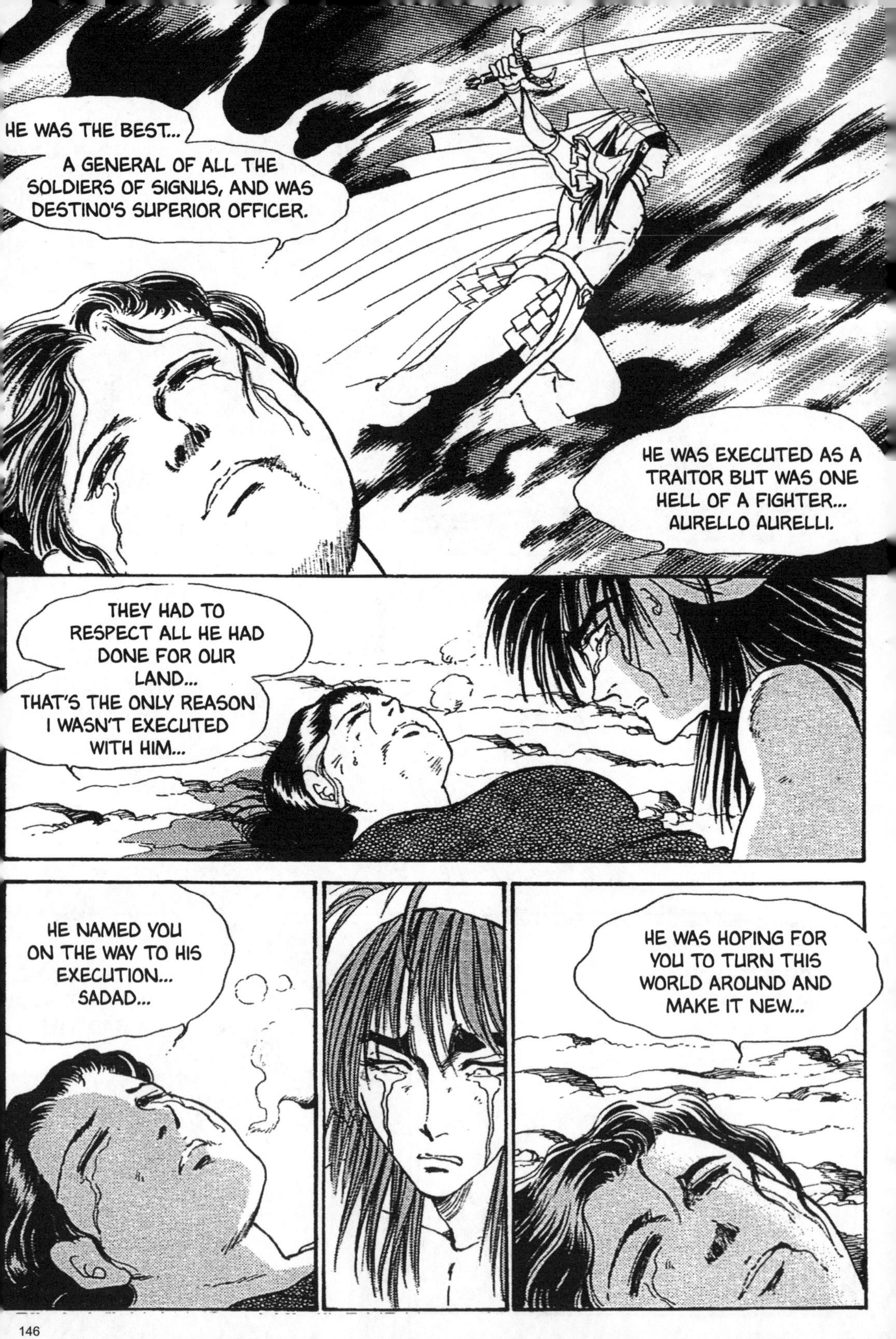

HE WAS THE BEST...
A GENERAL OF ALL THE SOLDIERS OF SIGNUS, AND WAS DESTINO'S SUPERIOR OFFICER.
HE WAS EXECUTED AS A TRAITOR BUT WAS ONE HELL OF A FIGHTER... AURELLO AURELLI.
THEY HAD TO RESPECT ALL HE HAD DONE FOR OUR LAND... THAT'S THE ONLY REASON I WASN'T EXECUTED WITH HIM...
HE NAMED YOU ON THE WAY TO HIS EXECUTION... SADAD...
HE WAS HOPING FOR YOU TO TURN THIS WORLD AROUND AND MAKE IT NEW...

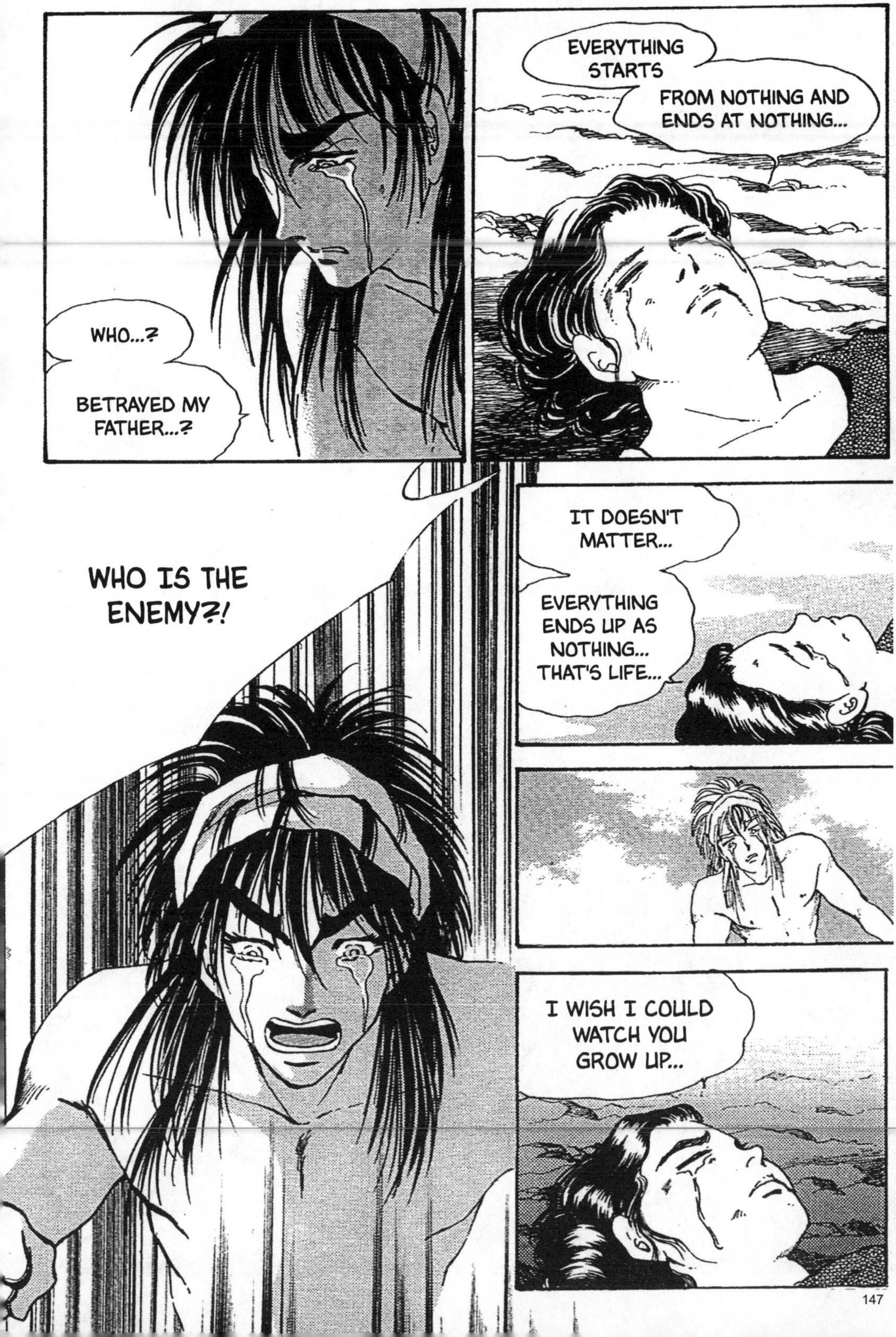
WHO...?
BETRAYED MY FATHER...?
EVERYTHING STARTS
FROM NOTHING AND ENDS AT NOTHING...
WHO IS THE ENEMY?!
IT DOESN'T MATTER...
EVERYTHING ENDS UP AS NOTHING... THAT'S LIFE...
I WISH I COULD WATCH YOU GROW UP...

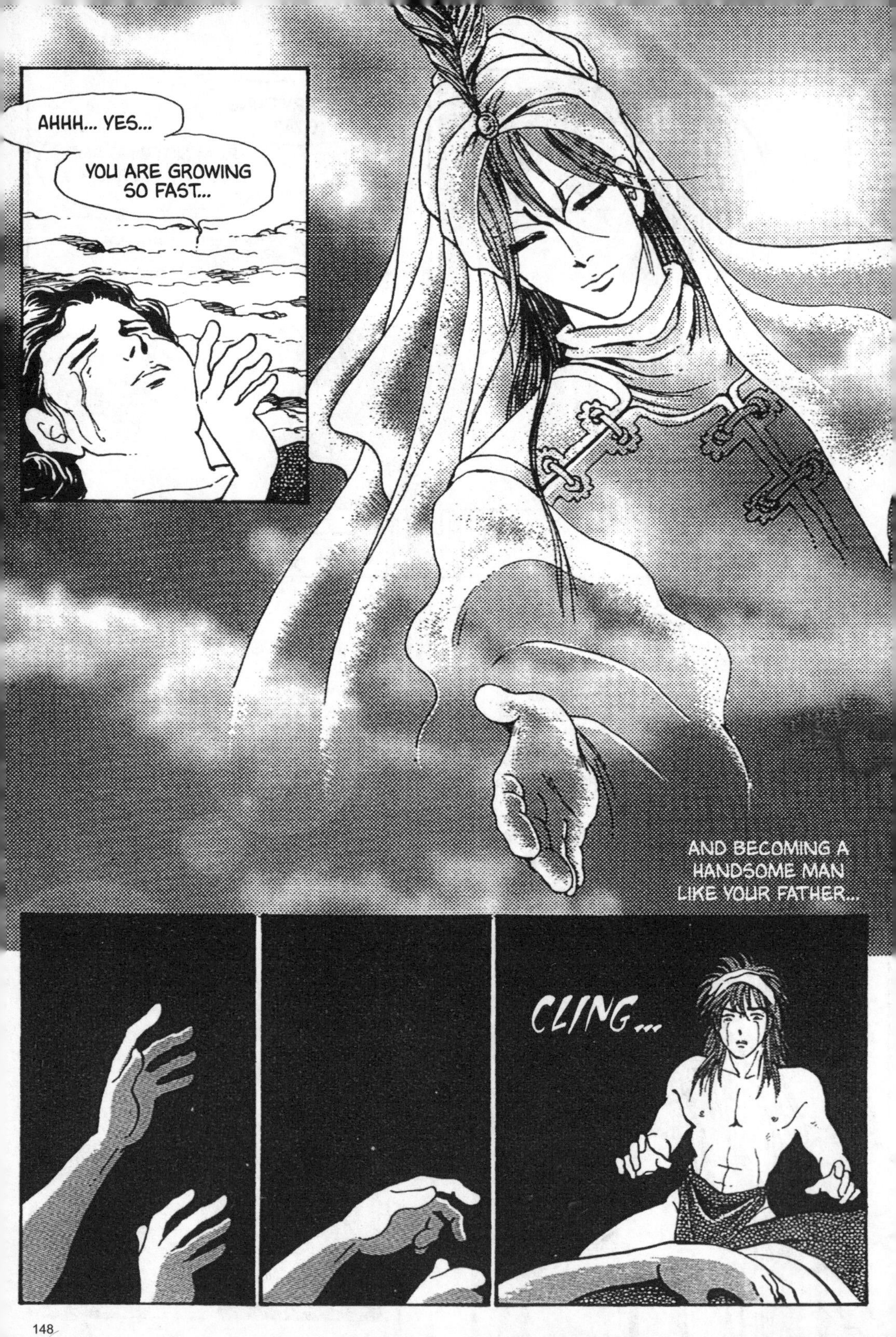
AHHH... YES...
YOU ARE GROWING SO FAST...
AND BECOMING A HANDSOME MAN LIKE YOUR FATHER...
CLING...

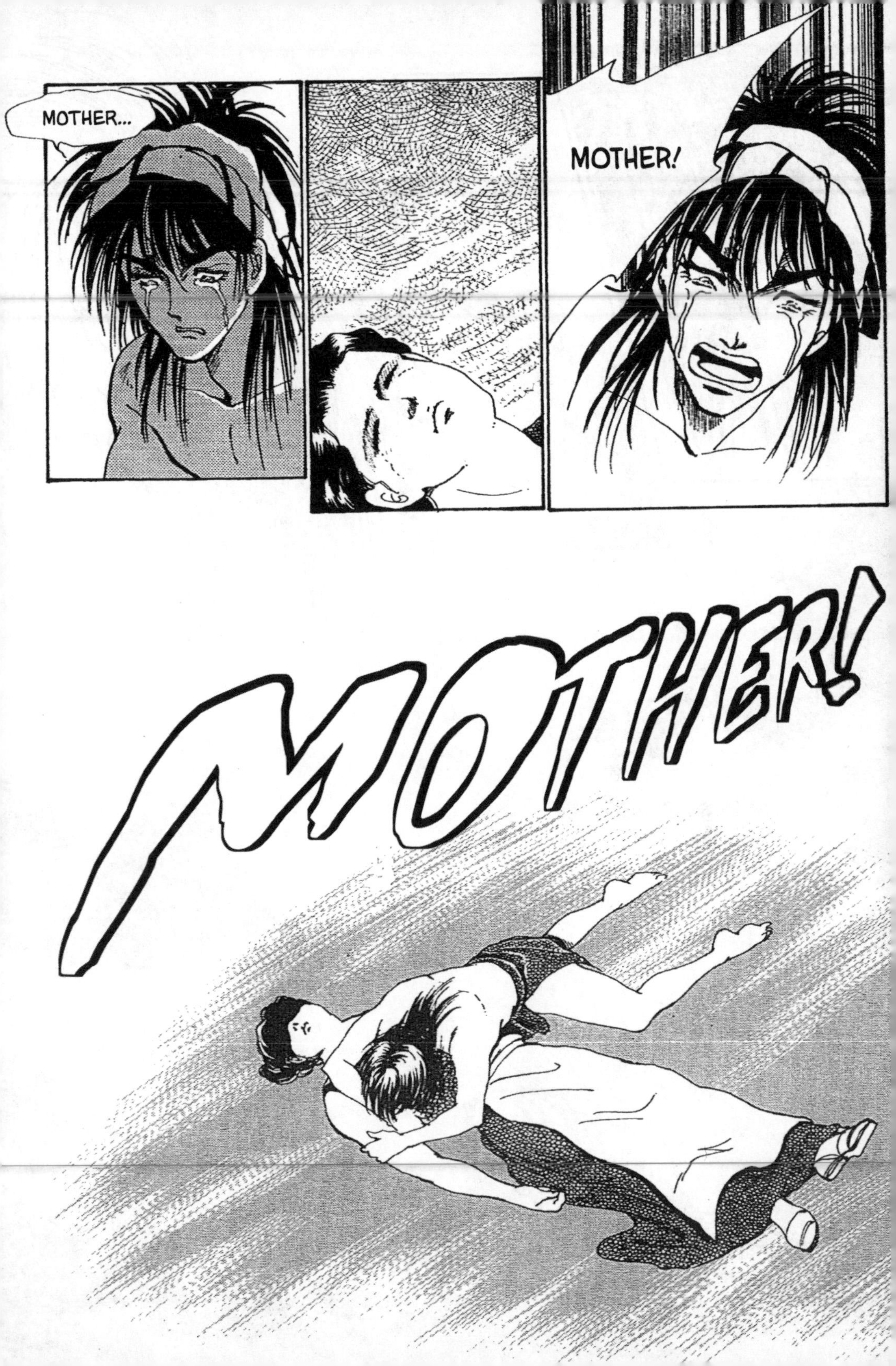
MOTHER...
MOTHER!
MOTHER!

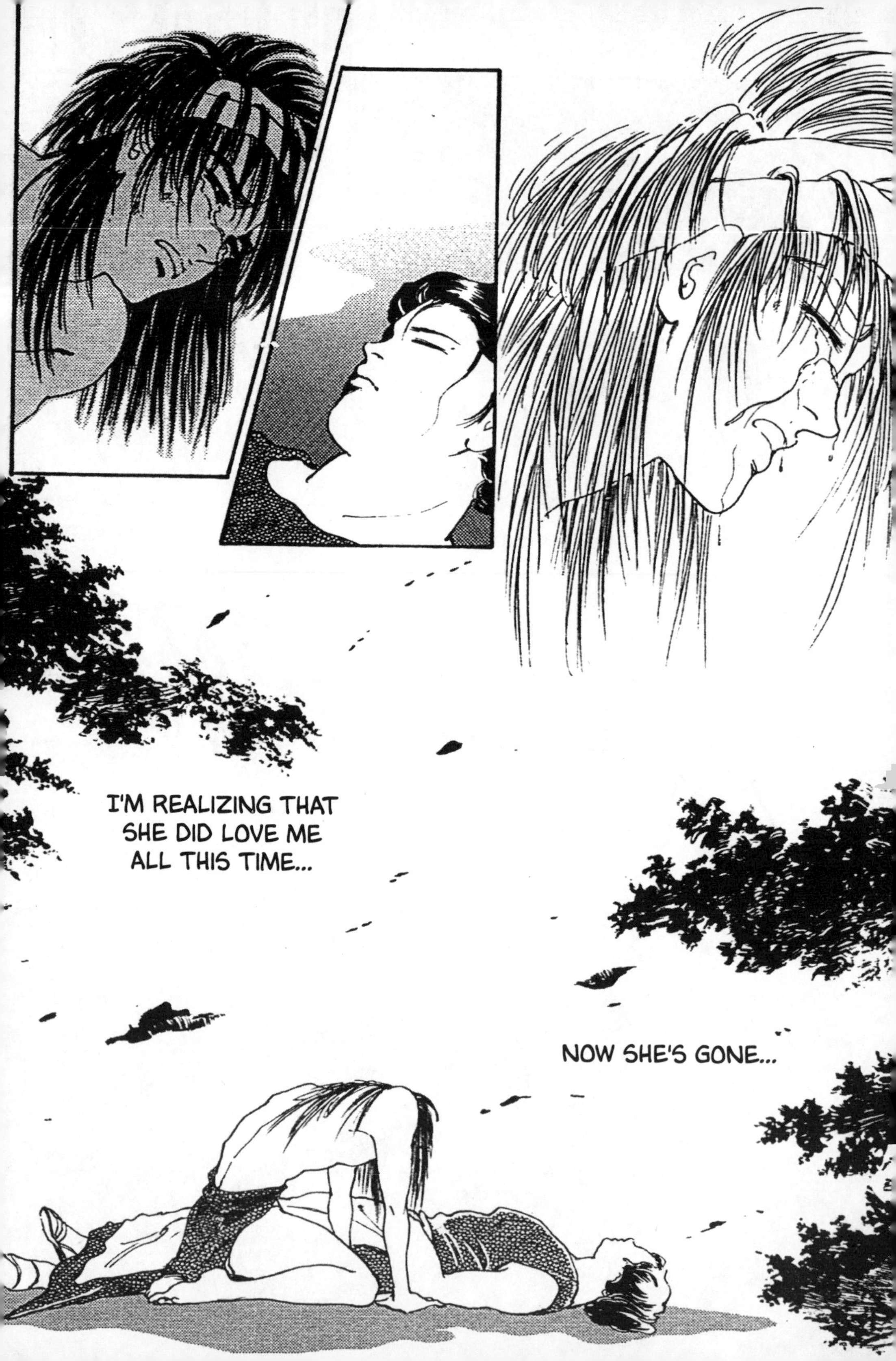
I'M REALIZING THAT
SHE DID LOVE ME
ALL THIS TIME...
NOW SHE'S GONE...

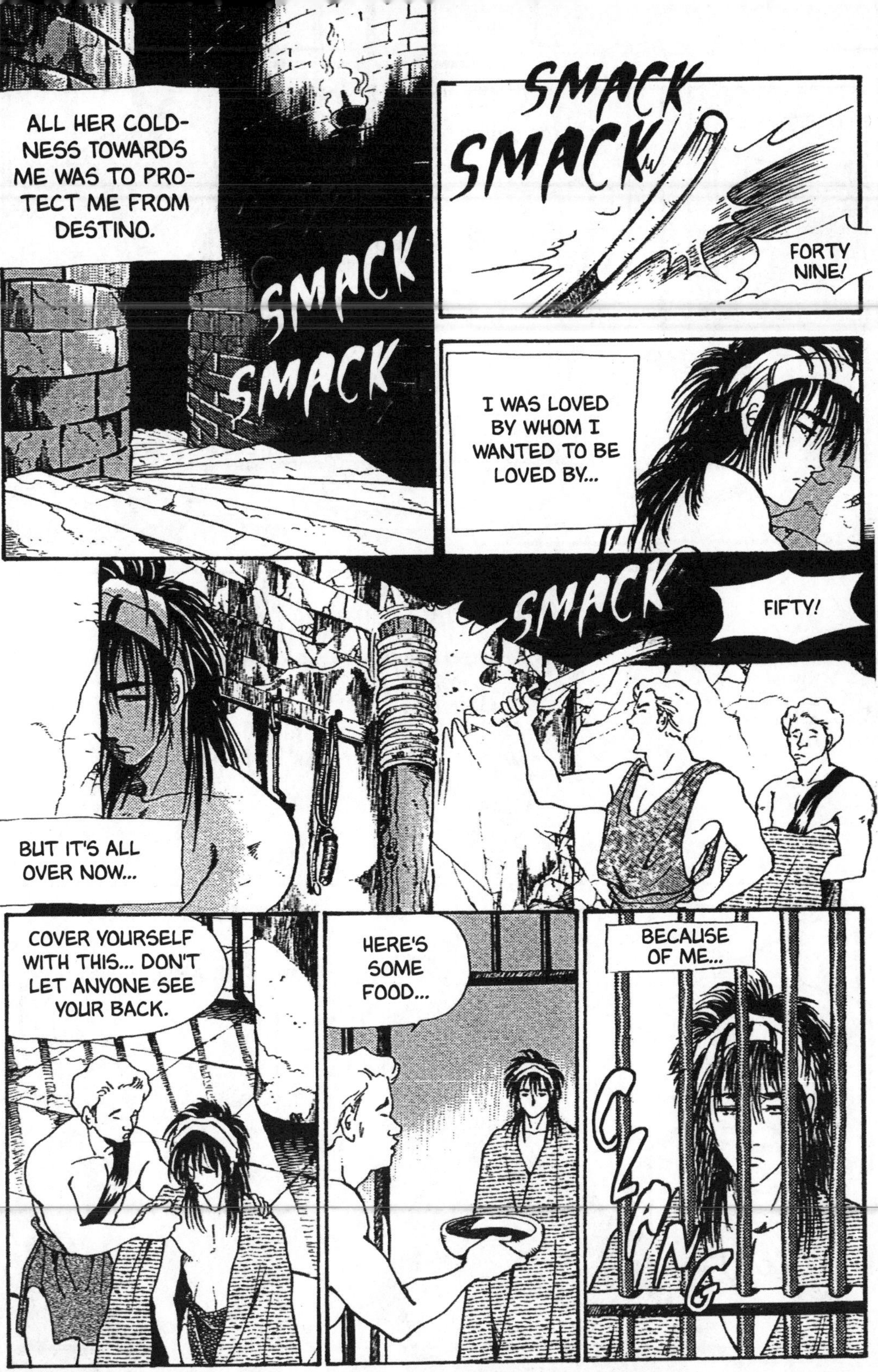
ALL HER COLDNESS TOWARDS ME WAS TO PROTECT ME FROM DESTINO.
SMACK SMACK
SMACK SMACK
FORTY NINE!
I WAS LOVED BY WHOM I WANTED TO BE LOVED BY...
SMACK
FIFTY!
BUT IT'S ALL OVER NOW...
COVER YOURSELF WITH THIS... DON'T LET ANYONE SEE YOUR BACK.
HERE'S SOME FOOD...
BECAUSE OF ME...
CLANG

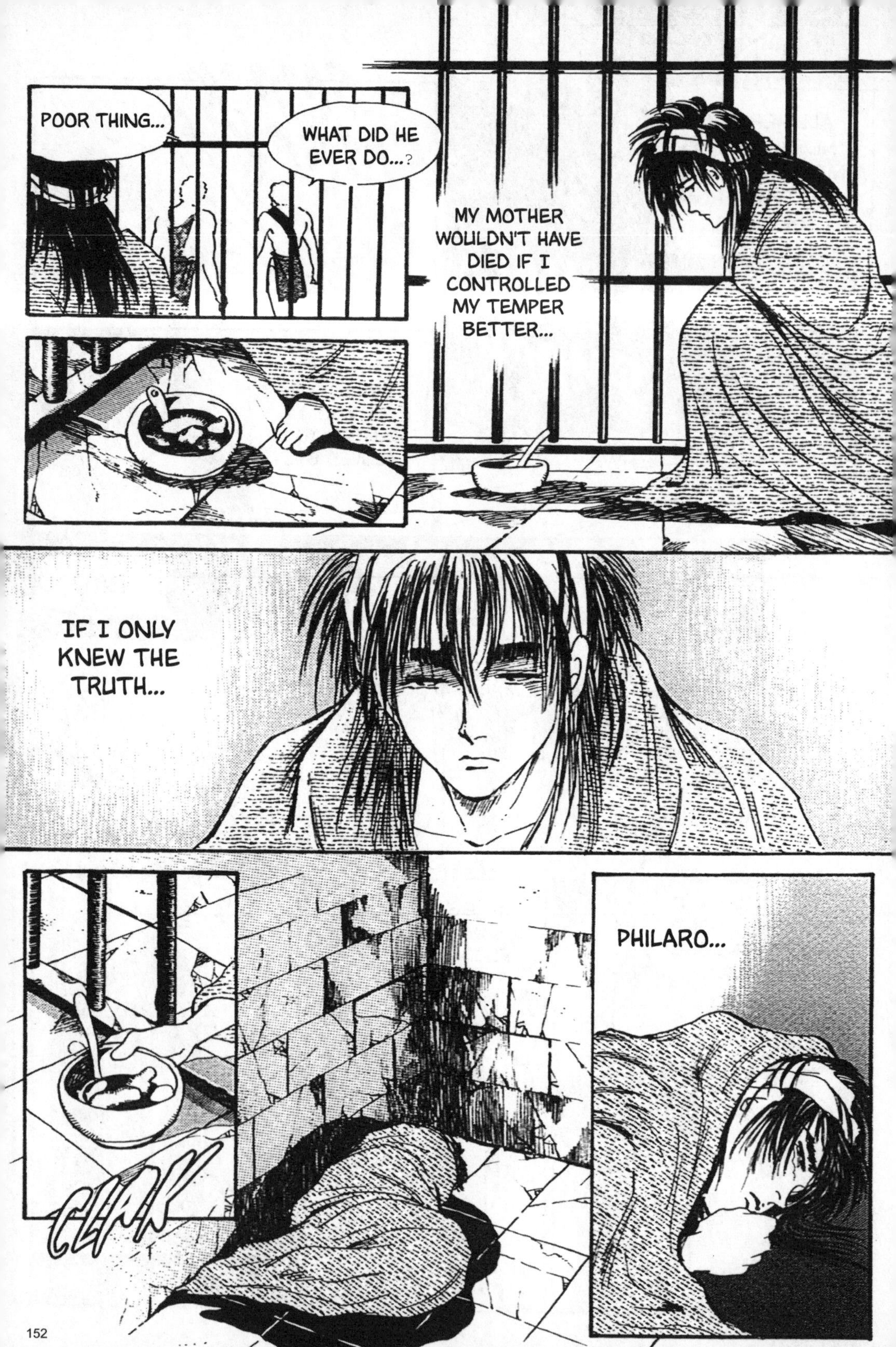
POOR THING...
WHAT DID HE EVER DO...?
MY MOTHER WOULDN'T HAVE DIED IF I CONTROLLED MY TEMPER BETTER...
IF I ONLY KNEW THE TRUTH...
PHILARO...
CLAK

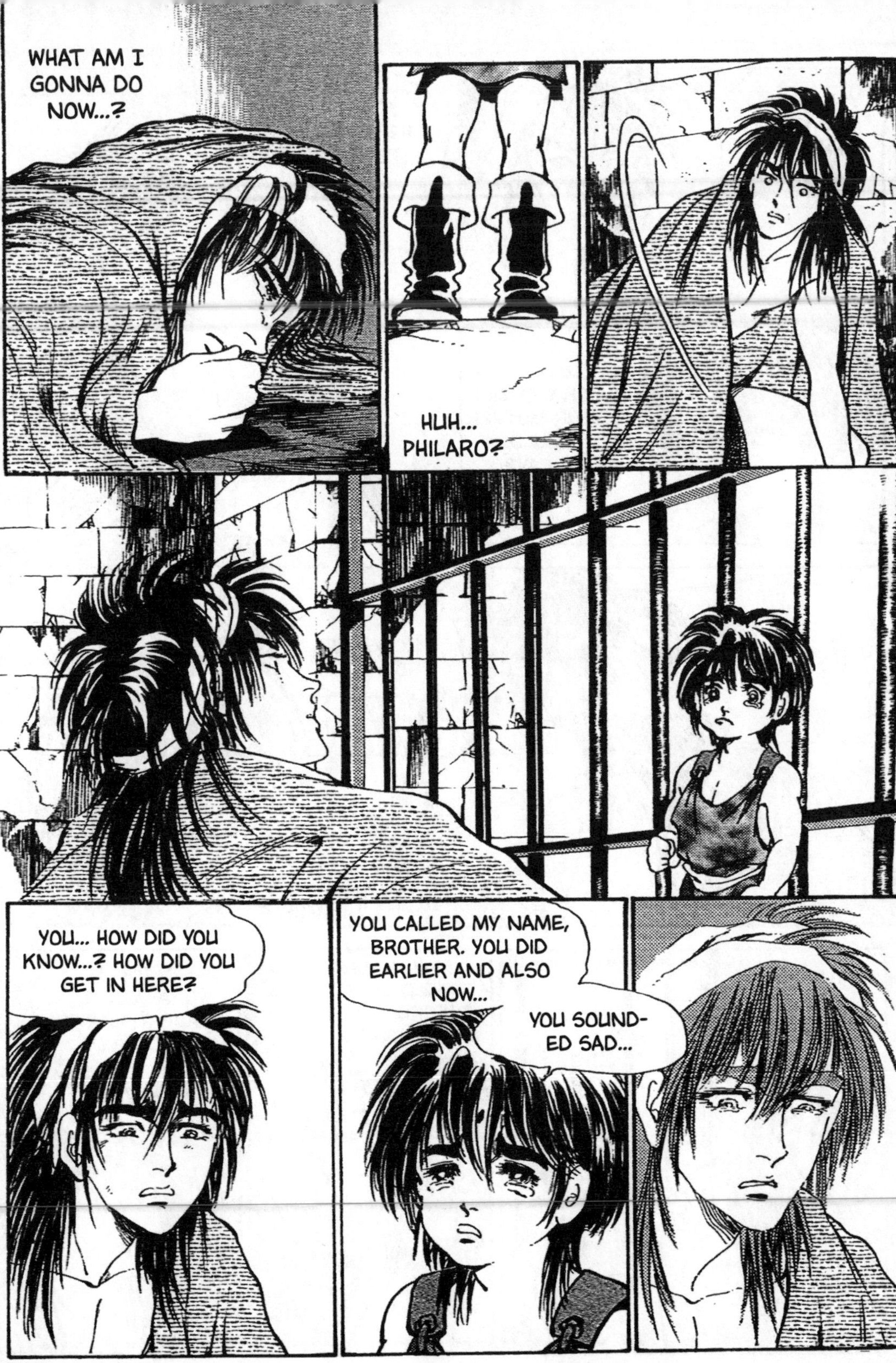
WHAT AM I GONNA DO NOW...?
HUH... PHILARO?
YOU... HOW DID YOU KNOW...? HOW DID YOU GET IN HERE?
YOU CALLED MY NAME, BROTHER. YOU DID EARLIER AND ALSO NOW...
YOU SOUND-ED SAD...

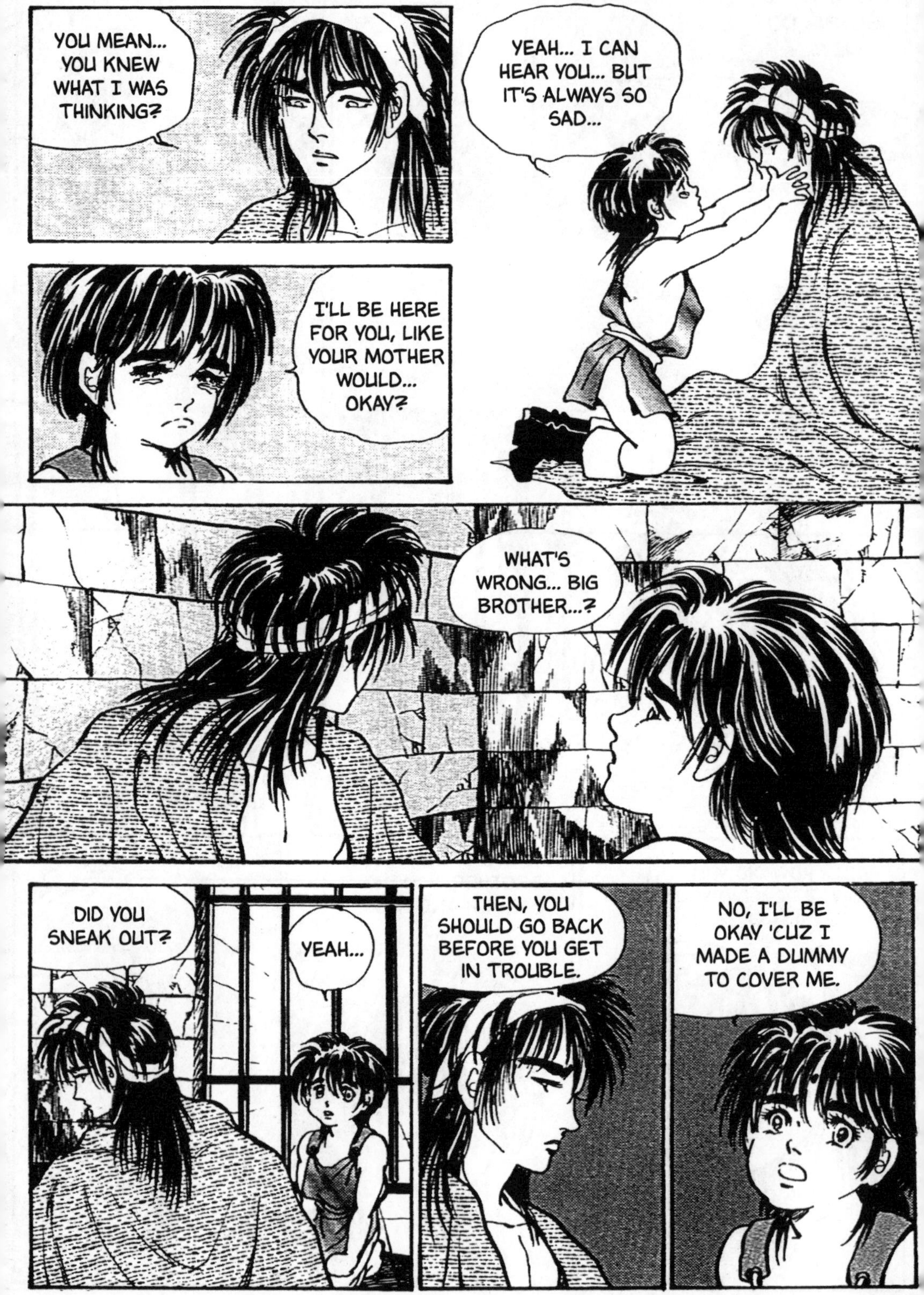
YOU MEAN... YOU KNEW WHAT I WAS THINKING?
YEAH... I CAN HEAR YOU... BUT IT'S ALWAYS SO SAD...
I'LL BE HERE FOR YOU, LIKE YOUR MOTHER WOULD... OKAY?
WHAT'S WRONG... BIG BROTHER...?
DID YOU SNEAK OUT?
YEAH...
THEN, YOU SHOULD GO BACK BEFORE YOU GET IN TROUBLE.
NO, I'LL BE OKAY 'CUZ I MADE A DUMMY TO COVER ME.

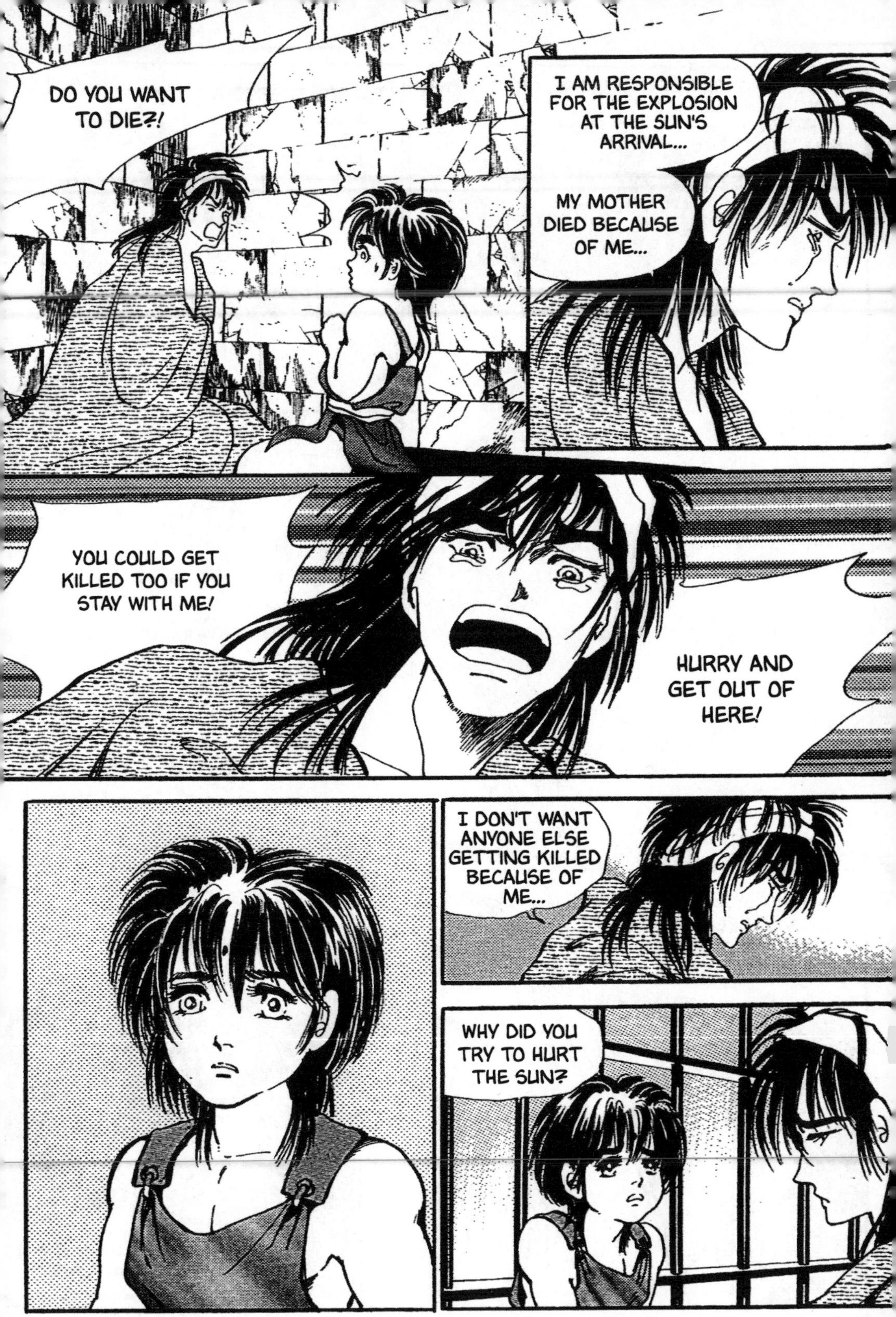
DO YOU WANT TO DIE?!
I AM RESPONSIBLE FOR THE EXPLOSION AT THE SUN'S ARRIVAL...
MY MOTHER DIED BECAUSE OF ME...
YOU COULD GET KILLED TOO IF YOU STAY WITH ME!
HURRY AND GET OUT OF HERE!
I DON'T WANT ANYONE ELSE GETTING KILLED BECAUSE OF ME...
WHY DID YOU TRY TO HURT THE SUN?

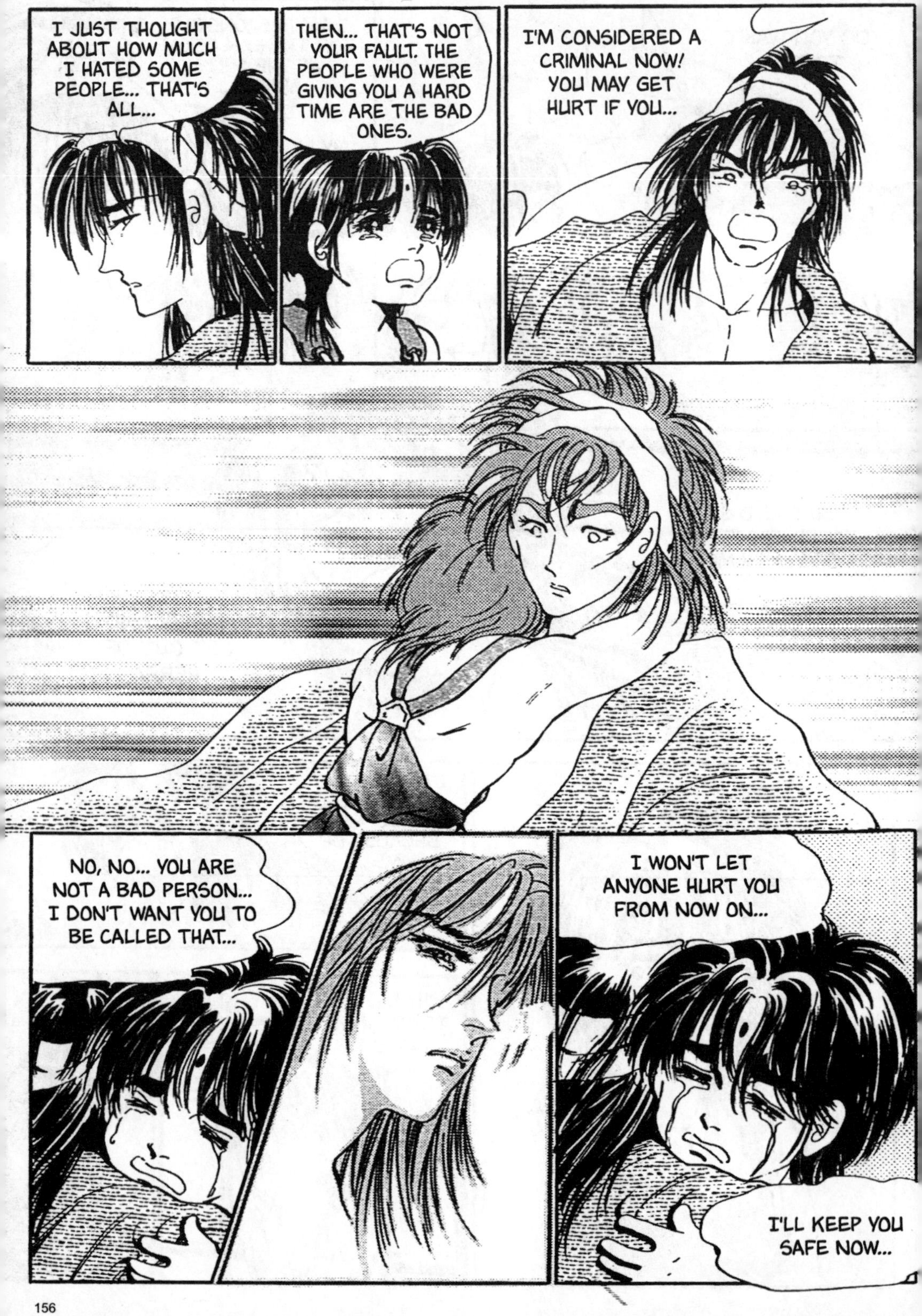
I JUST THOUGHT ABOUT HOW MUCH I HATED SOME PEOPLE... THAT'S ALL...
THEN... THAT'S NOT YOUR FAULT. THE PEOPLE WHO WERE GIVING YOU A HARD TIME ARE THE BAD ONES.
I'M CONSIDERED A CRIMINAL NOW! YOU MAY GET HURT IF YOU...
NO, NO... YOU ARE NOT A BAD PERSON... I DON'T WANT YOU TO BE CALLED THAT...
I WON'T LET ANYONE HURT YOU FROM NOW ON...
I'LL KEEP YOU SAFE NOW...

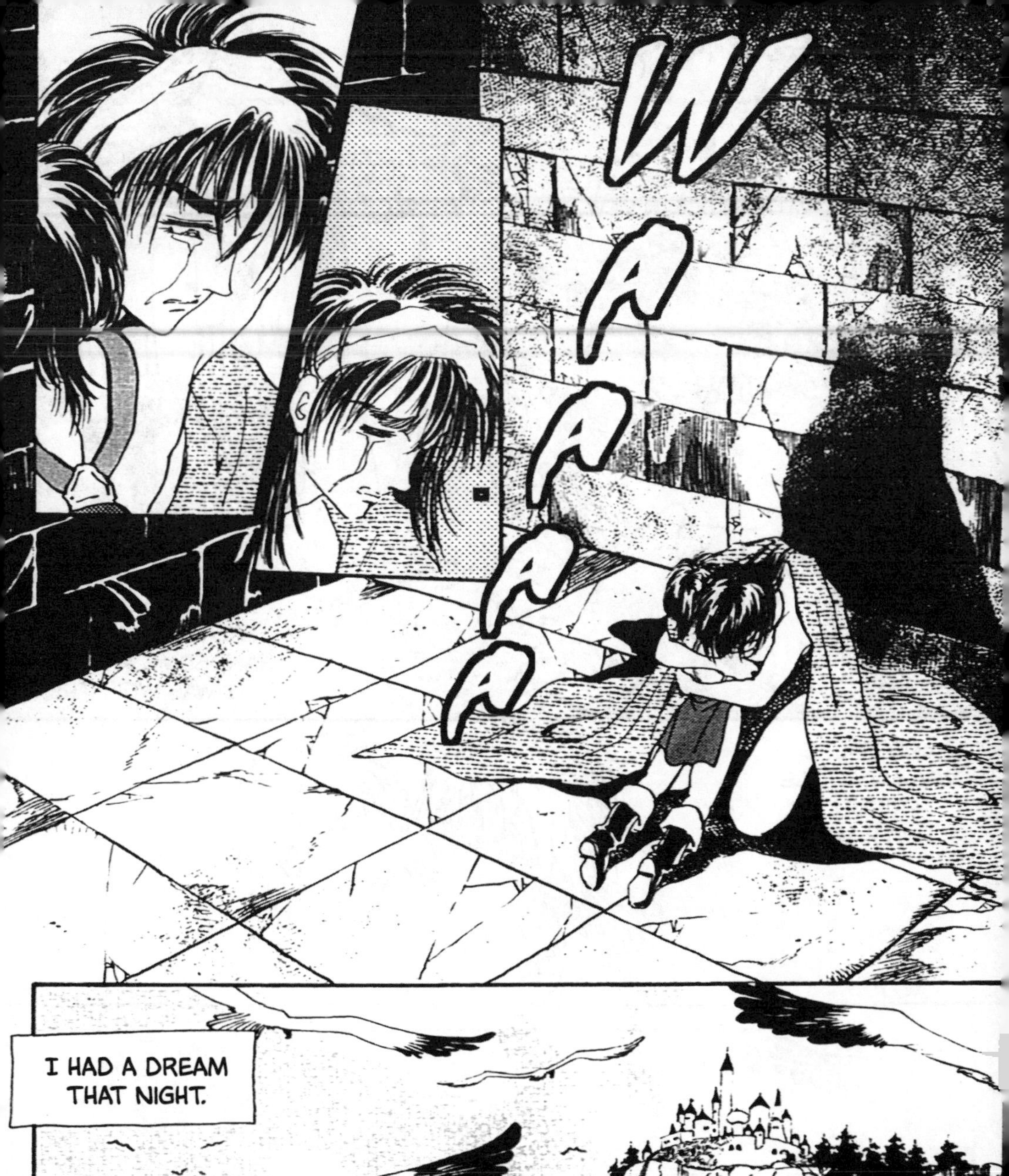
WAAAAA

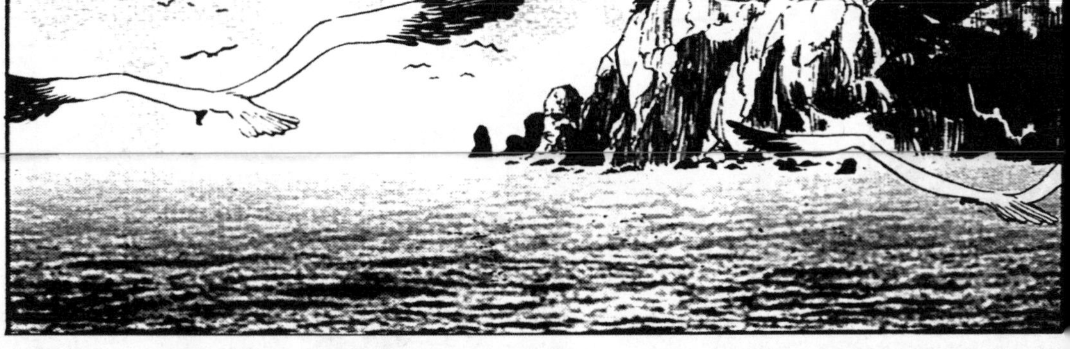
I HAD A DREAM
THAT NIGHT.

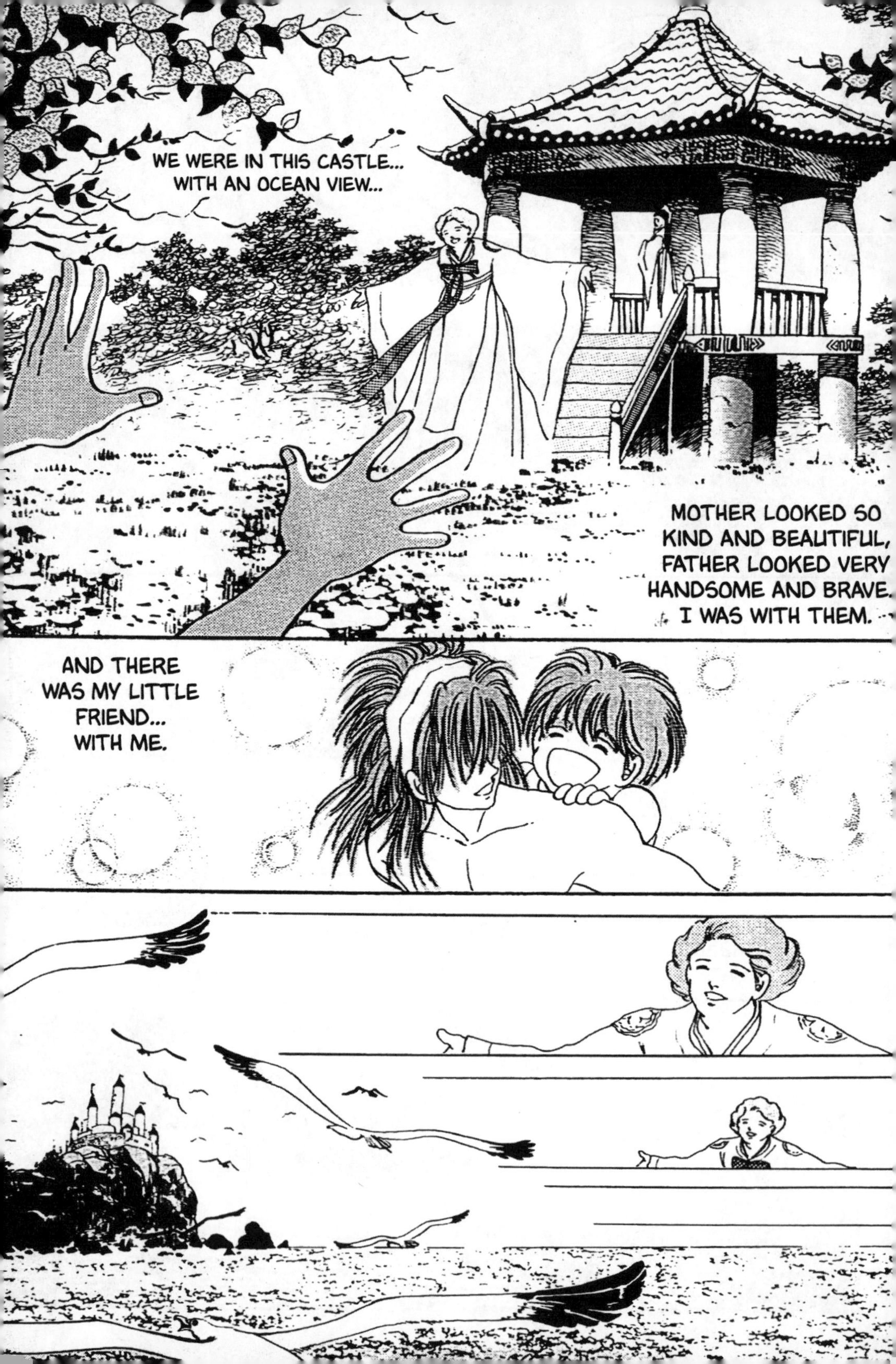
WE WERE IN THIS CASTLE... WITH AN OCEAN VIEW...
MOTHER LOOKED SO KIND AND BEAUTIFUL, FATHER LOOKED VERY HANDSOME AND BRAVE. I WAS WITH THEM.
AND THERE WAS MY LITTLE FRIEND... WITH ME.

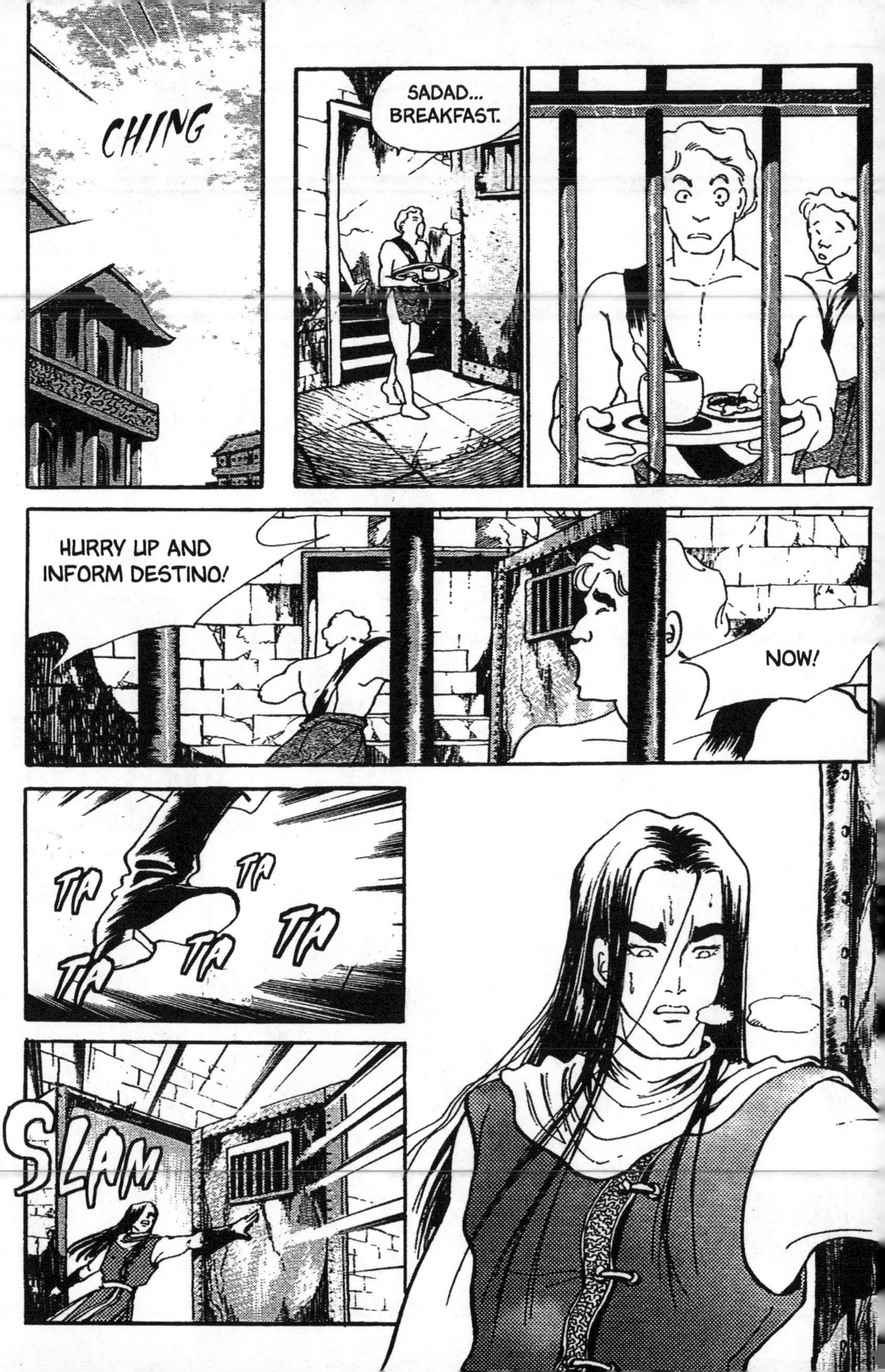
CHING
SADAD... BREAKFAST.
HURRY UP AND INFORM DESTINO!
NOW!
TA TA TA TA TA
SLAM

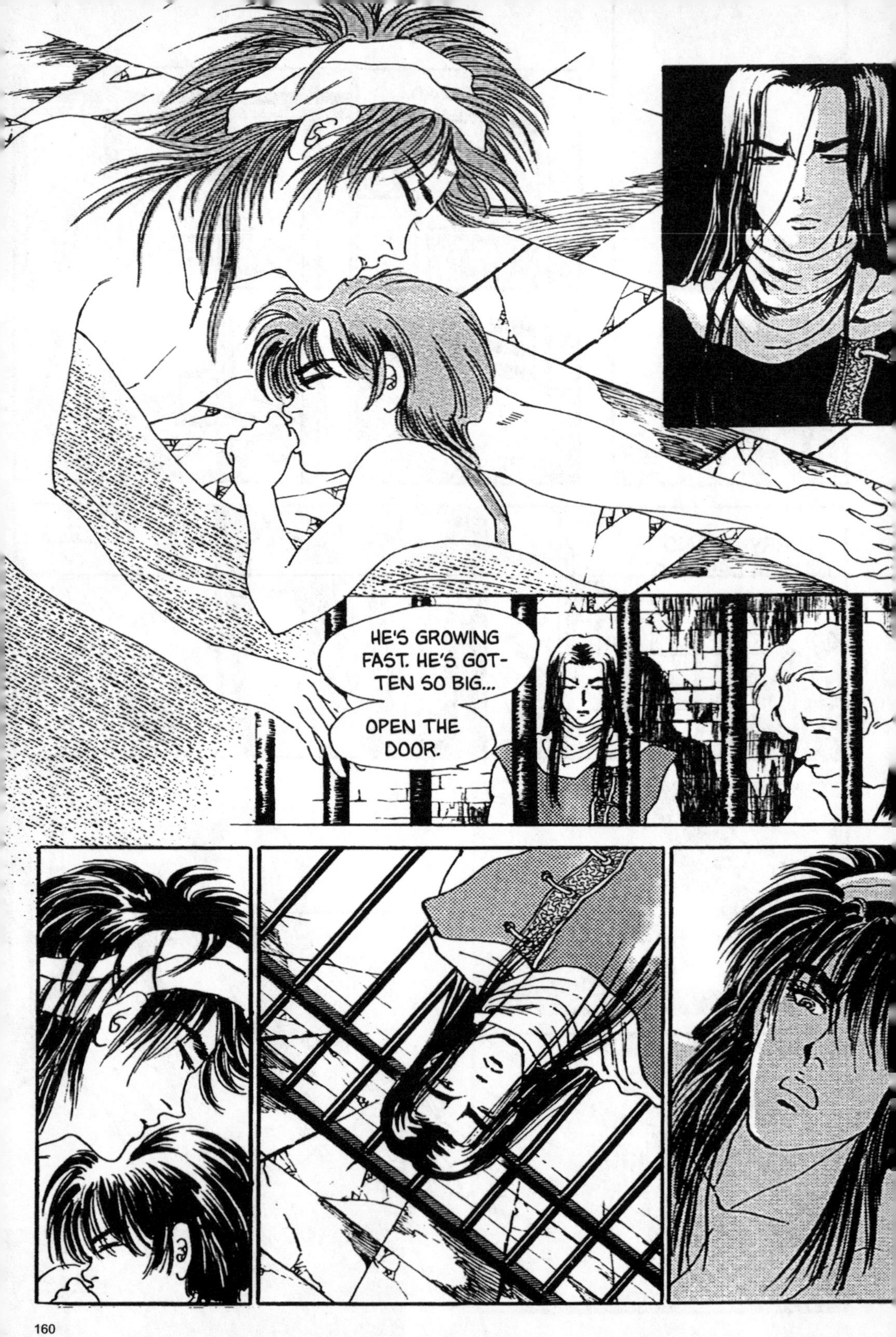

HE'S GROWING FAST. HE'S GOT-TEN SO BIG...
OPEN THE DOOR.

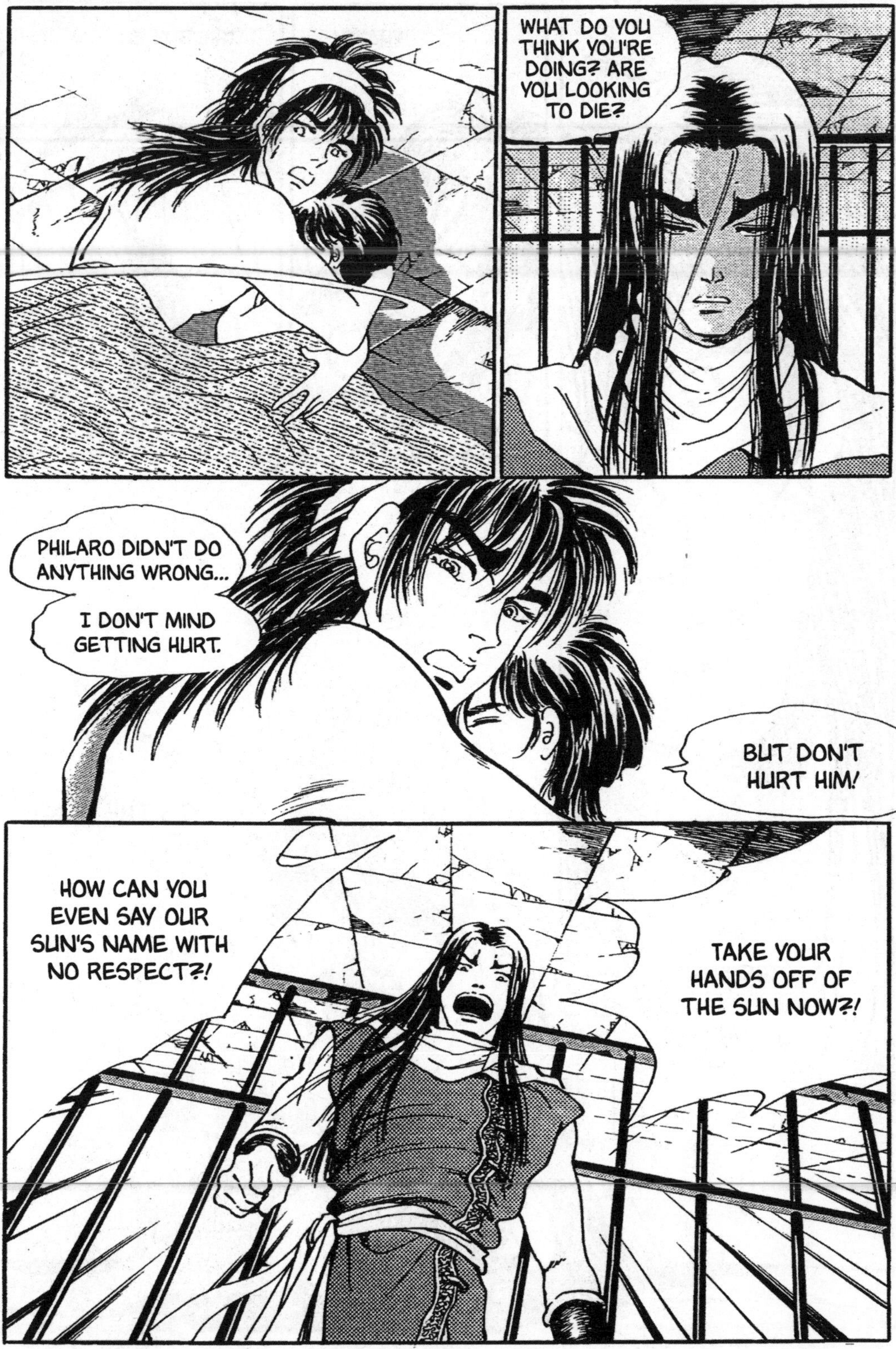
WHAT DO YOU THINK YOU'RE DOING? ARE YOU LOOKING TO DIE?
PHILARO DIDN'T DO ANYTHING WRONG...
I DON'T MIND GETTING HURT.
BUT DON'T HURT HIM!
TAKE YOUR HANDS OFF OF THE SUN NOW?!
HOW CAN YOU EVEN SAY OUR SUN'S NAME WITH NO RESPECT?!

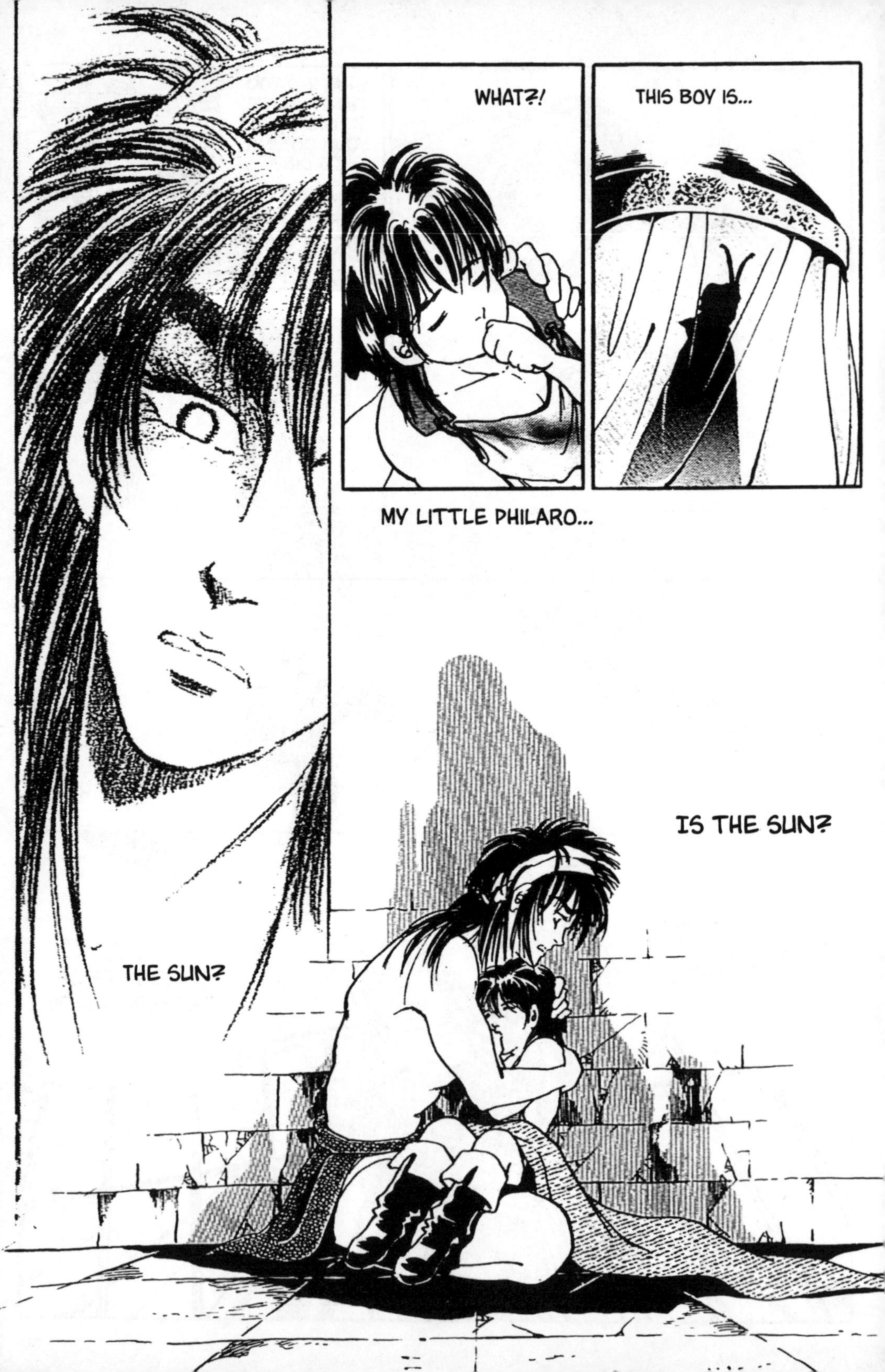

WHAT?!
THIS BOY IS...
MY LITTLE PHILARO...
THE SUN?
IS THE SUN?

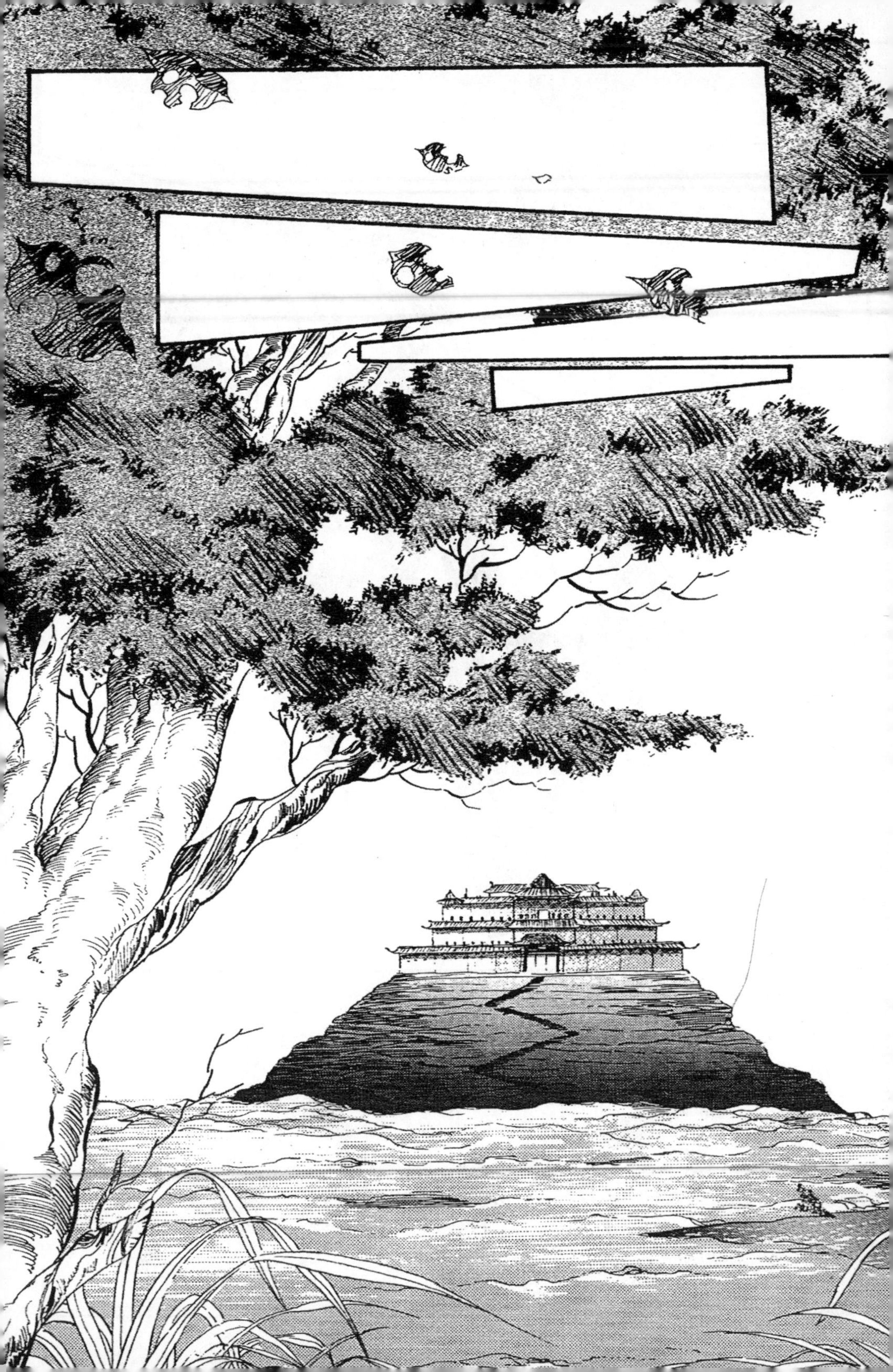

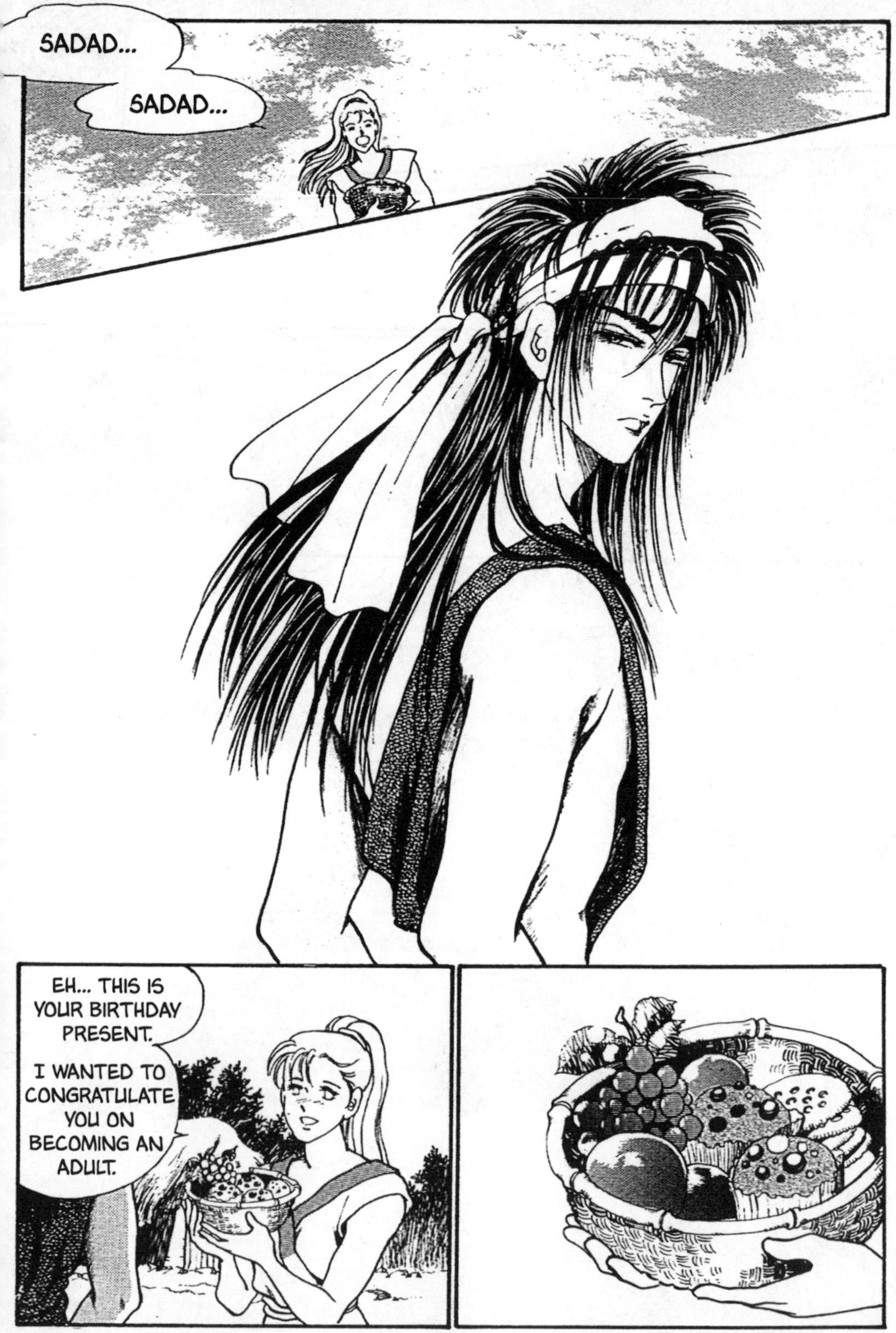
SADAD...
SADAD...
EH... THIS IS YOUR BIRTHDAY PRESENT.
I WANTED TO CONGRATULATE YOU ON BECOMING AN ADULT.

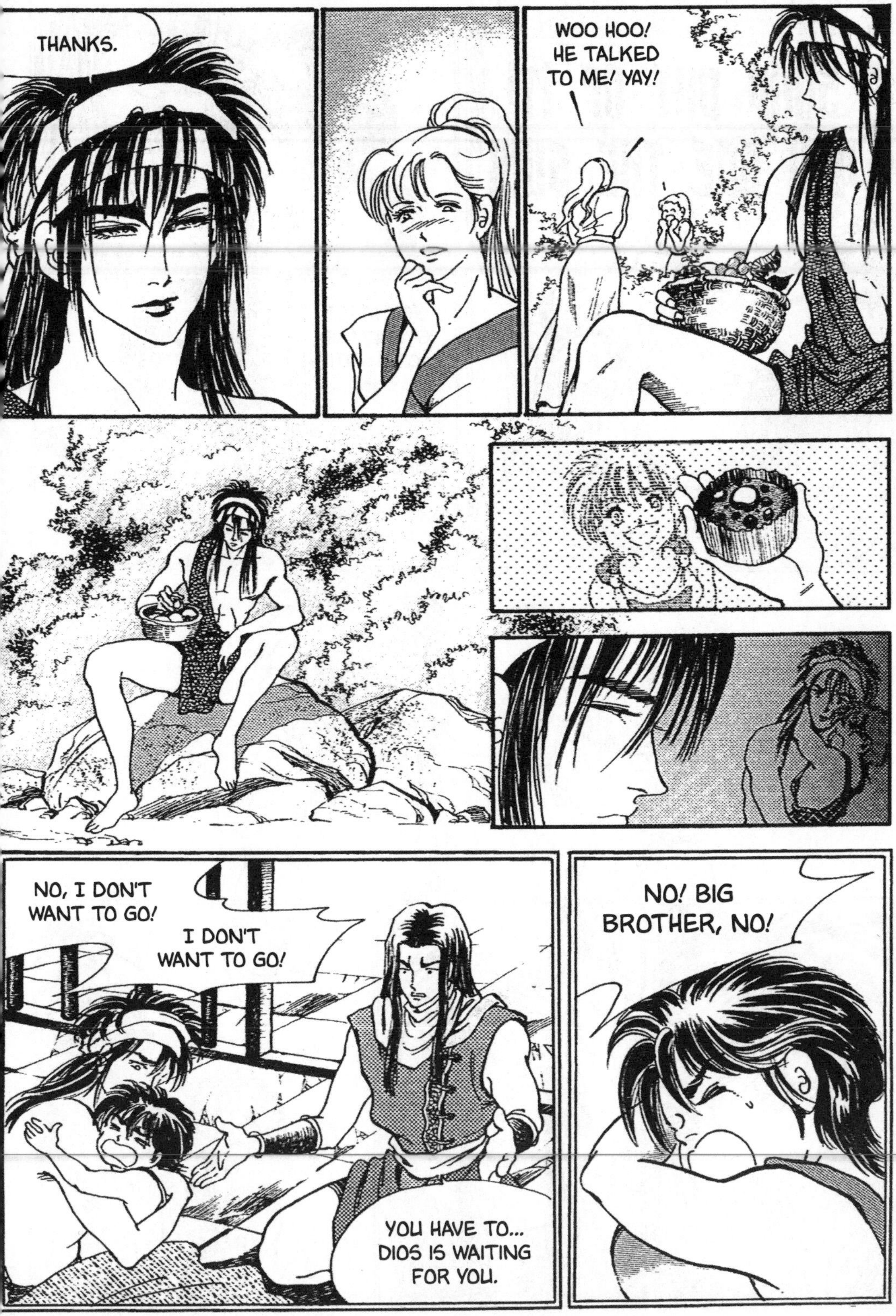
THANKS.
WOO HOO! HE TALKED TO ME! YAY!
NO, I DON'T WANT TO GO!
I DON'T WANT TO GO!
YOU HAVE TO... DIOS IS WAITING FOR YOU.
NO! BIG BROTHER, NO!

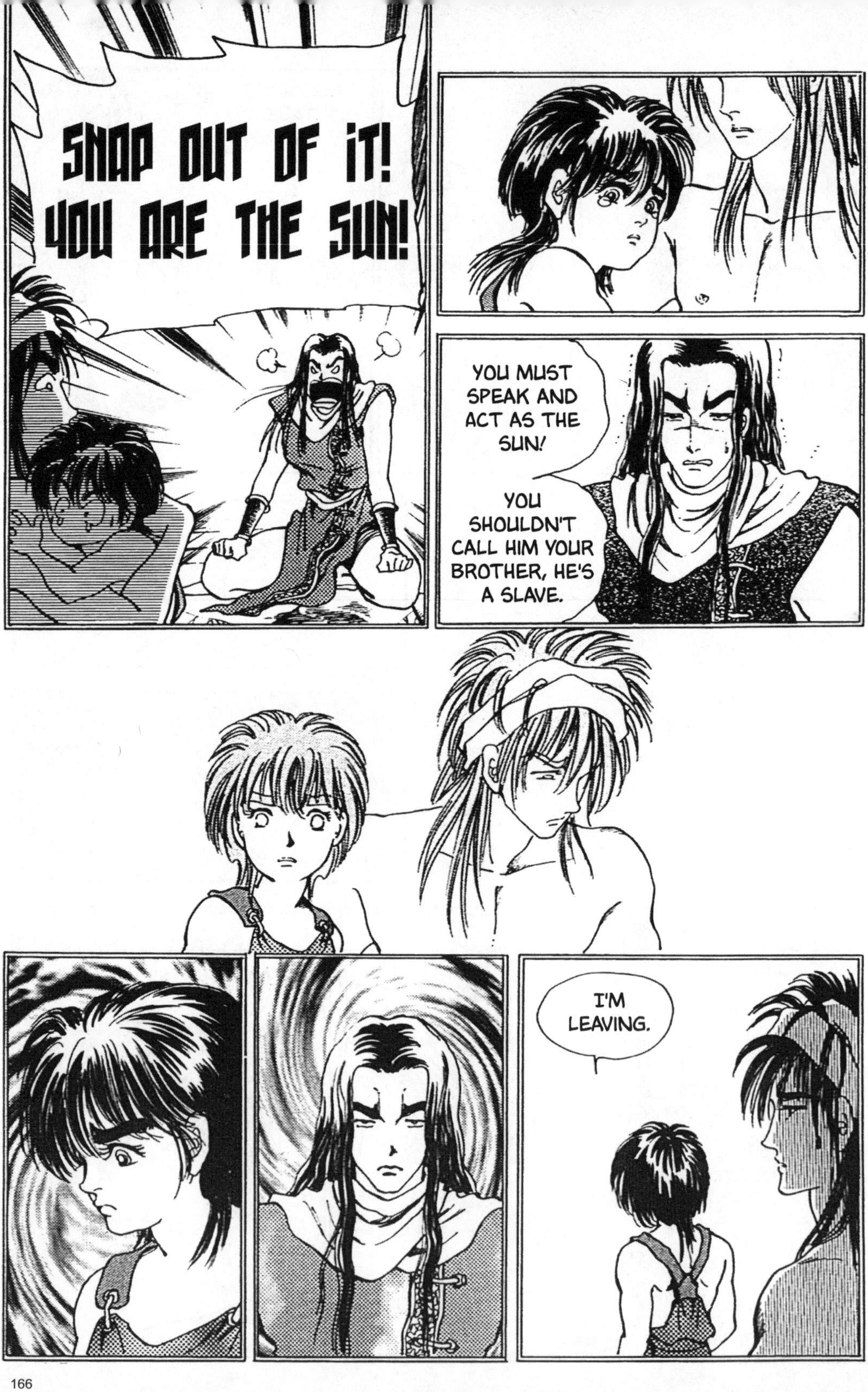
SNAP OUT OF IT! YOU ARE THE SUN!
YOU MUST SPEAK AND ACT AS THE SUN!
YOU SHOULDN'T CALL HIM YOUR BROTHER, HE'S A SLAVE.
I'M LEAVING.

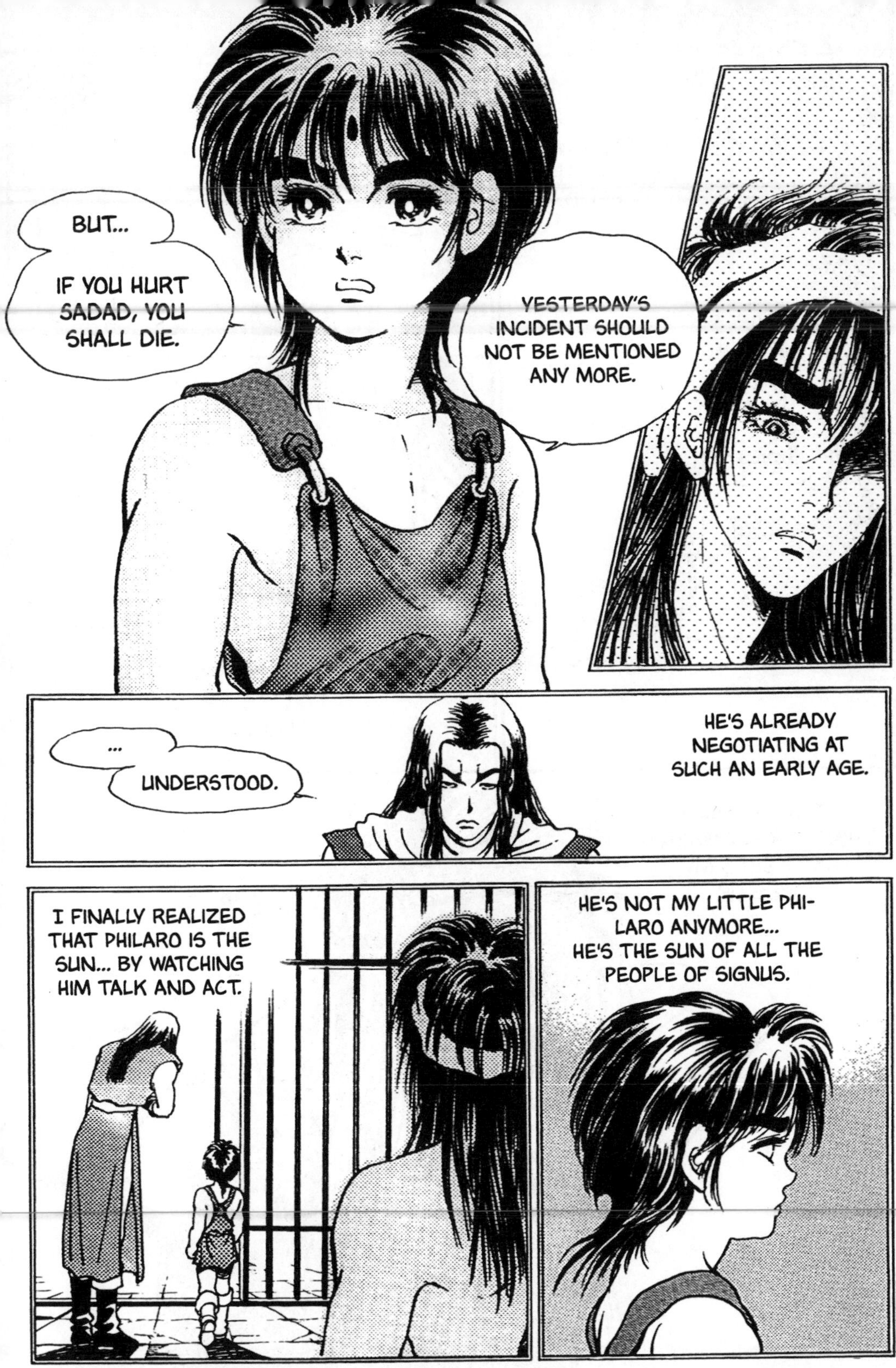
YESTERDAY'S INCIDENT SHOULD NOT BE MENTIONED ANY MORE.
BUT...
IF YOU HURT SADAD, YOU SHALL DIE.
HE'S ALREADY NEGOTIATING AT SUCH AN EARLY AGE.
...
UNDERSTOOD.
HE'S NOT MY LITTLE PHI-LARO ANYMORE... HE'S THE SUN OF ALL THE PEOPLE OF SIGNUS.
I FINALLY REALIZED THAT PHILARO IS THE SUN... BY WATCHING HIM TALK AND ACT.

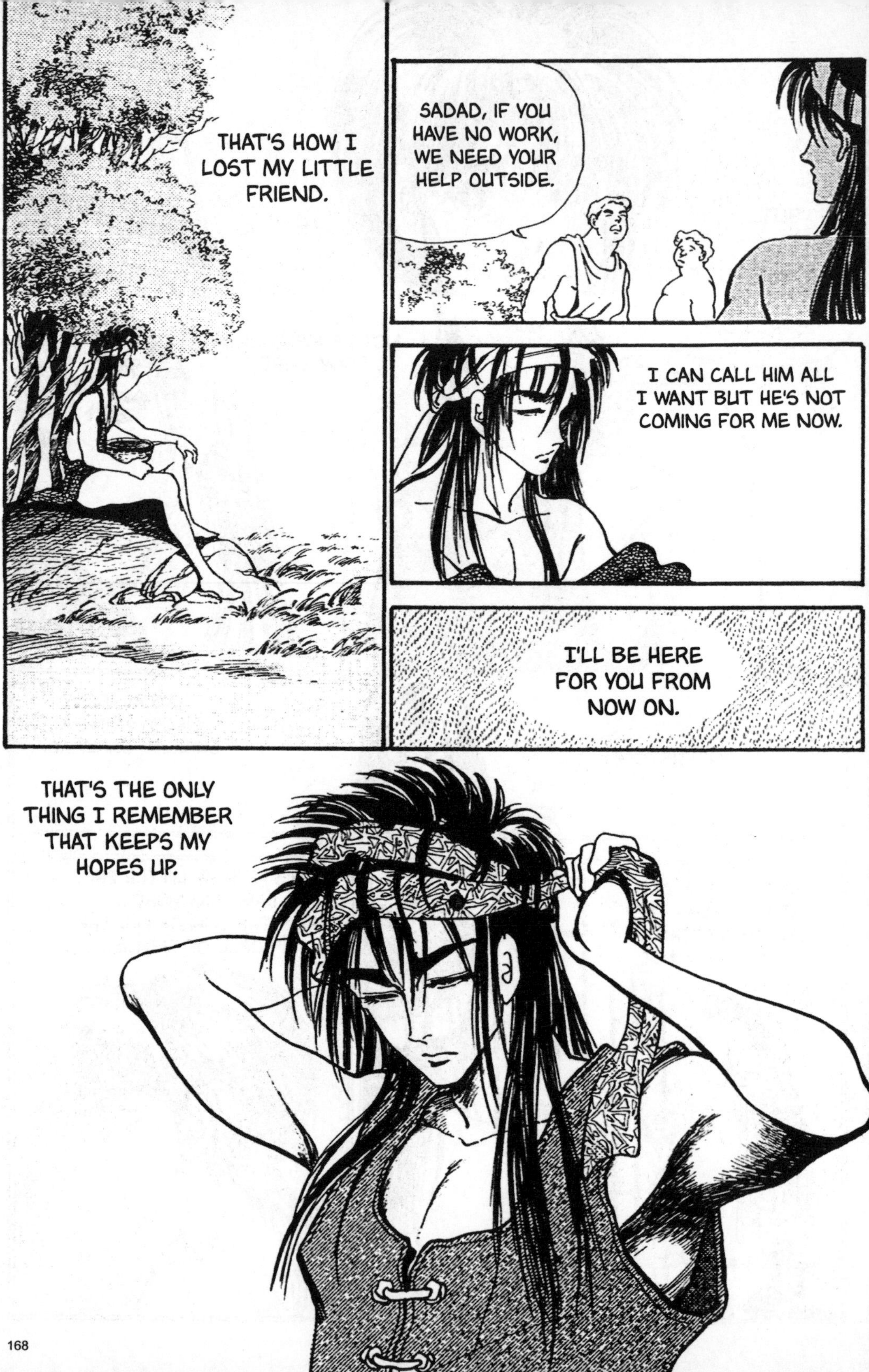
THAT'S HOW I LOST MY LITTLE FRIEND.
SADAD, IF YOU HAVE NO WORK, WE NEED YOUR HELP OUTSIDE.
I CAN CALL HIM ALL I WANT BUT HE'S NOT COMING FOR ME NOW.
I'LL BE HERE FOR YOU FROM NOW ON.
THAT'S THE ONLY THING I REMEMBER THAT KEEPS MY HOPES UP.

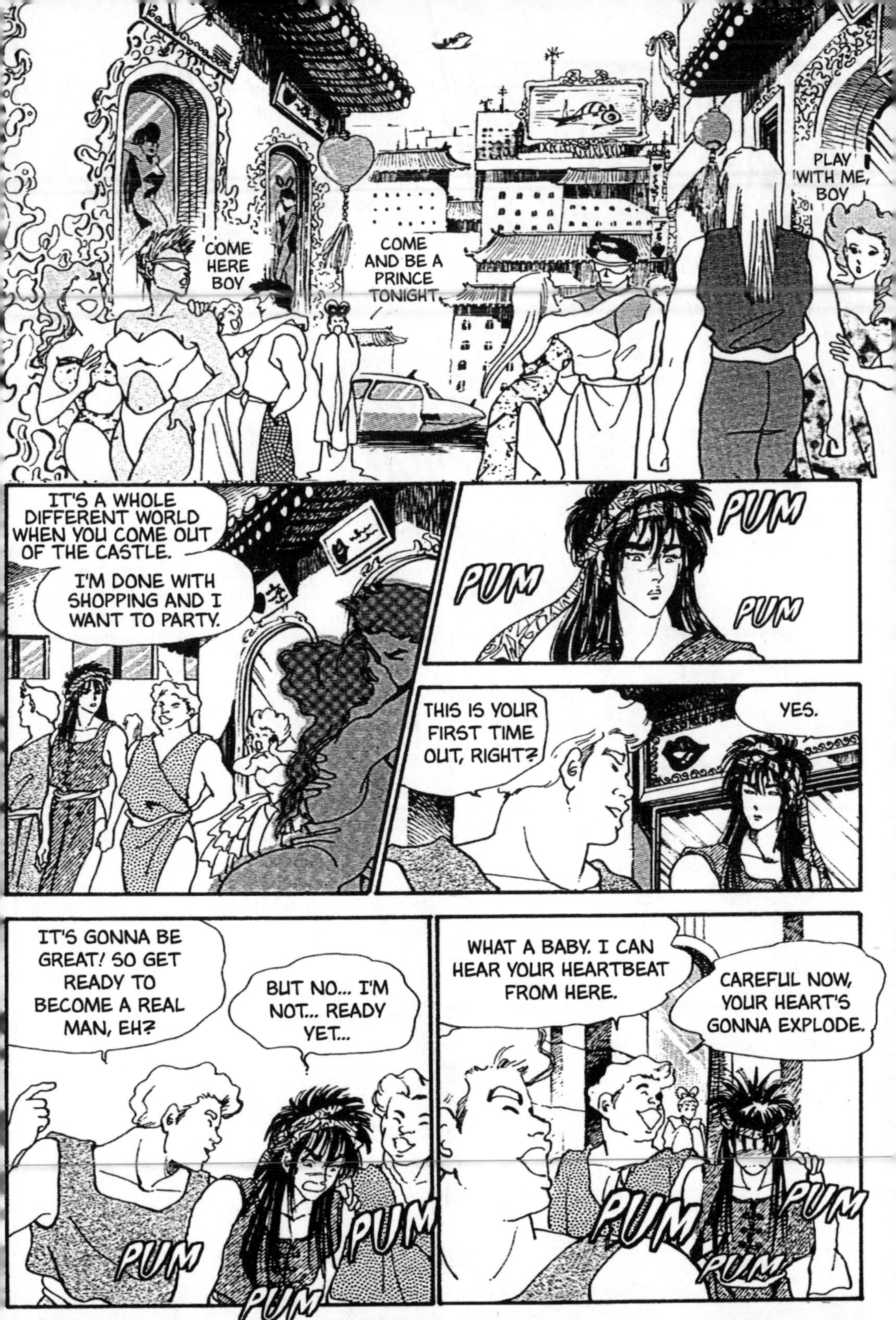

COME HERE BOY
COME AND BE A PRINCE TONIGHT
PLAY WITH ME, BOY
IT'S A WHOLE DIFFERENT WORLD WHEN YOU COME OUT OF THE CASTLE.
I'M DONE WITH SHOPPING AND I WANT TO PARTY.
PUM
PUM
PUM
THIS IS YOUR FIRST TIME OUT, RIGHT?
YES.
IT'S GONNA BE GREAT! SO GET READY TO BECOME A REAL MAN, EH?
BUT NO... I'M NOT... READY YET...
PUM
PUM
PUM
WHAT A BABY. I CAN HEAR YOUR HEARTBEAT FROM HERE.
CAREFUL NOW, YOUR HEART'S GONNA EXPLODE.
PUM
PUM
PUM

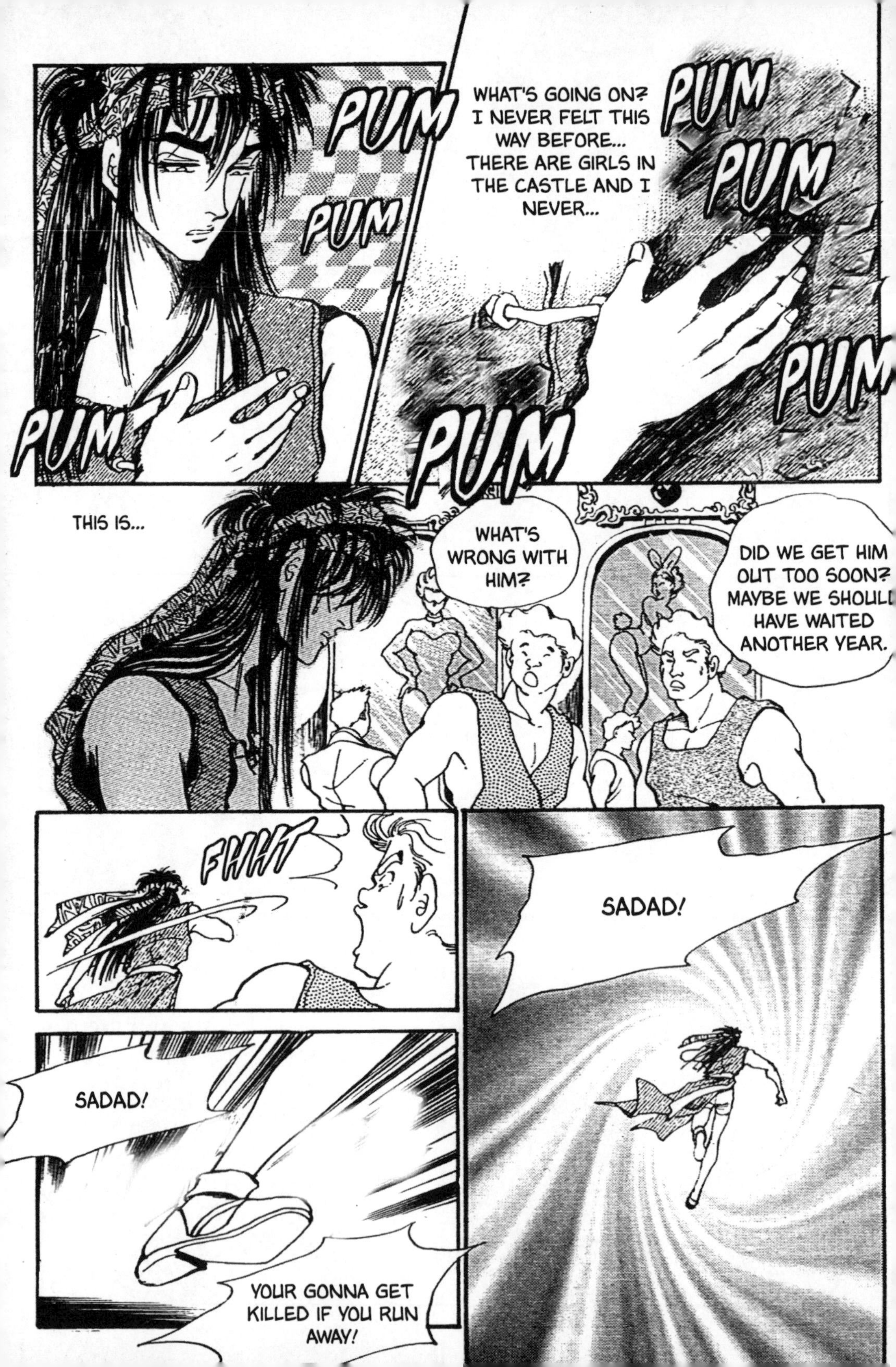
PUM
PUM
PUM
WHAT'S GOING ON? I NEVER FELT THIS WAY BEFORE... THERE ARE GIRLS IN THE CASTLE AND I NEVER...
PUM
PUM
PUM
PUM
THIS IS...
WHAT'S WRONG WITH HIM?
DID WE GET HIM OUT TOO SOON? MAYBE WE SHOULD HAVE WAITED ANOTHER YEAR.
FHHT
SADAD!
SADAD!
YOUR GONNA GET KILLED IF YOU RUN AWAY!

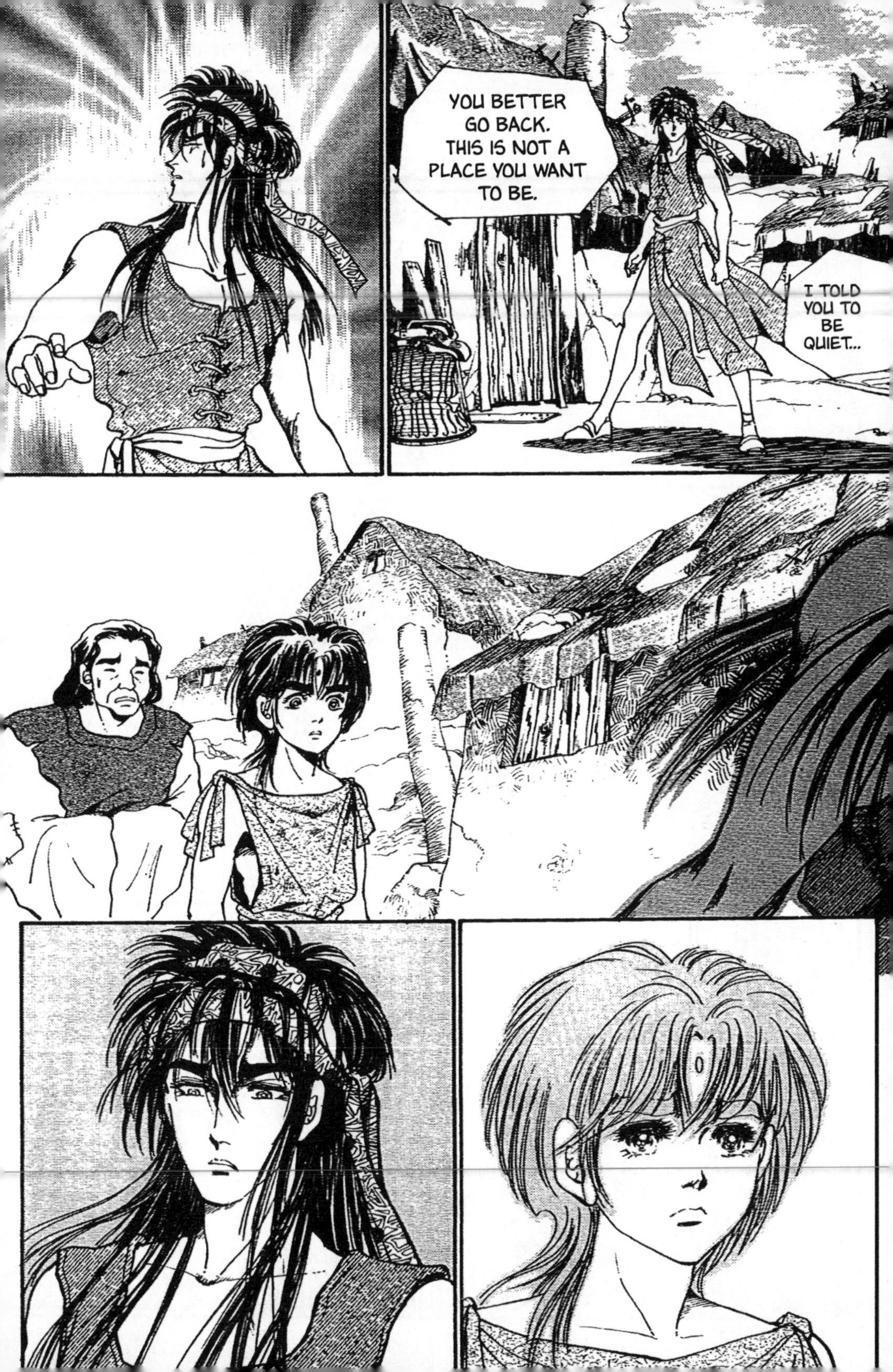
YOU BETTER GO BACK. THIS IS NOT A PLACE YOU WANT TO BE.
I TOLD YOU TO BE QUIET...

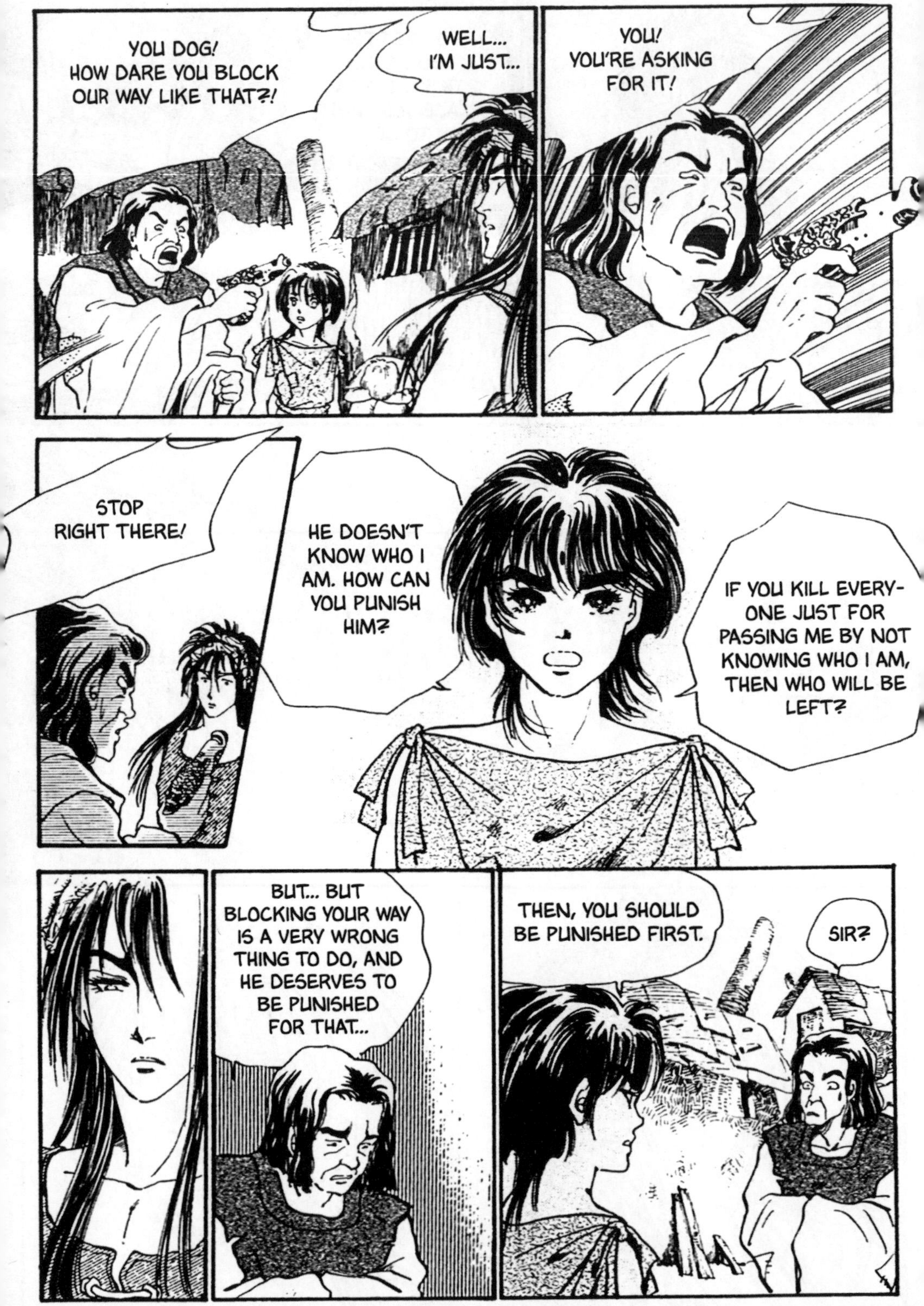
YOU DOG! HOW DARE YOU BLOCK OUR WAY LIKE THAT?!
WELL... I'M JUST...
YOU! YOU'RE ASKING FOR IT!
STOP RIGHT THERE!
HE DOESN'T KNOW WHO I AM. HOW CAN YOU PUNISH HIM?
IF YOU KILL EVERY-ONE JUST FOR PASSING ME BY NOT KNOWING WHO I AM, THEN WHO WILL BE LEFT?
BUT... BUT BLOCKING YOUR WAY IS A VERY WRONG THING TO DO, AND HE DESERVES TO BE PUNISHED FOR THAT...
THEN, YOU SHOULD BE PUNISHED FIRST.
SIR?

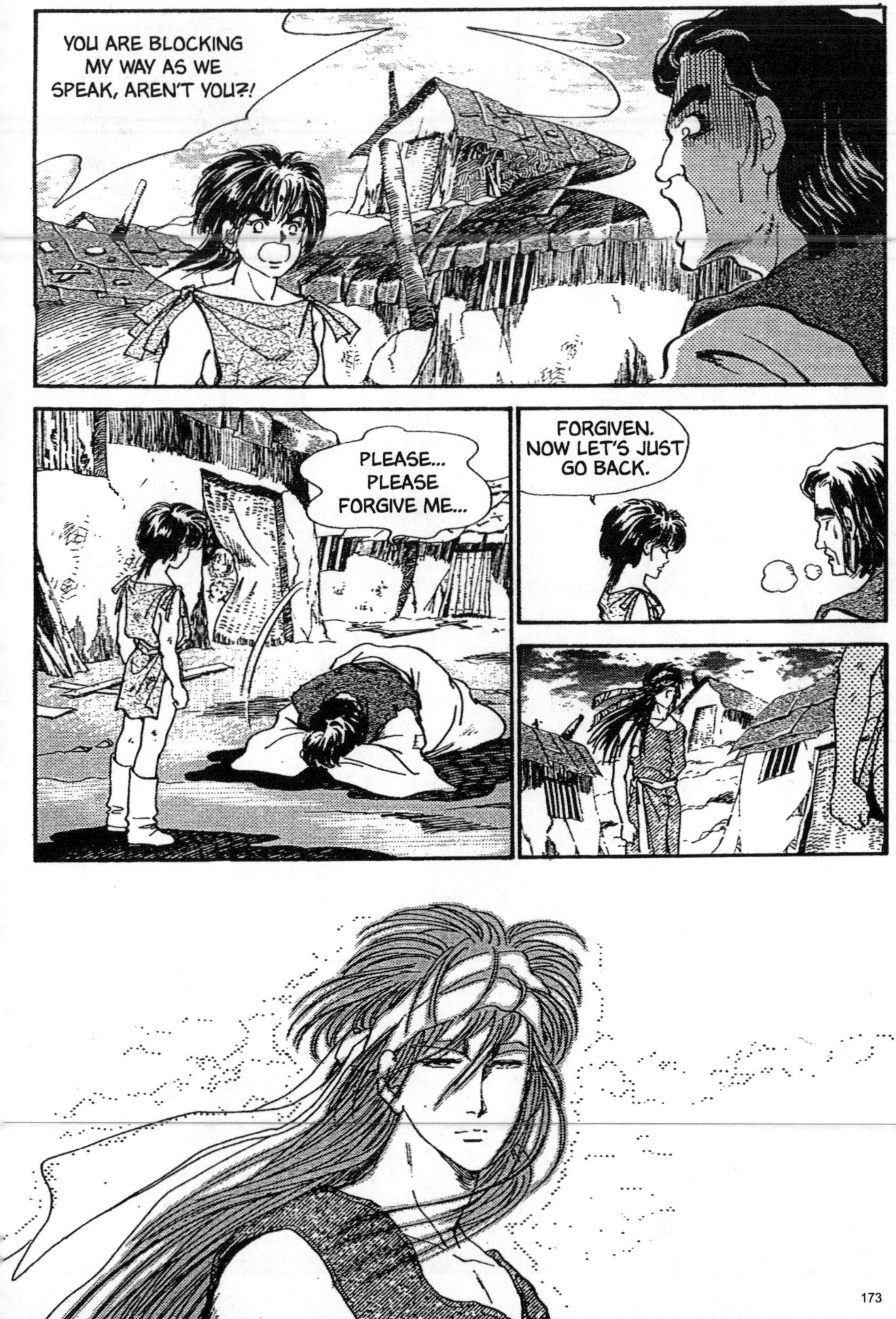
YOU ARE BLOCKING MY WAY AS WE SPEAK, AREN'T YOU?!
PLEASE... PLEASE FORGIVE ME...
FORGIVEN. NOW LET'S JUST GO BACK.

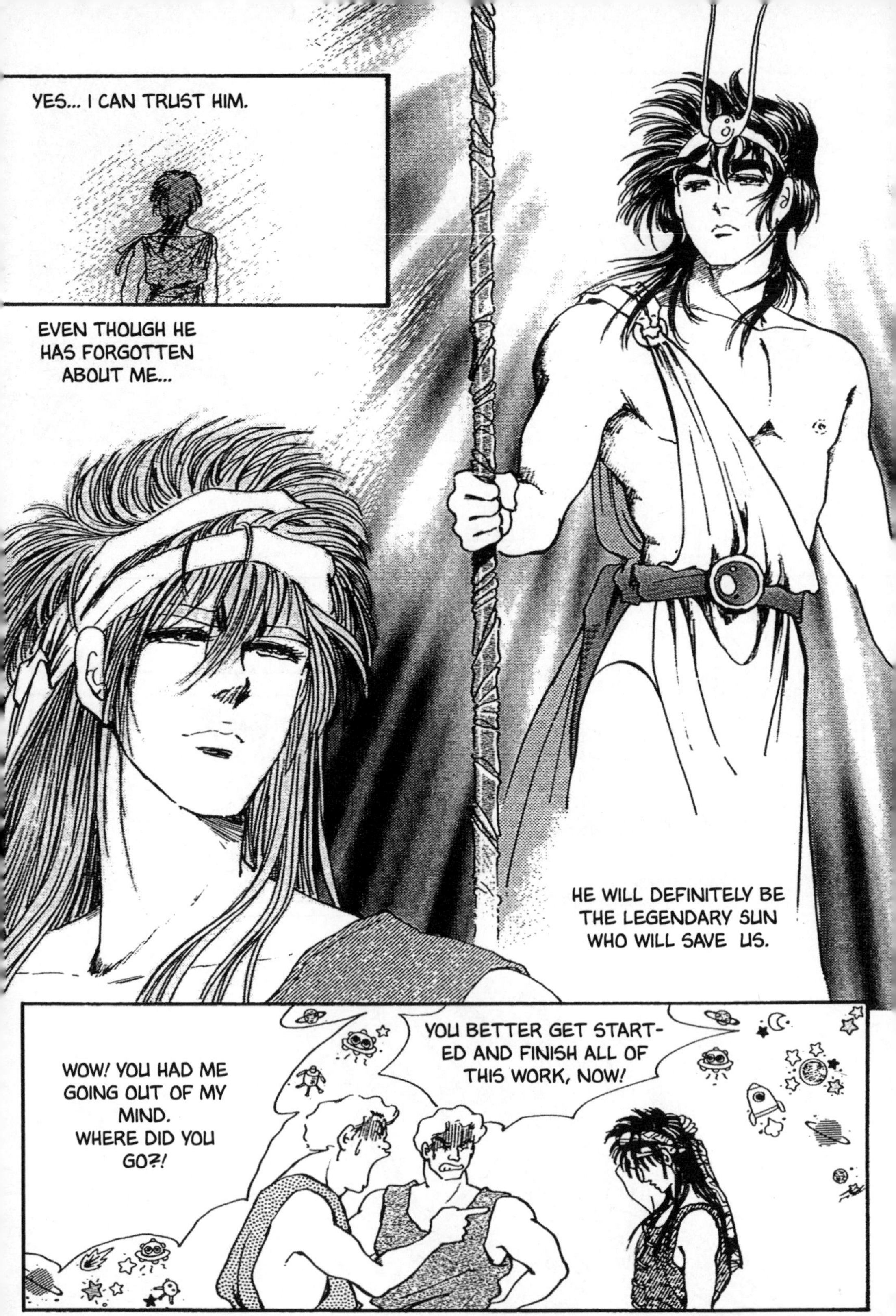
YES... I CAN TRUST HIM.
EVEN THOUGH HE HAS FORGOTTEN ABOUT ME...
HE WILL DEFINITELY BE THE LEGENDARY SUN WHO WILL SAVE US.
WOW! YOU HAD ME GOING OUT OF MY MIND. WHERE DID YOU GO?!
YOU BETTER GET START-ED AND FINISH ALL OF THIS WORK, NOW!

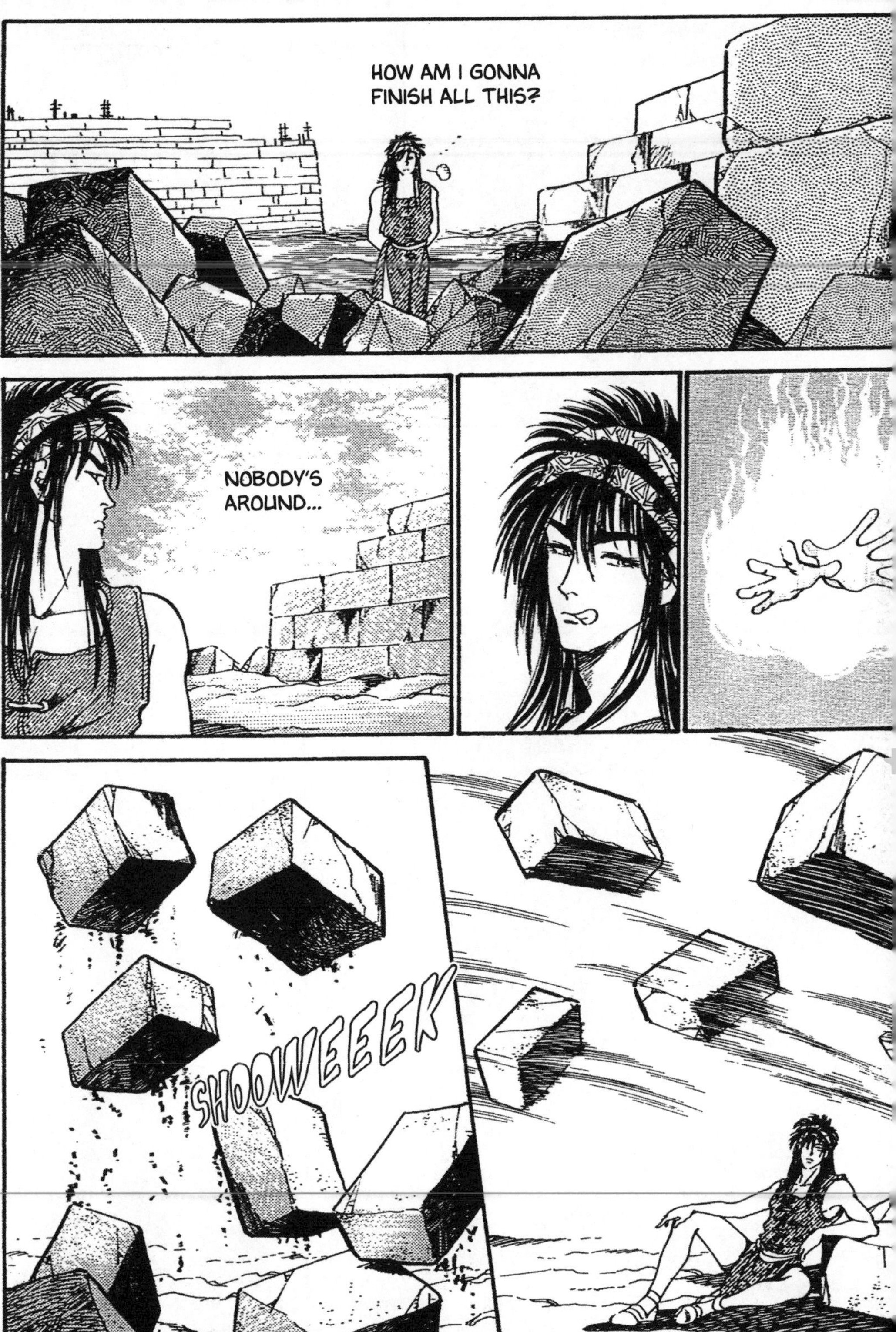
HOW AM I GONNA
FINISH ALL THIS?
NOBODY'S
AROUND...
SHOOWEEEK

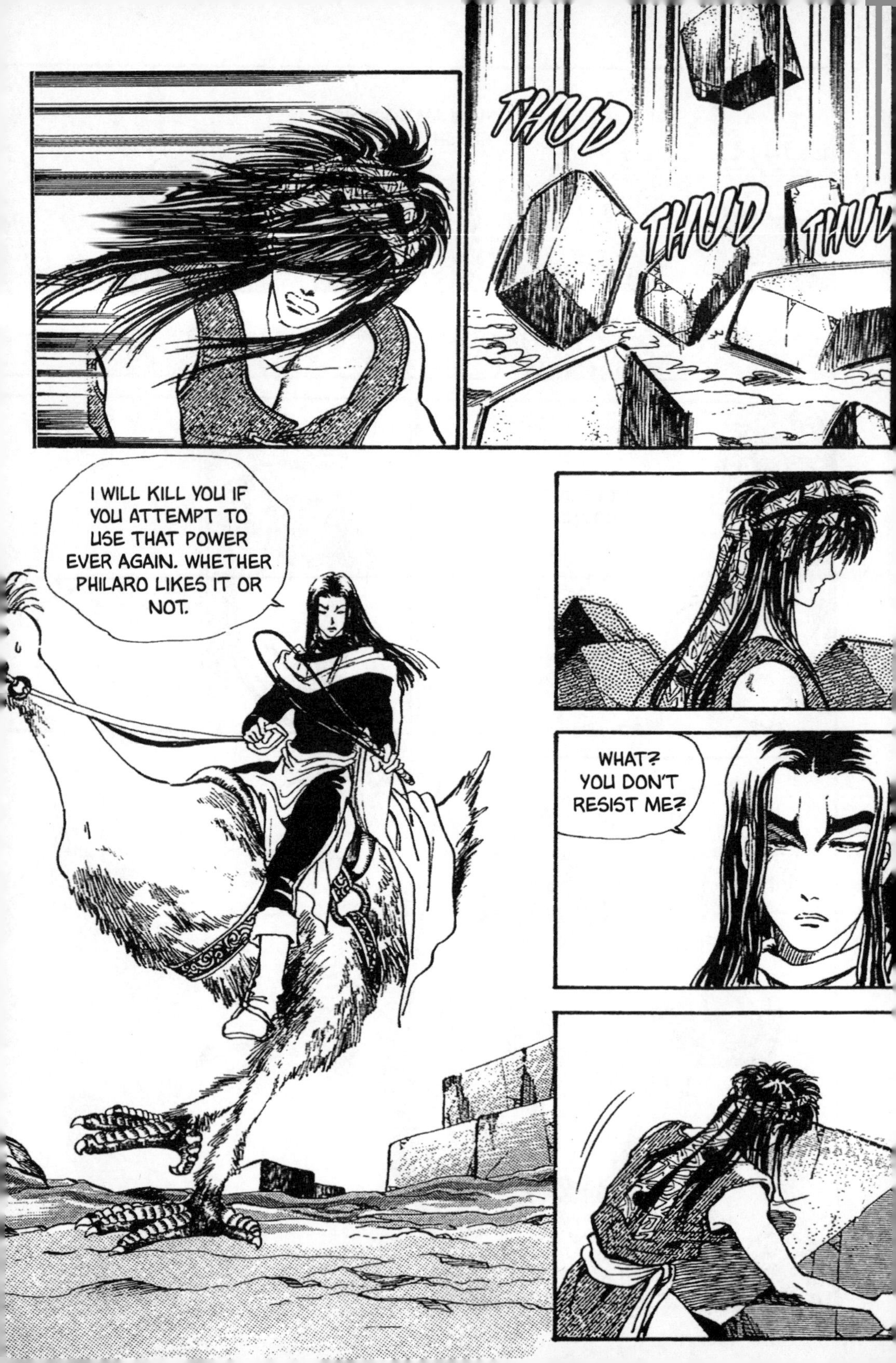
THUD
THUD
THUD
I WILL KILL YOU IF YOU ATTEMPT TO USE THAT POWER EVER AGAIN. WHETHER PHILARO LIKES IT OR NOT.
WHAT? YOU DON'T RESIST ME?

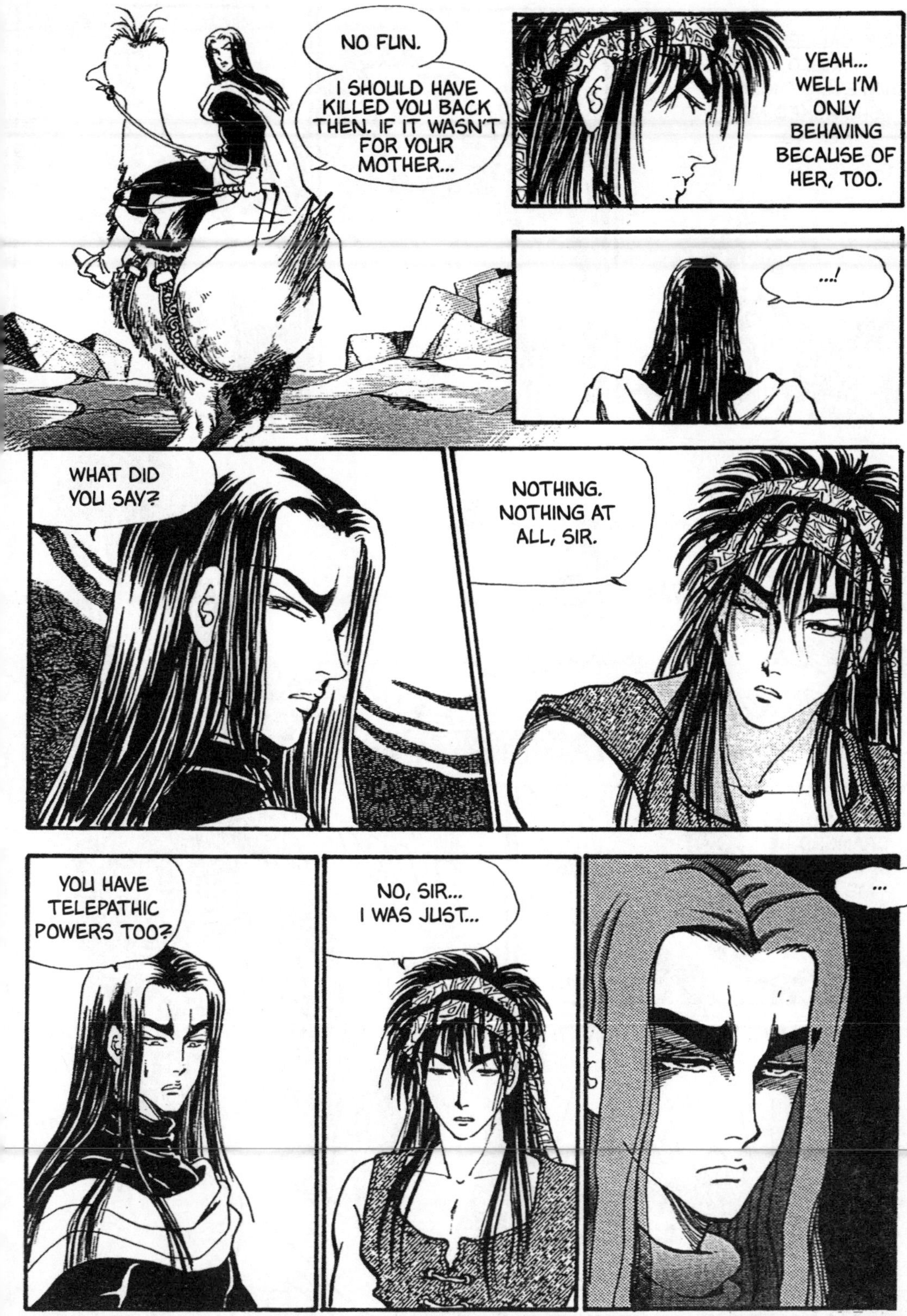
NO FUN.
I SHOULD HAVE KILLED YOU BACK THEN. IF IT WASN'T FOR YOUR MOTHER...
YEAH... WELL I'M ONLY BEHAVING BECAUSE OF HER, TOO.
...!
WHAT DID YOU SAY?
NOTHING. NOTHING AT ALL, SIR.
YOU HAVE TELEPATHIC POWERS TOO?
NO, SIR... I WAS JUST...
...

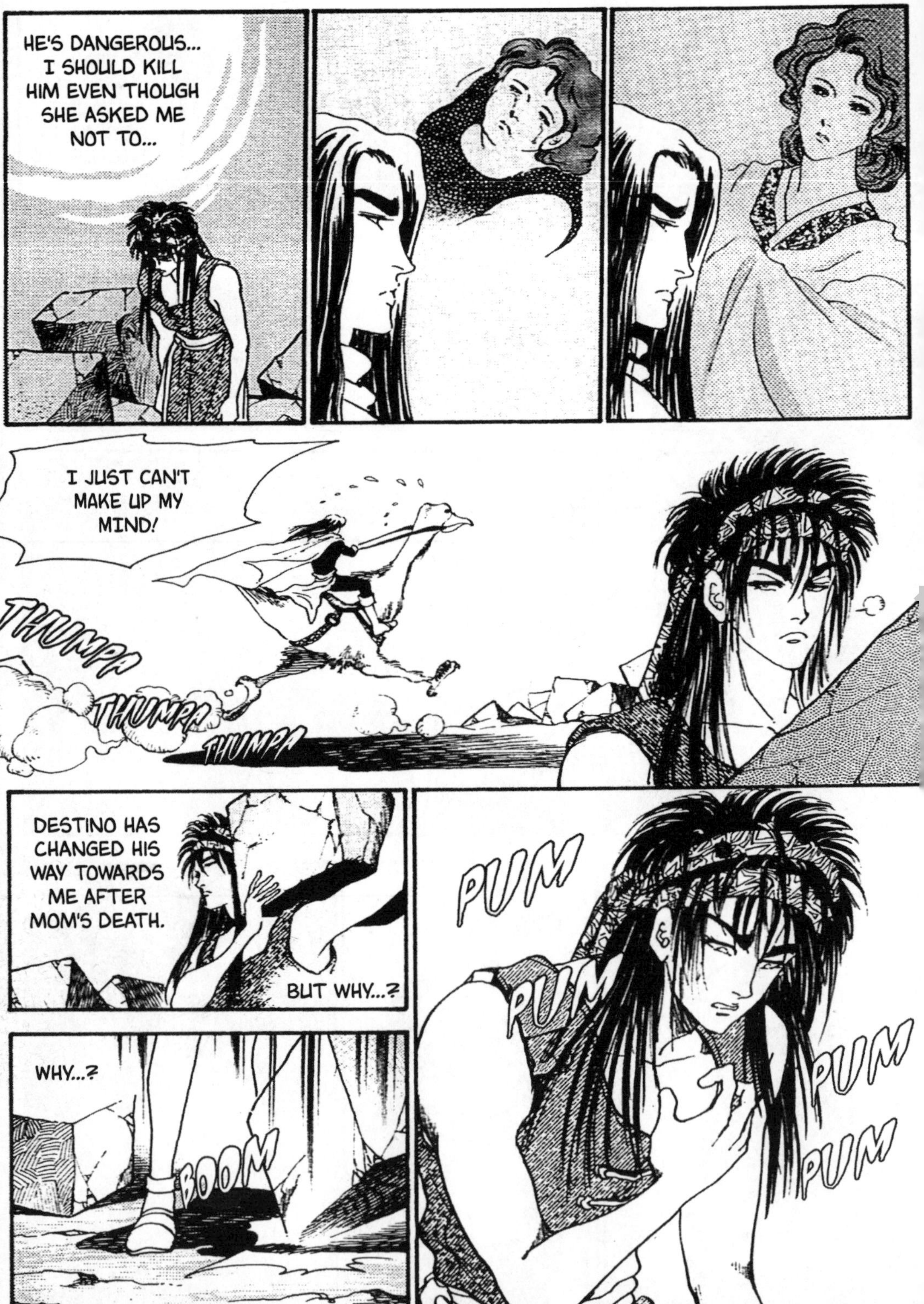
HE'S DANGEROUS... I SHOULD KILL HIM EVEN THOUGH SHE ASKED ME NOT TO...
I JUST CAN'T MAKE UP MY MIND!
THUMPA
THUMPA
THUMPA
DESTINO HAS CHANGED HIS WAY TOWARDS ME AFTER MOM'S DEATH.
BUT WHY...?
WHY...?
BOOM
PUM
PUM
PUM
PUM

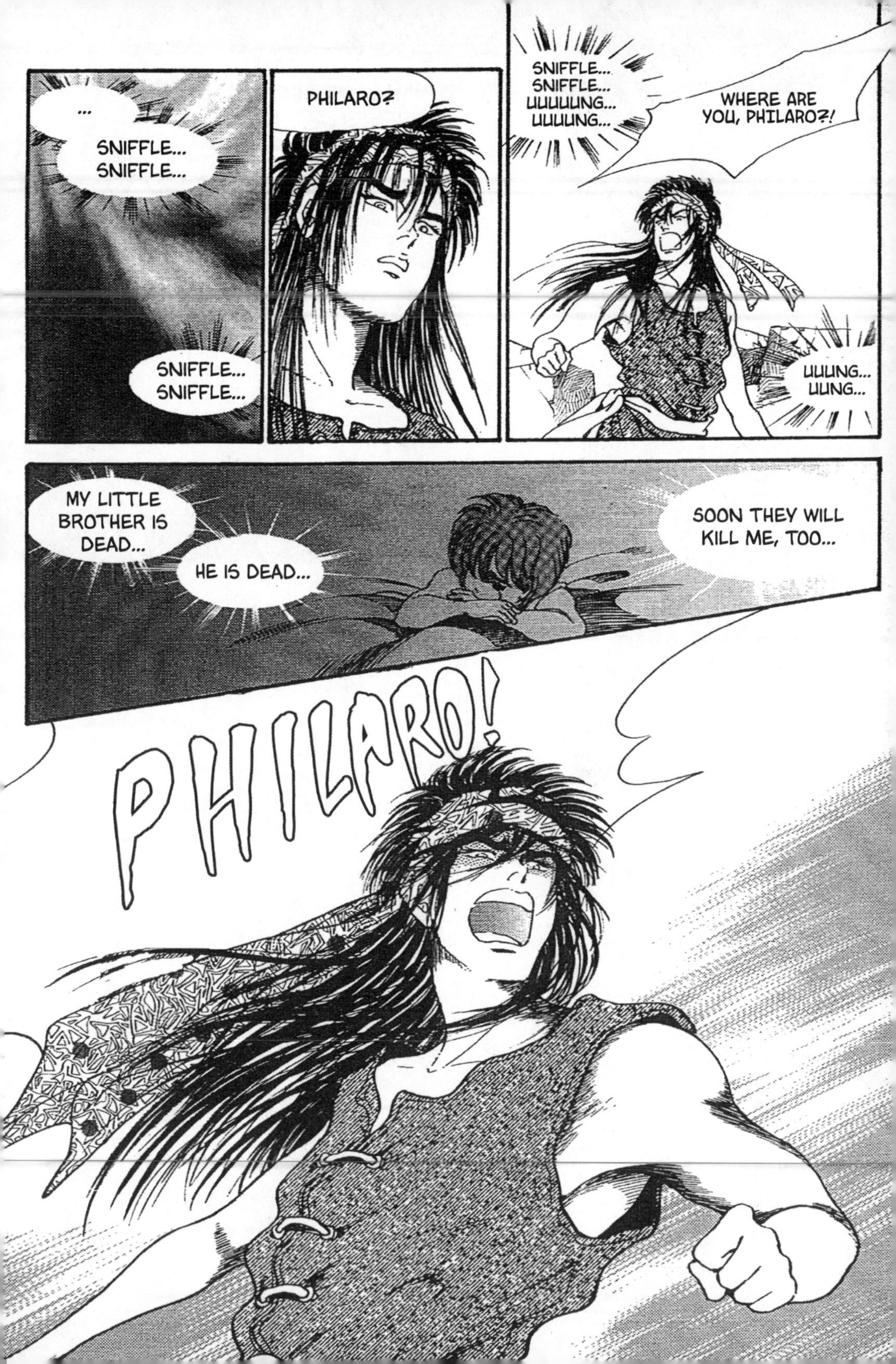
...
SNIFFLE... SNIFFLE...
SNIFFLE... SNIFFLE...
PHILARO?
SNIFFLE... SNIFFLE... UUUUUNG... UUUUNG...
WHERE ARE YOU, PHILARO?!
UUUNG... UUNG...
MY LITTLE BROTHER IS DEAD...
HE IS DEAD...
SOON THEY WILL KILL ME, TOO...
PHILARO!

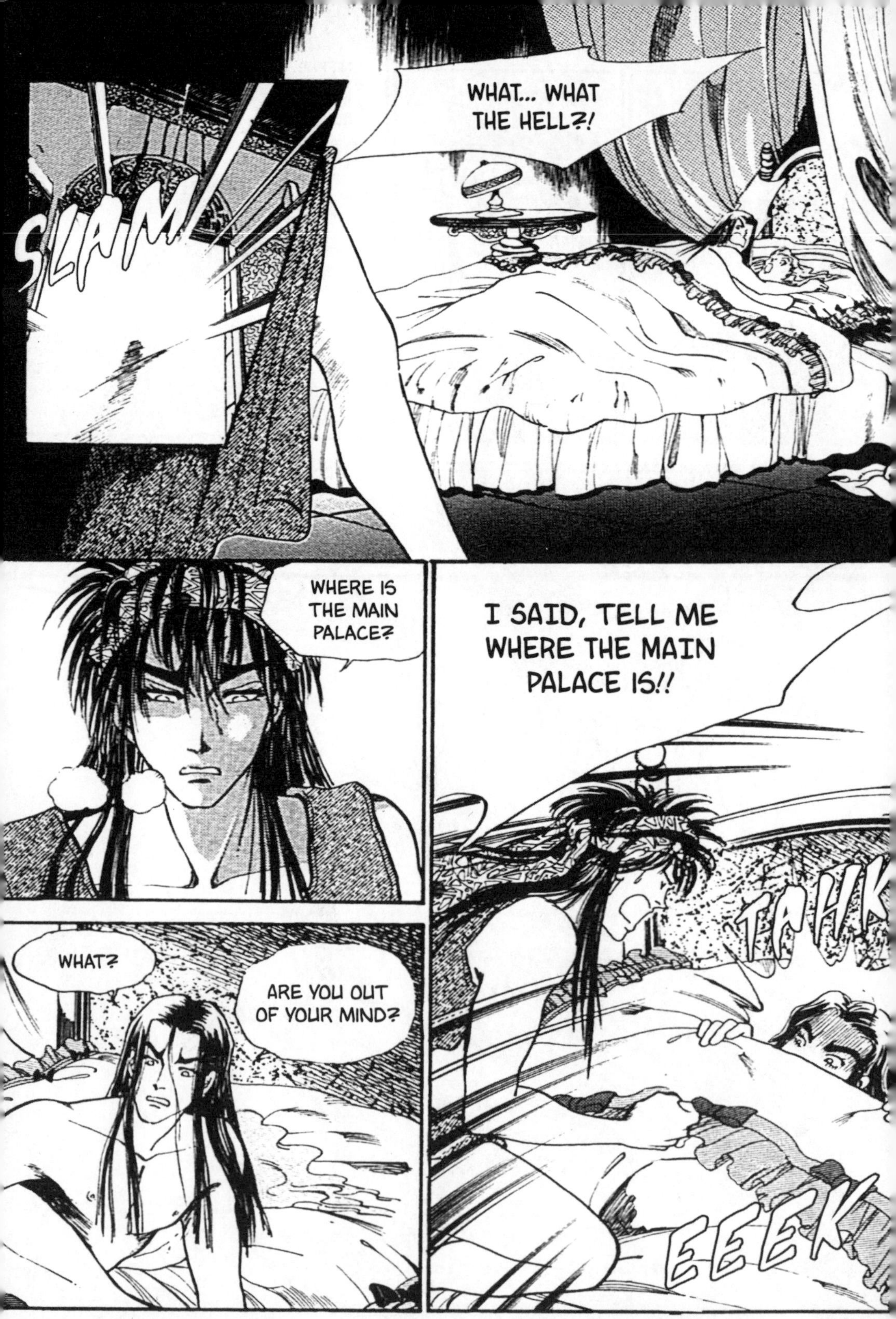
SLAM
WHAT... WHAT THE HELL?!
WHERE IS THE MAIN PALACE?
WHAT?
ARE YOU OUT OF YOUR MIND?
I SAID, TELL ME WHERE THE MAIN PALACE IS!!
TAHK
EEEK

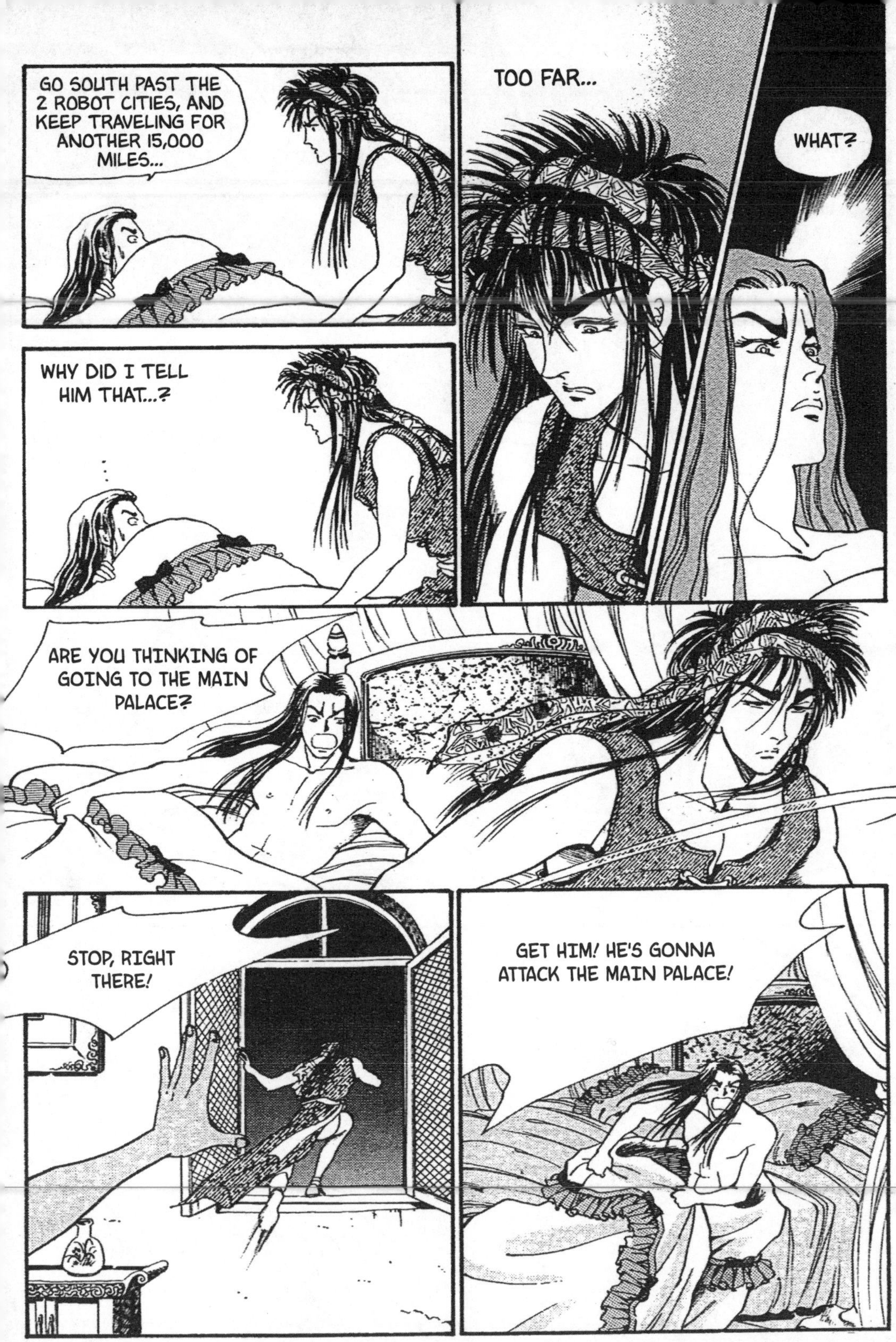
GO SOUTH PAST THE 2 ROBOT CITIES, AND KEEP TRAVELING FOR ANOTHER 15,000 MILES...
TOO FAR...
WHAT?
WHY DID I TELL HIM THAT...?
ARE YOU THINKING OF GOING TO THE MAIN PALACE?
STOP, RIGHT THERE!
GET HIM! HE'S GONNA ATTACK THE MAIN PALACE!

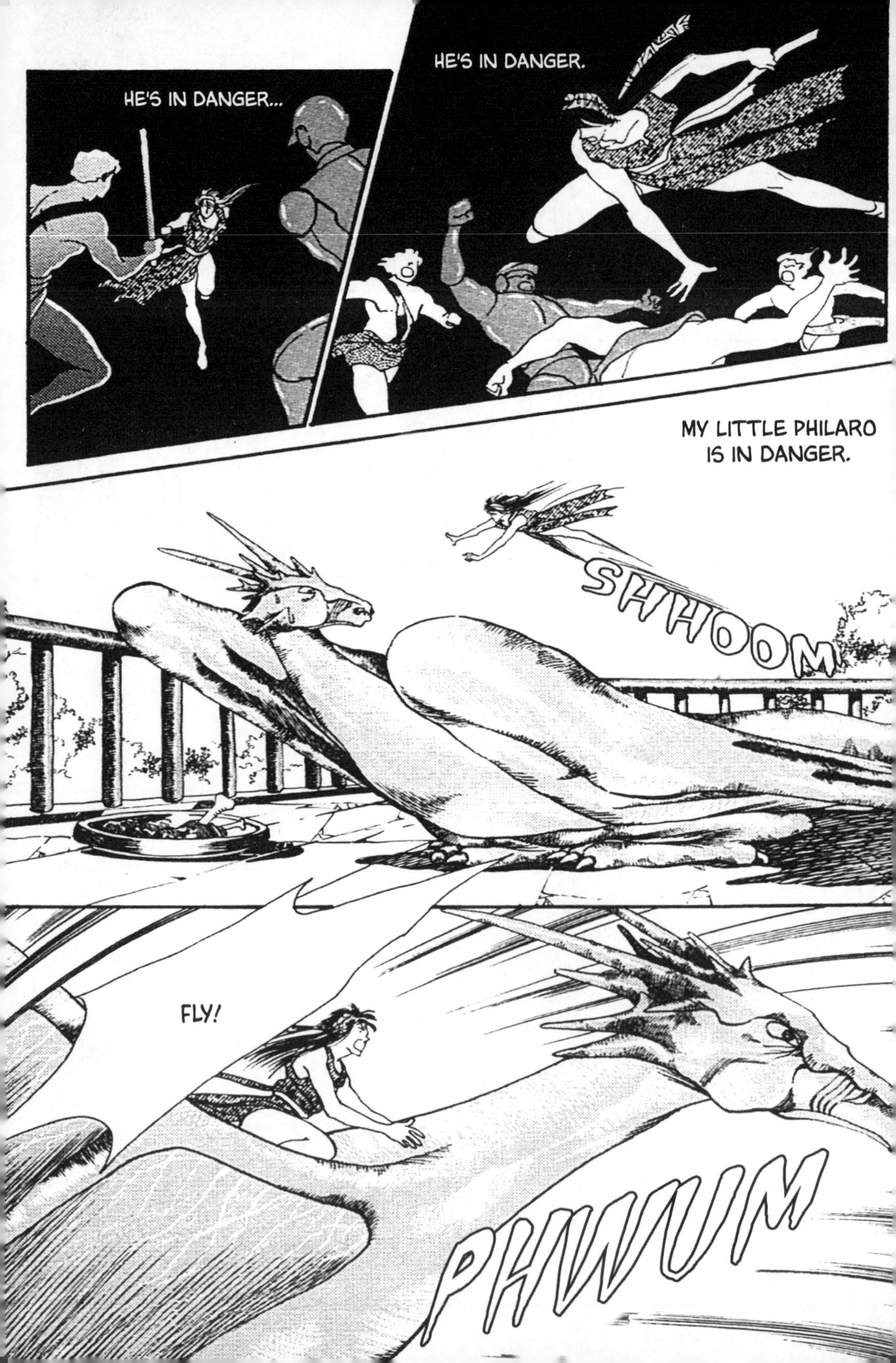

HE'S IN DANGER...
HE'S IN DANGER.
MY LITTLE PHILARO IS IN DANGER.
SHHOOM
FLY!
PHWUM

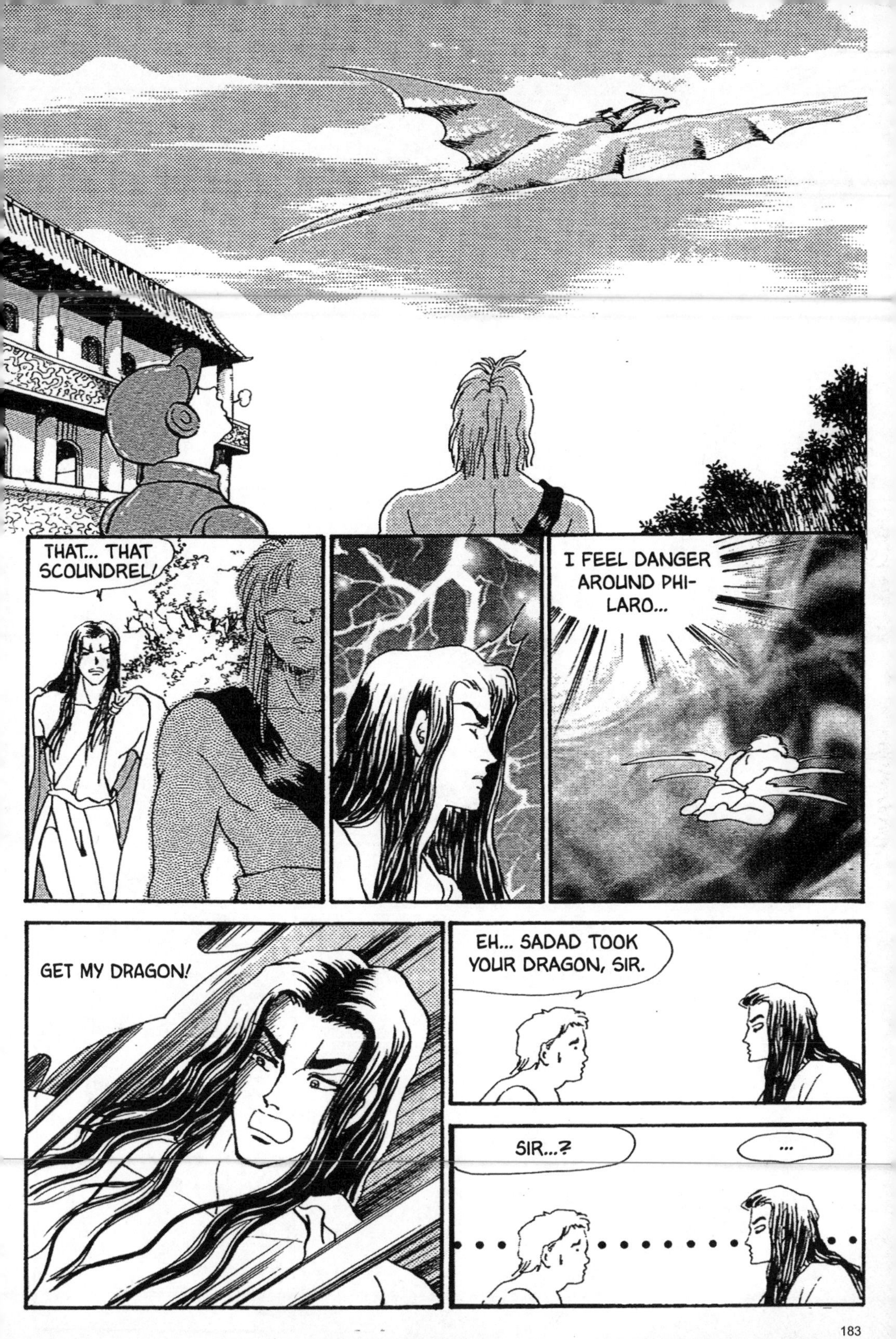
THAT... THAT SCOUNDREL!
I FEEL DANGER AROUND PHI-LARO...
GET MY DRAGON!
EH... SADAD TOOK YOUR DRAGON, SIR.
SIR...?
...

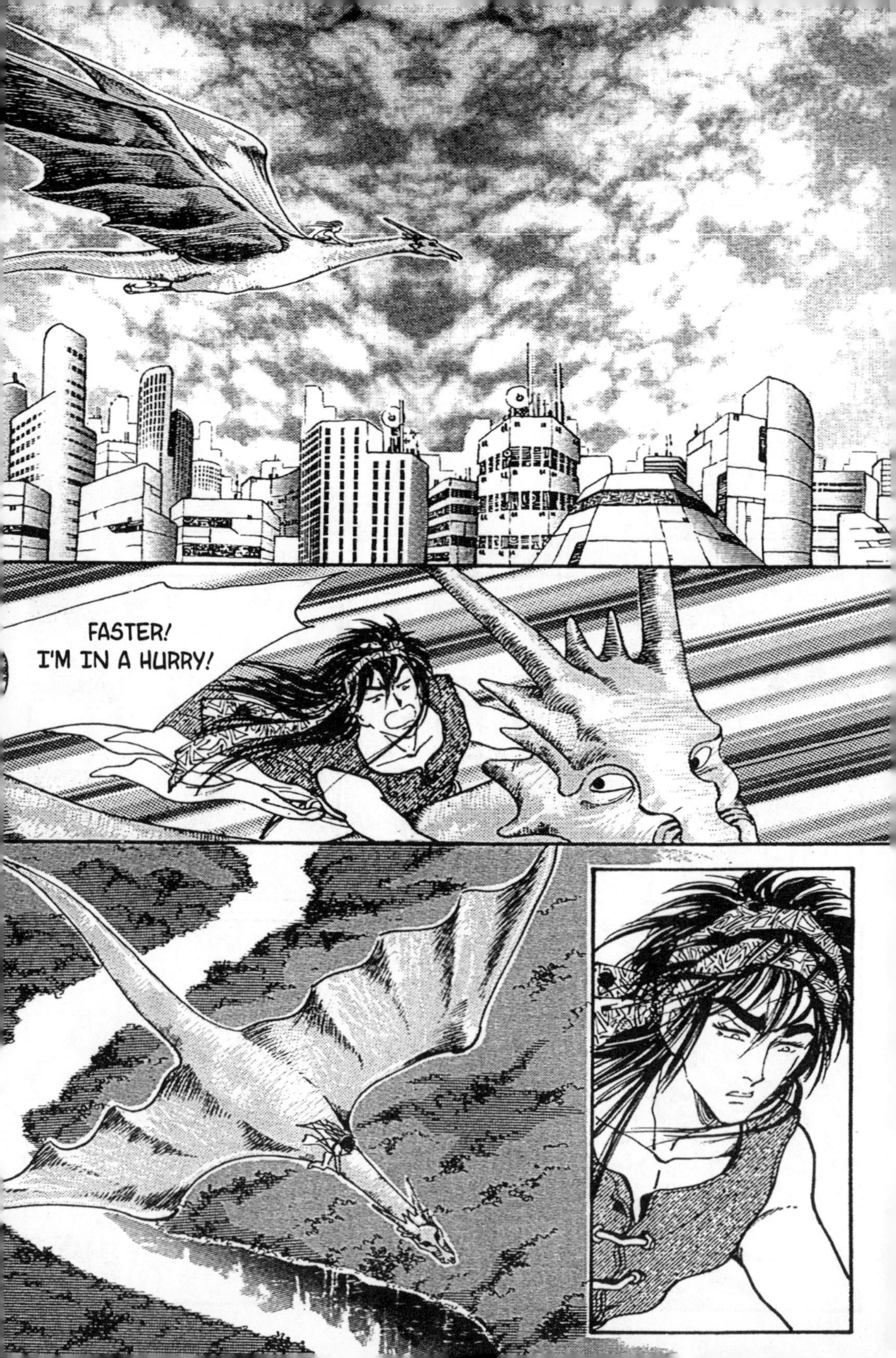
FASTER!
I'M IN A HURRY!

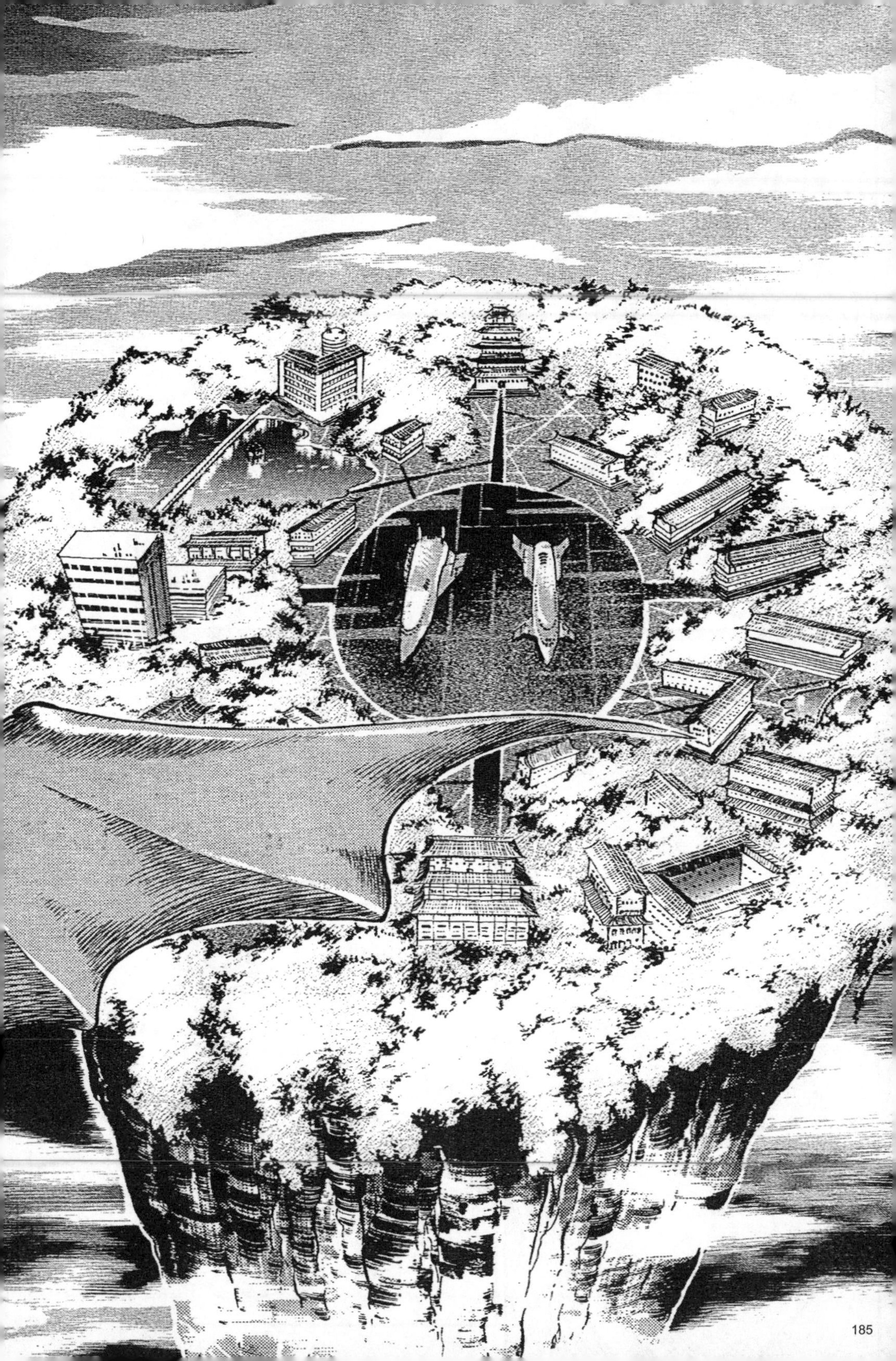

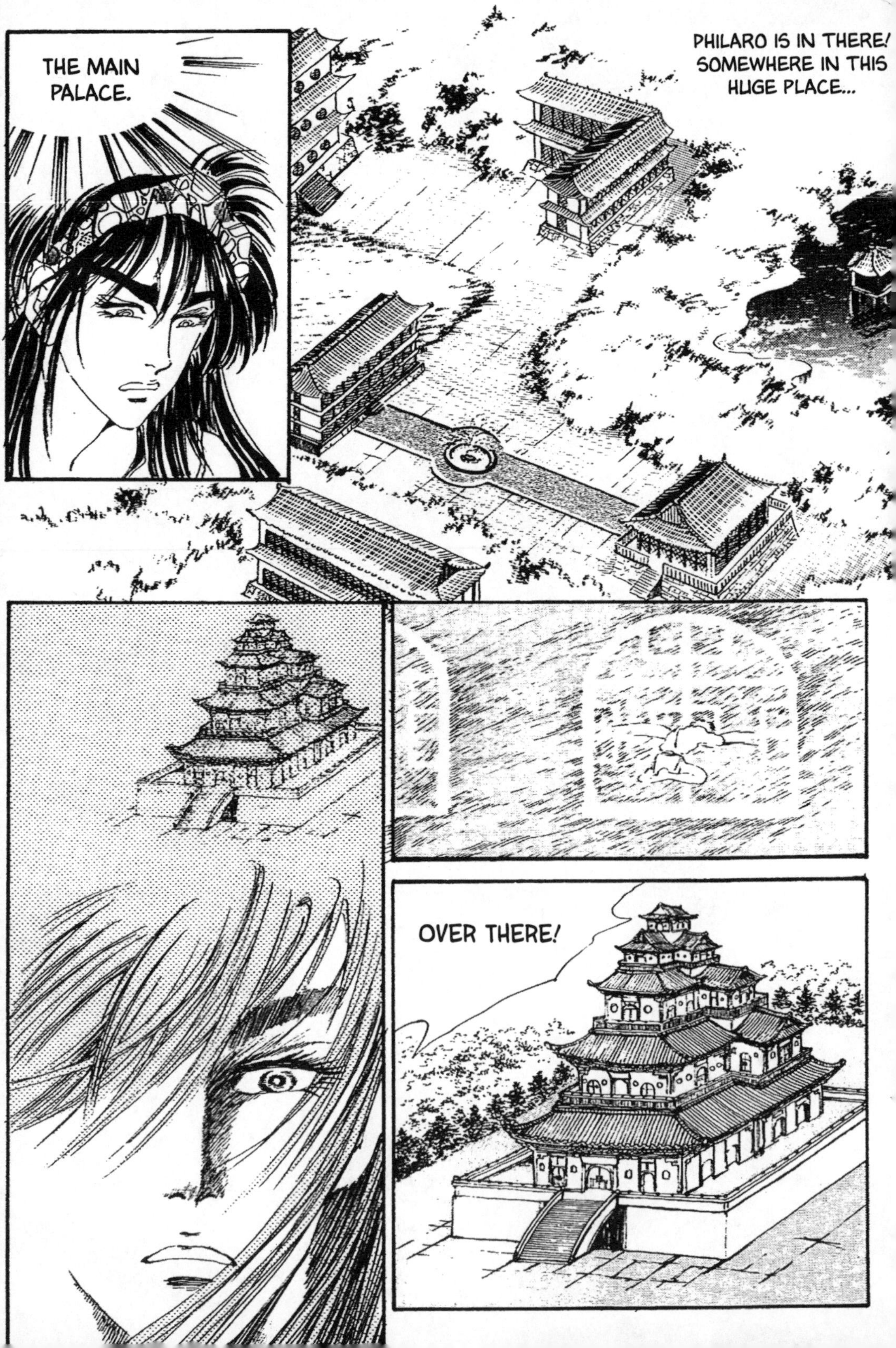
PHILARO IS IN THERE! SOMEWHERE IN THIS HUGE PLACE...
THE MAIN PALACE.
OVER THERE!

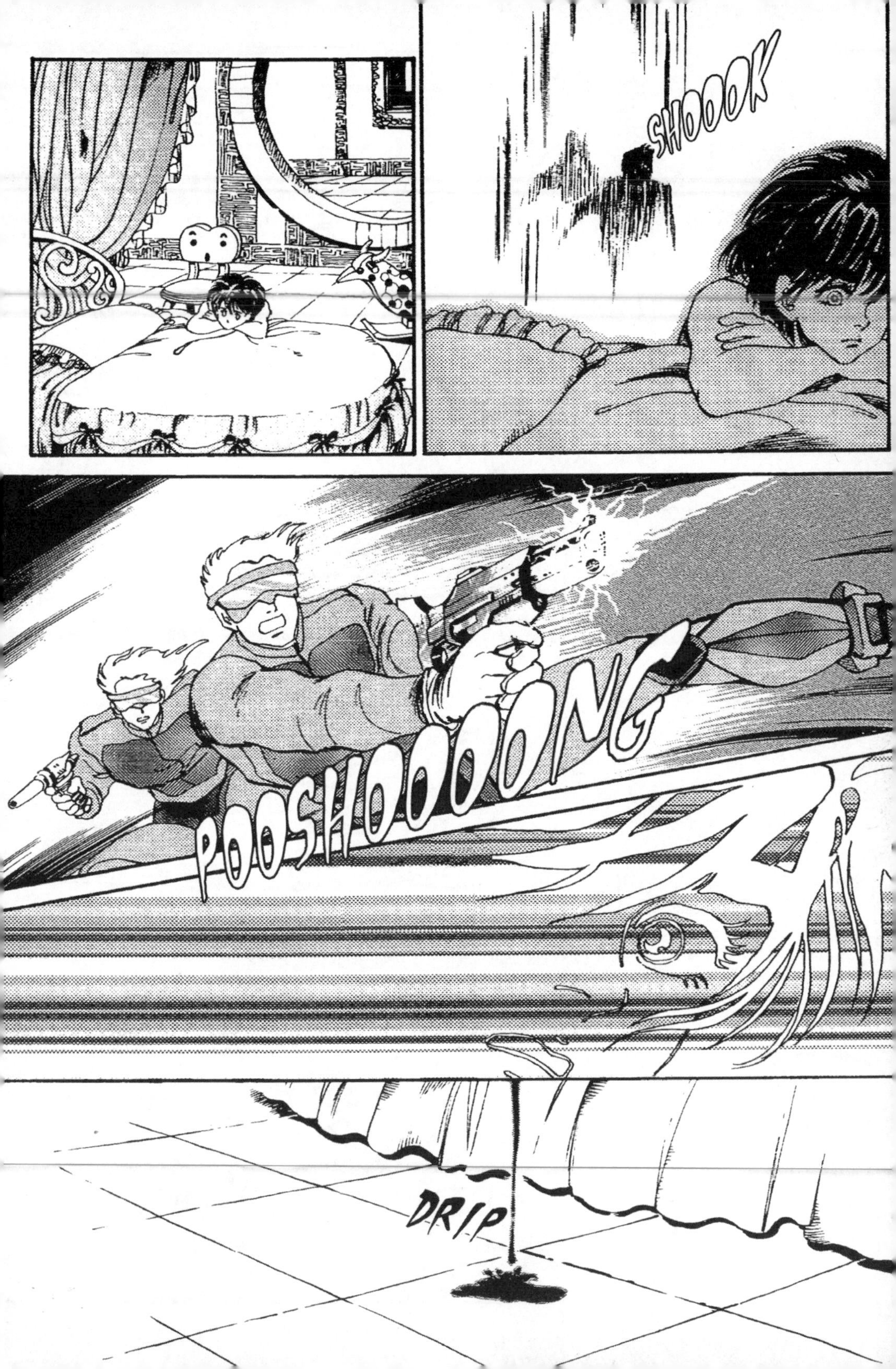
SHOOOK
POOSHOOOOONG
DRIP

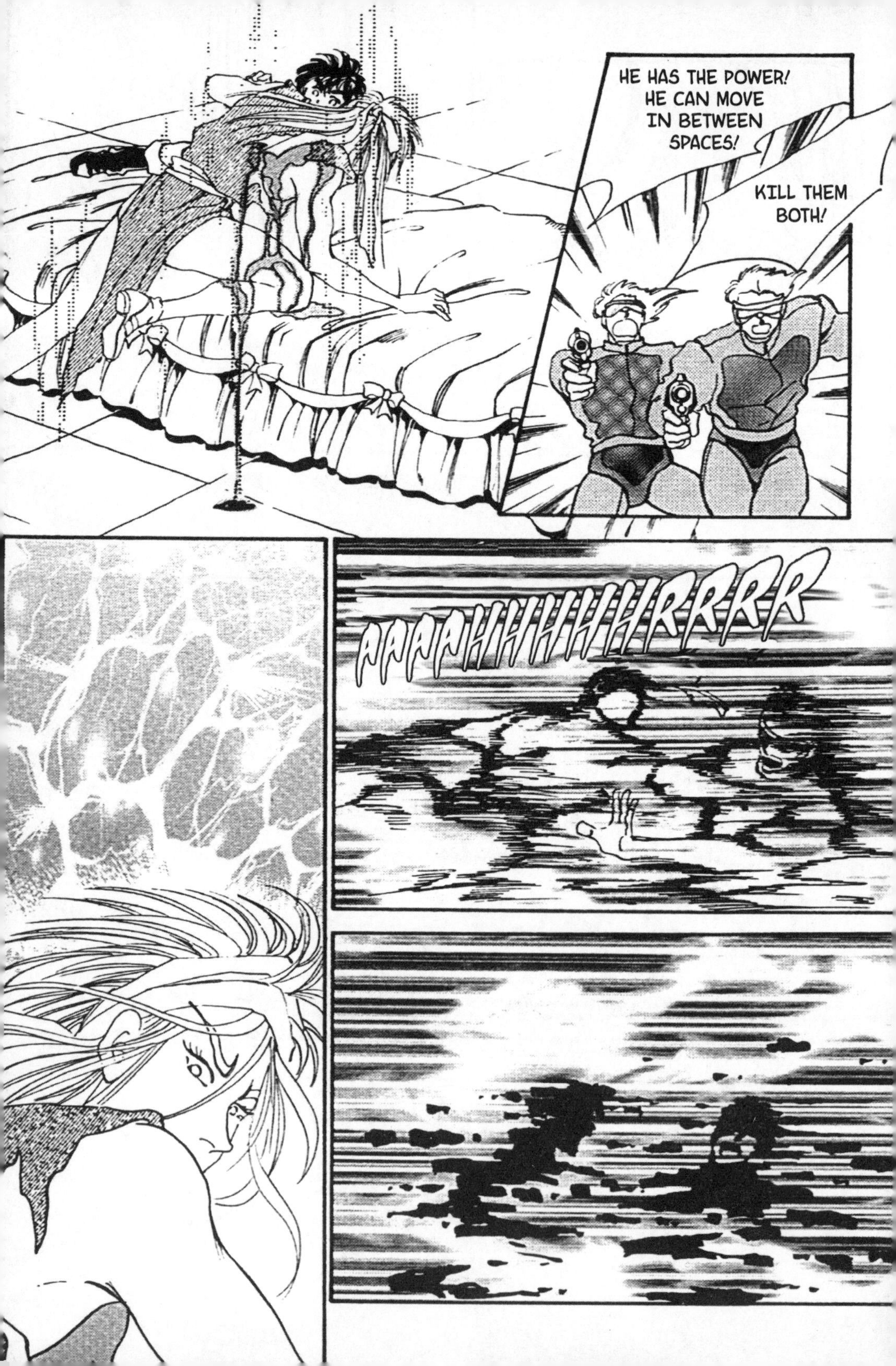
HE HAS THE POWER! HE CAN MOVE IN BETWEEN SPACES!
KILL THEM BOTH!
AAAAHHHHHHHRRRRR

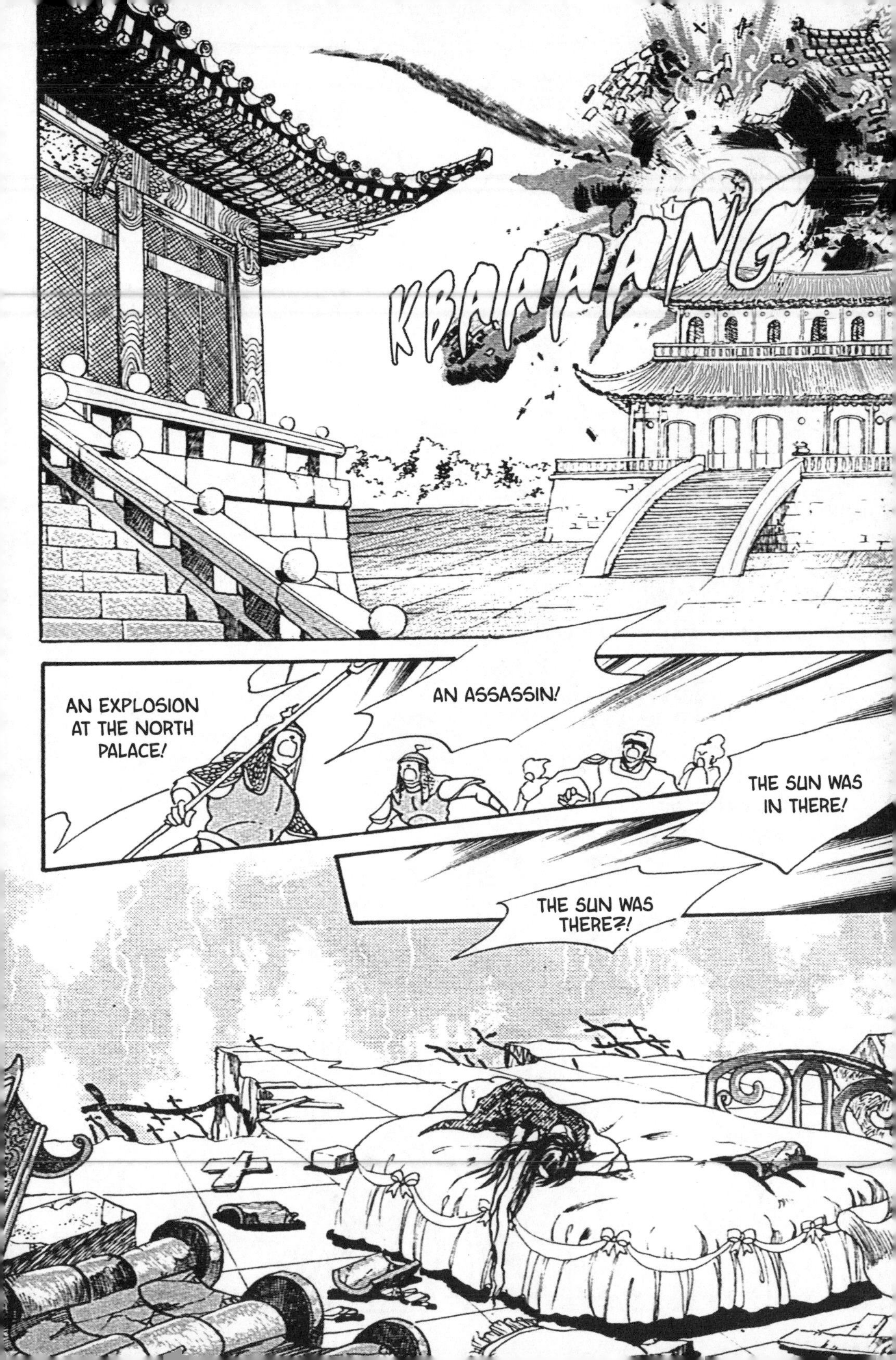
KBAAAANG
AN EXPLOSION AT THE NORTH PALACE!
AN ASSASSIN!
THE SUN WAS IN THERE!
THE SUN WAS THERE?!

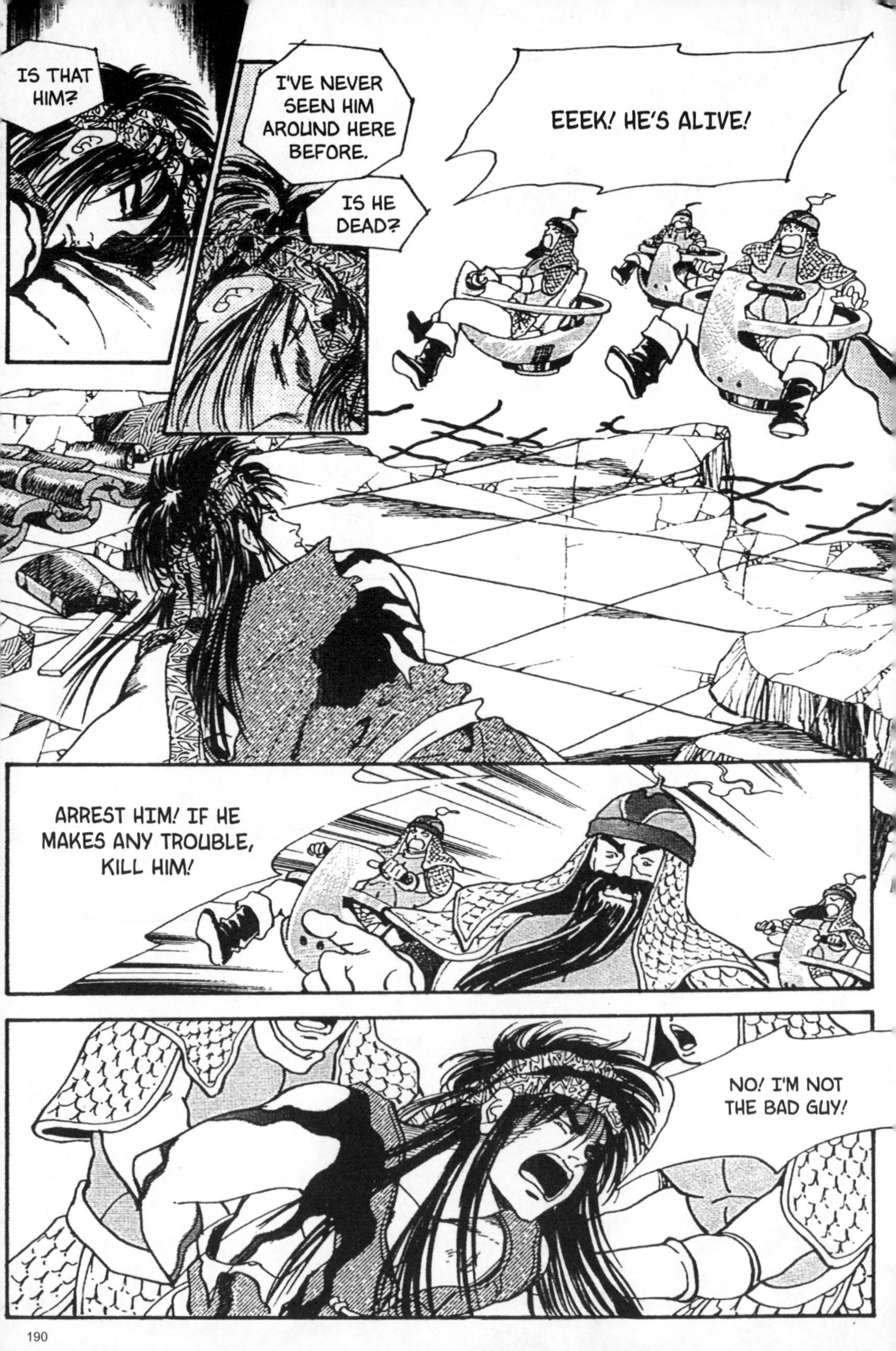
IS THAT HIM?
I'VE NEVER SEEN HIM AROUND HERE BEFORE.
IS HE DEAD?
EEEK! HE'S ALIVE!
ARREST HIM! IF HE MAKES ANY TROUBLE, KILL HIM!
NO! I'M NOT THE BAD GUY!

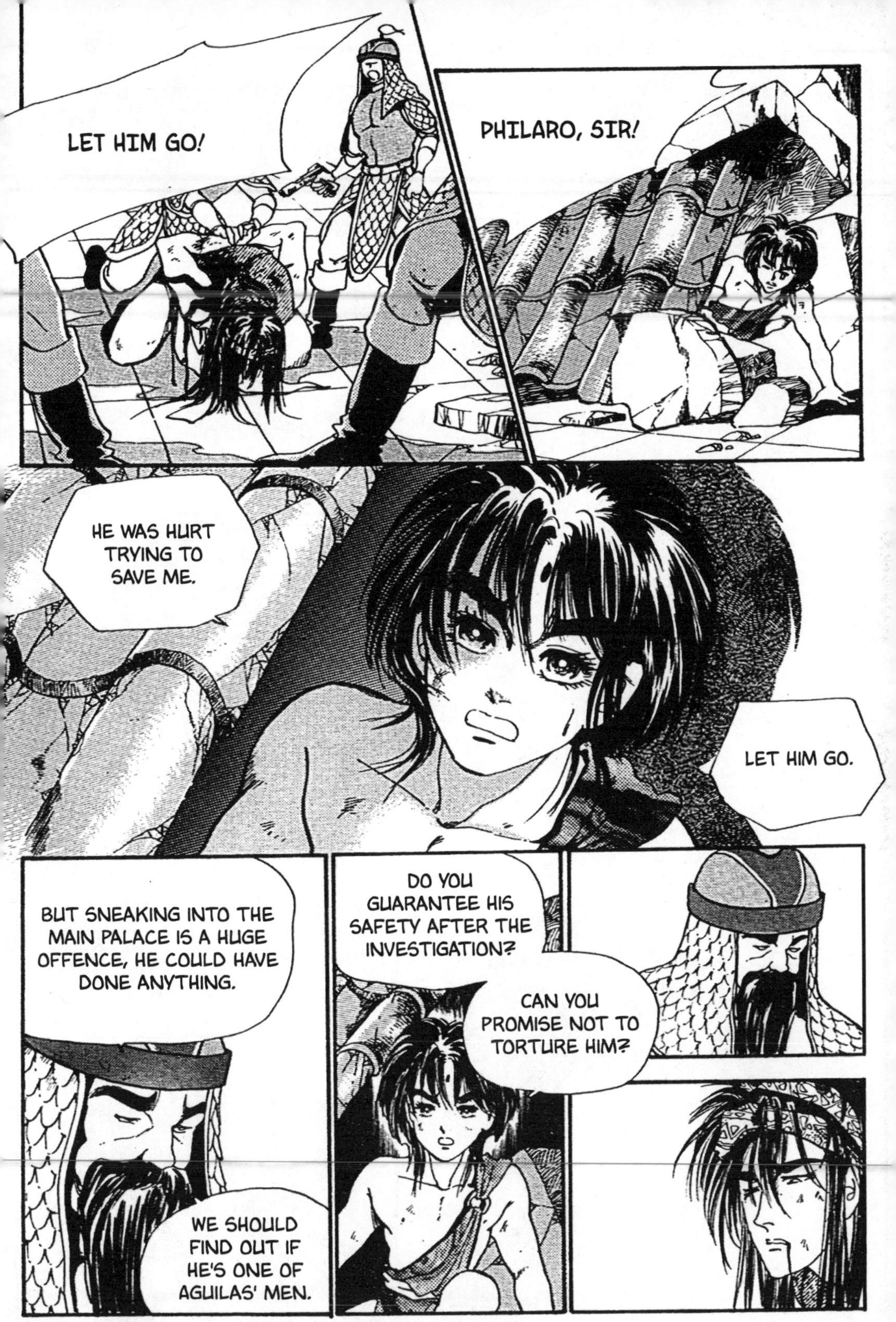
LET HIM GO!
PHILARO, SIR!
HE WAS HURT TRYING TO SAVE ME.
LET HIM GO.
BUT SNEAKING INTO THE MAIN PALACE IS A HUGE OFFENCE, HE COULD HAVE DONE ANYTHING.
WE SHOULD FIND OUT IF HE'S ONE OF AGUILAS' MEN.
DO YOU GUARANTEE HIS SAFETY AFTER THE INVESTIGATION?
CAN YOU PROMISE NOT TO TORTURE HIM?

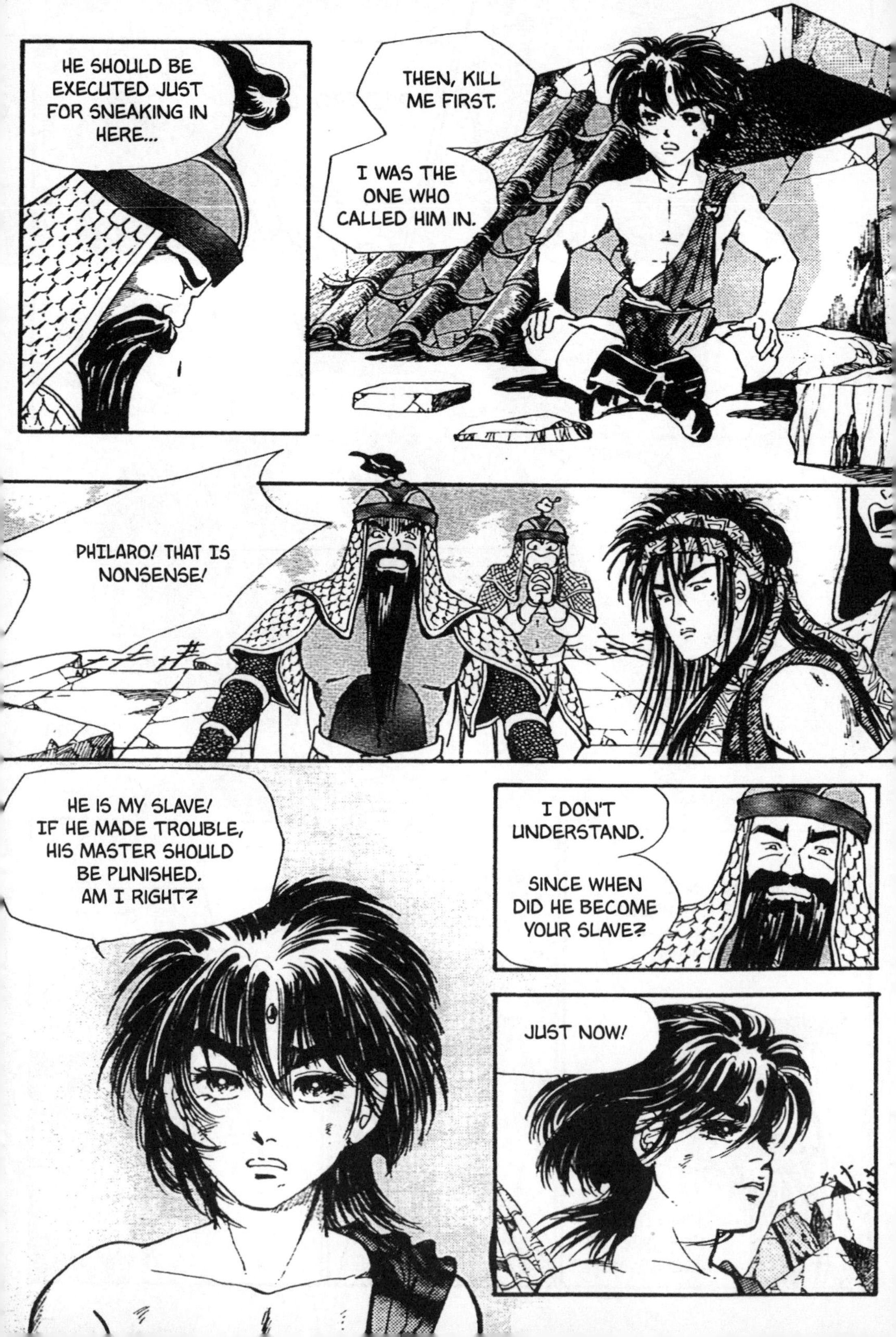
HE SHOULD BE EXECUTED JUST FOR SNEAKING IN HERE...
THEN, KILL ME FIRST.
I WAS THE ONE WHO CALLED HIM IN.
PHILARO! THAT IS NONSENSE!
HE IS MY SLAVE! IF HE MADE TROUBLE, HIS MASTER SHOULD BE PUNISHED. AM I RIGHT?
I DON'T UNDERSTAND.
SINCE WHEN DID HE BECOME YOUR SLAVE?
JUST NOW!

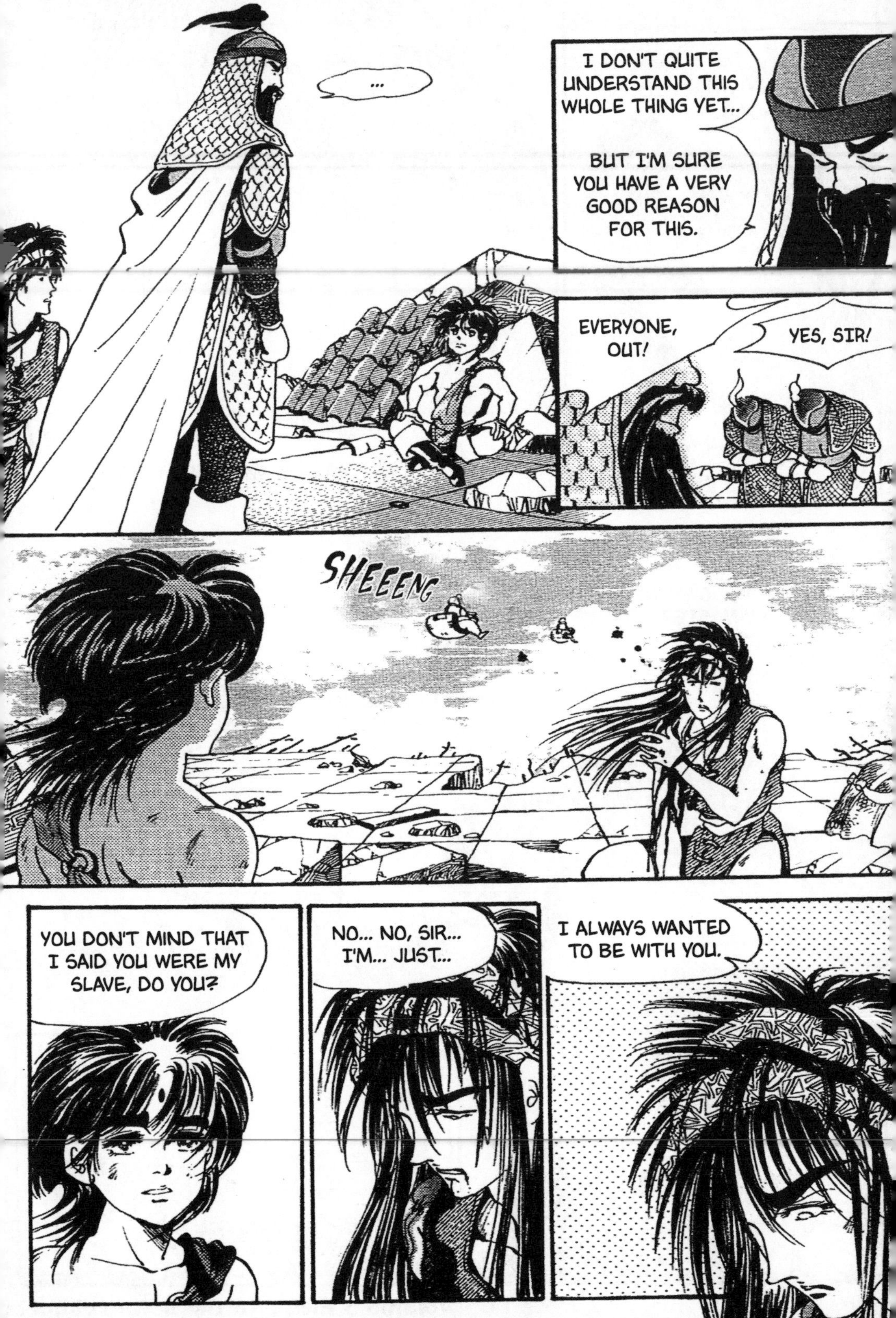
...
I DON'T QUITE UNDERSTAND THIS WHOLE THING YET...
BUT I'M SURE YOU HAVE A VERY GOOD REASON FOR THIS.
EVERYONE, OUT!
YES, SIR!
SHEEENG
YOU DON'T MIND THAT I SAID YOU WERE MY SLAVE, DO YOU?
NO... NO, SIR... I'M... JUST...
I ALWAYS WANTED TO BE WITH YOU.

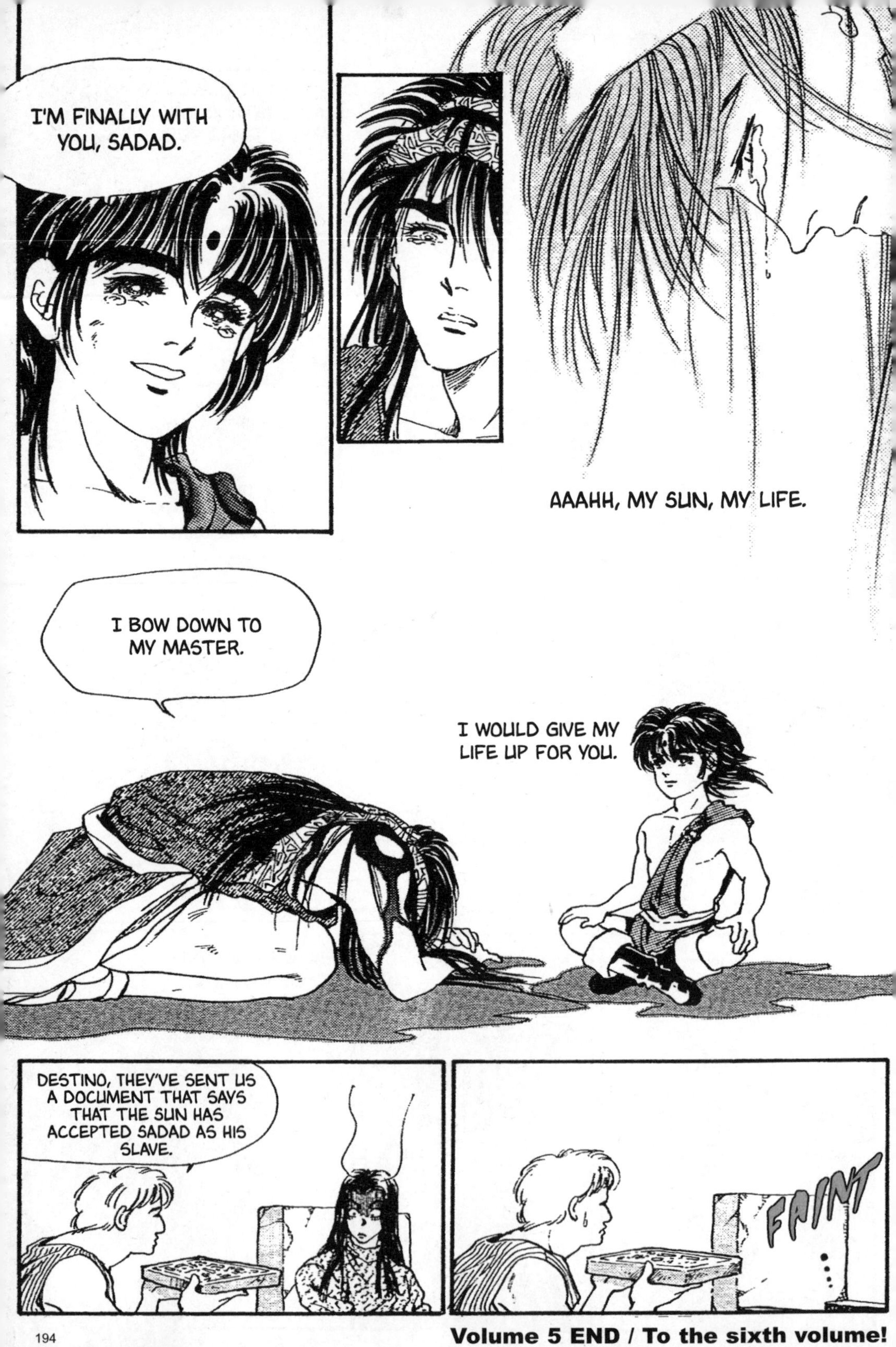
I'M FINALLY WITH YOU, SADAD.
AAAHH, MY SUN, MY LIFE.
I BOW DOWN TO MY MASTER.
I WOULD GIVE MY LIFE UP FOR YOU.
DESTINO, THEY'VE SENT US A DOCUMENT THAT SAYS THAT THE SUN HAS ACCEPTED SADAD AS HIS SLAVE.
FAINT

Volume 5 END / To the sixth volume!

KAZAN

Kazan is the last surviving member of a nomad tribe known as The Red Sand. When his village is wiped out by a vicious Water Demon, and his best friend Elsie is kidnapped, Kazan begins a journey to uncover answers that will span 10 years! Befriending a water woman, a cranky old lady, and a bizarre white Eagle, Kazan sets out for the legendary land of Goldene. Get ready for an action-packed ride through the desert as nomads, assassins, slave traders, thieves, and even giant centipedes cross paths with the young hero and his sharp-edged knife...

5 vols - 200+ pages B&W
Hardcopy US $9.95 each
eBook US $2.95 each

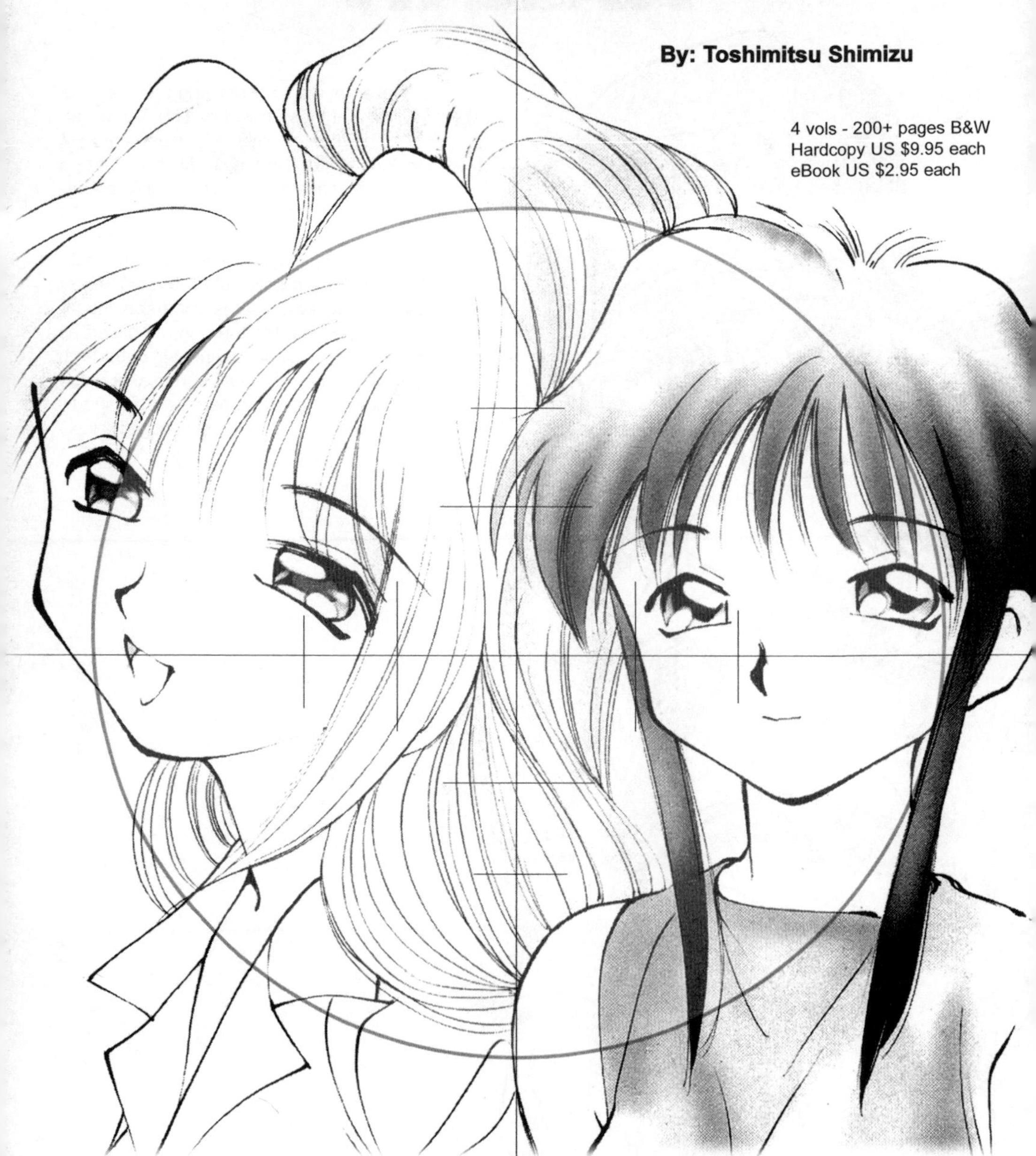

Flesh-Colored Horror

Flesh-colored horror is a collection of bone-chilling vignettes, centered on what at first seems like ordinary people...Tales of obsession, love, loss, beauty, and the perversities of nature will leave you afraid to turn off your lights before you got to bed!

200+ pages B&W
Hardcopy US $9.95 each
eBook US $2.95 each

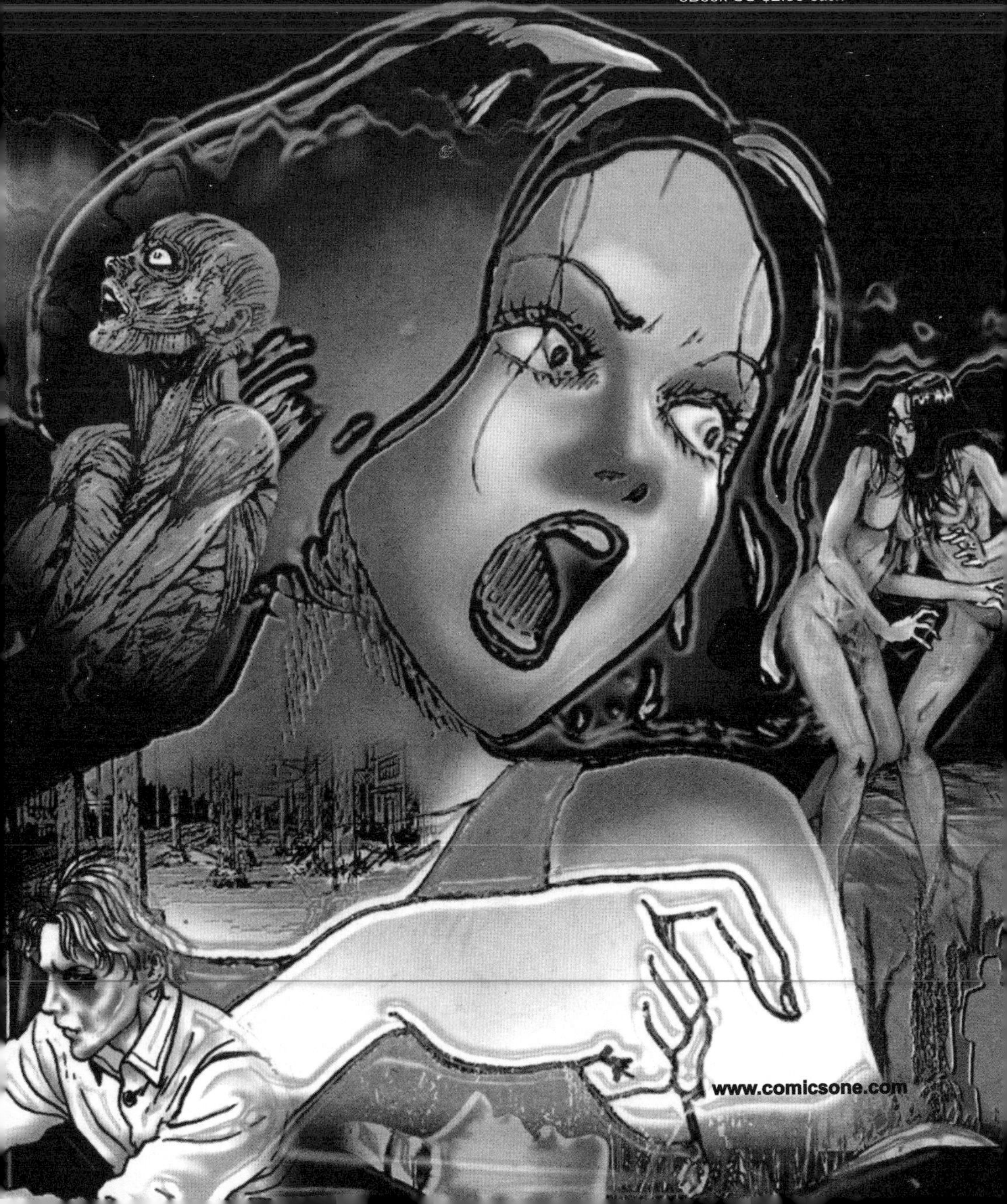

www.comicsone.com

Wounded Man

By: Kazuo Koike & Ryoichi Ikegami

Keisuke Ibaraki is not a man to be trifled with and the pornography company, G.P.X., makes a grave mistake when they kidnap his high school sweetheart, force her to do unspeakable acts and then make her commit suicide. Keisuke is now on a mission of vengeance and will stop at nothing until he vindicates the memory of his girlfriend. Travel with him through the jungles of Brazil as he exacts his revenge and tries to avoid a pure-as-white reporter out to get the story that will make her famous.

From the creators of *Crying Freeman*
Recommended for mature readers

9 vols -2- 400+ pages B&W
US $9.95-14.95 each

www.comicsone.com

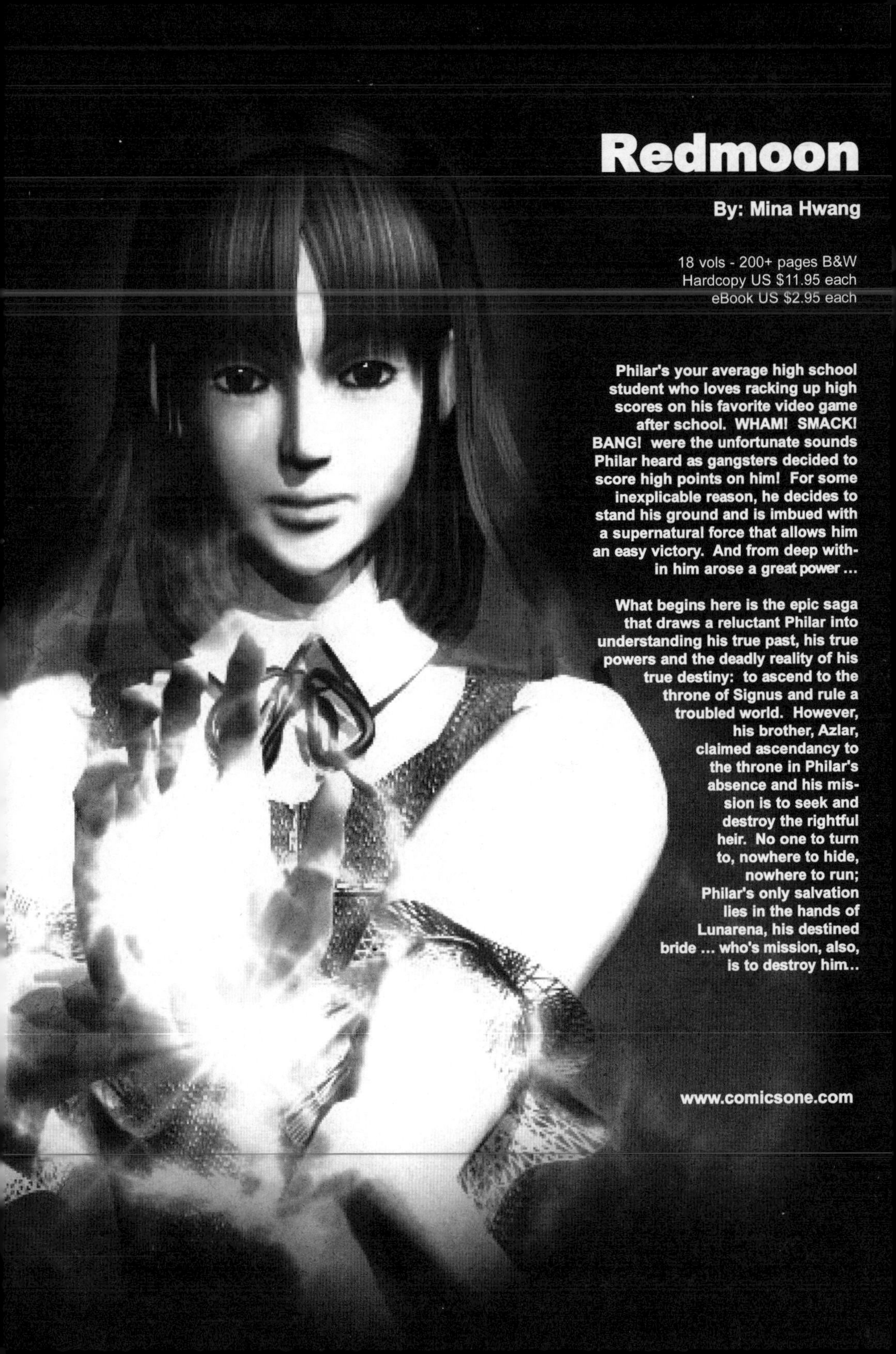
Redmoon
By: Mina Hwang
18 vols - 200+ pages B&W
Hardcopy US $11.95 each
eBook US $2.95 each
Philar's your average high school student who loves racking up high scores on his favorite video game after school. WHAM! SMACK! BANG! were the unfortunate sounds Philar heard as gangsters decided to score high points on him! For some inexplicable reason, he decides to stand his ground and is imbued with a supernatural force that allows him an easy victory. And from deep within him arose a great power ...
What begins here is the epic saga that draws a reluctant Philar into understanding his true past, his true powers and the deadly reality of his true destiny: to ascend to the throne of Signus and rule a troubled world. However, his brother, Azlar, claimed ascendancy to the throne in Philar's absence and his mission is to seek and destroy the rightful heir. No one to turn to, nowhere to hide, nowhere to run; Philar's only salvation lies in the hands of Lunarena, his destined bride ... who's mission, also, is to destroy him...
www.comicsone.com

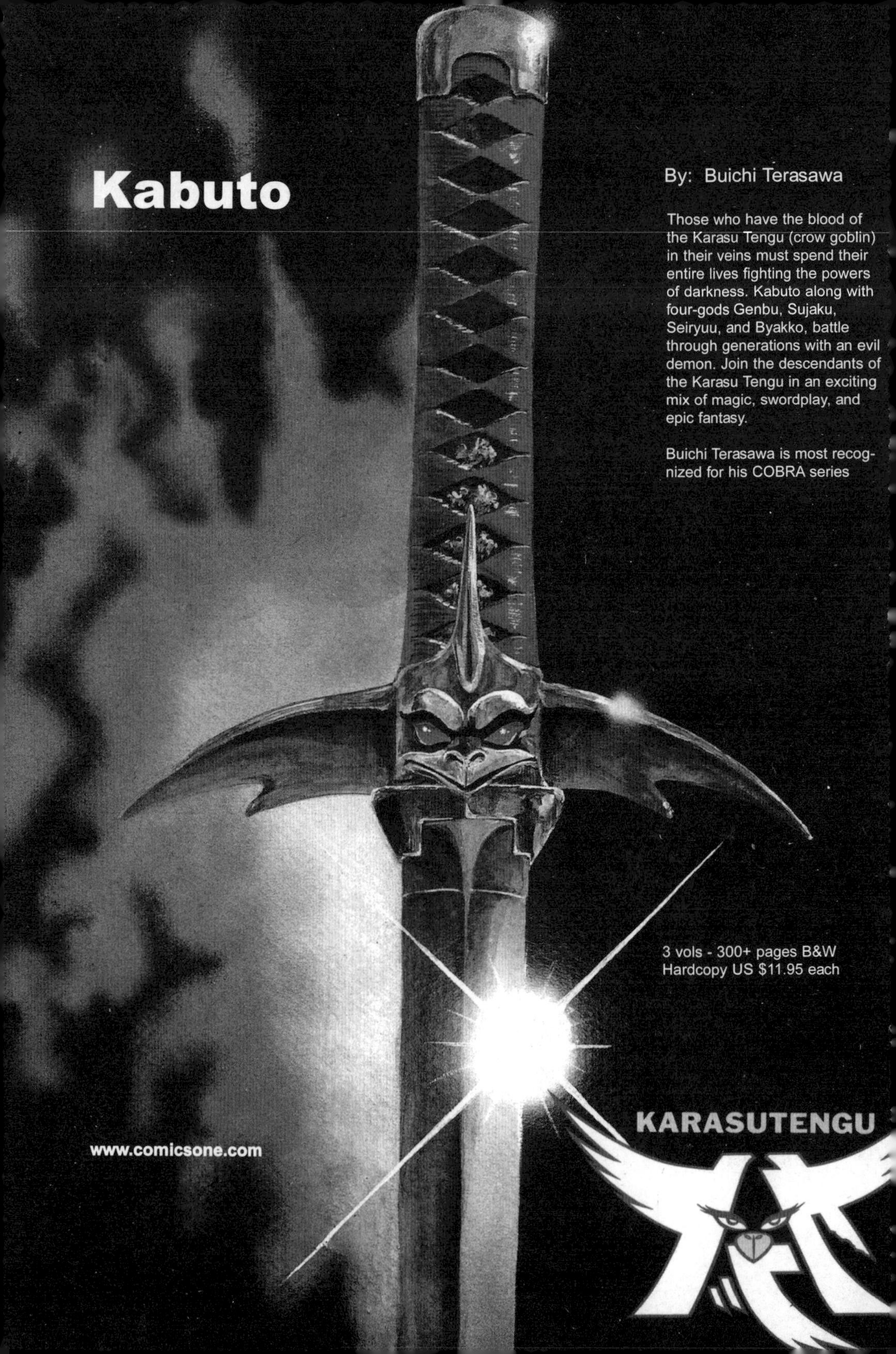
Kabuto
By: Buichi Terasawa
Those who have the blood of the Karasu Tengu (crow goblin) in their veins must spend their entire lives fighting the powers of darkness. Kabuto along with four-gods Genbu, Sujaku, Seiryuu, and Byakko, battle through generations with an evil demon. Join the descendants of the Karasu Tengu in an exciting mix of magic, swordplay, and epic fantasy.
Buichi Terasawa is most recognized for his COBRA series
3 vols - 300+ pages B&W
Hardcopy US $11.95 each
KARASUTENGU
www.comicsone.com